NATIVE PEOPLES OF THE NORTHWEST

A TRAVELER'S GUIDE TO LAND, ART, AND CULTURE

BY JAN HALLIDAY AND GAIL CHEHAK

IN COOPERATION WITH THE AFFILIATED TRIBES OF NORTHWEST INDIANS

SASQUATCH BOOKS
SEATTLE

Printed in the United States of America.
Distributed in Canada by Raincoast Books Ltd.

Cover and interior design: Lynne Faulk
Cover photograph: The mask on the cover was carved from cedar by Calvin
Hunt of the Copper Maker Carving Studio and Gallery, Fort Rupert Village,
Vancouver Island, British Columbia. It is transformation mask, and the two
sides of the eagle figure open to reveal a human face within. Hunt's work
is represented by The Legacy Ltd., a gallery in Seattle that has specialized
in authentic Native art since 1933 (located at 1003 First Avenue, Seattle,
WA 98104).
Foldout map: Barbara Dow
Interior maps: Karen Schober
Composition: Blue Fescue Typography & Design

Library of Congress Cataloging in Publication Data
Halliday, Jan.
    Native peoples of the Northwest : a traveler's guide to land, art,
and culture / Jan Halliday and Gail Chehak in cooperation with the
Affiliated Tribes of Northwest Indians.
        p.   cm.
    Includes index.
    ISBN 1-57061-056-8 (trade paper)
    1. Indians of North America—Northwest Coast of North America.
2. Indians of north America—Northwest, Pacific.   3. Northwest Coast
of North America—Guidebooks. 4. Northwest, pacific—Guidebooks.
    I. Halliday, Jan.   II. Chehak, Gail.   III. Affiliated Tribes of
Northwest Indians.   IV. Title.
    E78.N78H275 1996   95-52524

Sasquatch Books
1008 Western Avenue
Seattle, Washington 98104
(206) 467-4300
books@sasquatchbooks.com
http://www.sasquatchbooks.com

Sasquatch Books publishes high-quality adult nonfiction and children's books
related to the Northwest (Alaska to San Francisco). For more information
about our titles, contact us at the address above, or view our site on the
World Wide Web.

CONTENTS

Acknowledgments

This book is the work of many people. A heartfelt thank you to all who have helped. Special thanks go to the Native peoples of the Northwest, the executive board and staff of the Affiliated Tribes of Northwest Indians, the Tlingit/Haida Central Council, and the 54 tribal leaders and councils of the Northwest—for welcoming us into your territories, giving us permission to tell your stories, and identifying the tribal members and staff we could work with. We also extend thanks to the cultural committees and individuals, for your dedication to preserving and continuing the culture of the tribes, your assistance in gathering material for this book, and your careful reading of the manuscript. Without your help, this book could never have been written.

Another thank you goes to Sasquatch Books for their willingness to wade into uncharted territory in the guidebook genre. Special thanks to Stephanie Irving, who encouraged us to write the book; Joan Gregory and Sherri Shultz, who shaped our first drafts into a coherent manuscript in record time; and all the others at Sasquatch Books who helped us with design, maps, and encouraging words.

Finally, we thank our families, who brought us coffee and dinner, who provided for us financially and emotionally, and who insisted we break from the project at midnight. Faye and Chuck, Donovan and Kate, we couldn't have done it without you.

PREFACE

All of my great-grandparents headed west in the 1870s, most of them settling in eastern Washington on "government land"—the former lands of the Nez Perce, Cayuse, and Palouse people, who had been moved onto reservations. None of my family ever talked about the Indians whose lands they occupied. I was born in Seattle and have spent my adult life writing about the Northwest for newspapers, magazines, and guidebooks. But I can count on one hand the contacts I had with Native tribes before I began researching this book, and the contacts all stemmed from my work. Beyond that, most of what I knew about Indians came from anthropology books and museums—which talk about Indians in the past.

When I realized that there was no comprehensive guide to contemporary Northwest Indian culture, I started looking for an expert on the tribes. I called Gail Chehak, the tourism director for the Affiliated Tribes of Northwest Indians, and herself a Klamath Indian. Coincidentally, Gail had also decided it was time to write a guidebook to the tribes; in fact, when I called, she had been discussing the project in an ATNI staff meeting. The two of us met and decided to join forces. What you hold in your hands is the result of that collaboration.

When we set out, Gail and I assumed we would be writing a small guidebook, one that simply listed museums, heritage centers, and Native art galleries. However, after our first tour of a reservation with tribal members, we quickly expanded our goal. And it's been expanding ever since. Not only had we underestimated the number of the museums, centers, and galleries, we hadn't anticipated how many other experiences, destinations, and attractions should be included in this book. We made on-site visits to nearly every destination listed here—putting 20,000 miles on Jan's car; flying 5,000 miles on jets, float planes, and bush planes; and stepping aboard ferries, freighters, fishing vessels. In the end we found more than 1,000 things to see and do—from browsing art galleries and museums to attending powwows and celebrations.

We've loved every minute of researching and writing this book. It has been a joy to get to know the tribes and to experience the world through their eyes. We thank them, and with them extend an invitation to you: come and experience the culture, art, people, and land of the Native Northwest.

—The Authors

A Helpful Note

The question that non-Natives ask most often is whether or not it's acceptable to call Native Americans "Indians." The word "Indian" is fine as long as you think of Indians as wonderfully diverse, sensitive, strong individuals with a fascinating, complex, and unique heritage. If you are still imagining the stereotypic version of Indians (as in Indians vs. cowboys), then "Indian" is not okay. The Affiliated Tribes of Northwest Indians, a group of 54 tribal governments in the Northwest, as well as the Ketchikan Indian Corporation and the Metlakatla Indian Reservation, use the term "Indian." They would not do so if the word had negative connotations.

Numerous other terms have come into use besides the word "Indian." The term "American Indian" is used in legal documents regarding the relationship between Native nations and the U.S. government. In Canada, the term "First Nation" is used in reference to sovereign Native peoples and their relationships to the Canadian government. The term "Alaska Native" is used to refer to the special status of the aboriginal people of Alaska. "Native American" came into common usage in the 1970s as a respectful way of grouping American Indians into one general category. The term "Native peoples" has gained more acceptance internationally. (And it's easier to say than "the indigenous peoples of the Western Hemisphere.")

When greeting each other, Native people rarely use the words "Indian," "Native," "Native American," or "First Nation." Instead they describe themselves according to their tribal affiliation and ancestry. Someone who is an enrolled member of the Spokane Nation in Washington State might say: "I'm Spokane, with Coeur d'Alene and Welsh. My mother is Spokane, my father is Coeur d'Alene, and my grandfather is Welsh."

When you meet a Native person, just identify yourself as you would to anyone else. If you want to discuss heritage with a Native person, be prepared to know your own. For example, Jan Halliday might say "My family were lowland Scots who moved to Washington in the 1800s." What Jan is saying is that she descends from a long line of settlers. When Gail Chehak says, "I'm Klamath," she is saying that she descends from people who have lived for more than 500 generations on marshland in present-day southeastern Oregon. Encoded in both of these short introductions is a wealth of history and legend. What really matters, though, is the respect that Gail and Jan have for each other, and for each other's family history.

INTRODUCTION

Who would ever guess that you could raft down the wild and scenic Trinity River in northern California with members of the Hupa Indian Tribe and spy the ruins of old villages hidden along the banks? Or that you could ride out into Clayoquot Sound with the Nuu-chah-nulth, the great whalers of Vancouver Island, and see migrating gray whales? Or that in Southeast Alaska you could watch artists carving 30-foot-tall totem poles and visit a real clan house filled with Tlingit dancers?

These are only a few of the more than 1,000 activities, destinations, and attractions described in this book. *Native Peoples of the Northwest* is the first comprehensive guide to the art, culture, and land of contemporary Northwest Indians. More than 60 tribes live in the Northwest, many of them on some of the most beautiful and protected lands in the world. This book, written in cooperation with the tribes themselves, is an invitation and a guide to you—to visit the tribes and their lands; to learn about their lives, history, art, and culture from *them;* and to see the wonders of the Northwest through *their* eyes. You could spend your life in libraries and museums studying Indian culture and never meet an Indian. Also, most museum exhibits about Northwest history begin with colorful displays of Indian art, as a nod to the past, and then quickly segue into an exclusive focus on the 200 years of white settlement and development. They seem to ignore the fact that Indians continue to live, work, and create in the Northwest, very much tied to their traditional religions, cultures, and lands. This book is a guide to the vital Indian culture that thrives today on Native-held lands.

In the Northwest, there are more than 25 museums that house spectacular Native art, much of it collected at the turn of the century. These include the stunning Museum at Warm Springs, Oregon, named by the Smithsonian Institution as the top museum of its kind, and the University of British Columbia's Museum of Anthropology, one of the best cultural museums in the world. In coastal museums you'll find tall figures collected from abandoned villages, 30-foot-tall totem poles, cedar canoes, replicas of clan houses, ceremonial masks, and elaborate woven blankets. Inland museums display house styles such as tule mat, tepee, and wickiup, as well as hundreds of examples of beadwork. In addition, during the past thirty years, Northwest tribes have built fabulous cultural heritage centers, some of them reconstructions of actual villages, and filled them with wondrous things—weathered totem poles, carved cedar house screens, elaborate masks, beaded cradleboards, and baskets woven from cattail or cedar bark. The cultural center on the Makah Reservation in Washington houses one of the most important archeological finds in North America—the intact contents of an entire village that was buried in a mud slide more than 500 years ago. All of these museums and cultural centers are described in this guidebook.

For those who wish to purchase authentic Native art, this book recommends more than 50 Northwest galleries. We also introduce you to the Indian artists themselves—people who make everything from traditional dolls wrapped in buckskin to authentic Modoc bows and arrows and beaded cradleboards. You'll learn where you can buy authentic beadwork, watch totem poles being carved, and visit studios where you can see artists at work and perhaps purchase a piece from the very artist who created it. A special appendix describes how to ensure that the art you buy is authentic Indian, aboriginal, or Alaska Native. And we haven't limited our listings to visual arts. We also take you to see traditional performances with Native dancers and actors; we give you guidelines for attending powwows; and we list celebrations, rodeos, roundups, horse races, feasts, and powwows that are open to the public.

By visiting Native peoples and their lands, you can see and experience the magnificent landscape of the West through the eyes of the people who have lived here for generations. First-time visitors to reservations often notice only the administration buildings, schools, and modern housing—none of which resemble archival photographs of beautiful clan houses or tepee encampments. But there is far more than meets the eye. Tribal lands border magnificent national parks, such as Olympic National Park in Washington, Glacier National Park in Montana, and Crater Lake National Park in Oregon. Other tribal lands occupy parts of the isolated and rugged coasts of British Columbia, remote islands of Southeast Alaska, and vast stretches of hilly grassland between the Cascade Range and the Rocky Mountains. Many of the tribes offer first-class accommodations, resort hotels, and lake cruises, as well as fascinating eco- and cultural tours.

When you tour with a Native guide, it's like no other tour you've experienced. You see creation sites; hear legends, myths, and epic stories; and sometimes even meet the descendants of famous chiefs. On a guided raft trip with the Hupa Tribe in northern California, for example, you discover ancestral villages, learn about sacred dances, taste acorn soup, and watch how baskets are woven from maidenhair fern and wild grasses. In Montana, you can see buffalo, visit one of the first missions in the Northwest, attend a powwow with Flathead guides, and stay in a first-class hotel overlooking the mountains and lake. In British Columbia, you can tour the old village where the tribe hosted Captain James Cook in the early 1800s. The adventurous can go surfing with the Yakutat Tlingits in Southeast Alaska, ski with the Snohomish in Washington, or ride Appaloosa horses with the Nez Perce in Idaho. Or you can hike along a boardwalk through the oldest cedar grove in the world with the Nuu-chah-nulth on Vancouver Island, or enjoy a twilight cruise with the Salish-Kootenai on Flathead Lake in Montana. We also take you to some of the fish hatcheries in the Northwest, where tribal biologists are raising salmon, trout, and even sturgeon—the historic backbone of tribal economy and culture in the Northwest. Situated amid beautiful surroundings, the hatcheries are a fascinating combination of technology and nature, where visitors are always welcome.

We endorse Indian-guided tours because we've discovered that Native people, whose families have lived for more than 10,000 years on their lands, tell the best stories we've ever heard. There are creation myths, countless stories about Raven and Coyote, and hilarious tales of human error. Some are professionally told; many are shared casually. A story may begin with "See that rock up there?" and before you know it, your guide has covered centuries. Native people know their culture, their art, and their lands as no one else does.

History buffs can visit historic Indian battlefields, missions, totem parks, and old fur-trading forts, as well as petroglyphs and pictographs. On the Fort Hall Indian Reservation in Idaho you can examine the traces of the nine emigrant trails that crossed through the valley; in Sitka, Alaska, you can explore the battlefield where the Russian America Trading Company fought the Tlingits in a bloody skirmish; at Fort Clatsop near the mouth of the Columbia River, you can see the place where the Chinooks hosted explorers Lewis and Clark through a wet, rainy winter; and in eastern Washington, you can visit the Whitman Mission, site of the Whitman massacre.

This guidebook also takes you into the Northwest's metropolitan areas, where just the faintest glimmer of Indian culture seems to remain. Here too there's far more then meets the eye. Descendants of Chief Seattle still live in and around the city that bears his name. A short ferry ride from downtown Seattle, on the Port Madison Reservation, you can visit Seattle's homeland, grave site, and his tribe's cultural museum. In Vancouver, British Columbia, more than 100,000 aboriginal people live within the city limits. Their magnificent art is displayed in nearly every gallery in the city, as well as in a $4-million collection at the Vancouver International Airport, and at the University of British Columbia's outstanding Museum of Anthropology.

We wrote this guidebook with the help of the members of the Affiliated Tribes of Northwest Indians, a group of 54 tribes from Southeast Alaska, Washington, Oregon, northern California, Idaho, and western Montana. Based on their recommendations, we made on-site visits to nearly every place listed. Because the tribes themselves gave us their stamp of approval, you can be assured that you are welcome on reserves and reservations described here. And we're confident that if you visit just some of the places listed in this book, your grasp of traditional and contemporary Indian culture will be far more complete than with years of study in any library.

We welcome you to Indian Country—and some of the best cultural, eco-, and heritage tours available in North America.

How to Use This Book

Organization

This book is divided into six chapters, each covering a different region of the Northwest: Southeast Alaska; British Columbia; Western Washington; Western Oregon and Northern California; the Columbia River Gorge and Basin; and Idaho and Western Montana. Most often the parameters of a region were determined more by geography and natural features than by state boundaries, since it was geography that often shaped tribal connections and similarities. Thus, the Western Oregon and Northern California chapter focuses on the tribes that lived west of the Cascade Range in both of those states. The chapter on the Columbia River visits both eastern Oregon and eastern Washington tribes—those Natives who lived along the river and its tributaries and whose cultures were influenced by the yearly salmon migrations. The Idaho and Western Montana chapter explores the lands of Natives who have much in common with the Plains Indians, while the Southeast Alaska, British Columbia, and Western Washington chapters focus on coastal tribes.

Be sure to check the appendixes at the back of the book for information about sacred sites (including a special poem by Suzan Shown Harjo), attending powwows, annual events, buying Native art, Native-owned casinos, tribal administrative offices, and more.

Planning Your Route

At the beginning of every chapter is a map of the region. The chapter then takes you on a tour of tribes and tribal lands, moving step by step around the region in a manner designed to help you plan your visit. For example, in Southeast Alaska, we begin in Ketchikan in the south and travel from island to island until we reach Yakutat in the north. When planning an itinerary, you may want to read more than one chapter. If you are visiting the Portland area, for example, you should refer to both the Columbia River and the Western Oregon chapters.

Call Ahead

For every reservation, town, or city, we have listed numerous activities and destinations—everything from art galleries to powwows, Native-led walking tours to basket-weaving classes, houseboat rentals to tepee lodgings. For most of these, especially for those located in rural areas, we strongly suggest that you call ahead—to get directions, confirm hours or fees, or make appointments for tours. Remember that some of the businesses described in this book are operated out of private homes; many are run by tribal members who wear numerous hats. Use the phone number listed for the activity, or call the tribal office (tribal offices are listed in an appendix at the back of the book).

Coming Attractions

In this book we list only the attractions that were in operation at press time. Many new businesses and activities were being planned while we were writing this book: cruises up the Columbia River that focus on Indian history and culture; a live wolf exhibit on the Nez Perce Reservation; new tribal museums that will house long-lost objects that are being returned to the tribes from such institutions as the Smithsonian and the Chicago Field Museum. To keep abreast of new things to do and see in the Northwest's Indian country, you are invited to subscribe to our tourism newsletter, written and published by Jan Halliday and Gail Chehak four times a year. For a subscription, send your mailing address and telephone number, with a check or money order for $45, to "Chasing Raven and Coyote," PO Box 10223, Portland, OR 97210.

About the Authors

Jan Halliday has spent most of her life writing in the rural areas of the Pacific Northwest. The great-granddaughter of Scot-English pioneers who settled in the Northwest in the 1870s, she is a regular contributor to regional and national publications. She lives in Portland, Oregon.

Gail Chehak has worked for ten years in Washington, D.C., for the National Congress of American Indians, Morningstar Institute, and the Indian Arts and Crafts Shops. She is a Klamath Indian tribal member and director of tourism for the Affiliated Tribes of Northwest Indians. She lives in Portland, Oregon.

SOUTHEAST
ALASKA

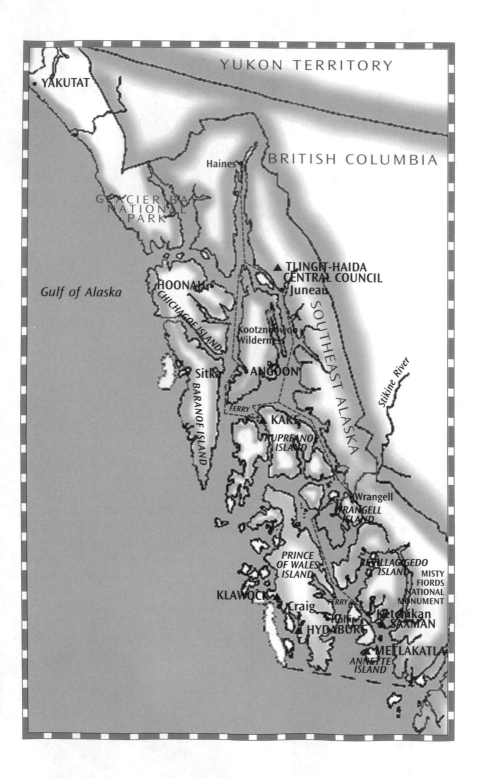

YUKON TERRITORY

YAKUTAT

BRITISH COLUMBIA

Haines

GLACIER BAY
NATIONAL
PARK

Gulf of Alaska

HOONAH

CHICHAGOF ISLAND

▲ TLINGIT-HAIDA
CENTRAL COUNCIL
Juneau

Kootznoowoo
Wilderness

SOUTHEAST ALASKA

Sitka

BARANOF ISLAND

ANGOON

Stikine River

FERRY

▲ KAKE

KUPREANOF
ISLAND

Wrangell

WRANGELL
ISLAND

PRINCE
OF WALES
ISLAND

REVILLAGIGEDO
ISLAND

MISTY
FIORDS
NATIONAL
MONUMENT

KLAWOCK

Craig

FERRY

Hollis

Ketchikan
▲ SAXMAN

▲ HYDABURG

▲ METLAKATLA

ANNETTE
ISLAND

SOUTHEAST ALASKA

Today, most of the Natives living in Southeast Alaska are Tlingit descendants, residing in towns and villages such as Angoon, Yakutat, Hoonah, and Kake. All Alaska Natives speak fluent English; some speak their Native languages as well. Many still practice subsistence lifestyles, gathering food in Alaska's rich fishing grounds (with whole villages occasionally ordering a planeload of Big Macs from Juneau's new McDonald's). There are also many Tlingit Natives living in the major Southeast Alaska towns—most of them ancient village sites—such as Ketchikan, Wrangell, Juneau, Sitka, and Haines. In all of these towns, you will find Native-run tours, totems, live theater, attractions, hotels, art galleries, shops, and museums. Distinctive Native art is everywhere you look: totem poles stand outside Kmart, and Raven and Eagle clan symbols adorn everything from bags of fresh-roasted coffee to beach blankets and T-shirts.

One of the most spectacular scenic waterways in the world, the 1,000-mile-long Inside Passage begins in the bays of Southeast Alaska and ends on the tideflats of southern Puget Sound. Carved by glaciers during several ice ages, the Inside Passage encompasses thousands of islands, which shelter water craft from the rugged Pacific Ocean. The Natives used the swift currents of the Inside Passage, which can run nearly 16 knots, to propel their huge, cedar-carved canoes. Turning river drainages into the equivalent of our highways, Natives also developed a network of trade far into the continent's interior.

Southeast Alaska reflects not only the cultures of the Tlingits, Haida, and Tsimshian Natives but also the impact of the Russian, British, and American traders of the early 1800s, the gold miners of the late 1800s, and the timber, fishing, and mining industries of the 1900s. Alaska Natives run their corporations dressed in business suits, then don ceremonial regalia to drum and sing during celebrations. Restaurants in the old Tlingit/Russian town of Sitka offer both smoked salmon and borscht on their menus. Even Sitka's public radio station, KCAW, is nicknamed "Raven Radio" in a nod to Native culture. And this mixing of cultures takes place amid glorious mountains, glacier-filled bays, emerald green seas, lush Sitka spruce and hemlock forests, sparkling lakes, and abundant wildlife.

"Given a choice, salmon will always choose the stronger current, knowing that the current leads the way through a passage. It is the same for a canoe. That's why so many canoes have salmon painted on the bow, to help them find the current, even in the strongest storms. The painting on the stern is something frightening, to scare off monsters, predators, or big swamping waves. Besides, it looks cool."

—Anon

Keep in mind that when you come to Southeast Alaska, you are visiting islands. Getting around is a real challenge, especially for first-time visitors. Ketchikan, Wrangell, and Sitka are very small towns on islands half an hour apart by jet. Alaska's capital city, Juneau, is on the mainland but at the base of a 4,000-foot-high sheer rock wall that no highway can penetrate; the only way to get to the city is by plane or boat. At the far north, Haines, also on the mainland, is accessible by highway, but the nearest town—Whitehorse, in the Yukon Territory—is 250 miles away.

Without a cedar canoe to catch the currents, residents and tourists alike take Alaska Airlines jets between major towns or catch four-seater bush planes and seaplanes to nearby islands. Ferries make stops daily or every three days, depending on the tides. Luxury cruise ships, such as Holland America, do a brisk business sailing the Inside Passage, as do smaller eco-tourism boats such as those operated by Alaska Sightseeing/Cruise West. The best news is that you can visit Southeast Alaska without a car. All the towns are so small that you can walk everywhere once you're there. And every town, no matter how small, has car rentals, taxis, and bus service, even in the middle of the night, when the ferries arrive. It is essential to make reservations for hotels and car rentals in advance, however.

*For an easy-to-understand description of Native people and their culture, the Tlingit and Haida tribes recommend **Alaskan Native Cultures, Volume 1,** which includes historical photographs and explanations of clans, trade, slavery, canoes, traditional art, spiritual life, ceremonies, and contemporary issues. Written by Tlingit, Haida and Tsimshian Natives; published by and available from the Native-owned Sealaska Corporation, Sealaska Heritage Foundation, One Sealaska Plaza, Suite 201, Juneau, AK 99001; (907)463-1844.*

Planning Your Trip

Getting around Southeast Alaska is an adventure in itself. Ferry landings can be miles from the nearest town (in one case, 30 miles away). When the weather abruptly changes, the little six-seater plane you were counting on might be grounded for as long as two weeks.

The big towns—Ketchikan, Wrangell, Sitka, and Juneau—are all served by Alaska Airlines' big jets. For that reason, travelers with inflexible schedules may wish to confine their exploration of Native culture to these areas. Travelers planning to visit less-traveled destinations, such as Metlakatla on Annette Island, Klawock on Prince of Wales Island, or Haines, need to have a more flexible itinerary. The Alaska State Ferry system is an excellent option, but it can have its downside. Sleeping cabins are often sold out well in advance, and the outdoor sleeping decks can be crowded, chilly, and damp. Ferries often arrive at their destinations during the wee hours of the morning, miles from town.

Fortunately, where there's a will, there's a way in Southeast Alaska—and even a four-block town has car rentals and taxi service. Buses meet planes and ferries at odd hours. Most Southeast Alaska towns also have floatplane service.

Of course, some journeys are more pleasant than others. The ferry from Ketchikan to Metlakatla, for example, is a relaxed couple of hours on a small ferry equipped with a snack bar and showers. You can also get back and forth from Ketchikan to Metlakatla on a noisy floatplane: a short hop across the water with great rhythm and blues on the headphones. Even in the height of the summer travel season, you could book both ferry and floatplane with a quick phone call half an hour before departure, with no penalty for last-minute reservations. However, it's best not to leave hotel reservations to chance, especially during the peak season between June 1 and August 30. An unscheduled arrival may mean no room at the inn.

How to Pack

No matter how you get to Southeast Alaska, travel light; lugging baggage down to a floatplane dock in the rain is a drag. And always take rain gear: a hooded slicker, waterproof boots, and nonslip shoes that dry quickly, such as kayaker's sandals. Bring layers of clothing— a T-shirt, shorts, turtleneck, wool sweater, hat, and lightweight slacks (jeans soak up rain). Silk long underwear or synthetic fleece are a must for spring and fall visits. Bring a camera and binoculars. If you forget anything, don't worry—all major towns have fully equipped outdoor stores.

Cruise Ships

In 1995, almost 350,000 travelers visited Southeast Alaska aboard cruise ships, an easy way to see the Inside Passage that also affords you the opportunity to book offshore excursions. Larger cruise ships dock in Ketchikan, Wrangell, Juneau, Sitka, and Haines. The smaller boats, such as those operated by Alaska Sightseeing/Cruise West, visit less-traveled destinations because they can maneuver into smaller docking facilities.

By late 1995, more than 500,000 travelers had already booked passage for cruises to Southeast Alaska. More than half of them said they were coming to Alaska to learn about Native culture, totems, and art. Indeed, Southeast Alaska is one of the few places one can learn about the Native perspective on life in a relatively unspoiled setting. A trip to the region makes a rewarding journey for luxury cruise ship passengers and backpackers alike.

To learn the most about Native culture, take the Native-guided tours listed in this book and visit as many different locations as possible. Inter-island transportation is relatively inexpensive: under $20 for a 6-hour ferry ride, under $50 for a hop to a nearby island on a floatplane. Although the generalities of Tlingit, Haida, or Tsimshian life may seem similar, each location has a unique history.

Getting There: *The Alaska State Ferry*

The only way to get around Southeast Alaska in your own car is to load it onto the Alaska State Ferry (also called the Alaska Marine Highway). The big boats load cars at Bellingham, Washington, (between Vancouver, B.C., and Seattle) for the trip north. You might want to weigh the cost (in terms of both money and time waiting in line) of taking a car versus renting one. The number of miles of road at your destination may make a car rental more economical. Revillagigedo Island, for example, where Ketchikan is located, has only 30 miles of road. Car rentals average about $35 a day and are available in almost all towns. The Alaska State Ferry accepts passengers without cars and provides overnight accommodations for travelers.

Food is served on board the ferry, and overnight cabins are available on all boats. (They're stark as a shoebox but have private baths, showers, bunks—and fresh linens on request.) Many people roll out sleeping bags, or rent pillows and blankets, and spend an often damp, but always memorable, night on the deck in reclining chairs. (People have also tried to erect tents on the deck for privacy, but we don't advise it—the wind rattles the tent all night long.) The ferries offer films and documentaries, and during the summer there may be on-board live entertainment. The smaller, interisland ferries all offer food service, comfortable chairs, and even a shower stall in the rest room.

The Alaska State Ferry schedule is a daunting 50 pages. To decipher it, first look in the table of contents for "Southeast Alaska/Inside Passage," a section about eight pages long. In that section, at the top of the page, look for the month you want to travel. Find the town you plan to leave *from.* Follow the column down to find the date you want to travel. Dates are coded, but are simple to figure out. For example, in the April section, under the town of Bellingham, "S1, 3:00 p.m." means the boat leaves the dock Saturday, April 1 at 3pm. Color codes don't mean anything; they just help you read the tiny print across the page. Weird times (such as 4am) are listed because the ferry travels long distances between towns and is subject to currents and tides.

If a town is listed on the ferry schedule, but there are no dates or arrival times in that column, look on the adjacent page for the interisland ferry schedule.

If you are taking a car in summer, make reservations a season in advance, prepaid by credit card. The back page of the Alaska State

Ferry schedule lists all information sources in the area serviced by the ferry, including U.S. and Canadian customs, Alaska State Parks, U.S. Forest Service, Alaska Railroad Corporation, and others. Once you've learned to use it, the schedule is an invaluable guide.

For a free copy of the ferry schedule or for reservations call (800)642-0066, Mon–Fri, 7:30am–4:30pm Alaska Standard Time. Credit cards accepted for reservations. Fares vary according to cars, trailers, number of passengers, and cabin reservations. Bicycles, kayaks, and canoes additional.

Jets, Bush Planes, and Floatplanes

Alaska Airlines, (800)426-0333, not only flies into Southeast Alaska from all major West Coast cities but also flies between Ketchikan, Wrangell, Juneau, and Sitka. It can save you hours on board the ferry. A flight from Juneau to Sitka, for example, is about 35 minutes; by ferry it's about 18 hours.

Ketchikan-based Taquan Airlines, (800)770-8800 or (907)225-8800, has the best safety record of any airline in Alaska and operates a Native-owned fleet of turbine-powered Otters and Caravan aircraft on floats and wheels. Taquan makes short hops between Ketchikan and Prince Rupert, B.C., as well as to nearby islands, offering some impressive tour packages to Prince of Wales Island villages (see the Prince of Wales Island section).

For a list of other floatplane and bush plane services, call the visitors centers in the town you plan to visit.

Visitor Information Services

The best visitors center we've seen anywhere is the Southeast Alaska Visitor Center in Ketchikan. Owned and operated by the U.S. Forest Service, this handsome building right across the street from the cruise ship dock is a great place to get oriented to Alaska. In the Trip Planning Room, you can relax in overstuffed chairs and watch videos about the state's different regions, read guidebooks, and browse topographic maps and nautical charts. You'll find information on all the public lands in the state of Alaska, including national parks. The other half of the building presents an overview of Southeast Alaska's Native culture, with exhibits and audiotapes. The center has a great bookstore, too.

Southeast Alaska Visitor Center, 50 Main St, Ketchikan, AK 99901; (907)228-6214. Open daily, May 1–Sept 30; Tues–Sat, Oct–Apr. Visitors may call ahead and request that packets of information be sent to them.

Resources

For free maps, accommodation lists, and information packets, contact:

- Haines Convention and Visitors Bureau, PO Box 530, Haines, AK 99827; (907)766-2234.
- Juneau Information and Visitors Bureau, 369 South Franklin Street, Suite 201, Juneau, AK 99801; (907)586-1737.
- Ketchikan Visitors Bureau, 131 Front Street, Ketchikan, AK 99901; (907)225-6166.
- Sitka Convention and Visitors Bureau, PO Box 638, Sitka, AK 99835; (907)747-5940.
- Wrangell Chamber of Commerce, PO Box 49, Wrangell, AK 99929; (907)874-3901 or (907)747-5940.

Ketchikan: *Tlingit*

In 1901, in a place the Tlingits called Kichxaan, a carver finished painting a 55-foot-tall totem pole and, with the help of those attending a potlatch (a traditional ceremonial feast in which the host distributes gifts), he raised the totem into place. The pole was carved in memory of the family of a Native chief (Chief Johnson) who had fished in the area for generations. The Native fishing camp had grown into the cannery town of Ketchikan, a crazy quilt of houses built on wooden pilings, scaffolding, and boardwalks along both sides of Ketchikan Creek.

In 1992, the town commissioned a young carver, Israel Shotridge, to carve a replica of the pole. It now stands on the original site, at the corner of Totem Way and Stedman Street, in downtown Ketchikan. At the top of the pole, in the place of honor, flies Kadjuk, the mythical eagle who lives at the top of a nearby mountain. The rest of the pole depicts the story of Fogwoman, who lives at the head of all the creeks calling the salmon home from the ocean to spawn.

The Ketchikan Visitors Bureau, located on Ketchikan's downtown cruise ship dock, has a free, easy-to-follow walking map of the city. Even if you take a Native-guided tour, the informative map is handy to have and makes a nice reminder of your visit. (131 Front Street, Ketchikan, AK 99901; (907)225-6166.)

Ketchikan and neighboring Saxman, a Native village, are the only towns on nearly roadless Revillagigedo Island, which is about 40 miles west of the also-roadless mainland. Ketchikan is the center of commerce for numerous surrounding islands. Saxman, a few miles south of Ketchikan, is the home of Tlingits whose families moved here in the late 1800s, from nearby Cape Fox and several other Tongass villages. Everyone comes to Ketchikan and Saxman by boat or plane. Because there are no highways, railways, or farmlands, staples are barged to the island from Seattle or Bellingham in Washington State; perishables are flown in by jet.

A two-night ride from Bellingham on the Alaska State Ferry, or a 90-minute jet ride from Seattle, Ketchikan is built on a lip of land so narrow that there's nowhere to land a plane. A runway was scraped out at the edge of a nearly uninhabited adjoining island; disembarking passengers walk down a covered ramp from the airport to a ferry, which acts as a bridge across the swift waters of Tongass Narrows to the west end of Ketchikan.

The town stretches for about 4 miles along Tongass Narrows, but the 6-square-block downtown area of restaurants, hotels, and shops is easy to explore by foot. The island's Native heritage is immediately apparent. Ketchikan and Saxman have more totem poles (more than 70) than any other city in Southeast Alaska. From downtown, you can walk up Ketchikan Creek to the salmon hatchery, ride the funicular up a granite cliff to Cape Fox Lodge, take several Native-guided walking tours, visit Native-owned art galleries, or see museum exhibits showcasing Tlingit, Haida, and Tsimshian life. Within driving distance are Totem Bight Park and Saxman's Totem Park. Both totem parks are filled with replicas of originals brought to Ketchikan and Saxman from abandoned Tlingit villages on neighboring islands. Some of the original 100-year-old poles are on display at the Totem Heritage Center, within walking distance of downtown.

Westmark Cape Fox Lodge

At the Kadjuk totem pole at Totem Way and Stedman Street, cross Ketchikan Creek on the boardwalk to the shiny, cherry-red tram. Built like a European funicular, the tram climbs a 130-foot granite cliff and delivers passengers to the Westmark Cape Fox Lodge, a spanking-new hotel overlooking Ketchikan. Built by the Native-owned Cape Fox Corporation, the hotel is filled with Native art, including hand-carved house screens, masks, and prints. Next to the stone fireplace in the hotel's great room is a framed ceremonial shirt, made of dark-blue wool and decorated with Beaver clan symbols, which dates back to the 1880s.

The views from the 72-room hotel are gorgeous. Below is the oldest part of Ketchikan—the boardwalk with its turn-of-the-century clapboard whorehouses; the wharf and small harbor sporting one-of-a-kind fishing boats; the cruise ship dock, which sparkles when the big white ships arrive; and the inexplicably pink 1950s federal building. Beyond stretch Tongass Narrows and the other islands. Rooms at the back open to views of forested mountains. Short, wide totem poles, carved by Lee Wallace, are set in a circle outside the hotel's front door. A flier at the desk briefly explains the meaning of each totem.

Like most of the guest rooms, the hotel's Heen Kahidi dining room has a great view of downtown through huge picture windows. The menu features seafood—especially salmon, halibut, fresh Dungeness crab, and shrimp—as well as fresh salads and perfectly steamed vegetables. Fish chowders are made with real cream and fresh seafood, and huge slabs of fresh salmon are served with a glaze of brown sugar and browned butter. Wine and beer are moderately priced.

Westmark Cape Fox Lodge; 800 Venitia Way, Kechikan, AK 99901. For reservations (essential): U.S. (800)544-0970; Canada (800)999-2570 or (907)225-8001. Rooms $116–$175. All major credit cards accepted; no out-of-state checks. Breakfast, lunch, and dinner, with Sunday brunch. Van pickup at the airport; hotel guests pay $5 for ferry crossing.

Meet the Tlingits, Haida, and Tsimshian

The Ketchikan Indian Corporation offers two unique tours of Ketchikan. One, a 90-minute walking tour led by a Native guide, begins downtown at the Southeast Alaska Visitor Center, where the guide adds his personal knowledge to displays of totems and culture. From there the tour follows the boardwalk and continues up the "Married Men's Trail" along Ketchikan Creek, where huge numbers of salmon thrash upstream throughout the year. The walk then follows the road to the fish hatchery and crosses the creek to visit the Totem Heritage Center.

A second 2-hour tour begins at the Deer Mountain Fish Hatchery with a video and orientation to the three Native cultures of Southeast Alaska: the Tlingit, Haida, and Tsimshian. Guests then enter the dance theater for a 25-minute live performance of "The Salmon Boy," narrated in all three languages, followed by a tour of the salmon hatchery. Both tours are highly recommended.

Ketchikan Indian Corporation, 429 Deermount St, Ketchikan, AK 99901; (800)252-5158 or (907)225-5158. Call for times and prices. (The Ketchikan Indian Corporation is a nonprofit organization incorporated in 1939 to preserve the heritage and welfare of 3,500 members of the Tlingit, Haida, and Tsimshian Tribes.)

Look for the Eagle Feather in His Cap

Joe Williams, a Tlingit, grew up in Saxman, went to public schools in Ketchikan, and studied in New Mexico and Texas before he earned his college degree in Alaska. A member of the Eagle and Killer Whale clans, Williams frequently lectures about Tlingit culture onboard cruise ships, with his three sons performing dances in their ceremonial regalia. Williams offers a 90-minute walking tour of Ketchikan, during which he teaches several Tlingit words and phrases; discusses totems, clans, chiefs, and shamans; and intersperses his talk with tidbits about Ketchikan local history.

Call Joe Williams in Ketchikan at (907)225-4314; prices vary according to group size; year-round, by appointment.

Deer Mountain Fish Hatchery

Perhaps it's true that Fogwoman draws the salmon home to spawn: they always return from the ocean to the creek where they were hatched. A small number of ready-to-spawn salmon making their way up Ketchikan Creek are diverted into the Deer Mountain Fish Hatchery; the rest of the fish go upstream to spawn naturally. The adult fish can be seen under the concrete raceway at the tribally owned hatchery. Steelhead come up the creek in early spring, Chinook (kings) arrive between April and mid-August, Coho (silvers) appear throughout the summer, and pinks (humpies) arrive late July through August. The hatchery also raises thousands of rainbow trout to plant in local lakes. Visitors can gaze into incubation modules and watch fry being fed in the rearing tanks. Mounted specimens of five species of salmon and trophy fish are on the wall. A 12-minute video about fish culture in Alaska plays continuously. The tribal gift shop sells smoked and canned salmon. The hatchery is a pleasant walk along Ketchikan Creek from downtown (pick up a free walking tour map from the Ketchikan Visitors Bureau on the cruise ship dock).

Ketchikan Tribal Hatchery Corporation, 1158 Salmon Rd, Ketchikan, AK 99901; (800)252-5258. (907) 225-6760. A short walk from behind Cape Fox Lodge and an easy hike from downtown. $2 admission includes guided tour. Open daily, year-round.

Saxman Native Village and Totem Park

In 1896, several bands of Tlingit Indians moved from their island villages to Saxman, near the newly formed American town of Ketchikan. Blustery winds, strong tidal waves, a change in salmon migration, and the promise of cannery work, a new church, and a school prompted the move. "We were a traveling people; we moved all over to hunt and fish," shrugs one elder. The Tlingits built a modern town, using house plans provided by the Presbyterian missionaries who built the church and school. The new village was named for Samuel Saxman, a white schoolteacher who disappeared with two other men while searching for the new village site.

Today, Saxman Native Village is the leading attraction in Southeast Alaska, drawing more than 65,000 visitors each summer. It is not really a village at all but a site adjoining Saxman's totem park. Buses leave Ketchikan's cruise ship dock every 2 hours for a well-orchestrated tour. Visitors walk in small groups through the community house, clan house, carving shed, and totem park with its replicas of poles brought from ancestral villages in the 1930s. No one lives in Saxman Native Village, but 498 people reside in the little town surrounding it.

"Clan houses, a representation of the cosmos, always face the water. The fire pit, in the center of the house, is the symbolic center of the universe, and is the intersection to the middle world dominated by man, the underworld, the upper world, the sea world, and sky world."
—Ketchikan Indian Corporation

A tour with Cape Fox Tours begins with a greeting, delivered in Tlingit at the community hall. On stage, the story of Eagle and Raven, Sun and Moon is narrated in English, while masked dancers reenact the story. A slide show briefly introduces Tlingit culture. As visitors leave the hall, they may meet several elders demonstrating crafts. The next stop is an old-style Beaver clan house. Constructed in 1990, it is the first authentic clan house built by Natives in Southeast Alaska in more than 100 years. Robed dancers discuss winter life in the clan house, then perform traditional dances and songs. Visitors are invited to try on carved headdresses and dance robes, and then to join the dancers in a final song.

A clan house is about as different from European housing as is imaginable. The interior of the Beaver clan house smells as fragrant as a new cedar chest. The rectangular room, built around a central square fire pit, is adorned with massive house posts and wall panels carved and painted with clan symbols. In the recent past, a clan house like this one might have lodged up to 50 members of an extended family during winter months, providing warmth and shelter from the wet, windy winters.

After leaving the clan house, visitors walk to a carving shed that is long enough to accommodate a 100-foot-long cedar log. Some of the best totem-, canoe-, and mask-carvers in the world (as well as their

When you speak to an elder (any gray-haired tribal member) you don't have to speak slowly or simply. While some elders speak Native languages fluently, all are fluent in English and often have, or are working on, college degrees. Elders are treated with deference and respect in the community because it is believed that they have lived long enough to have invaluable perspective, if not downright wisdom.

apprentices) are at work in this shed. Many of the totem poles carved here are commissioned; others are purchased by inspired visitors as the first chip falls, selling for $800 to $2,500 a foot. The carver himself may tell the story about the pole he's working on, a colorful narration designed to drive home a point. Outside, visitors take turns wielding an elbow adze, the primary tool used by Northwest Native carvers. When carvers use the adze, it seems to slide through the wood as if it were butter. It's not as easy as it looks.

Cape Fox Tours, PO Box 8558, Ketchikan, AK 99901; (907)225-5163. Tickets to Saxman Native Village ($30 adult, $15 child) are available only through Cape Fox Tours. They are sold in advance on board cruise ships and include transportation, which leaves from the Ketchikan cruise ship dock. Others may purchase tickets at the Village Store, a gift shop next to Saxman Totem Park. Times of tours always coincide with ship arrivals. A new 2 1/2-mile-long walking trail leads from Ketchikan along the road to Saxman; other transportation from Ketchikan to Saxman is by taxi (city buses do not run to Saxman). Open daily May–Sept Saxman Totem Park and the Village Store are free and open year-round.

Shotridge Studios

Israel Shotridge, a Tlingit Native, has carved a number of totem poles for the Southeast Alaska region, including a replica of the Chief Kyan pole carved in 1992 and now standing in Whale Park near Ketchikan's waterfront. Visitors to Shotridge's studio can easily while away an hour. Watch Shotridge and others carve, have a cup of fragrant herbal "Hudson's Bay tea," and settle into a chair to watch a video made for public television of Israel's mother, Esther Shea, an elder of the Tlingits' Tongass Bear clan.

There's an old Tlingit saying that when the tide is out, the table is set. Natives still harvest black seaweed during minus tides. The seaweed is dried slightly, sprinkled with clam juice, and then dried completely in the sun. Crunchy and highly nutritious, it's used in soups or eaten like popcorn.

Born in Quadra Island, British Columbia, in 1917, Esther Shea attended the Sheldon Jackson Indian boarding school in Sitka, then lived in Saxman most of her life, detached from the tribal ways. Ironically, at the age of 50 she was asked to return to the Sheldon Jackson School to teach the Tlingit language, which the boarding school had forced her to stop speaking as a child. In 1989, Esther led the first potlatch held in Southeast Alaska in 40 years, inviting the Bear clans of the entire Tlingit Nation to come forward. It was a momentous event for all of the clans, who soon began to hold their own potlatches once more.

Shotridge Studios, Ketchikan, AK 99901. By appointment only, (907) 225-0407.

Totem Heritage Center

The 33 totem poles stored at the Totem Heritage Center in Ketchikan are so weathered and aged that the original carvings are mere shadows on the cracked surfaces. Drained of color, the totem poles are silver with age and are crumbling with dry rot. Most of the poles, 95 to 100 years old, would have disappeared by now if they had been left where they fell in their abandoned villages. Tribal elders, the Alaska Native Brotherhood and Sisterhood, local historians, and the Tongass Historical Museum staff began rescuing the old totems in the 1960s. The Totem Heritage Center, the only major collection of authentic totem poles in the United States, has become an invaluable resource, especially for young carvers inspired by the old masters' work. Photos on the walls, many taken at the turn of the century, show the poles in their village of origin, most within a 50-mile radius of Ketchikan. The collection also includes house posts and other wood fragments.

Southeast Alaska Natives carved three kinds of totem poles. One kind commemorates an event, legendary or real. Another is a mortuary pole, with the family clan symbols on the front of the pole and the cremated remains of the deceased sealed in a hole in the back. The ridicule pole was used as a form of public humiliation.

Also available at the center is the Native Arts Program schedule of classes taught by Native artists from throughout the Northwest. The center's gift shop is owned and managed by the Ketchikan Indian Corporation.

Totem Heritage Center, 601 Deermount St, Ketchikan, AK 99901; (907)225-5900. Within walking distance of downtown, the center is located in a pleasant park that includes the old salmon hatchery ponds, the new hatchery, a bridge over Ketchikan Creek, and a self-guided nature path. $2 adults; under 12, free; Sunday afternoons, all free. Open daily, May 15–Sept 30; winters, Tues–Fri afternoons. Guided tours; wheelchair accessible; exhibits for the blind.

Tongass Historical Museum

At the Tongass Historical Museum is a small "This Is Our Life" exhibit consisting primarily of Tlingit, Haida, and Tsimshian artifacts, basketry, and stone tools. The museum is perched on the edge of rushing Ketchikan Creek, and also houses the public library. The totem outside the museum tells the story of Raven stealing the sun, probably the most oft-told Tlingit tale. There are two ravens in Tlingit myth. One is the great Nass Raven, who lives on the mainland at the mouth of the Nass River, at the border of Southeast Alaska and British Columbia, and who controls the sun, the moon, and the stars. The other is his grandson Scamp Raven, the lovable (and ribald) trickster. In the story carved in the totem outside the museum, Scamp

Raven brings light to the world when he steals the box of daylight from his grandfather. The totem pole is a new one, designed and carved by Tlingit Dempsey Bob and raised in 1983.

Tongass Historical Museum, 629 Dock St, Ketchikan, AK 99901; (907)225-5600. Open daily May 15–Sept 30; $2; winters, Wed–Sun afternoons; free.

Southeast Alaska Visitor Center

In the Native Traditions Room of the U.S. Forest Service's Southeast Alaska Visitor Center (a step away from Ketchikan's cruise ship dock), you can see a depiction of life in a typical Native fish camp, as well as displays showing how cedar shakes and planks were adzed and replicas of wood implements, including fish hooks and knives. The exhibit includes six audiotapes (a couple of minutes each) of elders describing life in a fish camp. The center also displays portraits of the elders who helped with the 5-year planning of the exhibit. Native people are on staff if you have questions. See if you can discern the stylistic differences among the Tlingit, Haida, and Tsimshian totem poles—this is the only place in Alaska where you'll see all three styles of totems together.

Southeast Alaska Visitor Center, 50 Main St, Ketchikan, AK 99901; (907)228-6214. Open daily, May–Sept; Tues–Sat, Oct–Apr. Free.

Totem Bight State Park

In 1938, carvers were hired by the U.S. Army Corps of Engineers to copy the old totems and to replicate a clan house. Fragments of old totems were laid beside new cedar poles and totem poles were re-created using handmade tools. The original poles had been painted with oil-based paint made from minerals and oil from crushed salmon eggs; unfortunately, the new poles were painted with glossy modern paint—and it shows. The clan house contains a central fire pit and hand-adzed, removable floor boards, underneath which household goods would have been stored. The doorway, facing the water, is so low that an adult must crouch to enter, an effective form of home security.

To learn more about totem designs and stories, look for The Wolf and the Raven, by Dr. Viola Garfield, anthropology professor, and Linn Forrest, U.S. Forest Service architect in charge of the Totem Bight restoration project. (University of Washington Press, 1948, 18th printing.)

Totem Bight State Park, Milepost 10 N, Tongass Hwy, Ketchikan, AK 99901; (907)247-8574. Follow trails through the woods to a point of land jutting into the Tongass Narrows. Access to beach, viewing deck overlooking poles, and the clan house is free or by donation.

Open dawn to dusk, daily, year-round. The clan house is open Mon–Fri, mid-May–mid-Sept, 8 am–8 pm; mid-Sept–mid-May, 9 am–3pm.

Art

Most of the galleries in Ketchikan carry Northwest Coast art, particularly the Village Store at Saxman and the Native-owned gift shop at the Totem Heritage Center in Ketchikan, where you'll find handsome wood carvings made by local carvers. Two Native-owned galleries are on the Creek Street boardwalk, directly below Cape Fox Lodge. Haida carver George Brown sells black argillite (a type of slate) carvings from British Columbia's Haida Gwaii at Hide-A-Way Gifts (18 Creek Street, Ketchikan, AK 99901; (907)225-8626); he also carves cedar on-site. Ask for a copy of Brown's father's memoir, which contains reflections on his visit to the Haida Gwaii village the family left in the 1800s. Also see photographs taken in the abandoned villages where relatives once lived in clan houses.

At Alaska Eagle Arts (5 Creek Street, Ketchikan, AK 99901; (907)225-8365), look for Diane Douglas Willard's exquisite Haida-style spruce root and cedar bark baskets, and Chilkat and Raven's Tail weaving. The majority of the gallery space is dedicated to owner Marvin Oliver's multimedia work and displays his glass castings, unusual screened prints, vests, denim jackets, T-shirts, cards, and unusual boxed stationery with a paper fold-out canoe on top of the box. Director of American Indian Studies at the University of Washington, Oliver is also on the faculty at the University of Alaska in Ketchikan, where he teaches the history of Northwest Coast art.

Metlakatla: *Tsimshian*

On a warm, windless evening in late July, the Alaska State Ferry *Aurora* quietly passes a small rocky island iridescent with pink fire weed and glides into the Metlakatla harbor on Annette Island. The boat docks at the foot of Purple Mountain, near a waterfall that streaks down a rocky face and splashes into the bay. In the distance the town's waterfront is defined by a small lumber mill, an old wooden cannery built on pilings over the water, and a weathered boathouse shaped like a dairy barn.

Metlakatla is 15 miles south of Ketchikan—a 15-minute hop on a floatplane that lands between the town's cannery and the boat basin, or an hour's ride on the ferry. From the ferry's upper deck, the land behind Metlakatla looks flat and treeless, as if it had been freshly logged, but it is really a huge wetland as beautiful as any Japanese garden. Created when glaciers scraped across Southeast Alaska during the last ice age, the wetlands, called "muskegs," cover hundreds of acres and are prevalent throughout the archipelago. Small, twisted pine trees and clusters of fragrant bog rosemary, leggy buckbean, and evergreen crowberry grow alongside hundreds of lilypad-filled ponds. Most of the trees are lodgepole pines, 400 to 500 years old, their growth stunted by the high acidic content of the bog's deep sponge of spagnum moss.

Rising from the middle of the muskeg behind Metlakatla is Yellow Hill, a geologic mystery of bright yellow, pillow-shaped rock, sanded smooth by winter's hard rain and high winds. Years ago Metlakatla's tribal historian and builder, Ira Booth, constructed a boardwalk through the rocks, across the spongy meadows, and alongside ponds, up to the hill's 546-foot-high summit. Although the boardwalk has collapsed in many places and treads have rotted away on the stairs, the easy climb up to the top is incredibly beautiful in midsummer, when hundreds of wildflowers, such as yellow and red Indian paintbrush and bluebells, nearly engulf the path.

The village site at Metlakatla, on the island's sheltered north end, was once occupied by Tlingit Indians. Although the Tlingits had left long before, their totem poles were still standing near the beach when nearly 1,000 Tsimshian Indians arrived on August 7, 1887, aboard a steamship trailing cargo canoes. They came from British Columbia with Scottish Anglican missionary William Duncan to build a utopian Christian community.

The Tsimshians came from "Old Metlakatla," 90 miles south of Annette Island, near British Columbia's Skeena River. Old Metlakatla, a model town composed of Tsimshians drawn from their villages by the charismatic Duncan, had existed only five years before trouble with church officials, who disliked Duncan's strong-headed ideas, forced the community to move. Duncan successfully negotiated with President Grover Cleveland for the entire 86,000-acre Annette Island in the newly acquired American territory of Alaska.

Annette Island wasn't just picked off the map. The Tsimshians had used it regularly as a summer fishing camp after the Tlingits had abandoned it. When the Tsimshians moved there permanently, they left behind everything they owned in Old Metlakatla except for a few personal belongings, which were packed in the canoes, and the

Ferry service to Metlakatla from Ketchikan can be sporadic, but three floatplane services operate daily. Metlakatla has a fully stocked grocery and sometimes a food booth, but no restaurants. Ethel Leask rents two comfortable rooms in her prefab house, one with its own bath. Continental breakfast and dinner (arrange in advance) for overnighters. Reservations essential. (PO Box 526, Metlakatla, AK 99926; (907)886-5275; $75–$115.)

community-owned sawmill, which was carried aboard the steamship.

The sawmill was soon put to use. New Metlakatla was designed by Duncan and built on boardwalks over the muskeg, a community consisting of wood-frame houses and the state's largest church, nicknamed the "Westminster Abbey of Alaska," which seated over 1,000.

Today the only Indian reservation in Southeast Alaska, Annette Island and its only town of Metlakatla is governed by a mayor and 12-member council. The village boardwalks are gone, but many of the old buildings remain. The cannery, rebuilt in 1918, still operates, and Duncan's humble little house is a repository of the island's history, with most of the minister's belongings intact. Metlakatla's charm is its patina, not its polish.

> *"The canoes pulled behind the steamship were not kayak-sized boats, but large enough to hold 60 men at a time, with 10-foot-high sides. How'd they paddle them? Didn't. They sailed them. With woven cedar sails."*
> —Ira Booth, Metlakatla tribal historian

Metlakatla Tours and Dance Performance

Visitors must obtain a permit if they wish to remain on Annette Island for more than 72 hours, and they must stay within the town limits or be escorted by a Metlakatla resident. These rules are strictly enforced by tribal police. Rules or not, the best way to fully appreciate Metlakatla is by guided tour. Tour guides will take you to areas you normally couldn't see from the road. You will get fascinating behind-the-scenes looks at the sawmill, cannery, council chambers, fish traps, William Duncan's cottage, and the village totems. Tours end at the longhouse with a performance by the Fourth Generation Dancers and a meal featuring salmon cooked over an open wood fire on the deck overlooking the boat basin.

For tour information, contact Solomon D. Atkinson, (907)886-1121; or the Metlakatla Tribal Council Chambers Office, Metlakatla, AK 99926; (907)886-4441.

Metlakatla's Totem Poles

Years ago, Father William Duncan shipped old totem poles left behind in Metlakatla by the Tlingits to Sheldon Jackson's museum in Sitka. Determined to replace their Indian culture with the European model, the Tsimshians carved no new totems. In the 1970s, Tsimshian Jack Hudson rekindled an interest in traditional Tsimshian culture when he taught himself to carve by looking at old photographs and talking with elderly carvers. Still, no totems were carved or traditional ceremonies held in Metlakatla until 1982, when another young Metlakatlan, David Boxley, who had taught himself to carve totem poles at the University of Washington, erected a pole and sponsored a potlatch in honor of his grandparents. Boxley also wrote songs and dances for the ceremonies. Two years later, more than 1,000 people participated in a memorial potlatch held for David's grandfather. Another pole was raised, this time in front of a new, traditional-style longhouse built near the shoreline.

Boxley was raised by his grandfather, a canoe carver who had given up his craft when he moved to Metlakatla. Boxley learned to carve by studying totems in museums. In 15 years, he created 42 poles and hundreds of bentwood boxes, rattles, masks, panels, and prints. Eleven of the thirteen poles now standing in Metlakatla were carved by Boxley, who now lives near Seattle, Washington, but spends summers at home in Metlakatla. Carver Jack Hudson lives on Metlakatla year-round, teaching carving at the high school and selling his own work at his home gallery, House of the Wolf (on the corner of Leask and Western, Metlakatla; (907)886-1936). Another outstanding Metlakatla carver is Wayne Hewson, who makes and sells exceptional native regalia, including museum-quality carved cedar headpieces trimmed with ermine and abalone shell. (At Hewson's studio on Haines Street, Metlakatla; (907)886-7051. By appointment.)

Father Duncan's Cottage and Museum

It doesn't look like much from the outside, but the inside of Father William Duncan's original house, where he lived from 1891 until his death in 1918, is a treasure. It feels like a small church, or perhaps someone's attic, with its dormer-style roof, unpainted walls, and fireplaces outlined with a simple painted white line. Most of Duncan's furniture, his narrow little bed, his books and personal items, and even a pile of his old shoes are displayed—some items looking like he carelessly tossed them in the corner a few hours earlier. Duncan, the island's only doctor, also served as the community's (harsh) judge and taught school as well. The museum preserves his unusual apothecary shop, his classroom, and his cylinder phonograph—a serious tool of early anthropologists and only the second one made and signed by his friend Thomas Edison. Visitors can look through Duncan's scrapbooks, which are filled with turn-of-the-century articles, clipped from newspapers all over the world, trumpeting Father Duncan's missionary zeal and the Metlakatla community's hard work.

Father Duncan's Cottage and Museum, Tait and Fourth Sts, Metlakatla, AK 99926; (907)886-7363. Free. Open year-round; Mon–Fri, afternoons; Sat, by appointment.

William Duncan Memorial Church

William Duncan died in 1918 and is buried on the grounds of the original church. The two-spired white church on the corner of Fourth and Church Streets is a replica of the second church on the site. Back in British Columbia, in Old Metlakatla, Duncan had enraged Church of England officials by teaching "some rituals and ceremonies to the Tsimshian Indians resulting in the church seizing Tsimshian land and jailing those in defiance," according to newspaper accounts of the time. The rest of the story is chronicled in *The Devil and Mr. Duncan,* available in most Southeast Alaska bookstores. Duncan's journals have been copied onto microfiche by historian Ira Booth; the original handwritten journals are stored in tribal archives. The church, nondenominational until 1945, now houses the local Assembly of God.

William Duncan Memorial Church, 4th and Spring Sts, Metlakatla, AK 99926; (907)886-6577.

The Old Cannery

It's modern inside, but the Annette Island Packing Company's old cannery building is a 1918 beauty. Three other historic buildings are on the premises: the old, barn-shaped boathouse, the cannery workers' mess hall, and the bunkhouse that housed Filipino and Chinese cannery workers.

The waters off Annette Island up to 3,000 feet deep belong to the Metlakatlans. They use surprisingly large fish traps or gill and seine nets to catch five different species of salmon. Salmon stocks are replenished at a busy hatchery on the island's south side. The packing company also processes salmon roe, sea cucumbers, sea urchins, herring roe, halibut, shrimp, and bottom fish. Gift packs of assorted smoked and canned salmon, with a label designed by Tsimshian Jack Hudson, are on sale.

Annette Island Packing Company, 100 Tait St, PO Box 10, Metlakatla, AK 99926; (907)886-4661. Due to safety and sanitation rules, the cannery is open for pre-arranged tours only. Call for details. Gift boxes may also be purchased at local stores.

The Fourth Generation Dancers

The Fourth Generation Dancers consists of 62 members of the community who wear gorgeous hand-crafted regalia and have learned and written songs. Their lead singer, Theo MacIntyre, has a voice that could call a kid from Ketchikan—without using the phone. The dancers are completely self-supporting, raising money for travel by holding bake and rummage sales. They dance in the tribe's longhouse, under a black-and-white cedar canoe suspended from the rafters.

Watching dancers dressed in traditional regalia sing, drum, and dance can transport you back to an earlier era, especially when they perform in a longhouse or clan house setting. The performance is so heady and exotic that it's easy to forget that the dancers have researched their tribe's past, sewn regalia, learned dances, and even relearned the native language, all while holding down full-time jobs, attending universities, and raising families. If you are at a loss for what to say to a dancer, ask him or her about the regalia—what the clan symbols sewn on button blankets represent, the number of hours it takes to make a headdress, the origin of a rattle or drum he or she is carrying. One singer we talked with described to us, using operatic terms, the way she uses her voice to fill the room.

Prince of Wales Island: *Haida*

Prince of Wales Island, west of Ketchikan, is one of the largest islands in the United States. Slightly smaller than Hawaii's "Big Island," it is largely unoccupied. Most of the 135-mile-long island lies within the Tongass National Forest, subject to logging by Native corporations. More than 1,000 miles of gravel logging roads wind over the rugged mountain terrain and through acres of hot pink fireweed that cover logged slopes.

Known for their intrepid seafaring in some of the world's most perilous seas, the Haida first encountered Spanish explorers nosing about their Queen Charlotte homeland in 1774. Astounded priests aboard a Spanish ship recorded the meeting: Haida oarsmen nonchalantly paddled out to meet the anchored Spanish ship at the height of a furious storm and proceeded to trade. When the British visited the Queen Charlottes in 1787, the northern group had left for Alaska.

The Alaska State Ferry serves Prince of Wales Island, but it lands 30 miles from the nearest town with services. Travelers might want to book an inexpensive and quick flight on Native-owned Taquan Air instead. Flights leave several times daily from Ketchikan to Prince of Wales Island; call (800)770-8800 or (907)225-8800. The narrow pass through the mountains to the west side of the island is "flightseeing" at its best: seaplanes soar between 3,000-foot narrow sawtooth ridges and jagged needles that are emerald green with moss, then dip so low over the bay as they come in for a landing that you can spot huge cloudy rafts of jellyfish in the water.

If you do decide to take your car on the ferry, prepare for a long drive, in the middle of the night, over a rough road prone to mudslides. If you fly, four-wheel-drive rentals are available in Craig. You'll need to reserve one in advance of your trip.

Sometime before the late 1700s, the Haida came to Prince of Wales Island from British Columbia's Queen Charlotte Islands, 90 miles to the south. On Prince of Wales Island, the Haida not only found abundant resources but also discovered abandoned Tlingit villages, where they erected their own clan houses and totem poles. By the early 1800s, the Haida were doing a booming business providing otter pelts for foreign fur traders.

But the advantageous trading with the Hudson's Bay Company and the Russian American Trading Company did not last long. Sea otters were hunted to near-extinction by 1834. Worse, smallpox and measles claimed not only many tribal members but most of the record-keeping storytellers. Missionaries arriving in 1878 found a desperate group of people battered by their losses: in just one generation, the Haida population on Prince of Wales Island had dropped from 10,000 to about 800.

Today, Haida and Tlingit descendants live in Craig, Klawock, and Hydaburg on Prince of Wales Island. Craig and Klawock are 7 miles apart; Hydaburg is about 30 miles from Craig over a narrow winding road. Three villages of Haida moved to Hydaburg at the turn of the century, so that all of their children could attend one school.

Craig

The heart and soul of Craig, by far the largest town on the island, is fishing. A large number of Natives live in Craig and own local businesses, including a grocery store. The town has most of the services you need, including ATM machines, car rentals, and even espresso. Two Native-owned lodgings are within easy walking distance of the floatplane dock. The Haida Way Lodge is a modest and well-used motel, a favorite of sports fishermen hauling out at 4am. The other, Sunnahae Lodge, is relatively new, with 10 rooms and a large dining room decorated with Mission-style furnishings. The Haida Way Lodge rents by the night, but at Sunnahae, lodging is sold only as part of a fishing package and includes a round-trip floatplane flight from Ketchikan, three meals a day, guided fishing aboard a fully equipped cabin cruiser, bait, tackle, rain gear, and equipment. Sunnahae Lodge is owned by state representative Jerry Mackie. He represents 37 coastal communities in Southeast Alaska during legislative sessions, but during the summer months, he's at the lodge and guides many of the guests himself.

Haida Way Lodge, PO Box 690, Craig, AK 99921; (907)826-3268. Located on Front Street. Some rooms have Jacuzzis. Also books fishing charters.

Sunnahae Lodge, PO Box 795, Craig, AK 99921; (907)826-4000 Around the block from the Haida Way, on Water Street. Three-day fishing packages begin at $1,950 per person. Extended fishing packages are also available.

Klawock

A short drive from Craig, Klawock has been used for centuries as a fish camp and permanent village site. To see the most interesting part of Klawock, go down by the picturesque old cannery buildings on the waterfront (the first built in Alaska, in 1878). Twenty-one totems stand in a circle on a grassy slope above the cannery. Some of the totems are original, some replicated, from the abandoned village of Tuxekan on the north end of the island. These totems are different from most of those you see in Southeast Alaska: they feature realistic, large figures, such as whales, bears, and birds with large staring eyes perched on top of tall poles. Klawock is also a great place to watch eagles, which flock to the beaches when fishermen gut their catches.

Klawock Totem Park, Bayview St, Craig, AK 99921. To find the park, turn from the Craig/Klawock Highway toward the harbor onto Bayview Street.

Taats Art/Designs

Kathy Kato-Yates (Taats), the granddaughter of the chief of the Haida Double-fin Killer Whale clan, Richard Carle, Sr., relies on word of mouth for advertising. And the grapevine has brought people from places as far away as Europe and Asia who have heard about her shop "Taats Art." When we talked with her, 10 young Texans had just left the shop. The kids had saved all their money to buy authentic Northwest Coast art, but could afford only her silk-screened post-cards. But Taats put on her button robe and hat for them anyway, and explained the meaning of each piece and how it was made. Then she sang them a Haida love song.

Kato-Yates is a versatile artist. She creates deerskin drums, silk-screened poster prints (limited editions may sell for $250 each), and tiny, 1-inch woven baskets with her trademark Russian blue beads sewn onto them. One of the few women carvers in Southeast Alaska, she makes masks and small replicas of the Klawock totem poles ($195 to $225 each) from red and yellow cedar that grows on Prince of Wales Island. When the cruise ships first came to town, her biggest sellers were three-dimensional cards made with felt and fur, which in 1989 sold for $4. In 1995 they were selling for $80.

Taats Art/Designs, 406 W St, Klawock, AK 99925; (907)755-2409. To find the totem park, follow the road down to the cannery area past the cold storage building, then take the next road to the right. The shop is 5 steps away from Taats' home. It's best to make an appointment, but you can find her most days.

Hydaburg

Founded in 1911 to centralize schools for three Haida communities, Hydaburg is the largest community (about 500) of Haida Natives in Southeast Alaska. It's also a very private place. In the middle of town, near the school, is a totem park, where poles from the three villages (Klinkwan, Sukkwan, and Howkan) were rescued and raised more than 50 years ago. There are no visitor services, but you are welcome to make the journey to Hydaburg and view the totems. The town is 30 miles south of Craig, via a narrow, winding road.

Prince of Wales Island Tours

Taquan Air, owned by Metlakatlan Jerry Scudero, has the best safety record in Alaska and offers five tours of Prince of Wales Island, in addition to regularly scheduled flights.

Alaska Bush Pilot Tour: Fly out with a bush pilot from Ketchikan on one of Taquan's daily mail, freight, and passenger routes to secluded wilderness areas on the island. Quick landings are made at historic villages, logging camps, remote fishing communities, and lodges. ($79 per person.)

Whales and Wildlife Cruise: Fly to the west coast of Prince of Wales Island for a day's guided eco-cruise aboard a cabin cruiser to see humpback whales, sea otters, seals, birds, and other marine life. ($279 per person; 10 hours; lunch included.)

Island Kayaking Adventure: On Prince of Wales Island, kayakers can explore 900 miles of coastline, bays, coves, inlets, points, and hundreds of small islands with some of the richest marine life in Alaska. The package includes flight to and from Prince of Wales from Ketchikan, 8 hours of fully equipped kayak rental, a detailed map, and guidance on currents. ($195.00 per person. Guides are extra; ask specifically if you want a Native guide. Additional days of kayak rental are available.)

Alaska Island Dive Fly-out: Diving in cold water is very different from diving in the Caribbean, particularly when whales are in the vicinity. Fly from Ketchikan to Craig for a half-day, two-tank dive with a divemaster. Drysuit and equipment, lunch, and time to explore in the afternoon included. ($295 per person; "C" card required.)

Fly-out Sportfishing: The floatplane rendezvous with a guided charter boat, fully equipped for saltwater sportfishing. Lunch and fishing equipment included. $285 per person. Or fly directly to Cape

Chacon on the southern tip of the island for fishing on an ocean-going vessel. ($295 per person; 10 hours.)

Taquan Air, 1007 Water St, Ketchikan, AK 99901; (800)770-8800 or (907)225-8800. Taquan Air's reservationdesk is at the Ketchikan International Airport. Tours vary according to season; call for more information.

Wrangell: *Tlingit*

After flying for nearly half an hour over uninterrupted sweeps of ever-green forest and blue-green water, the jet banks sharply and turns toward what looks like a wall of mountains before it touches down on Wrangell Island at the mouth of the Stikine River. Just before the plane lands, the tiny town of Wrangell appears below. Once an important trading post, Wrangell now consists mostly of a boat basin, a ferry landing, and a cruise ship dock.

According to their legends, the Stikine Tlingits arrived in the Wrangell area about 1,000 years ago. Coming from the interior, they were relative newcomers to the archipelago, which had been occupied for more than 10,000 years by other Tlingit bands. Long before the Russians occupied Alaska, the powerful Stikines controlled the entry to the Stikine River, a rare gap in the otherwise impenetrable wall of mountains that separates Southeast Alaska from British Columbia. The river reaches 330 miles into the interior, and by following it, the Stikine Tlingits could trade goods acquired from Pacific Coast tribes with interior tribes as far east as present-day Alberta and Montana.

Today, about a quarter of the population of Wrangell is Native, although not all are descended from the Stikine Tlingit. Schools and missions were established in Wrangell between 1870 and 1879, and Natives were brought into town from nearby islands. In the 1930s, the Native population changed dramatically when the Bureau of Indian Affairs built the Wrangell Institute, bringing Native students from all over Alaska for job training. Aleut people from the north were uprooted and relocated to Wrangell after World War II.

As with all towns in Southeast Alaska, Wrangell is small enough that a visitor doesn't need a car to see the town's major attractions. The Alaska State Ferry docks right downtown, but those flying in by jet will need to call a taxi for a short ride from the airport to town.

Wrangell is most famous for its reconstructed clan house, called Chief Shakes House. Surrounded by totem poles, it sits on the very spot where the original Shakes clan house was built prior to 1700. The Stikine elders and the Native Wrangell Cultural Heritage Committee have also beautified the downtown area with numerous totem poles and a totem park. There's a small museum with Indian artifacts. Less known is Petroglyph Beach, on a point overlooking the mouth of the Stikine River; it's well worth the 15-minute walk from downtown.

To get a map of town and directions, stop by the Wrangell Chamber of Commerce, located in a small A-frame on the corner of Outer Drive and Brueger Street near the city dock; (907)874-3901.

Petroglyph Beach

A 15-minute walk from the city dock, north on Evergreen Street, leads to a short trail to Petroglyph Beach. On the beach, turn to the right and look for boulders nesting in beach gravel. Petroglyphs are best viewed when the rocks are wet—in a rainstorm, after the tide has receded, or dampened with water from a spray bottle. As the rock darkens, faces, spirals, and totemic symbols, chipped in the rock with stone tools, whisper a forgotten language across the centuries.

The meaning of the petroglyphs is unclear. Some appear to be totemic and could illustrate portions of Raven story, while others seem to correlate with shamanic power signs. No one can say for sure. There is speculation that the glyphs may be the work of two separate cultures—one that may have been here as long as 35,000 years ago, the other a Tlingit community estimated to have been in Southeast Alaska 10,000 years prior to the arrival of the Stikines.

The beach, as unusual as it is, is taken for granted. Sunbathers throw their beach towels casually across the face of the petroglyph-incised rocks and lean against them to read, while kids dig in the sand around them. Washed by high tides, the area was used, literally, as a garbage dump until a few decades ago. Shell middens—cast-off clam shells thrown into piles by the first inhabitants—lie under a layer of broken glass and pottery sherds dumped in the last century.

Please do not remove or take rubbings of stones. More than 70 petroglyphs were once counted on the beach; in 1974 the count was 46, in 1995 there were about 27.

Petroglyph Beach, Wrangell. Walk from the ferry terminal north on Evergreen St, for ¾ mile to a gravel road leading to the beach. Watch for signs. An information kiosk is at the head of the short trail to the beach.

Chief Shakes House

A short wooden footbridge crosses to Shakes Island in Wrangell's inner harbor and ends right in front of Chief Shakes House. Surrounded by rustling cottonwood trees, a lawn speckled with white clover, and about a dozen totem poles, the hand-adzed plank house is painted with a figure that stretches from floor to roof. When the door is unlocked, you enter the house through a small hole in the figure's abdomen and step into the darkened single room, which is illuminated by a single hole in the roof over the center fire pit.

"Shakes" is an honorary title that was won for Wrangell's high-caste chiefs in a war with the Niska Indians, a Tsimshian tribe from British Columbia. To avoid being taken as slaves after losing the battle, the chief of the Niska gave his "Shakes" name and crest symbol to the victors. The Niska chief's killer-whale crest symbolized the right of Tlingit chiefs to use the title and crest forever. The title was passed down through Tlingit men, uncle to nephew, on the mother's side. The last direct hereditary chief, Chief Shakes VI, died in 1916. One more Chief Shakes was named in 1940. After his death, the title has remained unfilled.

Successive generations of chiefs, all with the name of Chief Shakes, lived in the first clan house built on this site after the clan moved in the 1600s to the Wrangell area from their village at nearby Kots-lit-na. The clan house you see here now was built in 1939 by the Civilian Conservation Corps during their totem restoration project.

All the totems that stand around Chief Shakes House are replicas of the originals. Natives inaugurated the new clan house with an authentic potlatch in 1940, one of the first held in Alaska since the ceremony was outlawed near the turn of the century.

Interior house posts were carved and raised inside the house in 1979, in the first of a series of new Native carving projects in Wrangell. They were carved by two men, one of them a Tlingit. The posts were copied from the original posts loaned by the local Tlingits to the Wrangell Museum.

A Chief Shakes memorial site is across the harbor from Chief Shakes House on Case Avenue, a short walk around the basin. Look for the three-story-high Wrangell Boat Shop. The memorial is across the street in a grove of trees: a rectangle of grass surrounded by a white picket fence with two carved killer whales erected on corner posts. It looks like a grave site, but no one is buried there. The remains of various Chief Shakes are buried in local cemeteries. The carvings look old, weathered by wind and rain, but were actually made in 1979, the third set of killer whales placed at the site.

One of the totems near Chief Shakes House features a realistic-looking black bear perched atop a tall pole. Bear tracks are carved into the pole all the way to the top. According to a story published in the 1940 *Wrangell Sentinel,* the pole commemorates a great flood that was of the same dimensions as the biblical flood. "When the flood came, the Shakes tribe was camped on the Stikine River near Cone Mountain, their summer camp. As the water rose, the people, frightened, fled to higher ground. Fighting their way up the mountains, through the tangled underbrush, they came across two grizzly bears who were also seeking refuge. The bears showed by their actions that they wanted to help the Shakes people, leading the people to safety. The party reached the pinnacle of Cone Mountain, where they stayed until the water receded."

Storytellers say that on the mountain today are impressions of ropes petrified into the stone where some of the people tied their canoes to the peak.

Chief Shakes House, Wrangell, AK 99929. Located at the end of Front St. Free. Chief Shakes House is locked except for special events. You can visit Shakes Island anytime between dawn and dusk.

Kiksadi Totem Park

About a block from Chief Shakes House is the Kiksadi Totem Park on Episcopal Street. The Sun House, a clan house similar to the Chief Shakes House, once sat on the site of the totem park. The tallest pole, in front, is a replica of the original, carved in 1890, that marks this site as belonging to the Kiksadi clan. Other totem poles are located throughout Wrangell.

Kiksadi Totem Park, Wrangell. On Episcopal St, 1 block from Chief Shakes House.

Detailed descriptions of the totems and the stories they tell were written by members of the Cultural Heritage Committee, a Native group, and are reprinted in "The Wrangell Guide," a free publication printed by the Wrangell Sentinel, (PO Box 798, Wrangell, AK 99929). The guide is also available from the Wrangell visitors center (on the corner of Outer Drive and Brueger Street).

Wrangell Museum

It's a little museum, full of the stuff of local history, but by far its greatest treasures are the old Chief Shakes house posts, carved about 1740, and other old totems from villages in the area. All are on loan from the Native community. The Tlingit baskets on display were woven in Wrangell and were sold as trade items or given as gifts. The beadwork shows the influence of both intertribal trade and post-contact trade demands. Subsistence technology is represented by halibut hooks, storage containers, gut parkas, fishing harpoons, and hunting points. The Eskimo baskets on display were made for trade and sold locally by students attending the Wrangell Institute between 1932 and 1975.

Wrangell Museum, 318 Church St, PO Box 1050, Wrangell, AK 99929; (907)874-3770. Admission $2; children 16 and under free. Open May–Sept, weekdays and Saturday afternoons; Sundays match ferry arrival times. Call for winter hours; also for tours and special events.

Juneau Metropolitan Area

From the outside, the house looks like any other tract home. But the living room furniture has been pushed aside, making way for a long dinner table. At the back of the house, the kitchen has plenty of room for guests to stand around, with an extra-large pantry stacked with china and dozens of glasses. This is a home where hospitality is taken seriously.

More than 30 guests—many of them heads of Native corporations—munch on appetizers before the main courses of salmon and halibut. Many of the appetizers are traditionally prepared Tlingit, Tsimshian, and Haida seafoods: various kinds of smoked salmon, octopus, crab, pickled gumboots (chiton), cockles, herring eggs, dried moose, dry fish strips, and ooligan oil. Dinner conversation turns from a story of flying a surfing-magazine editor to a remote beach to a discussion of the reorganization of the Bureau of Indian Affairs.

This is a side of Alaska that tourists, dazzled by Juneau's Mendenhall Glacier, the old town's narrow streets, the Alaska State Museum's collection of 19th-century Native art, and the totem poles and souvenir shops, rarely if ever see: Native Alaskans at home and Native corporations at work.

Juneau, the mountain-bound capital city of Alaska, is headquarters for several of the state's most influential Native organizations: the Central Council of the Tlingit and Haida Indian Tribes of Alaska; Goldbelt, Incorporated; Yak-Tat Kwaan, Incorporated; Huna Totem Corporation; Kootznoowoo, Incorporated; Klukwan, Incorporated; and Sealaska Corporation and its nonprofit Heritage Foundation. Some of the groups are housed in modern office buildings next to the state legislative buildings—all built on tailings from Juneau's AJ Mine, which honeycombed the town's Mount Roberts and filled in enough of the shallow bay for the city to expand.

The city mushroomed after gold was discovered in 1880. In October of that year, an Auk Tlingit named Chief Kowee showed prospectors Joe Juneau and Richard Harris where to find gold. In exchange he received 10 good blankets. Gold meant nothing to Kowee; his people used the rare dentalia shell as currency. But gold meant everything to the white prospectors, and its discovery brought hundreds more gold seekers to the Juneau area. They opened some of the most productive gold mines in Alaska and made the new, saloon-filled town of Juneau their headquarters.

The setting of Juneau is dramatic. Like all towns in Southeast Alaska, it fights for space between the deep fjord and the mountains, which here rise vertically nearly 4,000 feet within a block of downtown. The mountains closing in on Juneau are a boon to hikers but a barrier to highways from the interior; the only way in is by plane or boat.

When the gold miners arrived, the largest permanent Tlingit village was at Auke Bay, 14 miles north of what would become downtown Juneau. Four other villages were located in the area, including a fishing camp on the beach, right below the present-day governor's white antebellum mansion. The camp became a full-fledged village in the 1900s when the Tlingits abandoned Auke Bay to live and work in town. The modern office building containing the Haida and Tlingit headquarters sits there now, with a Victorian-era clan house behind it marked with clan symbols and two totems.

In the Alaska State Library, there's a picture of the Juneau Tlingit village, taken in the late 1800s. In it, modern houses have replaced the old clan houses. Another change is documented in such photographs: blatant discrimination against the Native people. Signs on restaurants proclaim in big block letters: "Whites Only" or "All White Help."

Probably one of the most important events that happened in Juneau, from the Native point of view, was the antidiscrimination bill passed by the state senate on February 8, 1945. The bill passed only after a nasty debate on the senate floor, which was finally ended by a stirring speech from Elizabeth Peratrovich, a Native Tlingit from the village of Klawoch on Prince of Wales Island. When she had finished talking, wild applause burst from the gallery and senate floor alike, and the bill was subsequently passed. Today several Natives are members of the state legislature.

The Native presence, once dismissed, is now everywhere you look in Juneau—from murals on the walls to public art to totems outside the Kmart. And every two years in June, Juneau is host to Celebration, a week-long gathering of Tlingit, Haida, and Tsimshian Natives from all over Southeast Alaska, who come to sing, dance, and celebrate their Native heritage.

Alaska Native Tours of Juneau

What distinguishes an Alaska Native tour from all others in Juneau is that it's narrated by Native drivers and includes both their own experiences and a Native's version of Juneau's history. The bus tour begins at the steamship docking area on South Franklin Street, near a mural of the Tlingit creation story. As the bus heads through town to the Mendenhall Glacier, the driver begins to sing a song in Tlingit, softly, like a lullaby. She brakes for an eagle she's spotted, then pulls the bus over to point out salmon running up a stream. Like all of Juneau's many bus tours, this one includes a 40-minute break at the glacier, 13 miles from downtown. By tour's end the passengers have learned the healing properties of several indigenous plants, as well as how to speak a few words of Tlingit, and are singing Native songs along with the bus driver, their mouths stained blue by huckleberries they've picked along the way.

Alaska Native Tours, 3235 Hospital Dr, Juneau, AK 99801; (907)463-3231. Tickets and tour times available at the cruise ship dock through Last Chance Ticket Broker; advance bookings through Alaska Native Tours. $15 per person. Tours last 2 1/2 to 3 hours. Bring a coat for the short walk to the glacier.

Naa Kahidi Theater

The sleek white cruise ship, four stories high and the length of two football fields, moored at Juneau's dock, is a startling contrast to the cedar-planked Naa Kahidi theater on the shore. Built in the style of a clan house of 200 years ago, the darkened theater's planked seats step down to a central fire pit.

Ravens, big-beaked, black birds twice the size of crows, have a distinctive croak and also make a sound like dice rattling in a cup. Masked raven dancers mime the bird's hopping walk and glimmering eye. In the flicker of firelight, the dancer spreads his wings, pulls the string on his mask, and slaps the wooden beak open and shut as the drum pounds.

Naa Kahidi is a professional acting company that reenacts Native Alaska's most powerful stories for their dramatic, emotional, and visual appeal. Narration in English accompanies the animated masked actors who dance the story. Costuming is extraordinary, particularly that of Raven, with his snapping beak and wings made of slats of wood strung over the actor's arms. Actors are drawn from 13 indigenous communities in Alaska. Naa Kahidi has toured Alaska, the lower 48 states, and Europe, supported in part by the Alaska State Council on the Arts, the National Endowment for the Arts, and Sealaska Heritage Foundation.

The stories are evocative, so much so that when actors wear carved wooden masks, audience members swear they see the masks' expressions change as the story unfolds. In a quick post-theater poll, the audience gave the theater a solid four stars.

Naa Kahidi, Sealaska Heritage Foundation, One Sealaska Plaza, Ste 201, Juneau, AK 99801; (907)463-4844. Located next to the Juneau library, in front of the Alaska steamship docking area, S Franklin St. Admission $15; children under 12, $9. Call for reservations; tickets also sold at the door. Summers, two performances daily, Tues–Sat; winters, the company travels and is available for educational seminars.

Free Films

Among the videos shown free at the U.S. Forest Service's Information Center's theater are ones specific to Native life. *Angoon, 100 Years Later* is a documentary about the Tlingit Native village of Angoon, and its rebirth. The video also includes footage of a potlatch. (Angoon is the only settlement on Admiralty Island, 15 miles west of Juneau. The town is gradually modernizing, but most Tlingit residents live a subsistence lifestyle.)

Two other films demonstrate how Raven's Tail blankets are woven and show Native carvers practicing their traditional art.

U.S. Forest Service Information Center, 101 Egan Dr, Juneau, AK 99801; (907)586-8751. In the Centennial Hall. Open daily in summer; weekdays only in winter. Free.

Auk Village Recreation Site

By 1900 the winter village at Auke Bay was nearly deserted, the Tlingits having left for Juneau to look for work in the mines. Today, where the village once stood, there are a small public campground, day-park, and harbor. The village site, still nestled in tall Sitka spruce with a rocky beach below, is commemorated by a Yax-te totem pole, raised in 1941. The Yax-te, the Big Dipper, was a crest of a clan that lived near Klawoch on Prince of Wales Island. It was given to an Auk chief for his clan's use after a battle.

> "When I go home from Juneau to my ancestral village, it just smells like home—the kelp at low tide, clean salt water on the cool breeze mixed with the scent of fresh fish and the smoke-house."
>
> —Carol Aceveda, Tlingit

Auk Village Recreation Site, administered by the U.S. Forest Service, Juneau Ranger District; (907)586-8800. Located off Glacier Hwy, about 18 miles from town and 1 ½ miles from ferry terminal. Primitive campground with 12 spaces; no showers. First come, first served.

Art and Artists

In Juneau, almost all galleries carry Native art. In Southeast Alaska, the primary artform is woodcarving based on distinctive formline designs. Art ranges from hand-carved wooden bowls, masks, and bent-wood boxes to full-size totem poles. Prices on hand-carved items can be quite high but worth it; some Native carvers have international reputations. Beware, however, of imitators. If authenticity matters to you, just ask the shopkeeper; dealers passing off non-Native art as the real thing are breaking federal law.

There are two Native-owned galleries in Juneau. Totem Twins is at the Juneau International Airport (1873 Shell Simmons Drive,

Juneau, AK 99801; (907)789-4672). Mount Juneau Trading Post is in Juneau's old downtown (upstairs, at 151 South Franklin Street, Juneau, AK 99801; (907)586-3426).

For names of artists, dance groups, singers, storytellers, and lecturers, contact the Tlingit and Haida Central Council (320 West Willoughby Avenue, Ste 300, Juneau, AK 99801; (800)344-1432 or (907)586-1432).

Alaska State Museum

The rich heritage of Alaska's four major Native groups—Eskimo, Aleut, Athabascan, and Northwest Coast people—are presented through a selection of tools, clothing, and regalia at the Alaska State Museum. Some of the more fascinating items in this museum include umiaks, kayaks, and a birch-bark canoe, as well as ingenious Eskimo raingear—made of transparent seal gut that gleams like alabaster. Modern-day raincoats look dull by comparison. Docent-led tours are the best way to get the inside story on the museum's collection.

The museum's largest exhibit is a Tlingit Frog clan house, with its four original house posts, on loan from Klukwan, a village near Haines.

A small ceremonial Frog hat on display is a treasure to Sitka's Kiksadi Tlingits, from whom it was taken more than 70 years ago. Like many ceremonial items that have left Southeast Alaska, the hat was sold without clan permission to a private collector prior to 1920. When it was offered at a Sotheby's auction in 1981, a consortium of the State Museum, Sealaska Heritage Foundation, and the clan successfully bid $65,000 for the hat, which is worth more than four times that today. The museum protects the hat, while the clan retains the right to use it for potlatch ceremonies.

"It's a new trend in museums," says collections curator Steve Henrikson. "Museums in the past tried to stop time, even though they put wear and tear on items by handling and displaying them. The uses of ceremonial objects by the original owners have equal, if not greater standing, than what the museum has been using them for." The arrangement has been mutually beneficial. Elders recently gave the museum a Chilkat robe worth at least $30,000 because they believe that ceremonial regalia should be stored and shown together.

Alaska State Museum, 395 Whittier St, Juneau, AK 99801; (907)465-2901. Open daily, year-round. Closed Sunday and Monday, Sept–Apr. Admission $3; children 18 and under, free. Gift shop.

Sitka: *Tlingit*

Sitka, built on the site of an ancient Tlingit village, is probably one of the most beautiful historic small towns in the United States. Once larger than San Francisco and considered the hub of European culture on the West Coast, it was regarded as "the Paris of the Pacific." Today, it's one of the hippest communities in Southeast Alaska. Sitka's public radio station, "Raven Radio" KCAW-FM (104.7), has been the subject of *New York Times* articles and a "60 Minutes" segment. The Island Institute's annual symposium attracts noted writers and thinkers from around the world. The Audubon Society's Christmas bird count draws an enthusiastic crowd. Other Sitka events include the Sitka Folk Festival, "Art on the Dock," International Museum Day, and a concert series.

Built on the west side of Baranof Island, Sitka is protected from the Pacific Ocean by an island-filled sound. Its Tlingit names, Sheet Ka and Shee Atika, mean "the village behind the islands" and "people on the outside edge of Shee facing the ocean," respectively. The pretty seascape is dominated by 3,102-foot Mount Edgecumbe, an extinct volcano as perfectly shaped as Japan's Mount Fuji. The Russians who burned down the Tlingit village to build their own town named the site "New Archangel" and operated a thriving fur-trading fort here until the 1860s, when Alaska was purchased by the United States. Today, Sitka's unique Tlingit-Russian heritage is everywhere in evidence. It's not unusual to find Russian borscht and alder-smoked salmon on the same menu. Public dance performances are in turn performed by Russian dancers and Tlingit; St. Michael's Cathedral, a Russian Orthodox Church, has a mostly Tlingit congregation; and businesses, such as the Sitka Rose Art Gallery, are even co-owned by people of Tlingit descent and people of Russian descent. In fact, the whole town appears to be quite harmonious today, happily capitalizing, without shlock, on its acrimonious past. Thirty-five years ago, the National Park Service, at the instigation of the Tlingit community, opened a cultural museum and totem park on the site where the Tlingits and Russians fought a bitter battle. And a few years ago, Tlingit Robert Sam led a campaign to clean up the old Russian cemetery.

Tlingit Cultural Tours of Sitka

Guide Tom Gamble, dressed in a handsome black-and-red jacket, introduces himself in Tlingit to the riders aboard his tour bus, holding up a recent photograph of his baby daughter. He translates what he's just said and begins to speak in English about his wife's labor and delivery in a local hospital. Gamble sounds like any other proud father until he segues into a description of his new baby's clan lineage and tells passengers that, in the old days, he and his wife would have kept this baby only until her fourth year, when she would have gone to live with her aunt and uncle, who would have raised her until she was ready to marry. As he puts the bus in gear, he gestures toward the site of Baronov's castle and the stockade that once surrounded the Russian settlement. Giving voice to something that is rarely spoken aloud, he says softly, "Baronov had to burn down my ancestors' homes to build it there." On Katlian Street along the waterfront, Gamble talks about the old village, which once had more than 40 clan houses facing the water, and the 2,500 Natives residing in Sitka today. He points out two ordinary houses, one gray and one white—clan houses behind their Victorian facades.

Tom picks local plants and wildflowers while his passengers visit the Sitka National Historical Park, a museum and interpretive center operated by the National Park Service. (Ironically, no Native interpreters are on the museum staff, and the Park Service does not allow Native guides to lead tours through the museum or the park.) When passengers return to the bus, Gamble passes around the plants he has picked and tells stories about each one, also describing some of their uses as medicine and food. At tour's end, he disappears to put on his robe and headdress and then takes his place with the Gaja Heen dancers for a short performance.

Sitka Tribe of Alaska, 456 Katlian St, Sitka, AK 99835; (800)746-3207 or (907)747-4915. Tour guides dressed in black-and-red uniforms sell tickets on the visitors' dock at the west end of Monastery Street. Two tours are offered; the longer tour (2 ½ hours) includes the dance performance. $10–$18 per person; children under 12 half-price.

Tracing Native Heritage

Members of a clan can trace their heritage back to one common ancestor. Each clan has a crest or multiple emblems, which are visual signals of some relationship between the clan and a supernatural or natural object. Crests, songs, dances, stories, and historical accounts are exclusive, clan-owned property, now protected by federal law just like corporate logos. No one can use a crest, song, dance, or story without permission from the clan. Clan crests are exhibited on ceremonial regalia, some of which is owned by the clan house or the whole clan, and some owned by individuals. The viewing of important crest items is an honor for the guests at potlatches and builds prestige for the host clan and the pieces shown. When a member of a clan, such as Tlingit carver John E. Bartel, identifies himself to another, it may sound like this:

"My name is John E. Bartels; my Tlingit name is KUU'-Ushgun. I was given Paul Willis' name, Ahnn-ka-la-seek, which is from the Eagle (Chh'a'ak') moiety. I am of the Chookaneidee clan. My Sitka house (Naak'a'Hitz'ee) is Iceberg House (Xaatl' Hit) and Iron House (Gaa yeis' Hit). My crest (At.oow) is Bear (Xoot's), Iceberg (Xaatl'), and Porpoise (ch'eech). I can also use Glacier Bay (Sit eeti Geey) and Woman in the Ice (Kaasteen).

"I was born December 6, 1949, in Sitka, Alaska, to Harry Bartel, half-Athabaskan and half-German, and Agnes (Nielson) Bartels (Kahh-dath), all Tlingit.

"My first introduction to totemic art was through my first teacher, my grandfather, Peter C. Nielsen (Aak'wa shoox'). His Tlingit name means "Laughing in the Lake." My grandfather's story is: 'Peter C. Nielsen, Tlingit name Aak'wa shoox', which is Raven moiety, Frog clan (Kiksadi). Born September 17, 1900, in Sitka, Alaska. I started my apprenticeship in 1926 under Jim Jacobs, i.e. Silver Jim (Yelth-Now-Yoo).'"

Sitka National Historical Park and Southeast Alaska Indian Cultural Center

The National Park Service's cultural museum and interpretive center, which sits on 107 acres at the mouth of the Indian River, was set aside as a public park by President Benjamin Harrison in 1890. Inside the museum is a collection of Tlingit artifacts (some of the most important pieces are on loan from the Tlingit people) along with a 10-minute film recapping the 1804 battle between the Tlingits and the Russians.

Look here also for a Raven's Tail robe, woven in one of the Native artisans' studios in an adjoining wing. The studios are operated by the Native-owned, nonprofit Southeast Alaska Indian Cultural Center, one of Sitka's major attractions. Master wood carver Will Burkhart, master silver carvers Louis Minard and Paul Galanin, wood carver Tommy Joseph, drum maker and ivory carver Jennifer Brady-Morales, and beader Catherine Pook demonstrate their crafts daily during the summer. The public is welcome to observe and ask questions. Apprentices train with the master artists; their first projects are added to the Sitka National Historical Park's permanent collection.

The museum faces a rocky beach that must look just as it did in 1804, when the battle between the Russians and the Tlingits took place at the mouth of the Indian River. Visitors can walk to the battleground and site of the Tlingit fort along a path interspersed with 15 totem poles. The poles are reproductions and, surprisingly, most are Haida, from Haida villages on Prince of Wales Island. The originals were collected in the early 1900s, with a $50,000 congressional appropriation, for the Louisiana Purchase Exposition of 1904. A few were sold in Louisiana; the rest were shipped to Portland, Oregon, for the Lewis and Clark Exposition, and were then shipped to Sitka, Alaska's first state capital, in 1905. The original Haida poles were erected on the park grounds, a lingering affront to the local Tlingit people. (The National Park Service sells a small, well-illustrated guidebook to the totem poles and house posts on the park grounds, called *Carved History;* available in the gift shop for $2.95.)

The path continues through the woods along the bank of the Indian River, across a stream by way of a wooden footbridge, and down the shore to the site of the Tlingit fort and Russian memorial (2 miles of trail).

Sitka National Historical Park and Southeast Alaska Indian Cultural Center, 106 Metlakatla St, Sitka, AK 99835; (907)747-6281. Free. Open daily; cultural center may be open winters (call first).

Sheldon Jackson Museum

A passionate collector who saved everything, including scrapbooks of pressed flowers, Dr. Sheldon Jackson traveled extensively throughout Alaska—first as a missionary and then as a general agent for education. He collected material from every remote village he visited, trading inexpensive cloth, needles, and kettles for valuable artifacts. Rich colleagues on the East Coast provided funds to house the collection in a fireproof concrete octagonal building constructed in 1895, next to the Sheldon Jackson Indian School (now Sheldon Jackson College).

Tethered live hummingbirds and young abandoned bear cubs were favorite pets of Tlingit children. If the cubs died, their skins were tanned, sewn, and then stuffed with dried plant material—the first "teddy bears."

The museum, now operated by the State of Alaska, is one of the most public-friendly anywhere. Items such as the Raven helmet worn by Tlingit leader Katlian are well displayed in eye-level glass cabinets and shelves, so you can walk around them and even look under them. There are items from everyday life, such as jewelry, miniature toys, gaming pieces, pipes, paintbrushes, and tools, all labeled in glass-topped drawers. More than 400 objects are available for handling and are often checked out to schools and libraries.

Sheldon Jackson Museum, 104 College Drive, Sitka, AK 99835; (907)747-8981. Adjoins Sheldon Jackson College, off Lincoln Street. Open 8am–5pm daily, mid-May to mid-Sept, 10am–4pm Tues–Sat. Gift shop.

"Raven Radio" KCAW-FM

Sitka's public radio station broadcasts National Native News daily at 8:30am right after the Raven Morning News, and replays it at 12:20pm. The station has put repeaters in remote areas such as Kake to make sure that Natives who have little access to media can keep abreast of breaking news. On Thursdays at 10:06am, you can catch Ut-Ka-Neek ("This Is My Story"), 90 minutes of local Native interviews and Native music, followed by Alaska Public Radio Network's Native talk show, broadcast from Juneau. This little radio station, on the top floor of an old World War I communication station, raises more money per capita than any other community radio station in the United States—about $75,000 a year. Souvenirs for sale—our favorites in Sitka—include T-shirts and sweatshirts emblazoned with the station's KCAW call letters and a goofy-looking black raven.

KCAW-FM, 2B Lincoln St, Sitka, AK 99835; (907)747-5877. Climb the back stairs outside the building to the second floor during business hours.

The Sitka Rose

Artist Teri Rofkar, a Tlingit Native, wove one of several ceremonial Raven's Tail robes on display at the Sitka National Historical Park. The Raven's Tail robe is a ceremonial robe that predates the elaborate yellow-and-black Chilkat blankets, and Rofkar's was the first such robe woven by a Tlingit in more than 200 years. The weaving took more than 700 hours, not including the six months spent spinning mountain goat wool and the time spent dyeing the wool with wolf moss (a type of lichen), iron, and hemlock bark.

Explorer Captain Cook's journals describe Tlingits wearing stunning black-and-white wool robes. A fragment of a robe found on Kruzof Island is in New York's Museum of Natural History. Inspired by her daughter's work, Teri Rofkar's mother,

"People ask me if it isn't odd to be selling my artwork to tourists, but it really isn't. My grandmother sat on the very same sidewalk in front of where my gallery is now and sold moccasins, baskets, and little totems to tourists. People pick up things that are 100 years old and want to know what they were used for. Many things were not used for anything functional but were carved and decorated for the tourist trade. People were going from a subsistence lifestyle to a lifestyle that depended on commodities. They had to pay for them somehow."

—Teri Rofkar, owner, Sitka Rose Gallery

Marie Laws, wove a robe herself, a work that took well over 1,000 hours. "What's so great about this," says Rofkar, "is that Mom was from that lost generation that was forced to go to boarding school, where they wouldn't let her learn any of her own mother's skills. She is one of our elders and had to teach herself how to weave."

Rofkar, co-owner of the multicultural Sitka Rose Gallery, also weaves traditional baskets from grasses, cedar bark, and spruce roots gathered from the Sitka area. She teaches, demonstrates, and lectures throughout Alaska and outside the state. Her work is included in the permanent collection of the Smithsonian Institution's National Museum of the American Indian in New York.

Sitka Rose Gallery, 419 Lincoln St, Sitka, AK 99835; (907)747-3030. Open year-round.

Native-Owned Lodging

Two elaborately beaded clan robes are framed and displayed behind the Westmark Shee Atika Hotel's registration desk, a nice introduction to the largest hotel in Sitka (100 rooms), built in the early 1970s and owned by Shee Atika Incorporated, a Sitka Native corporation.

Westmark Shee Atika Hotel, 330 Seward St, Sitka, AK 99835; (907)747-6241. A block from the old Russian Orthodox Church in downtown Sitka. Rooms $124–$175. All major credit cards and out-of-state checks accepted. The hotel's Raven Dining Room serves excellent seafood and salads; for reservations, call (907)747-6465.

At the Halibut Hide-A-Way, Tlingit Betty Jo Johns rents the one-bedroom apartment adjoining her house. Furnished with a double bed and a couple of futons, the apartment has a fully equipped kitchen and cable television. Pioneer Park is right across the street, with a trail through the park to the beach.

Halibut Hide-A-Way, 1972 Halibut Point Rd, Sitka, AK 99835; (907)747-4751. Three miles from town, toward the ferry terminal. One or two people, $65 with tax. Available year-round. Reservations.

You'll get a bed and a full breakfast with Margaret Gross Hope's family at Bed Inn, her duplex in the residential district, within walking distance of town. There are three bedrooms, each with a double bed. Full breakfast is included in the price.

Bed Inn, 518 Monastery St, Sitka, AK 99835; (907)747-3305. $50 single, $60 double. No alcohol, no smoking.

Haines: *Tlingit*

More than 300 years ago, Tlingit clans from Prince of Wales Island, Kupreanof Island, and British Columbia's Stikine and Nass River valleys moved to the north end of Southeast Alaska's Inside Passage. They established villages near a bridge of land between two rushing glacial rivers, the Chilkat and Chilkoot. It was a perfect spot for fishing and for building trade routes over the mountains to Athabascan villages in the interior.

The Haines Highway, which follows the Chilkat River from Haines to the interior, was originally a trade route. Whites nicknamed it "the grease trail" because the Tlingits used it to carry dried eulachon (a fish so rich in oil it can be used as a candle) and rendered fish oil over the mountains, where they traded withAthabascan tribes for ivory, beadwork, furs, and lichens used for dyes.

The Tlingits were also skilled navigators who had huge sea-going canoes and trade routes extending as far south as Monterey, California. When Russian and English fur-trading ships began appearing in the 1700s, the Tlingits were the middlemen in trading commodities, guns, iron tools, blankets, and other goods to the northern interior in return for pelts.

White influence came relatively late to the Haines area. In 1879, missionary S. Hall Young and naturalist John Muir chose it as the site for the Presbyterian mission.

In 1903, Fort Seward was constructed near downtown Haines, with fort buildings, including a carpenter and blacksmith shop, mule barn, carriage sheds, and Victorian officer's quarters, arriving by ship in pieces and erected around a 6-acre parade ground.

Decommissioned after World War II, Fort Seward was purchased by several veterans. The new owners tried to make it into a profitable enterprise, creating everything from a salmon smokehouse to a furniture factory on the site. Carl Heinmiller hit on a winner when he helped develop the Chilkat Dancers. This group draws on traditional Tlingit stories, dances, and songs and has been performing professionally, in Haines and internationally, for more than 30 years.

Today, the Tlingit village of Klukwan still stands about 22 miles upriver of Haines, a shadow of its former glory. The other original Native villages are gone.

Haines itself is in a strikingly beautiful location. Surrounded by glaciated mountains, it has the aquamarine Portage Cove on one side and the long estuary of the swift and shallow Chilkat River on the other. Although Haines is on the mainland and accessible by car, it's 250 miles by road from the nearest town of any size. It is far easier to fly to Haines from Juneau on a bush plane (a 45-minute jaunt), or to ride the ferry from Juneau (a 4-hour trip).

The main part of town consists of about 4 square blocks. A walk from downtown to the cruise ship dock, a distance of about 5 blocks, passes along the Portage Cove boat basin and by the unmarked mission cemetery. Directly above the cruise ship dock is the Victorian-style Fort Seward, where the Chilkat Dancers perform in the summer. Throughout Haines and on Fort Seward's parade grounds stand totem poles, most of them recently carved.

Two galleries in Haines are Native owned and carry authentic Native art from all over Alaska. The upper story of the town's small Sheldon Museum and Cultural Center is devoted mostly to the Tlingits of the Haines area. Although respectful travelers may be led to a carver's studio in a mobile home, the easiest access to authentic carvers in Haines is through one of the Native gift shops or Alaska Indian Arts, Inc., on the Fort Seward grounds.

Old Village Sites

Lutak Road is a scenic route that follows the blue-green Lynn Canal for a few miles north of Haines, past the ferry landing, to the mouth of the Chilkoot River, where it forks and abruptly ends. Near the bridge at the fork in the road is the site of an old camp where Natives caught eulachon and rendered them in pits. One village lined the banks of the river all the way to Chilkoot Lake, a short drive on a gravel road that ends at a large campground.

On the other side of Haines, on the Chilkat River, the village of Yendestakyeh was located on a wide meadow, adjacent to the Haines airport.

Klukwan, called by the Tlingits "the mother village," still exists on its original site (but not in its original form) on the banks of the Chilkat River, near milepost 22 on the Haines Highway. The clan houses, preserved in 1890 photographs, no longer exist, but the one-road village, with its weathered old Victorian houses and woodland cemetery, could tell a thousand stories. Don't let Klukwan's modest surroundings mislead you, though. The village's corporation, formed after Alaska Natives received a small financial reimbursement for lands confiscated in the 1800s, is one of the most profitable in Southeast Alaska. Plans have been under way for several years to build a cultural center here. Until villagers decide what they want to do with the place, tourists must respect their privacy. You may drive through at a reasonable speed, but no photographs, wandering in the cemetery, or knocking on doors, please.

Sheldon Museum and Cultural Center

Most of the upper floor of this small, browsable museum is dedicated to local Tlingit culture, including a rare, partially completed Chilkat blanket and the raw materials from which it was made. The Chilkat Tlingits were warriors and slave traders. The museum has a display of their wooden armor, worn over a moosehide shirt, an outfit strong enough to withstand Russian musket fire.

The museum is named after Stephen and Elisabeth Sheldon, who moved to Haines in 1911 and whose family donated Stephen's 50-year collection of Native art to the community under the care of the Chilkat Valley Historical Society.

Unfortunately the museum's clan house exhibit doesn't do justice to the real thing—it gives the false impression that Tlingits lived in woodsheds. Compare it with the museum's 1894 John Francis Platt photograph of the interior of the astounding Whale clan house that once stood in Klukwan.

Free printed handouts on Chilkat blankets, Tlingit history, dances, potlatches, spruce basket making, and other topics are in a rack by the door. Although the museum is accredited, tour guides are volunteers and may stumble over some of the more specific questions about Native culture. The museum's gift shop has a good selection of books as well as Native art from Southeast Alaska, interior Alaska, and Canada.

> *"Native people believed that the hole through a shell or stone was a portal for spirit power to enter and exit the 'real' world. So when traders brought Russian blue and red trade beads to Alaska, Natives willingly exchanged items of great value, such as otter pelts, for a few brightly colored beads."*
>
> *—June Simeonoff, Aleut educator*

Sheldon Museum and Cultural Center, Main and Front Sts, PO Box 269, Haines, AK 99827; (907)766-2366. Just above the city boat harbor. Admission $3; children under 18, free. Open summers daily 1pm–5pm; call for winter hours; extended hours for tours.

Chilkat Dancers

Potlatches were outlawed in 1910 by the U.S. government, and a whole generation of Indian children were reeducated in boarding schools where they were forbidden to speak their Native languages or practice Native dances or songs. In the early 1950s the prevailing attitude was that the old ways should be forgotten. But after Carl Heinmiller's racially mixed group of Boy Scouts went to the National Jamboree in Valley Forge, Pennsylvania, to perform dances with crude regalia they'd made after school, the Tlingit kids' grandparents jumped in. The kids were doing it wrong, and the elders couldn't stand to just watch any longer.

The elder Tlingits helped the young dancers obtain permission to use Tlingit, Tsimshian, and Athabascan dances and songs and showed them how to make authentic regalia. The newly trained and outfitted dance troupe won the dance award at the 1959 Intertribal Ceremonies in Gallup, New Mexico. From that auspicious start evolved a professional dance group, a performing arts hall, a replica of a tribal long-house on the Fort Seward grounds, and the Alaska Indian Arts carving shed and gallery, which was set up in the fort's old hospital building.

The dance group performs with a mixed group of Native and non-Native dancers, surprising an audience that expects to see all Native dancers. "We don't dis-criminate on the basis of race," says director Lee Heinmiller, the founder's son and himself non-Native. About 75 percent of the group is Native. Some of the non-Native dancers are married to Natives or have been adopted by the tribe. All of the dancers are paid performers, many of them children.

Performances last about an hour, are narrated, and include a dance that uses authentic Chilkat blankets as part of the costuming.

The Tlingit people learned to weave Chilkat blankets from the Tsimshian. The complex blanket, made with dyed goat's wool, took nearly a year to weave. Colors are always yellow and black, with blue accents. The "blue" in older blankets looks more green because the wool was boiled with copper ore and urine. The newer blankets have a more vibrant blue because the wool was boiled with the blue wool from white army officers' cast-off coats.

Alaska Indian Arts, Inc., PO Box 271, Haines, AK 99827; (907)766-2160. Performances are held in the Chilkat Center for the Arts Number 1, on Theater Drive, or in the Raven's Fort longhouse on Fort Seward's parade ground. Admission $10; children under 18, $5; children under 5, free. Tickets sold at the door. All shows, including those presold on the cruise ships, are open to the public. Performance schedules, which change monthly May–Sept, are posted at the theater and the Haines Convention and Visitors Bureau, Second St; PO Box 530, Haines, AK 99827; (907)766-2234. Dancers are available for photographs and dis-cussions after the show.

Raven's Fort

Raven's Fort, the tribal longhouse, was built in the middle of Fort Seward's grassy parade ground in the early 1960s. It was paid for by the state of Alaska, in an effort to employ Native carvers who were out of work because of several years of bad fishing. The project was spearheaded by Carl Heinmiller and was similar to the Depression-era Civilian Conservation Corps projects that put carvers to work repli-cating old totem poles. The longhouse (named Raven's Fort by el-ders) is used for commercial purposes, not tribal ceremonies. The Chilkat Dancers perform for small groups here, and the evening salmon bake is run by the Halsingland Hotel, housed in one of the old fort buildings nearby.

Raven's Fort, Fort Seward parade ground, adjacent to downtown Haines. For information, call the Halsingland Hotel, (907)766-2000.

Alaska Indian Arts, Inc.

In this workshop at Fort Seward, carvers coat a small totem pole destined for West Virginia with a fragrant mixture of beeswax and linseed oil. Located in the fort's old Victorian infirmary, the shop has a well-used look—open tackle boxes spilling odds and ends; a table of handmade carving tools, templates, and bandsaws; dried yellow flowers; and unfinished masks and silk-screened prints hanging on the wall. Scattered across the floor are an unfinished bear carved out of a piece of cedar, old olive oil cans, paintbrushes, and an oily chainsaw, all covered with fragrant cedar shavings.

Trivia: **The movie White Fang** *was filmed by* **Disney Studios in Haines.** *The cultural director and lead dancer of the* **Chilkat Dancers, Charlie Jimmie, is in the film,** *along with many locals.*

The workshop is open to any Natives who want to learn to carve. In years past, the workshop and the Chilkat Dancers provided the only employment for Natives in the Haines area. Alaska Indian Arts buys some pieces for the gallery adjoining the workshop and acts as a broker between carvers and customers commissioning projects.

Alaska Indian Arts workshop and gallery; (907)766-2160. At Fort Seward, in the old hospital building, next to the Chilkat Center for the Arts. Open daily 9am–5pm; year-round. Free.

Chilkat Valley Arts

Tlingit artist and Chilkat Valley Arts owner Sue Folletti is a silver carver whose designs are based on stylized animal forms similar to those found on totemic art in the region. A native of the Chilkat Valley, she trained with some of Alaska's best carvers. Her work has been selected for exhibition and sale by the Smithsonian Institution. Her gallery, co-owned for 10 years with her husband, Fred, is light and spacious, and contains local Native work as well as art from interior British Columbia and other Alaska tribes. She personally knows the artists whose work she carries; some, like stone carver Simon Koonook, even work on the porch outside her gallery during the summer months and are available to answer questions.

Chilkat Valley Arts, 307 Willard St, PO Box 145, Haines, AK 99827; (907)766-2990. One block from the visitors center, on the street behind Howser's Supermarket. Open daily, Mon–Sat, year-round.

Aatcha's Shop

June Simeonoff, an Aleut artist and educator, teaches Aleut basketry, beading, and skin-sewing throughout the slower winter months in Aatcha's Shop, her small gallery and supply store on Main Street in Haines. Simeonoff makes beaded elk, deer and mooseskin clothing, carries eskimo snow goggles and hunting visors, hand-cut ivory beads, trade beads, dentalia shells, ermine skins, and mammoth and walrus fossilized bone. She is also a well-known weaver of museum-quality Aleut baskets. Her husband, Charlie Pardue, an Athabascan, makes beaded moosehide gun cases and ivory knife handles. Ask June questions; she is extremely knowledgeable.

Aatcha's Shop, 22 Main St, PO Box 1311, Haines, AK 99827; (907)766-3208. Open summers, 10am until late evenings; closed on Sundays (available by appointment); call for winter hours. Classes are open to all.

Chilkat Bald Eagle Preserve

The eagle is a major Tlingit totemic symbol (the other is Raven). Each winter, about 3,500 bald eagles journey to the Chilkat River to feed on salmon. The best time see them is from the end of October to March. Stop along the Haines Highway, especially between mileposts 18 and 22, and park in the turnouts to watch the eagles fight over and gorge on select chunks of fish. Binoculars are useful; and photographers should bring a telephoto lens. Birds perch by the dozens in the cottonwoods along the riverbanks. Look for nests—piles of good-sized sticks, 8 feet wide and up to 7 feet deep—wrapped around the tops of hemlock and spruce snags.

For more information call the Haines Convention and Visitors Bureau, Second St, PO Box 530, Haines, AK 99827; (907) 766-2234.

Yakutat: *Tlingit*

The Yakutat Tlingits live in one of the most spectacular fjords in Southeast Alaska—and the residents are gearing up for eco- and cultural tourism. Immense, stunning glaciers and more than 200 miles of white sandy beaches surround the small fishing village of Yakutat. It lies near Hubbard Glacier, which in the last century advanced across Russell Fjord, creating an ice dam and a huge saltwater lake(an event some termed "the geologic event of the century"). To the west of Yakutat, the Malaspina Glacier—the size of the state of Rhode Island—flows from the St. Elias Mountains—the highest coastal range in the world. Yakutat is situated at the northernmost end of the

Tongass National Forest, a unique preserve of old-growth Sitka spruce forest. The area is a recreational paradise, with hiking trails, wildlife (black and brown bears, mountain sheep, trumpeter swans), down-hill and cross-country skiing (via air taxi), and some of the world's most outstanding surfing (demanding the protection of insulated dry suits, of course). Five clans of Yakutat Tlingits participate in the Mount St. Elias Dance group, and many are shareholders in Yak Tat Kwaan, Inc., a Native corporation. The Native corporation has pur-chased an air taxi service and is working with the clans on developing tourism.

For information on lodging or activities, contact Yak Tat Kwaan, Inc., at (907)784-3488. The town has a large, Native-owned hotel and several lodges (currently used primarily by sports fishers). Alaska Airlines makes two flights a day into Yakutat.

BRITISH COLUMBIA

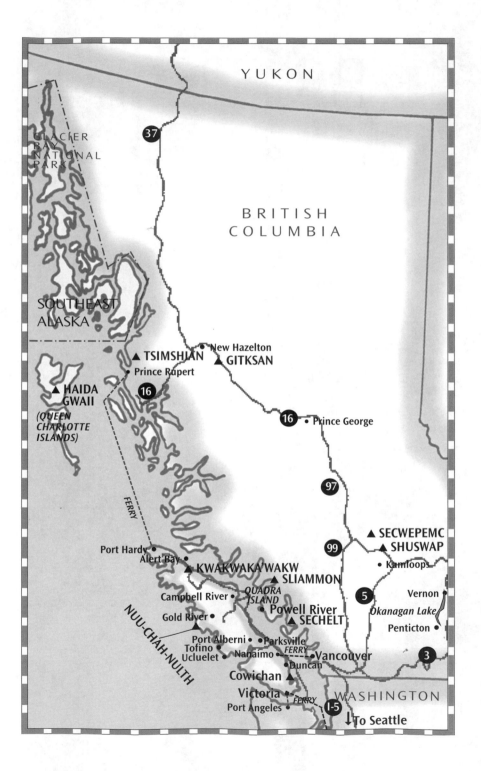

YUKON

BRITISH
COLUMBIA

GLACIER
BAY
NATIONAL
PARK

37

SOUTHEAST
ALASKA

▲ TSIMSHIAN
• Prince Rupert
16

• New Hazelton
▲ GITKSAN

16 • Prince George

▲ HAIDA
GWAII

*(QUEEN
CHARLOTTE
ISLANDS)*

97

▲ SECWEPEMC
▲ SHUSWAP

99

• Kamloops

FERRY

Port Hardy •
Alert Bay •
▲ KWAKWAKA'WAKW
▲ SLIAMMON

5

Vernon •

*QUADRA
ISLAND*
Campbell River •
Powell River
▲ SECHELT

Okanagan Lake

Penticton •

Gold River •

NUU-CHAH-NULTH

Port Alberni •
Tofino •
Ucluelet •

• Parksville
Nanaimo •
FERRY
• Duncan

Vancouver •

3

Cowichan ▲

Victoria •
Port Angeles •
FERRY
I-5

WASHINGTON

↓To Seattle

BRITISH COLUMBIA

Along the thickly forested coasts of what is today British Columbia, Native villages of magnificently decorated cedar houses once lined the shores of sheltered inlets. The fire-lit interiors of the bighouses and longhouses were animated by the presence of massive carved and painted figures of wolves, bears, and other animals. Visitors would have been served delicacies from the sea and entertained by masked dancers accompanied by songs and pounding drums. Travelers journeying upriver into interior British Columbia would have been invited into the warmth (or shade) of insulated underground pithouses and offered feasts of fresh venison, huckleberries, nuts, roasted camas bulbs, and other bounty.

More than 170,000 aboriginal people reside today in British Columbia, both in urban areas and on more than 350 reserves on ancestral lands. Some of their number continue to live by hunting and fishing in isolated or remote areas. Like Native people throughout the Northwest, First Nations people have their feet firmly planted in both the traditional and the modern worlds.

First Nations settlements are modern; many are fishing villages built on top of ancient village sites along the coastlines. Historic traditional structures, such as weathered totem poles and the remains of a longhouse, are few in number. Skungwaii (Ninstints), an abandoned Haida village on the southern end of Haida Gwaii (the Queen Charlotte Islands), is one such site; protected as a United Nations world heritage site, its fragile beauty is guarded by the Haida Gwaii Watchmen.

All of the bighouses and longhouses that once lined the shores are gone now, except for those constructed for Native heritage centers, such as the seven longhouses of the 'Ksan Historical Indian Village, which is open to the public near the town of Hazelton. There are also exceptional First Nations–owned museums in the province, such as the Kwagiulth museum on Quadra Island, which houses Winter Ceremony and potlatch items that were returned to the community by the Canadian government in the 1970s. Some First Nations sites and attractions are in or close to major cities and towns and are easily visited. Other locations, such as the islands of Haida Gwaii, are less easily reached. The Royal British Columbia Museum, in Victoria, and the University of British Columbia's Museum of Anthropology, in Vancouver, house significant collections of totem poles and artifacts, which have been brought together from many different places in the province. A mere 45-minute drive on the

For information and brochures on sightseeing, accommodations, brochures, and reservations in British Columbia, contact Tourism British Columbia, (800)663-6000. First-time visitors to British Columbia may be deceived by the distances between some destinations on the map. Vancouver Island's coastline is more than 400 miles long and nearly roadless. Both Prince Rupert and the Queen Charlotte Islands are about 600 miles north of Vancouver and just 100 miles south of Ketchikan in Southeast Alaska. Getting to the Queen Charlotte Islands by car requires both a long drive and an expensive ferry crossing. Please note that prices listed in this chapter are Canadian currency.

scenic highway north of Victoria's Royal British Columbia Museum is the Native Heritage Centre in Duncan, where you can meet people of the Cowichan Nation in person, watch totem-pole carving (and talk to the carver), sample traditional coast Salish culture, and purchase a warm, hand-knit Cowichan sweater. Just a few more miles north are two places where you can learn about extravagant potlatches from the people who still practice them: the Kwagiulth Museum and Cultural Centre on Quadra Island, and the U'Mista Cultural Centre at Alert Bay. Within 3 hours of Victoria, at Tofino, you can go whale watching across Clayoquot Sound with the Nuu-chah-nulth and take a tour of an old village site. And just a few hours east of Vancouver, you can visit the Secwepemc Native Heritage Park and discover the comfortable lifestyle of the inland Salish people, as well as stay in a modern hotel designed to resemble the *kekuli* (winter house) of the Little Shuswap Band, who own and operate the lodging.

As a companion to this book, we recommend two excellent guides: Pat Kramer's **Native Sites in Western Canada** *(Altitude Publishing, 1994); and Cheryl Coull's* **A Traveler's Guide to Aboriginal BC** *(Whitecap Books, 1996). Both are available from most western Canada booksellers for under $20.*

Vancouver Metropolitan Area

Several First Nation reserves lie within the city limits of cosmopolitan Vancouver, which also has a large Native population living throughout the city. The University of British Columbia's Museum of Anthropology is one of the finest museums of its kind in the world. In Vancouver you'll find Northwest Coast art in abundance, in public spaces and in most galleries, as well as the only restaurant in the Pacific Northwest featuring authentic Native cuisine.

University of British Columbia Museum of Anthropology

This modern museum is internationally renowned for its stunning collection of Northwest Coast art, three-story glass windows overlooking the sea, and calming use of natural light throughout. The pride of British Columbia and the First Nations, this is a museum for people who hate museums. You pass through an elegant bentwood box carved by 'Ksan master carvers into broad corridors and galleries filled with Northwest Coast art and artifacts. There are magnificent Haida, Tsimshian, Gitksan, and Kwakwaka'wakw totem poles, house posts, masks, woven cedar clothing and hats, and carved jewelry, coast Salish baskets, and carvings made of antler, stone, and wood—all exhibited in a respectful and well-ordered manner. Outside, Haida longhouses and totem poles face the water. It is a truly awe-inspiring and memorable experience to visit this museum.

Take the tram up the side of 4,100-foot Grouse Mountain, to see both the stunning view and Our Spirit Soars, a 35-minute video presentation about Vancouver and its First Nations cultures; shown every hour on the hour, year-round. Grouse Mountain, 6400 Nancy Greene Way, North Vancouver, BC V7R 4K9; (604)984-0661. Admission $14.95.

Call for the museum's calendar of events, including First Nations lectures and performances. A small gift store is on the premises. The museum is built on traditional coast Salish Musqueam territory. The Musqueam Reserve is about 3 miles south of the museum.

University of British Columbia Museum of Anthropology, 6393 NW Marine Dr, Vancouver, BC V6T 1Z2; (604)822-3825, 24-hour recorded message; (604)822-5087 museum office. The museum is on the UBC campus, west of downtown Vancouver. Open May 19–Sept 6, daily 11am–5pm; Sept 7–May 18, same as above except closed Mon and Dec 25–26. General admission $6; family rates available. Free on Tues nights in summer. Free all day Tues in winter. Group rates with guided tours if booked in advance.

First Nations Art at the Vancouver International Airport

If you fly into Vancouver, you can't miss the extraordinary collection of Northwest Coast art displayed in the Vancouver International Airport, one of the best public areas in the city to view First Nations art. In a small park near the airport's entrance are three 40-foot-tall totem poles, carved and restored by Gitksan carvers Earl Muldon and Walter Harris. Inside the amphitheater in the main terminal is Haida carver Bill Reid's masterpiece bronze *The Spirit of Haida Gwaii, The Jade Canoe*, an astounding 19-foot-long canoe filled with totem spirits and paddlers (its only other casting, *The Spirit of Haida Gwaii, The Black Canoe*, is in front of the Canadian embassy in Washington, D.C.). The $3 million Jade Canoe, purchased by the Vancouver

International Airport Authority, was the largest public art transaction ever made in Canada.

The airport also houses a rare collection of newly commissioned coast Salish art. The collection, in the rooms behind the security/customs gate in the International Terminal, includes two austere 17-foot-tall traditional Musqueam welcoming figures carved by Shane Point, an artist of Musqueam ancestry. Honoring the Musqueam's tradition of fine weaving is a 17-foot-high spindle whorl, carved from a single piece of red cedar by Musqueam tribal member Susan Point, and four large tapestries, woven in traditional patterns, which are suspended from the ceiling. Banners, prints, carved disks, eagle posts, split bears, thunderbirds, model totem poles, and two more welcoming figures, carved by Joe David, are also exhibited throughout the airport at various gates.

The airport authority has established a foundation to promote awareness of aboriginal art and to commission work from aboriginal artists for display in public buildings. It has also purchased First Nations artists' work in other media, such as copper, glass, wood, bronze, and paper. In the future, the airport hopes to offer tours of the collection led by Musqueam guides. Much of Vancouver and its airport (which is perched on an island in the mouth of the Fraser River) is built on traditional Musqueam territory.

Vancouver International Airport, PO Box 23750, Airport Postal Outlet, Richmond, BC V7B 1Y7; (604)276 6101. The airport is midway between the cities of Richmond and Vancouver on Hwy 99 or the southern end of Granville St.

Native-owned Art Galleries

Potlatch Arts Ltd (8161 Main St, Ste 100, Vancouver; (604)321-5888) is owned by Gene Joseph, head librarian at the First Nations House of Learning at the University of British Columbia. Potlatch Arts is a collector's gallery that sells the work of the First Nations' finest artists. These include Haida carvers Robert Davidson and Don Yeomans and coast Salish carver and glass sculptor Susan A. Point.

Internationally known totem pole carver and jeweler Norman Tait has opened his own gallery, Wilp's Ts Ak Gallery, "The House of the Mischievous Man" (2426 Marine Dr W, Vancouver; (604)925-5771). You can watch Tait and other artists carving wood, silver, and gold in the gallery.

Susan A. Point's Coast Salish Arts, a gallery exhibiting only her work, and her studio (3917 W 51st Ave, Vancouver, BC V6N 3V9; (604)266-7374) is on the Musqueam Reserve, a few minutes from the University of British Columbia. Point works in various media, including glass, wood, and stainless steel, as well as printing techniques such as intaglio aquatint. Open daily, 10am–5pm. Phone first for directions and to confirm hours.

Wickaninnish Gallery Ltd (Ste 14, 1666 Johnson St, Vancouver; (604)681-1057), in the Granville Island shopping area, specializes in authentic Northwest Coast carved silver and gold jewelry made by carvers throughout British Columbia. This is the place to compare carving styles.

Pieces of authentic gold and silver jewelry carved with Northwest Coast designs are some of the best high-quality souvenirs you can buy— handsome and easily portable. Carved bracelets were a favorite giveaway item at potlatches. To see some early examples of the craft, visit the University of British Columbia's Museum of Anthropology (6393 NW Marine Dr, Vancouver; (604)822-3825).

The Cedar Root Gallery (1607 E Hasting St, Vancouver; (604)251-6244) is a small, community-based gallery that draws its artwork from the more than 65,000 aboriginal people living on Vancouver's east side. The gallery, adjoining the Vancouver Aboriginal Friendship Centre, exhibits work by new young artists, as well as experimental pieces that combine tradition with contemporary art.

Khot-La-Cha (270 Whonoak St N, Vancouver; (604)987-3339), located on the Capilano Reserve, sells coast Salish handicrafts, including yellow and red cedar carvings, totem poles, ceremonial masks, silver and gold jewelry, Cowichan sweaters, moccasins, and prints.

Canoe Pass Gallery (No.115, 3866 Bayview St, Richmond; (604)272-0095) is 30 minutes from downtown Vancouver in the historic fishing community of Steveston, within the city of Richmond. The gallery is on the wharf overlooking the mouth of the Fraser River. Open daily.

Coghlan Art (6835 256th St, Aldergrove; (604)644-5285), off Highway 13, south of Vancouver, is a fine arts gallery and collection of artists' studios housed in a historic electric railway substation. Its co-founder is one of Canada's best-known First Nations painters, Norval Morrisseau. Look here for a dozen of Canada's finest First Nations artists, including George Hunt, Jr., Stan Hunt, Tom Patterson, Terry Starr, and Gary Meeches. Masks, paintings, vessels, and textiles are also for sale on the upper level, in a lofty three-story room with large clerestory windows. Outside, there's a covered area for artists to work on large commissioned pieces, such as totem and house poles.

Vancouver also boasts many non-Native–owned galleries, all of them listed in the Vancouver telephone directory. Among those recommended by First Nations artists are Images for Canadian Heritage (164 Water St, Vancouver; (604)685-7046), specializing in Northwest

Coast and Inuit art, and the Leona Lattimer Gallery (1590 W 2nd Ave, Vancouver; (604)732-4556), reflecting Lattimer's 45 years of collecting and selling First Nations art in British Columbia.

Authentic Northwest Dining at Liliget Feast House

Inspired by the renewed interest in First Nations culture, Dolly Watts and her family offer a unique experience in authentic Pacific Northwest dining in their Liliget Feast House. The dining room reflects longhouse-style design, with cedar walls and house posts, and has the same feeling as a Japanese tatami room, with seats flush to the floor. The most popular item on the menu is a potlatch platter, heaped with alder-smoked salmon, oysters, mussels, prawns, and venison, and served with wild rice, steamed ferns, and sweet potatoes. Appetizers include crab cakes with honey-garlic sauce, pan-fried *oolicans* (candlefish), and steamed herring roe. Soups range from a clear salmon broth to thick corn and crab chowders. They also serve a "Caesar Goes Wild" salad, topped with your choice of smoked salmon, duck, or venison. The house specialty is a smoked salmon entree; other entrees include barbecued duck, alder-grilled rabbit, and a pan-fried rainbow trout served with hazelnuts. Bannock bread is served with all meals. Unusual condiments, such as crunchy toasted seaweed and oolican oil for dipping, are examples of the extensive menu of Northwest Coast delicacies that was once served to guests during traditional feasts. Local wines are served; those originating from vineyards owned or managed by First Nations people get top billing (try Inniskillin's pinot blanc or Summerhill's Nordique from Inkameep Vineyards). Desserts include fresh berry tarts, gourmet cookies, and Indian wedding cake. Liliget owner Dolly Watts is Gitksan, from the village of Kitwanga on the Skeena River. She grew up in the Port Alberni area (Nuu-chah-nulth territory).

Liliget Feast House & Catering, 1724 Davie St, Vancouver, BC V6G 1W, (604)681 7044. The Feast House is open for dinner daily, 5pm–10pm. Reservations strongly recommended. Entrees range from $14.95 to $19.95. Catering menus are available by calling the restaurant during the day.

Sunshine Coast:
Sechelt & Sliammon

British Columbia's impressive coastline is broken by hundreds of inlets and channels, making road building an arduous task. The only coastal road on the mainland, Highway 101, ends at Lund, about 100 miles north of Vancouver. To travel the length of Highway 101, you must first cross Horseshoe Bay and Jervis Inlet, both 45-minute journeys on BC Ferries (or longer, if you count the wait in line at the ferry terminal). Ferries are equipped with restaurants, bookstores, and comfortable seating, making for a pleasant ride. A small amount of development has occurred on a narrow strip of coastline along Highway 101; the rest is mostly untouched, deeply forested wildlife habitat. Two First Nations are easily accessible on what hardy British Columbians call their Sunshine Coast. On the northern side of Horseshoe Bay, at the town of Sechelt, the Sechelt Nation has a museum, gift shop, and fish hatchery open to visitors. The Sliammon Nation is near the end of the road, between the town of Powell River and Desolation Sound Provincial Marine Park. Their fish hatchery is worth the drive just to talk with tribal members who have nursed the salmon back to the small stream adjacent to their reserve.

Sechelt Nation's House of Hewhiwus (House of Chiefs)

Right on Highway 101, at the town of Sechelt, is the Sechelt Nation's House of Hewhiwus. The modern complex includes the Sechelt Nation's administrative offices. Open to the public are Tsain-Ko Gifts, a privately owned gift shop selling art from all over British Columbia, the Sechelt Nation's Tem-swiya Museum, and the Raven's Cry theater. If for no other reason, you should stop to see the highlight of the museum, a rare stone carving of a mother and a child; the carving was excavated from nearby Davis Bay. The staff running the gift shop answers questions about objects in the museum. Both open and close at the same time; call ahead for hours, (604)844-4592. Raven's Cry is a local group that leases the Sechelt's theater and offers film festivals and live theater throughout the year.

Sechelt Nation's House of Hewhiwus (House of Chiefs), 5555 Hwy 101, PO Box 740, Shechelt, BC V0N 3A0; (604)885-2273. The Sechelt Nation's hatchery, with fish-rearing pens right in McLean Bay, is open 6am–2pm. For free tours and directions contact the Sechelt resource manager; (604)885-2273.

Wind Spirit Gallery/Powell River

This pretty gallery and restaurant, located in a remodeled, bungalow-style house overlooking the Malaspina Strait, contains the watercolor paintings, serigraphs, and limited-edition prints of April White. White is a direct descendant of Charles Edensaw, the renowned Haida artist of the Eagle clan (whose early work is in the University of

British Columbia's Museum of Anthropology). White was born on Haida Gwaii. Her work as a geologist in remote areas of the Canadian West and her marriage to a commercial fisherman give her paintings an authentic Northwestern feeling. This can be seen in her screen print *Balance,* for example, which depicts a glacial erratic nested on shale beach of Haida Gwaii and superimposed with images of Eagle and Raven. The gallery is just up the street from her workshop, Wind Spirit Printmakers.

Wind Spirit Gallery, 4643 Marine Ave, Powell River, BC V8A 2K8; (604)485-7572. The gallery is open Mon–Sat in summer, Tues–Sat in winter. Jitterbug Cafe, which features Pacific Northwest cuisine, is open for lunch and dinner. Dinner reservations recommended. Hours vary with the season; call first.

For a list of parks and a map of British Columbia's Sunshine Coast, contact the District Manager, Garibaldi/Sunshine Coast District, PO Box 220, Brackendale, BC V0N 1H0; (604)898-3678.

Sliammon Fish Hatchery

We almost passed this modest little fish hatchery on the grassy bank of Sliammon Creek, below the highway bridge, and should know better. First Nations–owned fish hatcheries are one of the best places for a visitor to meet aboriginal people. The day we were there, eagles perched in the trees, eyeing both the salmon running upstream and the hatchery workers who were dipping fish from the stream with nets. To allow visitors to see salmon spawning naturally, a shallow channel has been dug around a tree-covered island and the bottom filled with the size of gravel in which salmon prefer to lay their eggs. There are holding tanks full of fry and fingerlings, but the best part of this fish nursery is the cheerful people who run it. There is usually time for a free tour and lots of free salmonid literature. Please donate to the hatchery crew's doughnut and coffee fund.

Sliammon Fish Hatchery, RR 2, Sliammon Rd, Powell River, BC V8A 4Z3. On Hwy 101, north of Powell River. Open daily.

Kamloops: *Secwepemc & Little Shuswap*

Secwepemc Native Heritage Park

About four hours east of Vancouver, at Kamloops, on the main road to Alberta, is Secwepemc Native Heritage Park, which interprets the traditional culture and lifestyle of the interior Salish Secwepemc people. The park, built on a 2,400-year-old village site overlooking the Little South Thompson River, features a full-scale replica of a winter village with several *kekuli* (subterranean traditional winter homes with a central fire pit). A salmon-fishing station hangs over the riverbank.

In summer there are song, dance, storytelling, and live theater presentations along with pit-cooking demonstrations and salmon barbecues in a traditional summer lodge. In winter, visitors can view indoor museum exhibits and traditional Native art and crafts. Located on one of the major routes to the Rocky Mountains, Jasper, and Banff National Park, this is a great place to stop.

All guided tours begin with a 20-minute video. In summer, tours extend to 1½ hours when they include the outdoor heritage park. The gift shop includes locally published materials about Secwepemc life and culture.

Secwepemc Native Heritage Park, 355 Yellowhead Hwy, Kamloops, BC V2H 1H1; (604)828-9801. About 4 hours east of Vancouver, on the Coquohalla Hwy (Hwy 5). Northwest of Okanagan Lake on Hwy 97. The museum is open year-round; outdoor exhibits are closed in winter. Call for hours. Admission $5; group rates.

Quaaout Lodge

This new lakefront lodge, owned by the Little Shuswap Band, features a 40-foot-high lobby designed to resemble a *kekuli*. The lobby doors are ornately carved with traditional Salish designs, and the floor is decorated with copies of ancient Shuswap pictographs from a nearby site. From its spot overlooking Little Shuswap Lake, the 72-room lodge offers fishing, swimming, and a sandy beach, with 3.7 miles of jogging trails, an indoor pool, exercise area, sauna, and whirlpool spa. The lodge will also arrange sailing, golf, trail riding, and other family activities. Some rooms have fireplaces and hot tubs. The lodge restaurant, which also overlooks the lake, features First Nations cuisine in addition to regular fare.

Quaaout Lodge, PO Box 1215, Chase, BC V0E 1M0; (800)663-4303 or (604)679-3090. Located about 20 minutes east of Kamloops on Hwy. 123, just outside Chase, on the way to Banff National Park. Cross the Squilax Bridge over the Little South Thompson River. Open year-round. Room rates are $69–$108. The lodge dining room is open daily for breakfast, lunch, and dinner, as well as Sunday brunch. Reservations required for dinner; (604)679-3090.

Vernon: *Interior Salish*

Vernon, on Okanagan Lake, is north of Penticton in central British Columbia, about 4 hours from Vancouver, and north of Washington State's Colville Indian Reservation. Highway 97 parallels the Okanogan/Okanagan River in both countries. The tribes and bands who live on reserves in southeastern British Columbia are related to the interior-coast Salish people of Washington, Idaho, and Montana. For the tribes, the Canada–United States border is an artificial boundary between extended families.

Sen'Klip Native Theatre Company

In less than a decade, Sen'Klip has grown from a community-based local theater to an award-winning, internationally recognized performance group. The company is known for its unique adaptations of traditional interior-Salish legends, as well as for its recently created plays that blend traditional themes and contemporary issues. They perform each summer on an impressive earthen stage. Sen'Klip is based in Vernon, in the heart of British Columbia's wine country.

Sen'Klip Native Theatre Company, 2902 29th Ave, Vernon, BC V1T 1Y7; (604) 549-2921.

Vancouver Island

Access to Vancouver Island, nearly 400 miles long, is relatively easy from the mainland. As you'll see, there's much to do on Vancouver Island. We easily spent 12 days there, lingering on the island's spectacular west coast along the Pacific Ocean. Commuter planes from Seattle, Bellingham, and Vancouver land daily in Victoria, the island's largest city. Car and passenger ferries also service Vancouver Island year-round from Seattle, Port Angeles, and Anacortes in Washington State, and from Vancouver, Powell River, and Prince Rupert in British Columbia.

The Victoria Clipper, (800)888-2535, a fast passenger ferry, travels from Seattle, Washington, to Victoria's Inner Harbour four times a day. Travelers with cars can take the Victoria Line's car ferry from Seattle, (206)625-1880, or the MV *Coho* from Port Angeles, Washington, (360)457-4491. All three boats dock about two blocks from the Royal British Columbia Museum in Victoria. From Anacortes, the Washington State Ferry travels through the San Juan

Islands; one boat a day docks at Sidney on Vancouver Island, several miles north of Victoria.

From Vancouver, British Columbia, BC Ferries travel through the Gulf Islands and dock at Nanaimo on Vancouver Island. Ferries also leave Powell River and dock at Comox, about midway on the island's eastern shore. From Prince Rupert in the north, a ferry threads through the Inside Passage and arrives at Port Hardy on Vancouver Island's northern end, a 15- to 18-hour journey. For lists of accommodations, reservations, and other information, contact Tourism British Columbia; (800)663-6000.

Victoria Metropolitan Area

Royal British Columbia Museum

We've been visiting this museum for more than 20 years and never cease to be impressed by its memorable collection of Northwest Coast art. Totem poles and towering welcoming figures are installed alongside the escalators, so that visitors can see them close up while rising from the first floor to the second floor's First Peoples exhibit. The exhibit begins with a full-scale replica of the type of pithouse used by interior tribes, and then displays everything from household goods, such as looms and bentwood boxes, to canoes and ceremonial objects. The museum is filled with Northwest Coast carved masks, and there is one darkened gallery where you can sit and listen to narration as masks are illuminated one at a time. The Jonathan Hunt House, a traditional bighouse complete with carved house posts, screens, benches, and a glowing fire inside, is the centerpiece of the exhibit. The bighouse is named for the late Chief Kwakwabalasami of Fort Rupert. The house and all the carvings inside were created by the chief's son, Henry Hunt, and grandsons, Tony and Richard Hunt, members of an extended family that includes at least 30 artists (for more about the Hunts, see the Port Hardy section of this chapter). The Hunt family uses the bighouse for ceremonial occasions. Also visit Thunderbird Park, adjoining the museum, for one of the largest open-air displays of totem poles anywhere in British Columbia, as well as a full-sized replica of a traditional Haida house. The Wa'waditla House, carved by Mungo Martin, is also used for important Native ceremonies.

Royal British Columbia Museum, 675 Belleville St, Victoria, BC V8V 1X4; (800)661-5411 or (604)387-3701; (604)387-3014 for a recorded message. Located across from the Empress Hotel and the city's Inner Harbour. Open summer 9:30am–7pm; winter 10am–5:30pm. General admission $5.35. Groups of 10 or more should prebook their visit.

First Nations Art

Most Victoria galleries selling First Nations art are located along Government Street, anchored at the eastern end by the Royal British Columbia Museum (which has an excellent small shop selling aboriginal art and books on its first floor). Across the street from the museum, in the famous Empress Hotel, is the Art of Man gallery (721 Government St; (604)384-8111), representing some of the region's top First Nations and Native Alaska artists. Even if the prices are out of reach, you can see some of the finest artwork being produced in the region in this gallery.

If you can't make the hour-long drive to the Native Heritage Centre in Duncan to buy an authentic Cowichan sweater right where they are made, walk west along tourist-hungry Government Street to find four Cowichan sweater outlets: Sasquatch Trading Ltd (1233 Government St; (604)386-9033); Cowichan Trading Ltd (1328 Government St; (604)383-0321); Canadiana Gifts and Souvenirs (1012 Government St; (604)384-3123); and the Indian Craft Shoppe (905 Government St; (604)382-3643).

Lloyd and Frances Hill began selling Cowichan sweaters in 1946 from their Koksilak/Duncan General Store and post office, paying the knitters with groceries and wool. Today the Hill family has one store in Vancouver's Gastown shopping area and four stores on Vancouver Island. In Victoria, Hill's Indian Crafts (1008 Government St; (604)385-3911) has a wide assortment of masks and other items. Check with them for other store addresses. Also look for masks at Chinook Trading Company (1315 Government St; (604)381-3224).

Roy Vicker's Eagle Moon Gallery is the only aboriginal-owned gallery downtown (1010 Government St; (604)385-3911). Vicker's serigraph-print style is based on the look of Japanese woodcuts; he is also a skilled carver (most of his carved work is in his longhouse-style gallery in Tofino on Vancouver Island's west coast).

Duncan: *Cowichan*

Native Heritage Centre

One of the best First Nations attractions in British Columbia, the Cowichan Nation's Native Heritage Centre includes a tour through a bighouse, a carving shed, a multimedia show, an exhibit on the famous Cowichan knitters, and several galleries, one of which sells expensive First Nations fine art from throughout the region. Spread over 6 lovely acres on the north bank of the Cowichan River, the complex is filled with totem poles, carved screens, canoes, and working artists. A visit usually begins in the Longhouse Story Centre with a viewing of *Great Deeds*, a film about the history of the Cowichan Nation. Resident carvers demonstrate their skills while they carve works for the center and for private and corporate clients (local First Nations carvers have made the more than 60 totem poles that stand in the city of Duncan). During the summer, a fascinating 4-hour Feast & Legends program features traditional dances and a lavish six-course feast with storytelling inside the bighouse. Kids are encouraged to work with staff to make beaded name badges, headbands, and friendship bracelets on tanned moosehide, or try their hand at carving in the carving shed. This is also the place to buy an authentic Cowichan sweater. Made of undyed wool and knitted without seams, these sweaters are world-famous. If you don't find one that fits, knitters will custom-make one for you and mail it.

Native Heritage Centre, 200 Cowichan Way, Duncan, BC V9L 4T8; (604)746-8119. A 1-hour scenic drive north of Victoria on Hwy 1. The center is open daily, year-round. Guided tours are every hour on the half-hour, year-round. Admission $6.75, summers; $4 winters (includes guided tours). Midday salmon barbecues are held twice daily during the summer, with elders as guides, and there are masked dance performances; $24 per person. The longer Feasts & Legends program is held Fri only, during the summer; $35 per person. Please call to confirm dates, times, and prices.

More Art

Judy Hill Gallery and Gifts (22 Station St; (604)746-6663) carries the work of the region's top carvers, including Joe David, Robert Davidson, Richard Krentz, and David Neel.

North of Duncan at Chemainus, a cute little waterfront town and ferry landing, pick up a brochure of Native artisans' workshops and display galleries at Images of the Circle, 9272 Chemainus Rd, PO Box 75, Chemainus, BC V0R 1K0; (604)246-9920.

Tofino: *Nuu-chah-nulth*

The entire west side of Vancouver Island is Nuu-chah-nulth territory. For years in the Northwest we've usually referred to the Nuu-chah-nulth Nation as the Nootka, a name mistakenly bestowed by Captain James Cook, who misunderstood his first introduction to a Nuu-chah-nulth chief. Sprinkled north to south on Vancouver Island are 14 villages and bands: Kyuquot, Ehattesaht, Nutchatlaht,

Mowachaht, Hesquiaht, Ahousaht, Tla-O-Qui-Aht (Tofino), Ucluelet, Toquaht, Uchucklesaht, Ohiaht, Opetchesaht, Sheshaht, Pacheenaht, and Ditidaht. The Nuu-chah-nulth claim the Makah, on the northern tip of Washington State's Olympic Peninsula, as one of their own as well.

There are only three paved roads to Vancouver's west side. Most of the villages on this rugged coast are reached only by gravel logging road or by boat or float-plane. One of the paved roads, a two-lane highway, leads to Ucluelet and to the resort town of Tofino, which is at the end of a long spit adjoining Pacific Rim National Park. It's well worth the effort to get there. One side of the spit faces the rugged Pacific Ocean and has miles of public beach; the other side faces gorgeous Clayoquot Sound, where islands are covered with 1,500-year-old cedar trees—some of the last old-growth cedar forests in the world.

Tofino is a real jewel. It offers not only a first-class First Nations–owned hotel with its own private stretch of Pacific beach but truly extraordinary galleries, great feasts of cracked crab and salmon caught in the Sound, tours of a nearby First Nations village, salmon-fishing and whale-watching excursions, isolated hot springs, ancient rain forests, and even a 3-mile-long trail through a grove of ancient cedars, reached by a skiff that skims across Clayoquot Sound.

To get to Tofino, take Highway 1 to Parksville, then head west on Highway 4 to Tofino on a two-lane paved road that, during heavy rains, is drenched with spray from roadside waterfalls. (It's a pretty drive along the lakeshore and across roaring mountain streams, in spite of some severely clearcut slopes.) At the coast, you travel either south to Ucluelet or north to Tofino. The route to Tofino parallels Long Beach in Pacific Rim National Forest. For summer visits, it's best to make hotel reservations months in advance. In mid-winter, you'll have your choice of rooms, but tours may be limited. Plan on taking about 4½ hours from Victoria to Tofino, or about 2½ hours from the ferry landing at Nanaimo.

Take a Freighter to the West Side

At Port Alberni, halfway between Parksville and Tofino, you can board the 100-passenger MV *Lady Rose* or 200-passenger MV *Frances Barkley* to the

The Nuu-chah-nulth recommend **Wisdom of the Elders: Native Traditions on the Northwest Coast,** *by Ruth Kirk (Douglas & McIntyre, 1986), as the best book on the Nuu-chah-nulth, Southern Kwakwaka'wakw, and Nuxalk cultures.*

Look for Nuu-chah-nulth baskets, obsidian micro-blades traded from Oregon, gambling bones made from beaver teeth, and button blankets at the Alberni Valley Museum, 4255 Wallace St (in the Echo Activity Centre), Port Alberni, BC V9Y 3Y6; (604)723-2181. Open Tues–Sat, 10am–5pm.

Pacific coast and the Broken Group islands, a 4-hour trip each way. The working freighters make round-trips from Port Alberni to the oceanside towns of Ucluelet and the Broken Group islands in Barkley Sound from June to September, and to Bamfield year-round. From the ship's deck, you'll see the landscape as the Nuu-chah-nulth have observed it for centuries—from the water—and pass several First Nations reserves accessible only by boat. Kayak rentals are available at the dock. Ucluelet and Bamfield are both village sites—modern, with cafes and accommodations. Ucluelet is about 30 minutes south (by car) of Tofino. The Broken Group islands are a group of about 100 islands clustered at the mouth of Alberni Inlet. They have only campsites, best found by kayaking after the freighter drops you off. Those wishing to hike the West Coast Trail disembark at Bamfield. The 45-mile (72-kilometer) West Coast Trail is a 4- to 5-day hike over a challenging wilderness trail to Port Renfrew.

Pacific Rim National Park comprises three separate areas: Long Beach, the Broken Group islands, and the West Coast Trail. The park information center, with maps, videos, and brochures, is off Highway 4, between Ucluelet and Tofino. For information, contact Pacific Rim National Park, PO Box 280, Ucluelet, BC V0R 3A0; (604)726-4212.

Alberni Marine Transportation (Barkley Sound Service), 5425 Argyle St, PO Box 188, Port Alberni, BC V9Y 7M7; (800)663-7192 for reservations, Apr–Sept; or (604)723-8313. Fares are $38–$44.

Tin Wis Resort Lodge

Every room in this 56-room, two-story lodge faces a broad lawn overlooking the Pacific Ocean, as does the dining room with patio seating outside. All rooms have queen- or king-size beds; some have fireplaces. Located several miles from Tofino, nestled in the trees off the Pacific Rim Highway, the place is private and quiet, with its own quarter-mile of broad sandy beach. The lodge rents ocean kayaks, boogie boards, wet suits, and mountain bikes, and there's a spa and exercise room. The resort's boardrooms hold up to 40 people; the convention center accommodates 200 to 300 people. The dining room (open for three meals a day during the summer; for breakfast and dinner during the winter) offers such items as grilled chicory salad, steamed crab and clams, a sampler of smoked fish, and venison. Tin Wis (the name means "calm waters") is owned by the Tla-O-Qui-Aht First Nation band of Nuu-chah-nulth and is managed by Best Western.

Tin Wis Resort Lodge, 1119 Pacific Rim Hwy, Tofino, BC V0R 2Z0; (800)661-9995 or (800)528-1234 for the Best Western reservation line. Room rates $85–$140, depending on season. Children under 12 stay free with parents. Open year-round.

House of Himwitsa

The House of Himwitsa, a handsome building overlooking Tofino's wharf and seaplane dock, boasts a large waterfront restaurant; five classy, view suites for rent by the day, week, or month; and a first-rate art gallery. All of the artists represented in this gallery are First Nations people, and many are of the Nuu-chah-nulth Nation. The personable owners, Lewis and Cathy George, are Nuu-chah-nulth, and they and their staff are well acquainted with the artists and know the cultural history behind each work of art.

The gallery collection includes beautifully carved and painted Northwest Coast masks, engraved silver and gold jewelry, cedar bark baskets, limited-edition prints, totem poles, and pottery, as well as coats, capes, and distinctive Maquinna hats. Ask the gallery to send you their full-color catalogue ($3).

The restaurant on the lower level, the Sea Shanty, has a 180-degree view of the island-filled Sound and specializes in pasta and local seafood, including oysters and steamed crab. It's open for breakfast, lunch, and dinner most of the year.

On the top floor, overlooking the wharf and Clayoquot Sound, are five luxurious, spacious, well-appointed suites, all with fully stocked kitchens, decks, and large tiled baths. They are filled with Native art prints from the gallery downstairs. Our favorite room has a hot tub on the deck.

House of Himwitsa, 300 Main St, Tofino, BC V0R 2Z0; (800)899-1947 or (604)725-2017. The gallery is open daily, year-round. Restaurant reservations, (604)725-2902; open mid-Feb–Dec 1. Suite rates vary according to season, $80–$165. Make room reservations through the gallery's phone number.

Wilp Gybuu (Wolf House) Bed & Breakfast

Hosts Wendy and Ralph Burgess offer large, delicious breakfasts and sparkling conversation in their spotless, contemporary home overlooking Clayoquot Sound—all within walking distance of Tofino's attractions. Rooms have comfortable beds, private bathrooms, and absolutely all the amenities (slippers, candles, magazines, and thoughtful toiletries). Each room has its own private entrance; several have fireplaces. Ralph Burgess is a Gitksan Tsimshian who grew up in a village near Prince Rupert, on the mainland. He's also a first-rate gold and silver carver. The house has a well-stocked library on First Nations people. These are wonderful hosts (who thoughtfully leave an early morning tray of coffee outside your door). Make reservations months in advance.

Wilp Gybuu (Wolf House) Bed and Breakfast, 311 Leighton Way, PO Box 396, Tofino, BC V0R 2Z0; (604)725-2330. From Campbell St in Tofino, turn left onto First, right on Arnet Rd, left onto Leighton Way. Rates are $70–$80 and include breakfast. Nonsmoking; cat in residence.

Meares Island Big Cedar Trail

In Clayoquot Sound, the fight is on to protect the big cedars and other old-growth trees from logging. In 1984 the Tla-O-Qui-Aht Nation and other local residents stood on the shores of Meares Island and declared their intention to stop logging by MacMillan Bloedel Ltd, proclaiming the whole island a tribal park. A handful of Tofino residents first built the Big Cedar Trail on the island in 1981 so the public could see the ancient cedars growing there. In 1993, the Western Canada Wilderness Committee provided funding for Tla-O-Qui-Aht carpenters to build a mile-long boardwalk over the spongy forest floor, one of several "witness trails" now in the area.

A skiff takes you from the seaplane dock in Tofino across the Sound (a 10-minute ride, unless you pause to look at nesting eagles or whales) and drops you off at the trailhead, barely visible through the overhanging branches of hemlock trees and salal. The boardwalk, which looks like something out of a Swiss Family Robinson movie, threads through the grove of absolutely astounding cedars. They are each so old (1,200–1,500 years) and gnarled that every one of the 17 named trees seems to have a personality of its own. The boardwalk ends with a circle around the Hanging Garden Tree, British Columbia's fourth-largest western red cedar. The trail continues on bare ground for several more miles before looping back to the beach. Note: It's too wet to walk the bare trail in winter, but the boardwalk on a rainy day under the forest canopy is delightful if you're dressed for it. Take rain gear and wear nonslip-soled shoes. There are no handrails on some ramps.

The Clayoquot Valley Witness Trail Map and Recreation Guide describes wilderness hikes, lakes, and camps in the Clayoquot River valley, as well as fern meadows, boardwalks, old-growth sitka spruce groves, rock slab caves, cliffhanger log walks, rock gardens, and limestone sculptures—all in an area earmarked for logging by MacMillan Bloedel Ltd. Volunteers against the clearcuts have donated 15,000 hours to build "witness trails" through the forest. The guide is available from Tla-O-Qui-Aht First Nations, PO Box 18, Tofino, BC V0R 2Z0; (604)725-3233. Call for cost.

To hike the Meares Island Big Cedar Trail, book through Island Attractions Ltd, 300 Main St (located in the House of Himwitsa), Tofino, BC V0R 2Z0; (800)920-1072. $25 adults; less for kids.

Walk on the Wild Side

Take a 45-minute boat ride from Tofino on the heated, enclosed 31-passenger *Spirit of Marktosis* seabus to the Nuu-chah-nulth village of Ahousaht on Flores Island. The boat slows down so passengers can see sea lions, basking sharks, gray whales, orcas, and eagles. On Flores Island, passengers disembark for a 2-hour, fully guided "Spirit Walk," to learn the history of the village, explore traditions, and see "culturally modified" trees in which signs of the Ahousaht's earliest occupation are carved. Guides also take you to uninhabited Ball Beach, where you'll learn about foraging for edible sea plants and shellfish.

Walk on the Wild Side, General Delivery, Ahousaht, BC V0R 1A0; (800)665-9425 or (604)670-9602. Plan about 4 hours per trip; Adults $70; children 12 and under $60. Custom tours available for two or more people, and for schools and large groups by special arrangement.

Hot Springs Cove Lodge

Geothermal hot springs may be found in a sheltered inlet, about 25 miles (40 kilometers) north of Tofino, which was frequented for centuries by the local Hesquiaht Band. The water plunges down a stone cliff, then makes its way to the ocean through a series of pools, which are ideal for a hot soak. The surf pounds just 30 feet from the lowest pool.

Hot Springs Cove Lodge is just across the cove from the hot springs, next to the Hesquiaht Band's fishing village. Each of the six waterfront studios is self-contained, with fully equipped kitchenette, microwave, queen-size bed, and sofabed. Bring your own food. You can hike miles of Pacific beaches here. Charter boats may be reserved at the lodge for whale watching and sportfishing.

Hot Springs Cove Lodge, north of Flores Island. Book through Island Attractions Ltd, 300 Main S, Tofino, BC V0R 2Z0; (800)920-1072. Rates are $75–$100 plus $50 for water taxi to the lodge. Open year-round.

Whale Watching/Salmon Charters

Hundreds of gray whales pass Vancouver Island's shores during their spring (Mar–Apr) and fall (Sept–Oct) migrations; dozens of whales stay all summer in Clayoquot Sound, just a short ride from Tofino. The Nuu-chah-nulth once hunted whales and still are the best guides in the area. They tell some of the best whale tales you've ever heard, as well as stories of growing up on Vancouver's remote west side. The listings below are all whale-watching charter boats owned and operated by First Nations people:

The 32-foot MV *Clayoquot Whaler* leaves Tofino's wharf three times daily for a 2-hour eco-tour of the Sound. Prices vary (kids under 5 are free).

Al Keitlah, Jr., and his son, Neil, operate the 19-foot, six-passenger, open-cockpit *Raven Dancer* for whale-watching, sportfishing, and customized tours.

Felix Thomas has an enclosed, 12-passenger Cougar Island water taxi for whale watching as well as transportation to local destinations such as Flores Island, Meares Island, and Hot Springs Cove.

Daybreak Charters offers a 26-foot Tolly Craft with enclosed cabin and command bridge, and a skipper with 40 years' experience, for fishing charters (tackle supplied), whale watching, and water-taxi service.

Tickets and reservations for all of these boats may be obtained by calling Island Attractions Ltd, 300 Main St, Tofino, BC V0R 2Z0; (800)920-1072.

More First Nation Galleries

We found a wonderful sea lion mask, carved from alder by a local tribal member, in Marie and Colleen Martin's First Nations Visions & Images gallery at Long Beach, a few miles south of Tofino (221 Esowista, Long Beach; (604)725-2355). The Martins rely on fishermen to bring them artwork made in the remote west coast villages of Vancouver Island. Their store, a combination mini-mart and art gallery, offers carvings, baskets, beadwork, jewelry, limited-edition prints, and local T-shirts. We like this place because the Martins give young artists a chance to display their work. The store is in a small tribal residential area off the Pacific Rim Highway. Watch for signs.

In Ahousaht, you might recognize scenes and faces from I Heard the Owl Call My Name, a 1973 film based on the book by Margaret Craven. The story is about a Catholic priest transformed by his stay in a Nuu-chah-nulth village. Footage includes a brief part of the Ahousaht Maquinna families' most sacred dances. The book is available at the House of Himwitsa in Tofino.

Tsimshian graphic artist Roy Henry Vickers, from Kitkatla near Hazelton, British Columbia, has built the Eagle Aerie Gallery, a replica of a traditional Tsimshian longhouse complete with carved house posts and screens (350 Campbell St, Tofino; (800)663-0669 or (604)725-3235; open daily, year-round). The gallery displays Vickers' original serigraphs. He also owns the Eagle Moon Gallery in Victoria.

William Barr's hand-engraved silver and gold Native jewelry is sold at Barr's Native Jewelry & Art (346 Campbell St; (604)725-4482).

The Du Quah Gallery, built like a cedar longhouse, is on the main street of the charming little port of Ucluelet, about 14 miles south of Tofino (1971 Peninsula, Ucluelet; (604)726-7223). Chief Bert Mack and his wife, Lillian, sell masks, totem poles, silver, turquoise, Cowichan sweaters, leatherwork, and prints from all over British Columbia.

Campbell River: *Kwakwaka'wakw*

You'll see a number of totem poles in the town of Campbell River, but the most photographed is the Heritage Pavilion at Foreshore Park, overlooking Discovery Passage, right next to the ferry landing. Campbell River, best known for its salmon fishing, boasts a community museum with a new display of masks by contemporary carvers, as well as older ethnographic materials. From Campbell River, you can take the ferry to Quadra Island, to the Kwagiulth Museum and Cultural Centre at Quathiaski Cove, or take Highway 28 across Vancouver Island to Gold River, where you can board a boat bound for Nootka Sound and a stop at the village of Yuquot for a tour with the Mowachaht Band.

Campbell River Museum

The Campbell River Museum negotiated with a local Kwakwaka'wakw family for permission to tell the family story of a young man's adventures in the undersea world. Kwakwaka'wakw carvers created masks depicting Komegwey (the king of the undersea), sea monsters, spring salmon, octopus, and other sea creatures. These new masks, made by contemporary carvers, are outstanding proof that the First Nations artistic tradition and culture continue to thrive. The museum also contains an ethnographic collection, not always displayed, of Vancouver Island's three First Nations groups: the Nuu-chah-nulth, Kwakwaka'wakw, and coast Salish. Videos about First Nations history, based on archival materials, are shown in the museum's mini-theater. There's also a small museum store.

Campbell River Museum, 470 Island Hwy, PO Box 70, Station A, Campbell River, BC VPW 1Z9; (604)287-3103. Call for hours. Admission $2; family group rate $7.50.

Quadra Island

Quadra Island sits smack-dab in the middle of the Inside Passage, and for centuries the Kwagiulth people living on the island were the gate-keepers of the passage. There are two very good reasons to visit Quadra Island, which is accessible by a short ferry ride from the town of Campbell River: the Kwagiulth Museum and Cultural Centre at Quathiaski Cove, which houses the returned portion of the "Potlatch Collection" and offers one of the best explanations of the potlatch we've seen anywhere, and Tsa Kwa Luten Lodge (pronounced saw-kwa-looten), also tribally owned and operated, which is designed like a Kwagiulth bighouse and overlooks Discovery Passage.

Ferries leave Campbell River for Quadra Island once every hour, every day, year-round. For schedule and fare information, call (604)386-3431.

Kwagiulth Museum and Cultural Centre

Shaped like the spiral shell of a moon snail (a fist-sized mollusk common to Pacific Northwest waters), the Kwagiulth Museum and Cultural Centre was built in 1979 specifically to house the returned portion of the Kwagiulth's "Potlatch Collection." Masks, headdresses, coppers (a large object of hammered copper and a monetary unit that represents enormous wealth), and other objects were confiscated by a zealous Indian agent in the early 1920s, when a law banning the potlatch was enforced. The Kwagiulth were forced to surrender ceremonial objects and regalia used in Winter Ceremonies and potlatches or face imprisonment. The agent earmarked objects for the personal collection of Duncan Campbell Scott (Canada's superintendent general of Indian affairs), sold some of the items to George Heye, a New York collector, and packed off the rest to museums in Ottawa, Ontario. (You'll see objects from these private collections in every major museum in the world today.) After more than 60 years of negotiations, a portion of the Potlatch Collection was returned to Cape Mudge and to Alert Bay—in an emotional event documented on a videotape shown at the museum.

Look here also for photographs of Kwagiulth villages at the turn of the century, fiberglass casts of petroglyphs found on rocks on nearby beaches, and large wooden ceremonial flutes that you can pick up and play. The museum is overseen by the Kwagiulth's Nuymbalees Society and includes a well-stocked bookstore and gift shop.

Kwagiulth Museum, PO Box 8, Quathiaski Cove, BC V0P 1N0; (604)285-3733. From the ferry landing on Quadra Island, take Green Rd to Weway Rd (gravel road), and turn right into Cape Mudge Indian Village; continue along the beachfront, past the community center and cemetery. The museum is located next to the cemetery. Open daily, year-round; closed Sun in winter. Admission $3.

Tsa Kwa Luten Lodge

Located on a 1,100-acre forest overlooking Discovery Passage, the main lodge offers 26 sea-view deluxe suites and four cabins. Some have private verandas, fireplaces, and Jacuzzi baths. Overnight guests are welcome, but most people come here for a couple of days of salmon fishing in the fast tidal currents of Discovery Passage, at the mouth of the Campbell River. The lodge offers fishing packages that include lodging and meals. Fishing trips include boat, tackle, bait, all-weather gear, and a professional guide. Catches are cleaned, packaged, fast-frozen, and shipped for guests. The concierge also arranges boat cruises of the outer islands and Seymour Narrows, whale watching, scuba diving, and kayaking. Conference rooms accommodate up to 80 people and include fax, photocopying, and secretarial services.

Tsa Kwa Luten Lodge, The Resort at Cape Mudge, PO Box 460, Quathiaski Cove, BC V0P 1N0; (800)665-7745 or (604)285-2042. The lodge is open May–Oct. When the lodge is closed, contact the tribal office; (604)285-3316. Room rates vary. Seaplane flights can be chartered from Seattle, Vancouver, and Victoria (the lodge will help you make arrangements).

Yuquot: *Nuu-chah-nulth*

From Gold River board the MV *Uchuck*, a working freight boat, with a Mowachaht guide, and travel through the narrow inlets, passages, and channels of Nootka Sound to the oceanside village of Yuquot on Nootka Island. Also known as Friendly Cove, Yuquot has been the ancestral home of the Mowachaht/Muchalaht people for thousands of years and has been designated as a Canadian National Historic Site. Among the mariners the tribe hosted at Friendly Cove was Captain James Cook, who spent a month with the Mowachahts while his ship was being retrofitted, shortly before his death in the Sandwich Islands. When the Mowachahts traded otter pelts with the British in the late 1700s, Spain jealously responded by building Fort San Miguel at Yuquot in 1789 and seizing a number of British ships. The "Nootka Controversy" nearly ignited a war in Europe. At Yuquot, the hour-long tour of the village, the ruins of Fort San Miguel, and the site of the Mowachahts' sacred whaler's shrine is enriched with details of Mowachaht culture. You'll also see historic photographs of the village, as well as a fallen totem pole and several sets of carved house posts. The Mowachahts also maintain six new rustic cabins and a wilderness campground in Nootka Island's old-growth forest. Five cabins overlook the freshwater lake, just a few hundred feet from the Pacific Ocean; one overlooks the ocean beach. Cabins are equipped with kitchens and wood stoves. The campground has 18 tent sites, with fire pits, picnic tables, potable water, and pit toilets. To get to Gold River, take scenic Highway 28 from the town of Campbell River, west across Vancouver Island. At Gold River, turn left at the BC Information Centre, and follow the main road through Gold

River toward the mill. Ahaminaquus, from which the 100-passenger MV *Uchuck,* water taxi, and floatplanes depart, is about 8¾ miles (14 kilometers) outside Gold River. The MV *Uchuck*/Mowachaht tour leaves from Ahaminaquus every Wednesday during the summer months, July through August. The daylong round-trip, with a 1½-hour stop and tour in Yuquot and other stops in Nootka Sound, is less than $50. If you arrive by plane, water taxi, or personal craft, the hour-long village tour is $7.

Yuquot can also be accessed year-round from Gold River by Native-owned Maxi's Water Taxi, a 12-passenger enclosed boat (the 1-hour trip is $180 one way for one to eight people; (604)282-2282) or by Air Nootka charter floatplane, about $125 per person each way; (604)283-2255.

Book tours through the Ahaminaquus Tourist Centre, PO Box 1137, Gold River, BC V0P 1G0; (800)238-2933. Call the Mowachaht Band's office in Gold River for package rates that include transportation, tour, and accommodations; (604)283-2015. Cabins, campgrounds, and tours are open year-round; fees vary according to season. Most people come here May–Sept.

Alert Bay: *Kwakwa̲ka'wakw*

Alert Bay, one of Vancouver Island's most famous communities, is located on Cormorant Island, 40 minutes by ferry from Port McNeill, several hours north of Campbell River. Best known for its U'Mista Cultural Centre, Alert Bay was formerly used as a burial ground by the Nimpkish people. Today, handsome memorial totems still stand in the cemetery in the center of town.

Europeans settled in Alert Bay in 1870 and built a small fish saltery. Today the town numbers about 1,400. It is in the heart of orca territory, and there are a number of whale-watching and sportfishing tours, kayaking, and scuba diving. You'll find plenty to do here to make the long drive from Victoria (about 6 hours) well worth it. Accommodations on the island are limited, and reservations should be made far in advance of your visit. Contact the Alert Bay Information Centre, 116 Fir St, Alert Bay, BC V09 1A0; (604)974-5213. For ferry schedule information, call (604)956-4533.

U'Mista Cultural Centre

The Kwakwa̲ka'wakw community at Alert Bay lost most of their ceremonial masks, bowls, robes, and coppers after an 1884 policy outlawed Winter Ceremonies and potlatches and mandated the

confiscation of ceremonial items. The dances and ceremonies were held secretly until 1951, when the government dropped its law against potlatches. A large
number of confiscated items were returned in 1979
and are now safely ensconced in the U'Mista Cultural
Centre. The center, located a few feet from the rocky
beach, is built in the style of a cedar bighouse. On arrival, visitors watch *Box of Treasures*, a video explaining the long and fascinating journey of the confiscated
potlatch items from the village and back. The items,
many of them elaborately carved and painted masks,
are displayed around the inside walls in the order they
would appear at a potlatch. You can browse the collection alone, or join a Native-guided tour that takes
about an hour (recommended). Many more videos are
on hand at the center, and you're welcome to sit and
watch any of them. During summer months, there
may be regularly scheduled traditional masked-dance
performances. Private dance performances can be
arranged for groups of 50 or more. The gift shop sells
lovely carved jewelry, masks, silk-screened prints, and
many other items made by local artists, some of whose
work is internationally known.

*U'Mista Cultural Centre, Front St, PO Box 253, Alert Bay, BC V0N
1A0; (604)974-5403. Open year-round. Call for hours. Admission
$5; tours and dance performances are extra.*

*Don Smith, of Cherokee/
French ancestry, was
formally adopted and
given permission by the
James Sewid family in the
1950s to use their stories,
songs, masks, and cere-
monies. Smith, an ac-
complished woodcarver
who uses the Nez Perce
name "Lalooska," trans-
planted the Kwagiulth
culture to Washington
State, where he and his
family carve, perform
masked dances and do
storytelling in a replica
of a Kwagiulth long-
house, and showcase
their work in the
Lalooska Gallery, 165
Merwin Village Rd, Ariel,
WA 98603; (206)225-
8828. Ariel is off I-5, 45
minutes north of
Portland, Oregon.*

Port Hardy: *Kwakwaka'wakw*

From Port Hardy, at the far end of Vancouver Island, you can catch
the ferry to Prince Rupert on the mainland, the departure point in
northern British Columbia for Haida Gwaii (the Queen Charlotte
Islands) and roads leading to the northern interior.

The Copper Maker Carving Studio and Gallery

The Hunt family has produced some of the finest carvers in the
world, as well as more than 30 other working artists. This prodigious
outpouring by the last three generations of Hunts began in the 1850s,
when Robert Hunt, a Hudson's Bay Company employee from
England, married Mary Ebbets, the Tlingit daughter of a Tongass
tribal chief. Their offspring collaborated early in this century with

anthropologist Franz Boas and photographer Edward Curtis.

Calvin Hunt, who carved the transformation mask pictured on the cover of this book, owns, with his wife Marie, the Copper Maker Carving Studio and Gallery just outside Port Hardy. His work and the work of other Hunt family members—from pottery, prints, and jewelry to carving—is for sale at the gallery. Often family members work on larger commissions in the gallery's carving studio on the first floor. Commissions for authentic button blankets, as well as dance exhibitions, are also booked through the Copper Maker.

The Copper Maker Carving Studio and Gallery, 112 Copper Way, Fort Rupert Village; (604)949-8491. Open 9am–5pm year-round. The gallery is just south of Port Hardy. Call first; the gallery closes when the family travels to major exhibitions.

Prince Rupert: *Tsimshian*

There is an exceptional museum and harbor tour in Prince Rupert, a coastal town near the Southeast Alaska border and an ancient Tsimshian village site. The Skeena River is the mythical birthplace of the scamp Raven, protagonist of the Raven stories of the Northwest Coast. Tsimshians have occupied the area for at least 10,000 years, and Prince Rupert has the highest concentration of archaeological sites anywhere in North America. Today many Tsimshian people live in Prince Rupert and up the Skeena River.

Getting to Prince Rupert can be daunting, although it's a scenic trip no matter how you get there. BC Ferries, (604)669-1211, leave from Port Hardy, on Vancouver Island's northern end, cross Queen Charlotte Strait, and thread their way through the islands of the narrow Inside Passage to Prince Rupert, a 15- to 18-hour trip.

From the city of Vancouver, on the mainland, the Yellowhead Trans-Canada Highway 16 to Prince Rupert is about 935 miles (1,500 kilometers), or two very long days on the road. Greyhound Bus, (604)662-3222, makes the trip twice a day from Vancouver. The Canadian railway VIA Rail, (800)561-3949, goes from Vancouver to Prince Rupert via Jasper (Alberta), where passengers change trains. The trip takes two days and nights and arrives on the third day. The quickest route is by Air Canada, (800)776-3000, which flies 68-passenger jets twice a day from Vancouver to Prince Rupert.

For assistance with lodging and car rentals, contact Prince Rupert Visitor Information Centre; (800)667-1994. From Prince Rupert, you can continue to Southeast Alaska on the Alaska State Ferry (we suggest leaving your car behind), (800)642-0066, or visit the Queen Charlotte Islands on BC Ferries, (604)669-1211.

Museum of Northern British Columbia

Housed in a historic 1911 railway station on Prince Rupert's water-front, the Museum of Northern British Columbia is billed as British Columbia's "biggest little museum." Exhibits include the cultural history and ethnography of the coast Tsimshians. It also chronicles the history of European contact with the Tsimshians, early Hudson's Bay forts, William Duncan's mission at nearby Fort Simpson, and the village of old Metlakatla. The museum's gift shop gets rave reviews for having one of the best bookstores in British Columbia, with over 800 book titles, as well as an outstanding collection of Northwest Coast art for sale.

Museum of Northern British Columbia, 100 First Ave, PO Box 669, Prince Rupert, BC V8J 3S1; (604)624-3207. Open in summer, Mon–Sat 9am–8pm, Sun 9am–5pm; winter, Mon–Sat 10am–5pm. Donation.

Guided Archaeological Harbor Tours

Vistors begin with a slide show at the Museum of Northern British Columbia, then board a covered boat in Prince Rupert's harbor for a multicultural tour. Museum guides take you to a historic Finnish fishing village at Dodge Cove, built on the site of a 5,000-year-old Tsimshian village. Back on board the boat, guides pass around artifacts while pointing out dozens of archaeological sites, including rock carvings. At the modern village of Metlakatla, an Indian village for thousands of years, you learn about its brief history as a Christian utopian community (the entire village packed up and moved to Annette Island in Southeast Alaska in the late 1800s). Tours are co-sponsored by the Metlakatla Band of Tsimshians and the Museum of Northern British Columbia.

Museum of Northern British Columbia, 100 First Ave, PO Box 669, Prince Rupert, BC V8J 3S1; (604)624-3207. On the Prince Rupert waterfront. Buy tickets early in the day, as the tour is popular. Tours daily, June 19–Sept 4. Adults, $20; children 16 and under, $12; children under 5, free. Tours may be canceled on short notice due to sudden storms; money will be refunded.

First Nations Arts

Tribal Accents (526 3rd Ave W, Prince Rupert; (604)624-4417) is owned by Ken Humpherville, a Metis Cree and wood carver who has lived in Prince Rupert all his life. Kathy Humpherville is a Tsimshian from Metlakatla, Alaska, who makes garments using Northwest Coast designs, with other design elements such as leather fringes. Look here also for Tsimshian Heber Reese's outstanding masks and other fine cedar carvings. The shop, which specializes in Northwest Coast art, including argillite carving from Haida Gwaii, also carries Southwest art, as well as baskets from all over North America.

On the Prince Rupert waterfront, Eagle Wind Native Arts (203 Cow Bay Rd, Prince Rupert; (604)624-8313) has traditional Nisga'a art from the Nass River, carved on the premises by the Adams family. They also sell popular lathe-turned birch, alder, and yellow cedar carved bowls and 1- to 8-foot-tall totem poles, moon and sun masks, silk-screened prints, and carved gold and silver jewelry. Also look for hand-woven natural wool sweaters knitted by Nisga'a elders.

Totem Poles on the Skeena River

Prince Rupert has a number of carved totem poles around town. You can pick up a small book containing a walking map and explanation of the poles at the Prince Rupert Travel Information Centre or at the museum. Gitksan villages all along the Skeena River have totem poles as well, some now the oldest still standing in British Columbia. Look for them especially at the villages of Kitwanga and Kitwancool (between Hazelton and Prince Rupert, on Highway 37); at Kispiox (north of Hazelton); and at Kitsegyukla (south of Hazelton on Route 16). There are also totems at the 'Ksan museum near Hazelton.

Maps are available from the Travel Information Centre, at the junction of Highways 16 and 62, PO Box 340, New Hazelton District, BC V0J 2J0; (604)842-6571.

'Ksan Historical Indian Village

For thousands of years, Gitksan villages have occupied this site at the junction of the Skeena and Bulkley Rivers. Its narrow canyon made it a desirable spot to trap salmon as they made their way upriver to spawn. East of Prince Rupert, the 'Ksan Historical Indian Village, one of the most popular First Nations attractions in British Columbia, includes totem poles and reconstructions of seven traditional longhouses.

Three longhouses are named after Gitksan clans and furnished with cultural items. The Fireweed House of Masks and Robes contains contemporary masks and robes belonging to the 'Ksan Performing Arts Group. The Frog House of the Distance [sic] Past is furnished with everyday household goods that would have been used prior to white contact. The Wolf House of Feasts is furnished as if a 1920s-era potlatch were about to begin. Guided tours of the three furnished longhouses are available during the summer season only.

The other four longhouses are used as a gift shop, museum, and carving school and are open year-round to visitors. The museum contains Gitksan and Wet'suwet'en objects collected from within a 50-mile radius of 'Ksan. Each summer, on Friday nights, awe-inspiring "transformation" masks are worn and "danced" (to dance a mask is to bring the spirit it represents to life) as part of "the Breath of Our Grandfathers" performance by the 'Ksan Performing Arts Group. The gift shop contains outstanding carved masks, house screens, totem poles, and jewelry collected from all over British Columbia, as well as from artists perfecting their skills at the 'Ksan Historical Indian Village's Kitanmaax carving school.

'Ksan Historical Indian Village, PO Box 326, Hazelton, BC V0J 1Y0; (604)842-5544. 'Ksan is 180 miles east of Prince Rupert, near the town of Hazelton. Admission $7. Open year-round. Tours are mid-Apr–Sept. Due to severe weather, the three longhouses normally on the tour are closed in winter, but the gift shop, the Kitanmaax carving school, and the Treasure Room and Exhibition Centre are open daily, year-round. Please call for hours.

Queen Charlotte Islands:
Haida Gwaii

The archipelago of Haida Gwaii, known as Dida Cwaa in the Haida Raven stories, was named the Queen Charlotte Islands by the Canadian government in 1878. The islands are also often referred to as the Canadian Galapagos because of their unique flora and fauna. The archipelago lies about 60 miles off the British Columbia mainland. The 180-mile-long necklace of 150 islands (some of them no larger than a seal's nose) is the ancestral home of the Haida, a nation legendary for its art, frequent raids, and fierce domination of the inland waters all the way to Vancouver Island. The Haida have never ceded the islands to Canada, but many of their villages, now overgrown with moss-covered rain forests, were abandoned in the 1800s when smallpox epidemics forced the few remaining people to consolidate at Skidegate, on the northern end of the archipelago. Most visitors come to Haida Gwaii to visit and photograph the abandoned villages on the southern end of Moresby Island, known as Gwaii Haanas. You must make a reservation with the Canadian park service before you can visit any of the protected villages.

To get to the Queen Charlotte Islands, take the BC Ferry, (604)381-1401, from Prince Rupert across the Hecate Strait to Skidegate. The 6-hour crossing costs about $200 round-trip for car and driver. Ferries depart once a day May–Sept. In winter, ferries travel across the Strait three times a week. Flights from Prince Rupert to Skidegate take about 45 minutes.

At Skidegate, a town of about 500 residents, be sure to visit the Queen Charlotte Island Museum, where you can see Haida carvings of argillite (a type of slate), a totem pole carved by master carver Bill Reid, the *Lootaas* canoe, longhouses, and the Honna Fish Hatchery. Highway 16 links the towns of Skidegate, Masset, Port Clements, Tlell, and Queen Charlotte City. A car ferry links Graham and Moresby Islands, but south Moresby Island, the most popular tourist destination, is roadless and accessible only by personal watercraft, private charter, floatplane, or helicopter.

Free Travel Information

Parks Canada (PO Box 37, Queen Charlotte City, BC V0T 1S0; (604)559-8818) will send you a free travel planning guide with everything you need to visit Gwaii Haanas—from checklists, maps, and information about accommodations to boat and plane charters and guided tours. Note: The guide is necessary to plan your visit and contains not only a list of references and guidebooks but marine charts and where to purchase them on the mainland. To find out if there are tours or special events led by members of the Haida Nation, contact the Council of Haida Nations, (604)626-5252, or the Skidegate Band office, (604)559-4496. There are two Visitor Reception Centres on the islands—one at Sandspit, in the airport building, the other in the town of Queen Charlotte. Both have marine charts and topographic maps available to look at and marine VHF radio to check weather forecasts. *The Observer,* a Queen Charlotte City weekly newspaper, sells an 80-page *Guide to the Queen Charlotte Islands,* updated annually, for under $5; call (604)559-4680 for a copy. Another general guide available from Canadian booksellers is Neil G. Carey's *A Guide to the Queen Charlotte Islands* (Raincoast Books, 1995).

Queen Charlotte Islands Museum

Located just outside Skidegate is a fine museum dedicated entirely to Haida culture and history. Built on Qaykun (Sea Lion) point, on the site of an old Haida village, the museum is made entirely of cedar posts and beams, echoing Haida traditional bighouse style. Inside are four historic totem poles from the abandoned villages of Tanu and Skedans and contemporary Haida carver Bill Reid's first totem pole, commissioned by Shell Canada and donated back to the museum.

Reid's 50-foot Haida canoe *Lootaas* (wave eater), carved for Canada's Expo '86, is adjacent to the museum. The museum houses more than 500 argillite miniatures, including totem poles and carved plates, pipes, sculpture, and jewelry. Haida carver Robert Davidson, who began carving argillite as a boy and expanded into other media, also donated nine major pieces of his work to the museum. Contemporary work is for sale in the museum's gift shop, along with one of the most extensive inventories of books on Haida art and culture. The museum's multilevel decks overlook Skidegate Inlet. This is one of the best places in the world to see migrating gray whales in the spring and fall. They are drawn close to shore to feed in eelgrass meadows just offshore.

Queen Charlotte Islands Museum, RR 1, Second Beach Rd, Skidegate, BC V0T 1S1; (604)559-4643. The museum is just south of Skidegate on Hwy 16, on the Skidegate Reserve. In summers, open June–Aug daily: 10am–5pm Mon–Fri, 1pm–5pm weekends. In winter, closed Tues and Sun. Admission $2.50.

Argillite Sculpture

The Haida are the only people in the world allowed to quarry and work the rare black argillite, a fine, easily carved slate material found on Haida Gwaii. Argillite is sculpted into miniature totem poles, jewelry, plaques, boxes, and pipes. The most famous argillite carver is Charles Edensaw (also spelled Edenshaw). His great-nephew, Bill Reid, is among the best known of the Haida carvers. Robert Davidson, another famous Haida artist, was brought up in the north coast village of Old Masset and began carving argillite as a young boy. Both Reid and Davidson carve wood, silver, and gold as well. All three carvers' work is in major museums and private collections all over the world. Haida argillite carvings can be purchased throughout the Pacific Northwest coast and in Southeast Alaska, but the best place to buy them is Haida Gwaii. Contact the Queen Charlotte Museum or Council of Haida Nations for names of local carvers from whom you can buy directly; (604)626-5252.

Gwaii Haanas National Park Reserve

Dotting the southern end of Moresby Island (which the Haida call Gwaii Haanas) are the largest number of known abandoned Haida villages. The villages were set aside in the last decade as a national park preserve. Just off the southernmost tip, on Anthony Island, is the site of Skungwaii (Ninstints), today a United Nations world heritage site, from which the powerful Kunghit Haida once ruled Gwaii

Haanas. The Kunghit, who once numbered in the thousands, were hit hard by the smallpox epidemics, and by the late 1800s only 30 to 40 survivors were left.

The old village sites were documented by Victoria artist Emily Carr, who journeyed here alone in the early 1900s to paint the remains of Skungwaii and other villages. Dr. Charles F. Newcombe left a written record of the sites; in 1901, he circumnavigated and mapped old village sites in the southern portion of the islands in 1901 with Chief Ninstints, one of the last three or four surviving Kunghits.

Tours of the Skidegate Inlet in the Lootaas canoe may be available during the summer months. Contact Haida Gwaii Watchmen Native-Operated Tours, PO Box 609, Skidegate, BC V0T 1S0; (604)559-8225.

In the late 1950s, 11 of the best-preserved totem poles were removed and are today on exhibit at the University of British Columbia Museum of Anthropology in Vancouver and at the Royal British Columbia Museum in Victoria. Skungwaii today, which is about 95 nautical miles from any town, has only leaning mortuary poles, fragments of longhouses, and shell middens. The site adjoins a wildlife reserve, home to nesting puffins and petrels and herds of seals. Other villages on Gwaii Haanas, such as Skedans on Louise Island, are guarded by the Haida Gwaii Watchmen, tribal members who contract with the Canadian park service as guides and caretakers. In order to protect the sites, only a limited number of tourists are allowed to visit south Moresby Island each year. There are no facilities or roads in Gwaii Haanas National Park Preserve. Travel must be arranged by private charter, floatplane, or helicopter. Visitors must leave by dusk.

Gwaii Haanas National Park Reserve and Haida Heritage Site, Parks Canada, PO Box 37, Queen Charlotte City, BC V0T 1S0; (604)559-8818. To make arrangements to see abandoned villages, contact the Haida Gwaii Watchmen, PO Box 609, Skidegate, Haida Gwaii, BC V0T 1S0; (604)559-8225. June–mid-Aug are the best months to visit. The area is often foggy July–Oct.

WESTERN WASHINGTON

CANADA

VANCOUVER
ISLAND

▲ NOOKSACK

I-5

▲ LUMMI
• Bellingham

MAKAH ▲
• Ozette

112

Victoria

▲ SWINOMISH

▲ LOWER ELWHA S'KLALLAM
FERRY

Whidbey Island

Port Angeles •

Port
Townsend •

TULALIP ▲
• Everett

101

• Forks

QUILEUTE ▲

JAMESTOWN S'KLALLAM
PORT GAMBLE
S'KLALLAM ▲

▲ SUQUAMISH

OLYMPIC
NATIONAL
PARK

• Poulsbo
• Winslow
FERRY

SKOKOMISH ▲

101

• Seattle

109

I-90

▲ QUINAULT

• Taholah

▲ MUCKLESHOOT

• Tacoma

• Shelton

SQUAXIN ISLAND ▲

▲ PUYALLUP
▲ STEILACOOM

• Aberdeen

12

Olympia •

Nisqually
Delta

▲ NISQUALLY

▲ SHOALWATER BAY

I-5

101

▲ CHEHALIS

WASHINGTON

• Ilwaco

Columbia River

OREGON

WESTERN WASHINGTON

Most of the rivers in western Washington are named after the tribes who still live near them today: the Nooksack, Sammish, Skagit, Snoqualmie, Snohomish, Skykomish, Duwamish, Muckleshoot, Puyallup, Nisqually, Skokomish, Quileute, Hoh, Quinault, Queets, Chinook, Cowlitz, and Chehalis. The Lummi, Makah, Squaxin Island, Stillaguamish, Swinomish, Suquamish, Sauk-Suiattle, S'Klallam, Tulalip, and Shoalwater Bay tribes live in the area as well.

In 1854–1855, most of the tribes in western Washington signed treaties with the U. S. government. Territorial governor Isaac Stevens established several reservations, with the plan to later move the Indians to a single location on the Olympic Peninsula. The treaties stated that in exchange for signing away ownership to all of their land, the tribes could reserve forever the right to fish, hunt, and gather roots and berries at all of their traditional (usual and accustomed) places.

The Indian Wars of 1855–1856 followed as a result of the refusal of the Puyallup and Nisqually Tribes to move to reservation lands assigned to them. Battles pitted Indian warriors from both sides of the Cascades against American volunteers recruited by Stevens, as well as against the professional army stationed at Fort Steilacoom on southern

Puget Sound. On August 5, 1856, Governor Stevens met with the disquieted Indians to adjust details of the reservations and take into account the Natives' objections.

Today, it is difficult to imagine Native American life as it once existed in western Washington. Modern cities, highways, and industries dominate the landscape, and most of the original tribes have been scattered among reservations or assimilated into the onslaught of development. However, one can discover marvelous histories and artifacts, as well as thriving contemporary arts, crafts, and cultures, tucked away in unexpected corners. This chapter takes you around the rim of Puget Sound and onto the Olympic Peninsula, directing you to tribally owned museums such as the Steilacoom Tribal Cultural Center & Museum, housed in a 1903 church; to historic sites such as Chief Seattle's grave in Suquamish; to art installations such as the Salish *Ravens and Crows* at the University of Washington; and to contemporary Native events such as the Lummi's Stommish Water Festival and the Swinomish Annual Blues Festival. The chapter begins in southern Puget Sound, the southern end of the 1,000-mile-long "Inside Passage," a waterway that stretches from glacier-filled bays in Southeast Alaska to shellfish-laden tideflats in the Nisqually Delta.

PUGET SOUND

Olympia Metropolitan Area

Washington State Capitol Museum

The Washington State Capitol Museum in Oympia houses collections of art and artifacts from seven tribes living in the southern Puget Sound region: the Puyallup, Steilacoom, Nisqually, Squaxin Island, Skokomish, Chehalis, and Cowlitz. Its installation "Traditions and Transitions: The American Indians of South Puget Sound" is the only thorough explanation of Salish culture anywhere in the Northwest. Elders and cultural leaders helped design the hands-on exhibit, which includes the interior of a winter house furnished with household items, baskets, and tools. The exhibit also explains the transition of tribal culture from its original state to the European model introduced by the British Hudson's Bay Company in 1833. An adjoining gallery displays masterworks by contemporary artists. The archives contain a large number of Salish baskets, which are displayed for the public from time to time.

Washington State Capitol Museum, 211 W 21st Ave, Olympia, WA 98501; (360)753-2580. Seven blocks south of the state capitol grounds, off Capitol Way. Open Tues–Fri; Sat and Sun afternoons. Admission, $2.

Longhouse/Evergreen State College Campus

On the Evergreen State College campus, outside Olympia, Washington, is a full-scale adaptation (with modern restrooms, kitchen, and offices) of a traditional Salish longhouse. At one time a huge boulder, incised with Salish bear symbols, marked what is now the Evergreen campus as a gathering place for all the Salish nations. The current longhouse was built to house Evergreen's Indian Studies program, and was designed by Johnpaul Jones, a Native, with Seattle architectural firm Jones & Jones. Indian elders advised. It is open to the public.

Over the longhouse entrance perches a massive Thunderbird, carved and painted by Makah Greg Colfax and Skokomish Andy Wilber. Window covers are woven cedar-bark mats, illustrated with creation stories by Skokomish artist Bruce Miller. Other figures from Native American mythology adorn screens surrounding two fireplaces. The hoods over the fireplace are finished with hammered copper, the most common metal used by Pacific Northwest tribes prior to Europen contact. The building was sanctified with traditional ceremonies.

Evergreen State College, 2700 Evergreen Pkwy NW, Olympia, WA 98505; (360)866-6000. Take the Hwy 101 exit from I-5 at Olympia; follow 101 to the Evergreen State College exit. Tours should be arranged in advance.

Original Fort Nisqually Site

Today, the small town of DuPont is located near the site of the original Fort Nisqually, built on the fields overlooking the present-day Nisqually Delta Wildlife Refuge, between Olympia and Tacoma. It is one of the most important historic sites on Puget Sound. Established by the Hudson's Bay Company in Nisqually Indian territory in 1833, Fort Nisqually operated briefly as a fur-trading post, but soon developed into a completely different kind of enterprise. As the demand for furs decreased, the demand for other Northwest resources, most notably gold, became insatiable. In the late 1840s, the Hudson's Bay Company, with its fleet of cargo ships, began supplying animal and grain products to the developing Northwest. The company's new enterprise was centered in the Nisqually Delta and was renamed the Puget Sound Agricultural Company. Cattle driven from Mexico were fattened on the rich grassland, hundreds of sheep were tended at several sheep stations between the Nisqually and Puyallup Rivers, and acres of potatoes, corn, peas, and wheat were grown in present-day Pierce County. Farm managers were recruited from England and Scotland; day laborers consisted of Native Hawaiians, brought to the Pacific Northwest on Hudson's Bay ships, and local Squaxin, Nisqually, Chehalis, Cowlitz, Steilacoom, and Puyallup Indians.

The Hudson's Bay fleet of trading vessels shipped grain and products from the farm's creamery, as far south as San Francisco during the California gold rush, and as far north as Sitka, Alaska, to the Russian American Trading Company's headquarters. The farming operation also supplied nearby Fort Steilacoom and traded food for cedar shingles with new settlers clearing land in the Northwest.

The farm era ended in 1869. Pieces of the farmland were sold off; the buildings languished unused. In the 1930s, the DuPont Power Company, which had purchased the original Fort Nisqually site to manufacture explosives, donated the last two original buildings to the public. The factor's house and the granary were moved to Tacoma's Point Defiance State Park, 17 miles to the north, in 1940 (see Fort Nisqually Historic Site in the Tacoma section in this chapter).

Nisqually Delta and the Medicine Creek Treaty

You can still see the site in the Nisqually Delta where the Medicine Creek Treaty of 1855 was signed by the tribes of southern Puget Sound. Under a tree in a grove next to Medicine Creek (called She Nah Num by the Nisqually and now known as McAllister Creek), the terms of the treaty were presented to the assembled tribal leaders by Governor Isaac Stevens. Known by the local tribes as the "Treaty Tree," the old spar is in a closed, no-access area on the Nisqually Wildlife Refuge, but visible from the refuge. A kiosk displays information about the Medicine Creek Treaty. The refuge itself is a must-see—protected wetlands rich in bird and plant life.

A Medicine Creek Treaty monument can also be seen at the crossroads in the nearby town of Nisqually. A second monument, marking the very spot where Leschi was hanged, is at Thunderbird Square in nearby Lakewood.

When Stevens signed the treaties, he made several mistakes. He failed to dress ceremonially for the occasion, deeply offending the tribes. He also failed to fully translate the terms of the treaty into Salish dialects, instead choosing to use limited Chinook jargon to mask its intent. And he misjudged the innate intelligence of Nisqually Chief Leschi, who refused to sign the treaty. Leschi crossed the Cascade Range on horseback to warn the Yakama and other tribes in eastern Washington of Stevens's intentions. Upon the conclusion of the Indian Wars that followed, Leschi was captured and sentenced to be hanged for his trouble. Neither the members of the U.S. Army at both Fort Steilacoom nor the Brits at Fort Nisqually approved of the sentence. They refused to have gallows built at their forts and attempted to save Leschi during his second trial. However, they failed, and Leschi was eventually hanged.

Nisqually National Wildlife Refuge, 100 Brown Farm Rd, Olympia, WA 98516; (360)753-9467. From I-5, take exit 114, and follow signs to the refuge. Wildlife viewing trails (5 ½ miles of trail) through the delta are open to the public during daylight hours, year-round. The education center is open to the public on Saturdays only, 10am–2pm. Trails are open dawn to dusk, daily. No pets, no bicycles. $2 entrance fee per family.

Steilacoom: *Steilacoom*

Steilacoom Tribal Cultural Center & Museum

The oldest town in Washington, the little waterfront burg of Steilacoom was incorporated in 1854 by white settlers. Today the historic town, named after the tribe whose largest village was at the mouth of nearby Chambers Creek, still includes the original town hall and a 1903 church, which now houses the Steilacoom Tribe's Cultural Center and Museum. Nearby is the former site of Fort Steilacoom, an American military fort built in 1849. The old "Indian Trail," which extended from the fort (where Western State Hospital now stands) to the mouth of Chambers Creek, is still visible.

The Steilacoom Tribe is currently not recognized by the federal government. Nonetheless, they have continued to elect tribal leaders, and they own the restored 1903 church. The first floor of the two-story museum is dedicated to the Steilacoom Tribe's early history, with a replica of an archaeological dig that was conducted in the Chamber Creek village site. Charcoal from fire pits and petrified bone recovered from a butchering site date to the early 1400s. Buttons, trade beads, nails, and ceramics found at the site date to the early 1800s, when Europeans settled in the area and began trading with members of the village.

Upstairs is an exhibit of how one Steilacoom family maintained its cultural identity through eight generations. The second floor also has a gallery with touring Native American exhibits that are on display for six months to a year.

A small cafe serves traditional clam chowder (made without milk or tomatoes), smoked salmon–stuffed croissants, and other treats. The gift shop features unique handcrafted items made by local American Indian artists. Proceeds from the gift shop support the all-volunteer museum and cultural center activities.

Steilacoom Tribal Cultural Center & Museum, 1515 Lafayette St, PO Box 88419, Steilacoom, WA 98388; (360)584-6308. One block from the Steilacoom ferry landing. Admission $2. Children under 6, free. Museum memberships $15 a year include a newsletter. Guided tours and catered lunches for groups are available on request. Open Tues–Sun daily, year-round, 10am–4 pm.

Tacoma Metropolitan Area

Fort Nisqually Historic Site

Fort Nisqually Historic Site, reconstructed from the 1830s-era Hudson's Bay Company trading post and farm that was originally located in the Nisqually Delta, is in the 800-acre Point Defiance Park in Tacoma. Six fully furnished buildings recreate life at the fort during the period between 1833 and 1869. Two of the buildings, the factor's house and the granary, were moved to Point Defiance in 1940 from the original site. Self-guided tours include a fully furnished trade-goods store, a laborer's dwelling, a blacksmith's shop, the granary, a clerk's house, and the factor's original home. Special events include candlelight tours in October, several "living-history days" during the summer, and lectures on local tribes.

Fort Nisqually Historic Site, 5400 N Pearl St, #11, Tacoma, WA 98407; (206)591-5339. From I-5 near Tacoma, take the Bremerton exit and continue west to the 6th Ave, Point Defiance Park exit. Follow signs on Five-Mile Dr, within the park, to the site. Open daily, 11am–6pm summers, in winter only the museum and gift shop are open, Wed–Sun. Docent-led group tours and educational programs by reservation year-round. Admission, $1.25, summer. Free in winter.

Washington State History Museum

Both contemporary and historic Native American perspectives are included throughout the new Washington State History Museum in Tacoma. Enter the museum through a southern coast Salish winter home built by Lance Wilkie, a Makah longhouse builder. In the longhouse, visitors "hear" the conversations of family members as they mend nets and cook fern cakes in a basket. Another room includes a recreation of a petroglyph wall outcropping and videos of stories told by contemporary Indian elders. A gallery addresses the devastation caused by epidemics among Indian people; contemporary Indian artists' masks addressing the epidemics have been included in the display. Historic photographs appear throughout the exhibits and include pictures of the Cushman Indian School in Puyallup and portraits of Indian people on the Olympic Peninsula, taken by Indian agent Samuel G. Morse in 1896.

Special collections feature artifacts from all of Washington tribes, and include a handsome display of Indian basketry, as well as a rare set of bone tools and points, over 11,000 years old, uncovered in an eastern Washington apple orchard. Contemporary Indian perspectives are also incorporated in a variety of ways, such as taped interviews with nationally known, Indian leaders. There is a museum shop and a cafe, which offers outdoor dining on the plaza with views of Mount Rainier (Tahoma), historic Union Station, and Commencement Bay.

Washington State Historical Society, 1911 Pacific Ave, Tacoma, WA 98403; (206)593-2830. Opens summer, 1996. Open Tues–Sat, 10am–5pm; Thurs until 8pm; Sun 11am–5pm, year-round. The museum opens one hour earlier Tues–Sat during the summer. Admission $7.

Tacoma: *Puyallup*

The word *spwiya'laphabsh* means "generous" or "welcoming" in Salish. It's the original name of the tribe now known as the Puyallup. Their legends say the Puyallup people came into being in the foothills of Mount Rainier, behind what is now Sumner, Washington, many thousands of years ago. At the time, the waters of Puget Sound and the glaciers merged in the valleys. As the ice melted and the river valleys were formed, the Puyallup fished for salmon in the Puyallup River and in Puget Sound. They speared halibut and flounder and dug clams from Commencement Bay, now the industrial district of the city of Tacoma. The rich Puyallup River valley became a trading center for many tribes. The tribe prospered under the watchful spirit of Tacobet, which lives (still) within the snowy peaks of the mountain the Puyallup called Tahoma.

Published by the tribe, the Puyallup Tribal News covers local tribal news and national Native issues. Subscriptions are $10 a year; for single-issue fees, contact Puyallup Tribal News, 202 E 28th St, Tacoma, WA 98404; (206)593-0174.

In 1855, the Puyallup were among the many bands who signed the Medicine Creek Treaty. The Puyallup Reservation was established in 1856 when the tribe refused to move to other reservations. Today, the Puyallup Reservation covers 28 square miles and includes the city of Fife, much of the city of Tacoma, and stretches to the outskirts of the city of Puyallup. More than 95,000 people live on the reservation; only 2,050 are Puyallup tribal members.

Money from a recent land settlement has been earmarked by the tribe to clean up Commencement Bay, where industrial wastes from those occupying their land have polluted clam beds and decimated the salmon runs on the Puyallup River, which flows into the bay.

Puyallup Tribal Museum

In 1900, Thomas Stolyer, presiding chief of the Puyallup Tribe, gave his land to build a government school. The boarding school buildings included dormitories, a church, and a health clinic. In 1929, due to mounting deaths in the Northwest Indian community from tuberculosis, the buildings became the Cushman Indian Hospital, located on the outskirts of Tacoma.

Many Indian families were separated by prolonged stays in the hospital's sanitarium, which isolated patients for years at a time. "I remember looking up to the third window from the corner to see my mother," our guide tells us, looking up at the second floor of the hospital. "I was 3 years old. It was the first time I remember seeing her, my first memory."

A new hospital was built in 1942 and dominates the entire hilltop. It now serves as the tribal administration office. A totem pole at the entry softens the hard edges of the institutional setting.

On the first floor, in a small room that opens out into the reception area, is the small Puyallup Tribal Museum. The collection, some permanent, some for sale, was originally put together with contributions from tribal members. From floor to ceiling are baskets, several hundred years old, as well as contemporary artwork. The museum has a good selection of local Native art for sale, including cedar-plaited dresses and baskets.

Puyallup Tribal Museum, 2002 East 28th St, Tacoma, WA 98404; (206)597-6200. From I-5, take the 135 exit. Open 9am–3pm, weekdays.

Chinook Landing Marina

In 1993, the Puyallup Tribe built the 219-slip Chinook Landing Marina on the south shore of Commencement Bay to accommodate tribal fishermen as well as the public. The facility includes a convenience store, 24-hour security, pump-out station, electricity, shower, and laundry. Guest moorage is available. Waterfront restaurants are a short drive away. There are no lift, launch, or fuel facilities.

Chinook Landing Marina, 3702 Marine View Dr, Tacoma, WA 98422, (206)627 7676.

Medicine Creek College

Familiarize yourself with Native culture by taking a basket-making, beadwork, or totem-carving class at the Puyallup Tribe's Medicine Creek College, a 2-year community college open to the public. The school emphasizes outreach to other tribes and non-Native peoples. More than 28 tribes are represented in the student body. Curriculum includes art classes taught by various Native artists from throughout the Northwest region. "We want the students to see the differences in art from other areas," says president Kay Rhoads. "For example, each region made their baskets a little differently. We want our students to appreciate them all."

Medicine Creek College, 2002 E 28th St, Building 18, Tacoma, WA 98404; (206)593-0171.

Seattle Metropolitan Area

The city of Seattle is named after the famous orator Chief Seattle, son of a Duwamish mother and Suquamish father. The city of Seattle is built on the ceded lands of the Duwamish Indian tribes. The Duwamish Indians were Salish speakers, as were the other tribes who lived on the shores of Puget Sound.

Like other Northwest metropolitan cities, Seattle institutions say little about the city's Salish Indian heritage. Instead they focus on the art and culture of more northerly tribes. Most of the carved totems adorning Seattle, the Native art in the galleries, and the Native collections displayed in the city's major museums are not Salish, but Kwakwaka'-wakw, Nun-chah-nulth, Tsimshian, Haida, and Tlingit—the tribes of British Columbia and Southeast Alaska. In shops you'll also find a lot of Alaska Native stone and ivory carving. Even Tillicum Village, a major tourist attraction located on a former Salish fishing camp on Puget Sound's Blake Island, offers entertainment based on Southeast Alaska and northern British Columbia tradition. Why? One reason is that Seattle, with its train routes to the east and huge shipping port on the waterfront, has been the North American gateway to and from ice-locked Alaska ever since the Alaska gold rush in the 1800s. The souvenir trade of Native Alaska art and trinkets has been ongoing in Seattle for more than 100 years.

Just because Seattle hasn't trumpted its Salish heritage doesn't mean there isn't a huge underground wealth of knowledge. To learn more, visit the Northwest Manuscript Collection on the second floor of the Suzzallo Library, University of Washington, (206)543-1879.

Today, more than 26,000 Native Americans live in the metropolitan area, a third of them Alaska Natives, about half of them from tribes throughout the Puget Sound region.

The best place to meet the descendants of Seattle's Duwamish and Suquamish tribes is on the Suquamish Reservation, about 45 minutes from downtown Seattle. There you can visit the Suquamish Tribal Center and Museum and Chief Seattle's grave in the old churchyard in Suquamish.

Daybreak Star Indian Cultural Center

Daybreak Star Indian Cultural Center is named after a vision that came to Oglala Sioux holy man Black Elk more than 100 years ago: "I saw the daybreak star falling far and when it struck the earth, it rooted and grew and flowered, four blossoms on one stem." The building is divided into four wings, in observance of the four blossoms, the four directions, and the four races of man.

Built in Seattle's Discovery Park, on 20 acres overlooking Puget Sound, Daybreak Star is a Northwest Native American Grand Central Station, coordinating social services and events for Indians living in the metropolitan area. The exterior of the concrete and cedar shake building is modest. But inside, among massive cedar lodgepoles, is a permanent collection of art by some of the top Indian artists in the country, including Chippewa artist George Morrison, Caddo-Kiowa painter T. C. Cannon, and Aleut sculptor John Hoover. An entire wall is carved and painted by famed Tlingit artist Nathan P. Jackson. The center's Sacred Circle Gallery is small but holds some impressive shows and includes a sales gallery. Self-guided pamphlets explaining the art is available at the door, but gallery staff also lead narrated tours.

Indian Dinner Theater, featuring fresh salmon and authentic drumming, dancing, and singing by Native dancers, is available for groups of 100 or more, by advance reservation.

Daybreak Star Indian Cultural Center, United Indians of All Tribes Foundation, Discovery Park, West Government Way at 36th Ave, Box 99253, Seattle, WA 98119; (206)285-4425. Take Elliott Ave west from downtown Seattle to Emerson St (south of the Ballard Bridge), turn west on Commodore Way, and follow signs to Daybreak Star. Open daily 10am–5pm; Sun afternoons only. Free.

Annual Salmon Homecoming

In 1995, 35,000 people jammed the Seattle waterfront for September's third annual Salmon Homecoming. The event gets bigger every year. Four days of ceremonies, storytelling, forums, speeches, songs, and powwow fancy dancing honor the cultural, spiritual, and economic significance of salmon to the Northwest.

The homecoming begins on Pier 62 with ceremonies honoring salmon, followed by a colorful and joyous all-tribe "Dance on the Water." On the Salmon Stage are live performances by indigenous peoples of Hawaii, New Zealand, the Northwest Coast, and Alaska. Next door, visitors can watch adult salmon returning from the ocean to the Seattle Aquarium's fish hatchery to spawn.

Sponsored by the Indian Tribes of the Pacific Northwest, the City of Seattle, the Northwest Indian Fisheries Commission, and the Seattle Aquarium Society, as well as corporate sponsors such as the *Seattle Times,* the event each year kicks off a coastwide commitment to saving the salmon.

The Salmon Homecoming occurs each September on Seattle's waterfront at Pier 62, Waterfront Park, and the Seattle Aquarium. Free. For dates and schedule of events, contact Northwest Indian Fisheries Commission, 6730 Martin Way E, Olympia, WA 98506; (360)438-1180.

Burke Museum, University of Washington

The Burke Museum, on the University of Washington campus, is a treasure trove of Northwest Coast art. The collection, from British Columbia and Southeast Alaska, is one of the largest in the United States. Long-term exhibits include "Northwest Coast Journey: Northwest Coast Native Art and Artifacts." It includes a Sea Monster house front and interior screens, two full-height totem poles carved by curator Bill Holm (a non-Native), model canoes, baskets, and tools.

The museum also has a large collection of coast Salish art and artifacts in its archives, including baskets and stone figures that curators say will be coming upstairs as one of the museum's primary exhibits in the next few years.

Currently in the works is a videodisc and catalog of 25,000 slides of Northwest Coast artifacts residing in more than 200 museums and 100 private collections worldwide.

Burke Museum, University of Washington, DB-10, Seattle, WA 98195; (206)543-5590. On the northwestern corner of the UW campus at NE 45th St and 17th Ave. Park on campus. Admission $3. Open daily 10am–5pm.

Marvin Oliver Gallery

On a charming corner of Seattle's quirky Fremont neighborhood is Marvin Oliver's gallery, a spare, sunlit room where he exhibits his sculpture and framed, embossed serigraphs.

Of Quinault and Isleta Pueblo heritage, Oliver presents new forms of traditional art. He is director of Indian Studies at the University of Washington and teaches the history of Northwest Coast art at the University of Alaska in Ketchikan. Oliver's gallery includes affordable art such as gold-foil embossed cards and stationery (one of our favorites is a white box embossed with salmon, with a paper Salish canoe perched on top).

Marvin Oliver Gallery, 3501 Fremont Ave N, Seattle, WA 98103; (206)633-2468. Open Wed–Sun 11am–6pm or by appointment.

Other Seattle Galleries

The Legacy (1003 First Ave, Seattle; (206)624-6350), specializing in historic and contemporary Indian and Eskimo Art since 1933, is one of Seattle's best sources for authentic Native arts, including the work of British Columbia's Hunt family (more than 34 family members are carvers, printmakers, and jewelers). Owner Mardonna Austin-McKillop knows her artists personally and is buying contemporary work from the grown children of Native artists the gallery represented in the 1970s.

Summer Song Gallery (600 19th Ave E, Seattle; (206)329-1377) is the English translation of the Makah word *Kukooats Thlupaitch*. One room is dedicated to Makah art (see Makah section, in this chapter), including the basketry of master weaver Isabelle Ides, serigraphs by Greg Colfax, and masks by Spencer McCarty.

The Snow Goose (8806 Roosevelt Way NE, Seattle; (206)523-6223) carries the work of more than 200 Native artists, mostly Canadian Inuit and arctic carvers of ivory, whalebone, and soapstone. But also look for Northwest artists such as Skokomish artist Andy Wilber and Warm Springs basketweaver Pat Courtney Gold.

The Stonington Gallery (2030 First Ave, Seattle; (206)443-1108) carries the work of top Northwest Coast carvers and artists, including John Hoover, George Hunt, Jr., Tony Hunt, Jr., Larry Avakana, Joe David, and Susan A. Point. There are frequent one-person shows as well as lectures by artists throughout the year. Non-Native carvers instrumental in the renaissance of Northwest Coast art forms, such as Bill Holm, Steve Brown, and Duane Pasco, are also represented.

Seattle Art Museum

The Native American exhibits of the Seattle Art Museum are based on the collection of John H. Hauberg, who spent four decades collecting masks, sculpture, textiles, and household objects from the northern tip of Washington State to Southeast Alaska.

A Tlingit screen depicting Raven highlights a favorite story told from the coastal area of Washington State to Alaska. Haida art, from British Columbia's Queen Charlotte Islands, is represented in a small group of jet black argillite carvings from the 19th and 20th centuries, including works by Haida master carver and jeweler Charles Edensaw. Four elaborately carved full-scale interior houseposts, carved by

Arthur Shaughnessy around 1907, as well as Makah masks and cere-monial regalia, are also part of the collection.

Another gallery showcases the fiber and fabric art of coastal women, who used mountain goat and dog wool, cedar bark, spruce roots, and other plant fibers in their weaving.

The museum uses Native language terms whenever possible to help illuminate their creators' sense of the objects' identity. Native scholars and writers work with the museum to provide interpretation for the exhibits. The interactive audio installation in the performance gallery allows visitors to hear songs, oratory, and storytelling in a sam-pling of various Native languages.

The Spirit Within: Northwest Coast Native Art from the John H. Hauberg Collection a 304-page volume with full-color photos, as well as essays by contemporary Haida carver Robert Davidson and Tlingit poet and writer Nora Dauenhauer, is available in the museum gift shop's book section.

The Seattle Art Museum, 100 University St, Seattle, WA 98122; (206)654-3100. Downtown, between 1st and 2nd Aves, 2 blocks south of the Pike Place Market. Admission, $6 adults. Gift shop, cafe, library. Open Tues–Sun.

Seattle Public Art

Ravens and Crows is one of Seattle's more delightful public art instal-lations; more than 100 of the mischievous birds circle the patrons of the University of Washington's Allen Library. Some are painted on walls; some hang on unseen wires with bits of twig in their beaks—or with a stolen symbol, such as a crescent moon or a letter of the al-phabet, in a nod to the delightful Northwest Coast story of Raven stealing the sunlight. Look for the words "Raven Brings Light to this House of Stories," written in English and in Lushootseed Salish, on the library foyer's eastern wall. A handmade book of Raven stories also sits in the middle of the room on a carved cedar table.

A very few pieces of Seattle's public art either honor Northwest Indians, such as the carved Chief Seattle Fountain in Pioneer Square, or are created by Indian artists, such as a manhole cover design of a Tlingit whale etched by Alaska Native Nathan Jackson. The city is also adorned with various totem poles (only some of which were carved by Natives).

A Field Guide to Seattle's Public Art, with self-guided tours, essays (including a short discussion of Lushootseed art), and maps can be purchased from the Seattle Arts Commission, 312 1st Ave N, Seattle, WA 98109; (206)684-7306.

Tillicum Village on Blake Island

Boats leave daily from Pier 55 and 56 in Seattle for lunch and dinner theater at Tillicum Village, a longhouse-style performance center built on the northern point of Blake Island in Puget Sound. All 473 acres of tree-covered Blake Island, an ancestral fishing camp of the Suquamish Indians, is now a state park with views of the Olympic and Cascade mountains and towering Mount Rainier.

The boat ride to Blake Island takes about 30 minutes. Native people, costumed in the traditional blue and red button capes and headpieces worn by Southeast Alaska and British Columbia tribes, greet passengers with cups of steaming clam broth on the walkway to the longhouse. Inside, diners line up at the buffet to load up plates with all-you-can-eat fresh salmon, new potatoes, salad, and warm bread. Salmon is cooked in the traditional style on alder skewers in front of open fire pits. After everyone is seated, "Dance on the Wind," a choreographed stage performance showcasing legends, masked dancing, and song, begins with a drumbeat.

Tillicum Village was the brainstorm of a chef and Boy Scout leader, who was looking for a way to combine traditionally prepared salmon and Indian crafts with Boy Scout "Indian" dancing. This dancing was all the rage in the 1950s and 1960s, when mostly non-Native Boy Scouts competed nationally for dance titles. Over the years the attraction has become more authentically Native. Today, Tillicum Village hires Native staff to greet visitors, cook, and perform in the stage show. The village reflects mostly Southeast Alaska and British Columbia coastal art and tradition.

Tillicum Village & Tours, Inc, 2200 6th Ave, Ste 804, Seattle, WA 98121; (206)443 1244. Call for reservations and brochures. Ticket stands are on the Seattle waterfront between Piers 55 and 56. Boats leave twice a day most months; tours are 4 hours long. Adults $46.50; teens, $30; children 6–12, $18.50. Senior discounts.

Suquamish: *Suquamish*

The territory where the Suquamish Tribe once lived comprises most of Seattle, half of the Kitsap Peninsula, and most of Puget Sound's larger islands—Whidbey, Bainbridge, Vashon, and Blake. The Suquamish's Port Madison Reservation and the town of Suquamish, where Chief Seattle is buried, are about 45 minutes from downtown Seattle. The name Suquamish comes from the tribe's ancient village, D'Suq'Wub, on the shores of Agate Pass, a narrow waterway that separates Bainbridge Island from the Kitsap Peninsula. In the village of D'Suq'Wub, "the place of clear saltwater," stood "Ole Man House," a longhouse 60 feet wide and over 500 feet long, surrounded by madrona, cedar, and fir trees. The village site is memorialized with a small park in the present-day Port Madison Reservation.

The most famous of the Suquamish is Chief Seattle. Born on Puget Sound, perhaps on Blake Island in the latter part of the 18th century, he witnessed the arrival of the first white explorers, led by Captain George Vancouver, in 1792. He gave an eloquent speech during treaty negotiations of 1854 that is a masterpiece of mature observation and oratory. A peacemaker with the whites, and chief of Puget Sound's allied tribes, Chief Seattle's vision and negotiating skills are the reason there were few wars or skirmishes as white settlers began to claim native lands. An old man when his tribe was moved from their homelands to the Port Madison Reservation, he died in 1866, shortly before his worst fears for his people were realized.

A small fold-out book of hand-tinted archival photographs and excerpts from Chief Seattle's speech, published in cooperation with the Suquamish Tribe by Sasquatch Books, is available from the tribal museum's gift store. The tribe also offers a full-length version of the original speech.

Pressure on the Suquamish Tribe began early on when the tribe refused to learn to farm or to accept commodity food provided by the army on the Port Madison Reservation. The Suquamish insisted on retaining their hunting and fishing rights, as promised by the treaty they had signed. After Seattle's death, and while families were gathering food during the summer of 1870, Ole Man House, of great spiritual significance to the Suquamish community, was burned to the ground by the U.S. military. The military's already-stated goal was to force the Suquamish to give up their traditional lifestyle; yet the military claimed the lodge was burned to keep epidemics from spreading. Either way, the house was destroyed without the Suquamish people's consent. The village that surrounded Ole Man House continued to thrive for 20 more years, until the army forced the tribe to move to individual allotments upland. The remainder of their land was sold by the U.S. government to a real estate and advertising agency, which then resold it for summer homes.

The Port Madison Reservation today comprises about 7,800 acres, half of which are in Indian ownership. The rest, most of it valuable Puget Sound waterfront, is owned by non–Indians. Two major Indian communities are at Suquamish and Indianola.

The tribal headquarters and the two small communities of Suquamish and Indianola are strung along the bay, making them easy to reach if you are walking the shoreline or paddling along in a canoe (however, they are not easy to reach by walking along roads). In a canoe you can paddle from the tribal headquarters on Agate Pass;

under the Agate Pass Bridge; past the site where Ole Man House once stood on the beach; around a wide point to the old ferry landing at Suquamish, where Chief Seattle is buried on the hill behind the church; and across the mouth of shallow Miller Bay to the wharf at Indianola. Indianola is a charming little place in the woods, with a single grocery store near the wharf, churches tucked into groves of madrona and fir, and cottage-sized houses—reminiscent of Puget Sound towns in the 1930s. (To find Indianola from Suquamish, follow Miller Bay Rd north, and take a right on S Kingston Rd NE).

In the last few years, the Suquamish Tribe of under 800 members, which includes Chief Seattle's descendants, has become an enthusiastic participant in the resurgence of the canoe culture. Joining with other shoreline tribes from British Columbia and Washington State they've formed a "Canoe Nation." Members are not only paddling some of the arduous routes of their seafaring ancestors but have hand-carved, from single-trunks of old-growth cedar, their own 6- to 11-man canoes.

Suquamish and Port Madison Indian Reservation are off Hwy 305 on the Kitsap Peninsula, north of Bremerton and just west of the Agate Pass Bridge from Bainbridge Island. The Suquamish Tribal Center and Museum is on Sandy Hook Rd; watch for signs on Hwy 305. Suquamish is on Miller Bay Rd (Suquamish Way), which heads north from 305 just west of Agate Pass.

Chief Seattle's Grave

Chief Seattle is buried in the small tribal cemetery behind St. Peter's Catholic Church in Suquamish.

In 1902, Chief Seattle's body was moved to St. Peter's churchyard after the tribe was forced off the valuable waterfront property, and its first church was torn down. A Suquamish Native gave 5 acres of his own allotment for a new church and cemetery. Chief Seattle was reburied there with a marker bearing his baptismal name, Noah Sealth, a name adapted from the Salish.

The doors and windows of the white-steepled St. Peter's Catholic Church are from the original church. The two canoes suspended over the grave were erected in 1976 to commemorate the Suquamish's traditional way of burial. A graveside memorial service is held in the cemetery each August during the Suquamish's Chief Seattle Days.

St. Peter's Catholic Church and cemetery are on South St, about a block from downtown Suquamish. From Hwy 305, take Miller Bay Rd (Suquamish Way) to Augusta Ave and turn left up the hill to the church parking lot on the right.

Ole Man House at Chief Sealth Park

Squeezed in between two waterfront homes in a housing development, a little 1½-acre park and sandy beach commemorate the site where Ole Man House once stood. Ole Man House was actually a series of longhouses, attached to each other, which housed multiple families. The site has been occupied for at least 2,000 years of the tribe's 15,000-year occupation of the area. Ole Man House, burned by the military in 1870, is the most well known of 17 longhouses of similar dimension, occupied only during the winters when the weather was more severe. A life-size replica of a portion of the longhouse is in the Suquamish Museum.

To reach Chief Sealth Park, turn right from Hwy 305 on Suquamish Way to Division Ave, turn right on Division, then left on McKinstry St. The park is at the end of McKinstry, open dawn to dusk.

Suquamish Museum

Two permanent exhibits are on display at the Suquamish Museum: "The People and Way of Life at D'Suq'Wub" and "The Eyes of Chief Seattle." The museum is set up for a self-guided tour, with well-written interpretive captions. There are also guided tours through the museum that elaborate on food gathering, summer dwellings, fishing, and the boarding schools that tribal members attended in Puyallup, the Tulalip Reservation, and in Seattle—all the topics that international visitors inquire about most frequently. Look also for the Pacific Northwest Land Company's 1920 advertisements of their "Chief Seattle Park" housing development on the Suquamish's Port Madison land. The museum gift shop sells an "Eyes of Chief Seattle" exhibit catalogue and two videos are shown in the museum daily: *Comes Forth Laughing: Voices of the Suquamish People,* tribal elders' accounts of the past, and *Waterborne: The Gift of the Indian Canoe.* Visitors can observe a cedar canoe being carved outside the museum.

Chief Seattle Days is the third weekend in August and open to all. First celebrated in 1911, the festival features a salmon bake, canoe races, traditional dancing, Indian arts and crafts, a powwow, baseball tournament, and a graveside memorial service to Chief Seattle. Call the Suquamish Tribe for information at (360)598-3311.

Suquamish Museum, 15383 Sandy Hook Rd, PO Box 498, Suquamish, WA 98392; (360)598-3311, ext. 422. Turn left about a quarter mile past the Agate Pass Bridge, Hwy 305, onto Sandy Hook Rd and watch for signs. The museum adjoins the tribal center. Admission $2.50 adults; includes a self-guided map to major sites on the reservation. Museum tours are $15 per person and must be arranged in advance. Summer hours, May 1–Sept 30 are 10am–5pm daily; winter hours, Oct 1–Apr 30, are Fri–Sun only, 11am to 4pm, or by appointment.

Marysville: *Tulalip*

The Tulalip Tribe's ancestral home, Hebolb, is at the mouth of the Snohomish River. The 22,000-acre Tulalip Reservation, once home of one of the largest Indian boarding schools in the Puget Sound area, is located west of Marysville and 12 miles northwest of Monroe, Washington. The reservation possesses areas of cultural and spiritual significance, scenic views, magnificent waterfront properties, and freshwater streams and lakes. The present-day Tulalip Tribe is a confederation of tribes from the northern Puget Sound area.

Tulalip Museum

In 1988, the Tulalips carved their first traditional canoe in over 100 years. Made of a single cedar trunk, it holds 20 people and more than a ton of cargo, and is paddled with the aid of a canvas sail, soon to be replaced with a sail woven of cedar or tule reeds. The canoe, stored in the tribe's carving shed, is part of a small exhibit of photomurals, carvings, totems, baskets, and blankets, all housed in one of a group of modules that looks like a high-tech longhouse. This may be a small exhibit, but it's attracted members of the British Parliament and a delegation from Nigeria, among others. When the new museum building is completed, the tribe will be able to display ceremonial items long absent from view. Plans include a boardwalk into adjoining wetlands where tribal members still gather traditional basket-weaving materials. Be sure to ask to see the tribe's fascinating Lushootseed language videos.

Tulalip Museum, 6410 Ave NE, Marysville, WA 98271; (360)651-4000. Open weekdays. Call in advance for tours. Cost is by donation. All proceeds go to the building fund for the new museum building.

Indian Shaker Church

Although it's on the National Register of Historic Places, this historic site is not open to the public except during services, but you can see it from the outside. This active church was built in 1924 (the sign says "1910" because that's the date the government sanctioned the Indian Shakers as a bona fide religion) and is one of the best-preserved churches in the region. When an episode of the TV show *Northern Exposure* was filmed here a few years ago, the film company put a new roof on the building and reinforced the steeple—a gift to the membership.

The Indian Shaker religion (not related to the Massachusetts Shaker religion) was founded in 1881 in a little church still operating on the Squaxin Island Reservation near Shelton, Washington. Historic Shaker churches are on or near many Northwest reservations today.

Indian Shaker Church, N Meridian Ave, Marysville, WA 98271. From Marysville, go past the casino and west on Marine Dr about 2 ½ miles to N Meridian; turn right (the sign may say Shaker Creek Rd) about ½ mile.

St. Anne's Roman Catholic Church

On the National Register of Historic Places, St. Anne's white late-Victorian gothic-style church overlooks Tulalip Bay. Built in 1867 in a cedar grove, the church burned in 1902 and was replaced in 1904. A statue of the Virgin brought from France was rescued from the fire and still stands in the church today. Most of the congregation are Tulalip tribal members; all are welcome to attend Sunday services.

St. Anne's Roman Catholic Church, Mission Beach Rd, Marysville, WA 98271. Worship service times are posted on the door.

Tulalip Fish Hatchery

Catching spawning salmon in fish ladders and broomstick weirs in March and May, the Tulalip Fish Hatchery raises over a million coho and chinook and 4 million chum salmon each year. Indian-run fish hatcheries are among the best places to visit on reservations, and this one is no exception. Visitors are welcome; large groups are asked to make arrangements in advance.

Tulalip Fish Hatchery, 10610 Waterworks Rd, Marysville, WA 98270; (360)651-4550. Located a few miles from Tulalip Bay, at the confluence of Battle Creek and Tulalip Creek. Open weekdays. Free.

Stevens Pass: *Snohomish*

Snohomish tribal member Francine Long and her staff instruct all ages and all levels in downhill skiing and snowboarding near the top of 4,061-foot Stevens Pass (Highway 2), which winds over the Cascade mountains between Everett and Leavenworth. Ask her anything about the Snohomish Indians who once used the slopes and river valleys in the mountains as their summer territory.

Clancy's Ski School, 5031 27th Ave W, Everett, WA 98203; (206)348-3622.

La Conner: *Swinomish*

The picturesque little town of La Conner, located north of Seattle and built on the east bank of the Swinomish Channel, was first a trading post, founded in 1867 by John Conner before railroads came to

Washington State. The town's historic waterfront is as picturesque as
it gets. Its 100 small shops and 25 restaurants are a favorite tourist destination, especially in the spring when the adjacent Skagit Valley tulip
fields are in full bloom.

Across the narrow channel from La Conner, on Fidalgo Island, is
the Swinomish Reservation, home to the descendants of the four
tribes who lived in the present-day lower Skagit River valley, coastline, and estuary. Their 7,000-acre reservation was assured by executive order in 1873.

Early on, the Swinomish traded with Russian and British traders
who arrived in the area in the 1830s. It's estimated that 85 percent of
the Native population died from the ensuing smallpox epidemics.
La-hail-by, son of Huah-le-tsa (He of the Magic Robe) was one of
the few who survived. La-hail-by became known as "The Prophet."

The Swinomish Reservation can be reached by crossing the
"Rainbow Bridge" (named for its bow-shape), which connects La
Conner and the Swinomish Reservation at the south end of La
Conner.

In La Conner, the Swinomish Tribe owns a small open-air market on a waterfront pier, where you can buy smoked salmon and a
seafood lunch and sit at picnic tables overlooking the channel and the
undeveloped beach of the Swinomish Reservation. Below the pier
are a fishing dock and a couple of spots for boaters to tie up. The
Swinomish, Kikallious, Samish, and Lower Skagit Tribes were and
still are fishers.

Swinomish Ways

The Swinomish used a number of methods to fish: drift netting and
tidal traps, weirs, hook-and-line troll fishing, gill nets, trawl nets,
beach seines, dip nets, harpoons, leisters, and gaff-hooks. Nets over
100 feet long, made of nettle fibers, were used to trap ducks; deer
were hunted on what is now Whidbey Island. Seals, sea lions, and
other marine mammals were taken in the exposed reefs and rocky
headlands. Beaver, muskrat, otter, mink, elk, and bear were hunted in
the fall. The meat was used fresh or dried for storage. Traditional
homes were large cedar buildings up to 1,000 feet long that housed
several extended families.

In winter, the village community gathered in longhouses around
the fire pits, with smoke rising through the hole in the roof. Benches
surrounded the fire, serving as seats by day and beds by night. During mild summers temporary camps were constructed, some with
A-framed structures made of woven cattail mats called wickiups.

Swinomish Smokehouse

There's a special silence found only in churches and other sanctuaries, such as the Swinomish Smokehouse, located on the reservation, right across the channel from La Conner. As you walk through the large wooden doors handcarved with eagles, the sounds of youngsters playing baseball in the field below are left behind. All you can hear is the rustle of wings from birds perched on beams high overhead. The Swinomish practice their traditional religion in this 200-foot-long longhouse.

Built in traditional longhouse style and situated in a cedar grove, the Smokehouse seats up to 1,200 people on bleachers set on an earthen floor. It is easy to imagine a time when the trio of fires, with smoke curling through the openings in the roof, warmed the people of the tribe—who in the old days would have slept comfortably here. Eight floor-to-ceiling poles are placed around the hall. Some signify the great spirits of Eagle or Salmon; others depict shamans and important stories, such as the "Maiden of Deception Pass."

For centuries traditional coast Salish Indian religions were practiced in smokehouses. And for years traditional Indian religions have been closed to outsiders, forced into secrecy by federal regulations. Money to build the smokehouse came from a settlement negotiated by three tribes along the Skagit River that were impacted by three dams licensed to Seattle City Light. The Smokehouse includes a kitchen and dining hall and a smaller room used for local gatherings. Outside, a barbecue pit under the trees is used to cook salmon—a staple at all gatherings of the Swinomish people.

Tours of the Smokehouse interior are by appointment only, usually offered in the spring, summer, and early fall. For tours call Maxine Williams, (360)466-4525.

Swinomish Annual Blues Festival

In August, the Swinomish Reservation is transformed as it hosts the Swinomish Annual Blues Festival. Native drums, dancers, and singers are joined by groups such as Roy Rogers & the Delta Rhythm Kings, Burnin' Chicago, Little Bill & the Blue Notes, Rantin & Raven, and many others during a weekend of music, culture, food, and fun. Proceeds from the event—first held in 1991 and nominated as one of the best blues festivals in the state—support the Smokehouse.

The Swinomish Annual Blues Festival is held in the John K. Bobb Ballpark, below the Smokehouse, the third weekend in August, Fri–Sun. Tickets are available at a number of outlets in La Conner, Mount Vernon, Seattle, and Bellingham. Kids 15 and under are free. For information, call Jimmy and Ava Goodman, (360)466-3052.

St. Paul's Catholic Church

Built in 1868, picturesque St. Paul's is the second oldest church in Washington State. Behind it is a new wing, called the Swinomish Spiritual Center, used jointly by other denominations. New stained-glass windows incorporate orca, deer, and feather designs.

St. Paul's Catholic Church is on Pioneer Way, on the Swinomish Reservation. The church faces La Conner and is usually open. For more information call Beverly Peters, director of the Swinomish Spiritual Center, (360)466-5737.

Walk Along the Channel

A short paved walkway follows the Swinomish Channel, with interpretive signs about the wetlands and beaches. The welcoming plaque says "Gwu'sh-book-wahk-bcyou sjool-eel"—"For all people to enjoy." The project was started when the tribe built its seafood processing plant. They wanted to make sure that displaced plants would grow farther upstream and original wetlands would be reestablished. A great picnic spot, with a great view of La Conner.

To reach the Swinomish Channel, follow Pioneer Way to the cedar-shake-covered Community Services buildings. Follow the driveway toward the water and the path along the water.

On the reservation's small Swinomish dock is a carved eagle totem and a wooden cross. Each year when the salmon return, Indian fishers gather there for the blessing of the fleet. The public is welcome to attend. For information, call the Swinomish Indian Tribal Community at (360)466-3163.

Kevin Paul Studio

When the doors of Kevin Paul's carving shed are thrown open, feel free to stop by and visit. He and his father have carved a number of the poles for the Swinomish community, including those inside the casino and a replica of a pole carved by Charlie Edwards that formerly stood on Pioneer Way. In Paul's studio are 4-inch totems, large poles, and carved screens. One of the best-known carvers from Swinomish, Paul went to Canada to learn his craft from relatives.

Paul Carvings, PO Box 1147, La Conner, WA 98257; (360)466-3906. His studio, surrounded by piles of raw cedar and totems, is on Pioneer Way, a few doors down from St. Paul's Catholic Church. Open by appointment.

Swinomish Pier in La Conner

Several vendors serve food and espresso on the Swinomish Pier, across the street from the Native-owned Legends Art Gallery on La Conner's waterfront. Puget Sound Smokers offers free samples of delicious peppered, garlic, and honey-smoked salmon, prepared according to owner Vern Mcleod's grandmother's recipe. Legends Salmon Bar sells large portions of fresh barbecued salmon, fried oyster sandwiches, Indian fry bread served with fresh berries, jam, and butter, salmon Indian tacos, and other fast foods for under $7. If they have time, vendors will point out the differences between gill-netters, purse seiners, and other fishing vessels tied up at the La Conner docks.

Swinomish Pier, 708 First St, La Conner, WA 98257; Legends Salmon Bar, (360)466-5240; Puget Sound Smokers, (360)466-4129.

Legends Art Gallery

Legends Art Gallery, on La Conner's waterfront, is first-rate, with a sales gallery in the front and exhibit space in the back. Owned by a Swinomish tribal member, Legends carries mostly Northwest Coast art, including the work of Canadian carvers. Look for Simon Charlie's gorgeous coast Salish carved codlures; Upper Skagit-made wooden boxes; and masks, cards, stationery, engraved silver and gold jewelry, and silkscreened ties and scarves. There's an excellent book selection as well. The gallery is easy to spot among the other shops on La Conner's First Street—you can't miss the carved whale totem outside.

Legends Art Gallery, 705 1st St, La Conner, WA 98257; (360)466-5240. Open daily.

Skagit County Historical Museum, La Conner

In addition to vignettes on early 1900s farming, fishing, logging, mining, and pioneer life, the Skagit County Historical Museum has the only exhibit of local Native history in the area. See basketry, fishing spears, early tools, horn spoons, historical photographs, and a 39-foot, shovel-nosed canoe buried in mud near the Skagit riverbank, found by the Boy Scouts in 1948.

Skagit County Historical Museum, 501 S 4th St, La Conner, WA 98257; (360)466-3365. Open afternoons, Wed–Sun. During the annual Skagit Valley Tulip Festival, generally in early April, the museum is open daily. $1 adults. Reserve tours in advance.

Viking Cruises

Your sense of the Swinomish Reservation will forever be changed once you travel through the Swinomish Channel past the mouth of the Skagit River and around the south side of Fidalgo Island to Deception Pass. From the La Conner dock, you may board Viking Cruises' yacht and spend a pleasant few hours learning about the

Skagit estuary, bird life (a rare white eagle was spotted here recently), and Swinomish history. Groups of 25 or more may request a Swinomish tribal member guide to accompany them onboard.

Viking Cruises, 109 N 1st St, PO Box 327, La Conner, WA 98257; (360)466-2639. In the Lime-Dock building. Boat capacity 49, with inside and outside viewing. Winters, weekends only. Summers, daily. Reservations a must.

Padilla Bay National Estuarine Research Reserve

The land spreading from the foot of the ridges to Padilla Bay, north of the Swinomish Reservation, was once a huge salt marsh that was fed by the rushing Skagit River—a haven for juvenile salmon, shellfish, and waterfowl. In the 1800s, settlers began diking the river, changing its course to the south. By 1900, nearly the entire estuary and salt marsh was diked and filled as well, creating the agricultural lands and tulip fields you see today in the Skagit Valley. Very little natural salt marsh is left.

The Breazeale Interpretive Center, on the ridge overlooking the old salt marsh, has a few small exhibits and a resource library where you can learn more about the old marsh as it was in the days when 11 tribes subsisted on its bounty. The Padilla Bay shore trail, 2½ miles long, has many interpretive signs describing the area's history, waterfowl, tidal marsh, and sloughs.

Padilla Bay National Estuarine Research Reserve and Breazeale Interpretive Center, 1043 Bayview–Edison Rd, Mount Vernon, WA 98273; (360)428-1558. From I-5, take exit 230 to Anacortes on Hwy 20. Fifteen miles west on Hwy 20, at the Farmhouse Inn Restaurant, turn north on Bayview–Edison Rd and watch for signs. Open Wed–Sun, all year long. Free.

Bellingham Metropolitan Area

Whatcom Museum of History and Art

The Whatcom Museum, in downtown Bellingham, includes a fine collection of local Native art. It consists mostly of baskets donated by University of Washington linguist Melville Jacobs, who worked with Northwest tribes in the 1930s. The museum also received a collection of 50 to 60 unidentified Northwest baskets from a private collector. Contemporary Lummi weavers helped the museum identify both individual weaving style and designs, which are family-related trademarks and passed down through generations. The museum is housed in Bellingham's former city hall (built in 1892), and three adjoining buildings. Watch for traveling exhibits pertaining to Native culture.

Whatcom Museum, 121 Prospect St, Bellingham, WA 98225; (360)676-6981. Open Tues–Sun, afternoons. Free.

Bellingham: *Lummi*

The Lummi Indian Reservation is on a peninsula jutting out into the Strait of Georgia, 10 miles west of Bellingham. The tribe's casino overlooks the beach, next to a small car ferry that crosses the channel to Lummi Island. The island is not part of the reservation, but was part of Lummi ancestral territory, as were portions of the adjoining San Juan Islands. One of the largest groups of basket weavers in the Puget Sound area lives on the Lummi Reservation, and Lummi artists have been active in celebrating and teaching Salish culture and art.

Annual Stommish Water Festival

Every June, the Lummi Nation and American Legion host the Stommish Water Festival to honor Native American veterans of all wars. (Native Americans have consistently had the highest number of volunteers for U.S. military service of any minority people; 80 percent of Lummi men have been involved with the military through the years.) The festival features canoe races, with 11-man teams from throughout the Northwest racing 55-foot war canoes through Hales Passage. Other events include foot races, tugs-of-war, traditional dancing, salmon barbecue, traditional bone-game tournaments, and arts and crafts sales. The public is welcome to attend.

Stommish Water Festival. For information, contact the Lummi Indian Nation, 2616 Kwina Rd, Bellingham, WA 98226; (360)384-1489. Stommish grounds are located 1 mile east of the Lummi casino at Gooseberry Point. Dates for the June festival depend on the tides. A small admission fee.

St. Joachims Catholic Mission Church

A historic landmark, St. Joachims Catholic Mission Church is one of the oldest churches still standing in Washington State. Following the signing of the Treaty of Point Elliott, which established the Lummi Reservation, the Roman Catholic Church sent the Reverend Eugene Casimir to set up a mission among the Lummi. The church, built in

1861, has been used continuously since that time and is now open only during Sunday Mass.

St. Joachims Catholic Mission Church, Kwina Rd, Bellingham, WA 98226. From I-5, take Haxton Rd to the Lummi Reservation and follow it to the shoreline. Turn left on Kwina Rd to the church on the corner of Kwina and Lummi Shore Rd. For Mass hours, call St. Josephs Church in Ferndale, (360)384-3651.

Northwest Indian College

This small college, founded in 1973 as a school of aquaculture, is today one of the fastest-growing colleges in the Northwest. A major institution in the preservation of local Native languages, it maintains distance-learning satellite links with extension campuses on the Nisqually, Swinomish, Nooksack, and Makah reservations, as well as with major cities in the Northwest. The college's main focus is preserving Lummi culture, language, and traditional skills such as basket and textile weaving. It also hosts workshops and conferences. Non-Natives are welcome to attend classes.

Northwest Indian College, 2522 Kwina Rd, Bellingham, WA 98226; (360)676-2772. For distance learning class schedules and information, call (360)733-3995.

Sharing of the Culture

Many fine Lummi artists produce their work on the reservation, which is also home to one of the largest basket-weaving groups in the Puget Sound area. Lummi art is showcased in one of Whatcom County's most celebrated annual exhibitions, "Sharing of the Culture," held in conjunction with Allied Arts of Whatcom County each June in the Bellingham area. Lummi artists include wood carvers Jewell "Praying Wolf" James, Dale James, and Harry Cooper; Salish basket weavers Anna Jefferson, Joyce Tommy, Ted and Marina Plaster, and Fran and Bill James (who also weave traditional Northwest wool blankets); sculptor Yvonne Thomas, and drum maker Joe Page.

For information about Lummi art and Sharing of the Culture, contact the Lummi tribal office, 2616 Kwina Rd, Bellingham, WA 98225; (360)384-2338.

Basket-weaving Classes

Wild cherry, red cedar bark, and beargrass are some of the materials used in Lummi baskets. Weaver Anna Jefferson teaches basket weaving through the Northwest Indian College, as well as through other institutions such as the North Cascades Institute's weekend seminars.

The public is welcome to learn the complexities of gathering materials and weaving.

Northwest Indian College, 2522 Kwina Rd, Bellingham, WA 98226; (360)676-2772. North Cascades Institute, 2105 State Route 20, Sedro Woolley, WA 98284; (360)856-5700. Free catalogs of classes are available from both.

Eagles Haven RV Park

Privately owned by tribal members Dean and Sherry Williams, Eagles Haven is approximately 1 mile from the Lummi casino. This well-kept park includes full-service hookups, hot showers, laundry, security, and convenience store. The store includes books, snacks, and gifts. Williams has an affinity for nostalgic prints featuring romanticized images of Native peoples that were produced in abundance in the 1950s. They decorate the store and can be purchased. In addition to the usual hot dogs and donuts, you'll find espresso and salmon jerky.

Eagles Haven RV Park, 2924 Haxton Way, Bellingham, WA 98226; (360)758-2420. 12 miles west of Bellingham, from I-5, take the Slater Rd exit.

Deming: *Nooksack*

Thirteen miles east of present-day Bellingham, the Nooksack people lived in about 13 villages near the Nooksack and Sumas Rivers on the west flank of Mount Baker. "Nook" means "people"; "sa'ak" means "bracken fern root." Fishing grounds extended from Bellingham Bay to British Columbia, but the people also gathered hazelnuts, huckleberries, and bracken fern roots. The fern roots were baked in hot ashes, ground into a fine powder, and used as thickening or cereal. Forced to abandon villages near present-day Lynden, Washington, they settled into one traditional village and five settlements made up of homesteads adapted from the European model, with garden plots and domestic animals.

Unlike other tribes, the Nooksacks had a good friend in an early settler, John Bertrand, who helped them collect recommendations from whites and file the lengthy applications for homesteads. In order to file a claim for a homestead, individual tribal members had to promise to sever ties with their tribe. Many other settlers provided assistance and served as witnesses to help defeat later attempts to oust the Natives from their lands.

Today, you can walk on one of the original family homesteads, pioneered by the Nooksack Williams family, who own it still. In 1993, they gave the tribe permission to use their land to bring the salmon back to Williams Creek. Choked by canary grass that had been brought in by settlers and planted for hay, the creek had nearly disappeared. To kill the grass by shading it rather than using herbicides, the Nooksack Fish and Wildlife Department planted weeping willows along the creek. The willows' shade also cools the water for salmon. Tribal young people helped build two short walking trails that cross the secluded stream on wooden bridges and benches overlooking the water made of alder entwined with vine maple. The hatchery, a mere 6 feet square, is fed by clear spring water and has replenished the creek with chum salmon, coho, and steelhead. It's an inspiring spot. Trails end at a little park with just one picnic table.

Nooksack Tribe Administrative Offices, 5048 Mount Baker Hwy (Hwy 542), PO Box 157, Deming, WA 98244; (360)592-5176. Contact the tribe for directions and permission to visit (or a tour).

OLYMPIC PENINSULA

Blyn: *Jamestown S'Klallam*

The S'Klallams once occupied much of the coastal strip along the Strait of Juan de Fuca, all the way to Port Townsend and inside Puget Sound. Although the S'Klallams once dominated the northern Olympic Peninsula, today there are very few reminders of their presence. Clallam county, on the northern end of the Olympic Peninsula, is named after the S'Klallam Tribe. Port Townsend, a Victorian seaport where ships from the Strait of Juan de Fuca round the point and enter Puget Sound, was once an important trading center, used for centuries by all the tribes in the area. At Point Hudson, an old cedar canoe—found on nearby Protection Island and thought to be of Makah origin—is displayed under a shed roof. It is one of hundreds of canoes that were once pulled up on these shores. A few blocks away at the Jefferson County Historical Museum (210 Madison Street, Port Townsend (360)385-1003) are a few photographs of unidentified Indians, presumed to be S'Klallams, camping in tents with their long canoes pulled up on the Point Hudson beach.

Walk north on the public beach from Point Hudson and you'll find Chetzemoka Park, named after and honoring a S'Klallam chief. Very few people know, however, that Chief Chetzemoka's descendants live just 30 minutes away, in a small residential community called Jamestown, near Dungeness, north of Sequim.

The Point No Point Treaty, signed in 1855, forced the S'Klallams to give up all their land. In 1874, several S'Klallam families pooled $500 to buy the Jamestown 210-acre plot. Some of the acreage of the original Jamestown has been sold over the years, but a core of S'Klallam-owned land remains in the small community. The Jamestown S'Klallam struggled along on their own for more than a century until they were finally recognized by the federal government in 1981.

Under the direction of tribal council chair Ron Allen, the Jamestown S'Klallam Tribe recently resurfaced on the Olympic Peninsula in a most visible way. They purchased land on Highway 101 on Sequim Bay, at Blyn (halfway between Port Townsend and Port Angeles) and built a striking tribal center overlooking Sequim Bay. They stocked three art galleries, one of which is the centerpiece of their large casino (a second is at the tribal center, a third is in Port Townsend), and also bought investment properties on nearby Bainbridge Island, a bedroom community of Seattle. Visitors are welcome at the Jamestown S'Klallam Tribal Center and its small public park on the Blyn waterfront (watch for signs, you can't miss it). The tribe also sells fresh and smoked oysters at the facility overlooking their oyster beds near Dungeness Spit, which is one of the longest natural spits in the Pacific Northwest and a great place for birdwatching and a picnic.

Northwest Native Expressions

Northwest Native Expressions is the name given to all three Jamestown S'Klallam galleries. This trio of galleries, each at a different location, houses an exceptional collection of Native American art. On display are some of the finest Northwest Coast and coast Salish baskets, masks, clothing, and limited edition prints. Serious browsers and buyers might cruise all three galleries, which feature many one-of-a-kind works of art and craft. The galleries also sell Northwest Coast–style art made by non-Natives, but all pieces are carefully labeled.

One gallery is located in an historic waterfront building at 637 Water Street, Port Townsend, WA 98368; (360)385-4770. A second showcase gallery, built in the style of a longhouse, is inside the 7 Cedars Casino, 5 miles east of Sequim at 270756 Hwy 101 E, Sequim, WA 98382; (360)681-6757. The third is across the highway from the casino at 1033 Old Blyn Hwy, Sequim, WA 98382; (360)681-4640.

Dungeness Oyster House

Dungeness Bay is protected by three natural sand spits, fed by Pacific Ocean seawater and cold mountain water from the Dungeness River. The cold water in the pristine bay makes for prime oyster-growing conditions, and fresh Pacific oysters are harvested year-round. You can buy live oysters in the shell (great for baking over a campfire), shucked, or smoked at the tribe's Dungeness Oyster House, a water-front wholesale/retail store. Ask there for directions to Dungeness Spit, one of the best birdwatching spots on the Strait of Juan de Fuca.

Dungeness Oyster House. JKT Oyster Farm, Inc., 1033 Old Blyn Hwy, Sequim, WA 98382; (360)683-2025. From Hwy 101 at Sequim, take Marine Dr to the Dungeness Scenic Loop and watch for signs. Call for hours.

Those interested in the S'Klallam Tribes may also contact the Port Gamble S'Klallam Tribe, outside Kingston and across the bay from historic Port Gamble, at (360)297-2646, or the Lower Elwha S'Klallam Tribe, near the mouth of the Elwha River west of Port Angeles, at (360)452-8471. Both tribes are involved primarily in aquaculture and salmon enhancement projects.

Neah Bay: *Makah*

The Makah Reservation is literally at the end of the road. Highway 112, which stretches from Port Angeles to the Makah Reservation at Neah Bay, has been patched many times; winter mudslides may shut it down for as long as 2 weeks at a time. Built along a narrow brim of land on the northern edge of the Olympic Mountains, the road ribbons in and out of clearcut slopes and dips down to narrow, rocky beaches and pockets of sand along the Strait of Juan de Fuca. It leaves the last town behind at Clallam Bay and enters the Makah Reservation 23 miles later.

The last 23 miles of Highway 112 is the only road into Washington State's rugged northwest corner, the westernmost point in the Lower 48. The Makah Reservation includes Neah Bay, a well-known salmon fishing port, and Cape Flattery, a windy promontory that noses into the Pacific Ocean, guarding the entry to the Strait of Juan de Fuca—the southern gateway to the Inside Passage.

The Makah, relatives of the Nuu-chah-nulth tribes of western Vancouver Island, inhabited this region of mountains, dense forests, and open seas. They were excep-tional seafarers, harvesting every kind of fish and marine mammal,

Years after the last Makah longhouse was destroyed, an elderly chief kept one of the remaining longhouse boards nailed to the wall above his sickbed, saying that it made him feel good to sleep under it as he had as a child. The weathered, hand-adzed board, silvery with age, now hangs on his grand-son's wall.

including migrating gray whales. The surrounding rain forest's massive 1,000-year-old cedar trees provided pliable fiber that the Makah pulled off in strips and wove into waterproof clothing and hats, floor coverings, and even sails. The Makah used the roots in baskets, steamed the wood into storage boxes, or adzed it into planks for houses. Whole tree trunks were carefully carved and steamed into efficient, seaworthy canoes.

Today, the Makah Reservation encompasses 47 square miles. Four of the five original Makah villages, which once were occupied year-round, are within the present-day reservation: Deah, Bahaada, Waatch, and Sooes. The site of the fifth village, Ozette, is about 15 miles south of Cape Flattery. The multiple-family longhouses that once existed at these village sites all faced the water. Made of planked cedar, they had shed roofs that could be opened to fresh air and sunlight, and rain gutters made of whalebone. Average houses were 60 by 30 feet, with 15-foot-high ceilings.

To keep cedar bark clothing from scratching sensitive skin, the Makahs intertwined the weave with hummingbird feathers, the soft fibers surrounding cattail seeds, and dog wool.

Before the turn of the century, missionaries and Indian agents forced the Makah to pull down most of their longhouses and abandon their villages in favor of single-family dwellings. Most were built on platted streets facing Neah Bay. During World War I, the U.S. military, occupying Cape Flattery for the sake of national defense, bulldozed and burned the last remaining village of longhouses. Recently two new longhouses have been built on the reservation by Lance Wilkie, the only federally registered longhouse builder in the world.

The fifth Makah village, Ozette, was buried some 500 years ago in a massive mudslide. The tribe knew about it but did not disturb the ruins or reveal their existence until artifacts began washing onto the beach after a series of pounding storms in the late 1960s. Excavated by a team of anthropologists and their students in the 1970s, Ozette yielded more than 55,000 mostly intact artifacts, proving the existence of the incredible cultural heritage the Makah had always claimed.

One square mile surrounding the original Ozette village site, outside the reservation boundary, was returned to the Makahs in 1970; Tatoosh and Waadah Islands, off Cape Flattery were returned to the tribe in 1984. Today, about 800 of the 2,200 enrolled tribal members live on the reservation, many of them commercial fishers. When you enter Neah Bay, the only town on the Makah Reservation, you are entering the original Deah village site. Motels, owned and built mostly by non-Indians on land leased to them by the Makah Tribe, have replaced the longhouses that 100 years ago lined the beach.

There are no plans to rebuild longhouses for living quarters, but plans drawn for a new 200-slip marina promise to revitalize the waterfront. Most visitors to the Makah Reservation come here to see the Makah Cultural and Research Center, the only museum in North America displaying artifacts found in Ozette Village. Visitors can also kayak in the bay and on the river, camp overnight, photograph Tatoosh Island from a lookout, walk the beaches, or take a tour of the area with a tribal member (see below).

Makah Cultural and Research Center

The discovery of the Ozette village site is considered by many anthropologists to be the most significant find in North America. Like the ashfall that buried Pompeii, the mud interred Ozette villagers in the middle of their daily routines. Proof of the Makah's rich heritage came when the site yielded perfectly preserved household, fishing, and hunting items. Among the items recovered was a fishing tackle pouch. Inside were weights, tackle, stone fishhook shanks, and codfish, bonefish, and halibut hooks. Other unusual finds include a cedar carving of a female killer whale's dorsal fin studded with more than 700 otter teeth, as well as metal tools predating European contact by about 300 years.

In the Makah Cultural Center is a miniature model of Ozette Village, built by tribal members Greg Arnold and Alex McCurty. Details include a woman with her dog in the forest, whale bones alongside the houses, petroglyphs on the rocks, and a baby cradled in a bentwood box.

Also recovered from Ozette was a centuries-old fishing net made of twined and woven nettle fibers. Modern-day Makah fishers, who had fought for decades in federal courts for the right to fish with nets, could finally prove their claim that ancestors had fished with nets made of nettle fibers. When they presented the net as evidence in court, the case was won with no further argument.

Today, the entire collection is housed in the $3 million Makah Cultural and Research Center in Neah Bay. The board of trustees consists of members of the tribe's strongest families. The center's director is Makah tribal member and Dartmouth University graduate Janine Bochak.

Lights in the cultural center are dimmed to protect fragile wood and fiber, lending a mystical air to the objects. The museum includes a life-size replica of the interior of a longhouse, full-size canoes, and objects found at a second archeological site, estimated to be about 2,500 years old, on the nearby Hoko River.

The pinecone-shaped "Ozette potato," believed to have come to the Washington coast from Peru with Spanish explorers, has been cultivated on the cape since the late 1700s—and is still grown in some gardens on the Olympic Peninsula. Baked and skinned, the little potato was a welcome addition of carbohydrate to the Makah's diet.

The gift shop offers a good selection of books, videotapes of the Ozette excavation, carved masks, bentwood boxes, and woven baskets.

Makah Cultural and Research Center, PO Box 160, Neah Bay, WA 98357; (360)645-2711. The museum is on the left, just inside the gateway to the Makah Reservation, on Hwy 112 at Neah Bay. June 1–Sept 15, call for hours. Sept 16–May 31, 10am–6pm; closed Mon and Tues. Admission $4; children $3; under 4, free. Tours are led by museum staff for a small extra fee; please make tour arrangements 2 weeks in advance.

Donna Wilkie's Native American Adventures

Makah tribal member Donna Wilkie drives her van up a steep, graveled road west of Neah Bay to a spot near the top of Cape Flattery. As she drives, she discusses the clearcuts visible on surrounding reservation hills. The logging has helped finance the Makah Tribe when no other money was forthcoming, but it's caused rifts between those tribal members wanting to preserve the reservation as a wilderness and those favoring logging—a common conflict in the Pacific Northwest.

Near the top of Cape Flattery, a half-mile trail along the cliffs overlooks Tatoosh Island, the westernmost spot in the Lower 48. Rather than hike the usually muddy trail, Wilkie drives past a No Trespassing sign (one of the advantages of traveling with a Native tour guide) and pulls into a clearing overlooking the Pacific Ocean. Far below, the ocean swells crashing on the rocks of Tatoosh Island form a white meringue around the barren, rocky shoreline, and we marvel at the difficulty of beaching a canoe on such dangerous ground. Wilkie tells us that potlatch celebrations, outlawed by the government, were held secretly on the island until 1924, when a change in the law made them legal and also granted American citizenship to the Native people.

Donna Wilkie's tours vary in length from one to three hours. Depending on the tour, they may include the Makah Cultural and Research Center, a circle of the town and the four historic villages, the vantage point overlooking Tatoosh Island, and the ocean beaches and nearby archaeological sites. Wilkie has lived on the reservation all her life, is a professional jazz singer, makes earrings and necklaces with dentalia shells (once valued as money for trade with coastal and inland tribes), grows Chinese ginseng in her garden, and is among the most genuine people on the planet.

Native American Adventures, PO Box 57, Neah Bay, WA 98357; (360)645-2554 or (360)645-2201. By appointment, year-round.

Makah Artists

The Makah Tribe boasts many talented artists, among them fine canoe and mask carvers. They also make feathers of cedar, so thin and etched with lines that they seem real. Black stems of maidenhair fern decorate baskets; jewelry is made of olive-shaped shells indigenous to Neah Bay. Ceremonial drums may be painted with clan symbols. One family of accomplished basket weavers makes woven baseball hats, dolls, and earrings and weaves grasses around glass balls, lamps, and bottles, a tradition that stems back to the 1900 souvenir market. Artists are listed with the Makah Tribal Planning Department, which publishes a brochure of names, addresses, and phone numbers. Check the Makah Cultural and Research Center's gift shop for art and inexpensive mugs and T-shirts; also peek into Washburn's General Store, (360)645-2211, in Neah Bay (you can't miss it; it's the only supermarket, and is just about the largest building in town).

Group art tours or meetings with individual artists can be arranged in advance through the Makah Cultural and Research Center, PO Box 160, Neah Bay, WA 98357; (360)645-2711.

Sandy Beaches

Three sandy Pacific Ocean crescent beaches on the Makah Reservation are available to the public. Waatch Beach is west of the Cape Flattery Tribal Center. A gentle stream, which runs through a meadow near the beach, is deep enough for kids to kayak or innertube in and is also accessible to the public. Hobuck Beach has a grassy berm with campsites and a few rental cabins and is open for picnics (no fires), horseback riding, and surfing in certain areas from June 15 to August 30; (360)645-2422. Access to Tsoo-Yas Beach is allowed by paying private landowners a parking fee, posted on the road. The public is also welcome to walk along the breakwater and the beach on the Neah Bay waterfront.

Cape Flattery is a famous bird-watching spot each March. Bird lists naming 239 species on or near the cape are free from the Makah Tribal Planning Office, PO Box 115, Neah Bay, WA 98357; (360)645-2201.

By the time this book is printed, there may also be public access to Shi Shi Beach from the reservation, if the tribe has acquired private landholder easements to reopen an existing trail. Until then, the trail is posted with No Trespassing signs. Shi Shi boasts some of the most colorful, and most photographed, tide pools on the Washington coast.

Check with the Makah Tribe first for a list of which beaches are open to the public, as well as for maps, rules and regulations, and fishing permits.

Makah Tribal Planning Office, PO Box 115, Neah Bay, WA 98357; (360)645-2201. The tribal office is in Building 12, at the old Air Force station near Cape Flattery, 6.7 miles southwest of Neah Bay. Follow Hwy 112 along the Neah Bay waterfront to the west end of the bay, turn left, and watch for signs. If you get lost along the way, ask anyone you see for directions.

The Hike to Ozette Village

The trail through a roadless wilderness corridor to the site of the Makah village of Ozette at Cape Alava is one of the premier hikes on the Olympic Peninsula. A cedar-plank boardwalk, which resonates like a drum under your boots, winds through dark cedar groves, wetlands filled with broad-leafed skunk cabbage, and prairie resplendent with blue camas (a type of edible lily) in the spring. The trail ends at the cape, where haystack rocks rise dramatically offshore from a sea of kelp-covered stones and tidepools filled with sea stars, sea urchins, anemones, limpets, barnacles, and other sea creatures. Campers pitch their tents in well-worn but unusually clean primitive campsites among the exposed roots of the cedar trees that overhang the eroded bank. Deer are tame, and often bring their newborn fawns within a few feet of visitors.

During the summer you must make a reservation to hike the trail to the Ozette Village site. Although there's little trace of a village left at Ozette, it continues to draw hundreds of visitors a day.

The Ozette village site, excavated in the 1970s, is about 500 yards north of the trail's end. The crows like to perch on top of the small cedar longhouse built recently by the Makah to memorialize their ancestors, who perished when the village was buried by a mudslide. On our visit, park ranger and Makah tribal member David Corpuz stood by the longhouse to answer the questions asked by some of the thousands of travelers who hiked the 3-mile trail to Ozette. From Ozette, you can also hike 1 mile south on the beach to Wedding Rock's petroglyphs. From Wedding Rock, the trail continues another 2 miles south to Sand Point, where a second boardwalk loops back through the woods and skirts Ozette Lake. Also at Sand Point, adventurous hikers can continue hiking down the wilderness coastline to Rialto Beach and the Quileute Reservation, a distance of about 25 miles, or all the way north to Neah Bay. Since it rains about 146 inches annually here, even day hikers should wear sturdy shoes and take poncho-style rain slickers with hoods, a change of pants and dry socks and shoes, as well as food and water. Water from the creeks is full of natural tannin and not potable.

The road to Lake Ozette is paved, but there are no services for 21 miles from the turnoff (between Hoko and Seiku) on Highway

112 to Ozette. The ranger station at the trailhead has modern rest-rooms, potable water, and kiosks with tide charts, wildlife, and trail information.

From Port Angeles, follow Hwy 112 past Clallam Bay to Seiku, and watch for well-marked signs to Lake Ozette. From Forks, take Hwy 101 north to Sappho and continue north on Hwy 112 (Burnt Mountain Road) to the town of Clallam Bay. Continue west 4 miles to the turnoff at Seiku. There are no stores or restaurants at Ozette. Food and supplies (even rain gear) may be purchased at supermarkets in Forks, Clallam Bay, or Neah Bay. Potable water is available at the ranger station at the trailhead. There are 15 free camping sites on Lake Ozette: first come, first served. Backcountry camping permits are required for free coastal sites. To make a reservation and get a confirmation number, call Olympic National Park headquarters, (360)452-0300. Pick up your permit from the ranger station at Ozette, (360)963-2725, when you arrive. Tide charts for hiking the beaches are essential. No pets.

La Push: *Quileute*

Few people live in a more beautiful setting than the Quileute Tribe. Surrounded by the rain forests of the Olympic National Park, their one-mile-square reservation at the mouth of the Quileute River faces a sandy, crescent beach, haystack rocks, and open ocean. Isolated on the undeveloped Washington coastline that is protected by the park, the Quileutes live midway between the Makah and Quinault Reservations. The village of La Push is at the end of a 14-mile paved road. The logging town of Forks, the only town of any size on the west side of the Olympic Peninsula, is inland on Highway 101.

From the 1950s to the early 1970s, when salmon were plentiful, La Push was a thriving salmon charter-boat port. Local fishermen still supply the Quileute's fish processing plant with crab, salmon, and bottom fish. But the little village is best known for the unpretentious Ocean Park Resort (which offers some of the best views for the best prices on the Washington coast), and for the tribe's beach, a drift-wood-covered, sandy crescent with sloughing cliffs at one end and the Quileute River jetty at the other.

The resort is the first thing you see when entering La Push. Beyond it is the village, less than eight square blocks facing the river. The village looks poor and it is. Almost a third of the households earn less than $7,000 a year. The Quileute Tribal School, once housed in the picturesque 1920s-era Coast Guard station, is now located in a new building overlooking the ocean. The school has won national awards for its outstanding cultural education program, in which elders teach the Quileute language and carving and basket-making skills.

The tribe is currently building a longhouse and planning a pot-latch to welcome a contingent of Native canoes and paddlers who will arrive at La Push by water from as far away as Alaska and New Zealand in 1997. The Quileutes are calling the canoe celebration *Aklat,* the Quileute word for potlatch, a ceremony still held in the area.

The Quileute Tribe's dreams for the future include building an interpretive center and museum on an 11-acre island east of the vil-lage, accessible by footbridge, containing studio and workshop space for tribal members. The island is currently a well-trampled pasture favored by a herd of Roosevelt elk, which swim the Quileute River to reach it.

Most visitors to La Push come to the resort to relax, walk on the beaches, and watch the sunsets. Few stray into town, but they are wel-come to walk along the boat dock (you may see one of the tribe's traditional canoes tied up at the dock), visit the fish processing plant, and see the tribe's few displays of baskets in the tribal center. Across from the resort, in a shop attatched to a trailer, is elder Helen Harrison's gift shop, Paddler's Sun, with local art for sale and fresh, hot coffee.

The Quileutes of the Past

For thousands of years before the "White Drifting-House People" arrived in their ships, the Quileute Indians lived, fished, and hunted sea mammals along the mouths of the rivers that flow from the gla-ciers of the Olympic Mountains to the island-strewn Pacific beaches. Legends indicate that the Quileutes may be among the oldest inhab-itants of the Pacific Northwest, their lineage stretching back to a time when ice covered most of the land and the people nearly starved to death. According to their origin myth, the Quileutes were created from wolves by a wandering supernatural Transformer. The Quileutes speak a unique language, unrelated to any root language in the world.

The Quileutes' stories say that their only kin, the Chimakum, were carried away by a great flood through the Olympic Mountains and deposited on the other side of the Olympic Peninsula. The present-day crossroads of Chimacum, south of Port Townsend on Puget Sound, is named after the Chimakum who lived there until the 1860s, when the Suquamish Indians, under Chief Seattle, wiped them out, leaving the Quileutes with no known relatives.

From cradleboard to burial canoe, Quileutes depended on the help and inspiration of supernatural powers. Youths sought their own *taxilit* (personal guardian power) on solitary spirit quests. Rituals such as the first salmon ceremony guaranteed the goodwill of the salmon spirits, assuring the great fish would continue to fill the river each year and allow themselves to be caught. There were also a terrifying array of monsters, such as *daskya,* the kelp-haired child snatcher, lurking in the area.

The Quileutes signed a treaty with the U.S. government in 1856, agreeing to move south to the Quinault Reservation, the home of their traditional enemy. They didn't actually move, however, either because they didn't understand what they'd signed or because they decided to hold their ground. In 1889, President Grover Cleveland agreed the Quileutes could stay at La Push, at the mouth of the Quileute River. However, out of all their lands, including the three rivers that flow into the Quileute, they were allowed only 1 square mile of land surrounding the village. No sooner had they secured their reservation, however, than the village was burned to the ground by several white men who wanted their land. The elders (left behind in La Push while the rest of the tribe was picking hops in the Puyallup Valley), were unable to save the tribe's houses or any of their ceremonial items when the village was engulfed by flames.

The Quileutes survived the boarding school years, when their children were removed from the village and indoctrinated with white values. Once great seal hunters and fishermen, they have continued to fish, first with outboard motors strapped to the sterns of their canoes, and then with the modern fishing vessels one sees today.

The Paddle to La Push

In the summer of 1990, members of several Northwest tribes made the 1,200-mile round-trip canoe journey from La Push to British Columbia's island of Bella Bella. More than 30 Quileute tribal members, paddling eight- to ten-man traditional cedar canoes, launched their craft in the Quileute River and paddled up Washington's coast to Vancouver Island, where they joined canoes from other Puget Sound and British Columbia tribes. Together the tribes followed a route through the Inside Passage, crossing the Queen Charlotte Strait at the northern tip of Vancouver Island and continuing up the coast of mainland British Columbia to Bella Bella. The route had not been traveled by Native canoes in more than a century. Bella Bella, located on an island off the roadless British Columbia mainland, is the home of the Heiltsuk band of the Kwaikutl Tribe, who welcomed the paddlers with traditional songs on the beach and a huge potlatch celebration.

The Quileute Tribe is preparing to host a similar event in July of 1997, Native paddlers from the Northwest, as well as from New Zealand and Hawaii, will arrive on the beach at La Push.

124 • **WESTERN WASHINGTON**

La Push Ocean Park Resort

The glorious beach, relaxed atmosphere, and views are what bring travelers to Ocean Park Resort and adjoining Shoreline Resort year-round, in spite of relentless winter rain. Ocean Park also offers the only oceanfront accommodations between Neah Bay and Kalaloch, about 100 miles apart, on the northern Washington coast. Accommodations range from A-frame cabins under the trees, where guests cook on a hot plate, heat water for washing (there's a nearby shower-house with hot water), and sack out in their own sleeping bags; to new three-bedroom townhouses with fireplaces, fully equipped kitchens, and barbecues on the deck. Newer cabins are equally spiffed up, and most cabins have fireplaces or glass-fronted wood stoves. Split, dry firewood and kindling are provided free in a box at the doorstep. The two-story Thunderbird and Whale motel units are nothing fancy, but have decks and fully equipped kitchens. The resort's new water system pipes in clear, fresh spring water. Tent camping and RV hookups are also available. Pets are allowed in some units ("Please do not feed the local dogs so they will go home," reads one brochure).

Whale watchers take over the place in March, April, May, and the first part of June when the gray whales linger just beyond the breakers; July and August are equally popular. November through March the storms hit with full force, with a few dazzlingly sunny days in between. Weekends are always busy. There are no restaurants at the resort or at La Push. A small grocery store is in an old building across the street from the resort; full-service grocery stores are in Forks, about 16 miles away. From December through June you can buy freshly caught, iced Dungeness crab in the shell at Quileute Seafood, a short walk from the resort (see below). Espresso, video-tapes of the Quileute tribes' first canoe project, printed information about the tribe, and gifts are available in the resort office.

Ocean Park Resort, PO Box 67, La Push, WA 98350; (800)487-1267 or (360)374-5267. Take the La Push/Quileute exit from Hwy 101 and stay on the road until the beach is visible. Ocean Park Resort office is on the left. Prices range from $10 a night for camp sites, to $36 for campers' cabins; $50 for a motel unit to $125 for a fireplace cabin. Reservations strongly advised.

James Island: A La Push Landmark

James Island, a prominent haystack rock covered with tall firs, sits off-shore on the north side of the Quileute River. It is named after a settler who once perched his house up top. James wasn't an island, however, until the U.S. Army Corps of Engineers changed the course of the Quileute River, which isolated the haystack from the village.

Shaped like a horseshoe, with access to the top on the ocean side, James Island had many uses. It was a temporary home to the Quileutes, who moved their entire village of longhouses to the top to defend themselves during seiges by the neighboring Makahs. It was also the burial ground for chiefs. Bodies were wrapped in blankets woven from dog's hair and laid in a cedar canoe. The tribe also grew nettles 10 feet high in a tended patch on the island's top, later harvesting them and twisting them into fine twine to use in weaving fishing nets.

Basket Weaving

One of the best things about meeting basket weavers is talking with them about collecting materials. Leila Morganroth remembers bedding down for the night in the canoe with her grandmother when out gathering cattails and other materials near Lake Ozette. Elder Lillian Pullen, a fluent speaker of Quileute, learned to weave beside her grandmother, one of the best weavers in the tribe. Mrs. Pullen has also taught other tribal members how to gather and prepare the inner bark of cedar (no easy task) for baskets and traditional woven clothing, which includes rainproof hats, vests, and cedar bark skirts. Her daughter-in-law, Eileen Penn, and great granddaughter, Ann, are weavers as well. They also incorporate Mrs. Pullen's weaving designs into knit sweaters, vests, hats, and mittens.

To make an appointment to meet local weavers, contact the Quileute Museum at (360)374-4366. To make an appointment with Lillian Pullen or one of her family, call (360)374-5842 or (360)374-9896.

Quileute Seafood

Early in the day you can climb up on the jetty, find a flat rock to sit on, and watch fishing boats chugging out to sea, and fishermen standing in skiffs checking their nets in the river. The boom time for the fisheries was in the 1950s to 1970s, when more than 300 fishing boats moored in La Push. Now there are 20. At Quileute Seafood's cold storage plant next to the dock, you can buy freshly caught, iced Dungeness crab in the shell (in season), tasty with cocktail sauce, as well as whole coho and pink salmon, black and red sea bass, and other fish either singly or in quantity.

Quileute Seafood, 100 Main St, La Push, WA 98350; (360)754-5533. Look for crab pots stacked in front of the blue building and the old firetruck parked in the lot. Open daily, hours vary according to the catch.

Four Sparkling Beaches to Explore

Deer have been observed leaping in the surf on Olympic National Park's mist-shrouded beaches, but most two-legged visitors rarely immerse themselves in the icy sea: hypothermia is a real threat to anyone staying in the water more than 10 minutes. Except for the surfers and ocean kayakers, who dress in insulated wet or dry suits, most visitors come to Olympic National Park ocean beaches for their unspoiled beauty. The beaches near La Push are some of the best on the coast. Two of them are easily accessible by road; two others are accessible only by trail.

First Beach, in front of Ocean Park Resort at La Push, is open year-round, with paths through the driftwood to the sand. Permits for beach fires are available from Ocean Park Resort for $2. Second Beach is less than a mile south of La Push, separated from First Beach at La Push by an impassable headland. Park in the well-marked lot next to the road and hike through deep, quiet forest on reservation land for less than a mile to the beach. Steep portions of the trail have broad stairs with handrails to make the descent easier, and benches to rest on during the tiring ascent back to the parking lot. Second Beach faces the Quillayute Needles, impressive spikes of rock that are part of the offshore national marine sanctuary, accessible at low tide for tidepool exploring.

Third Beach is even farther south, separated from Second Beach by Teahwhit Head. Park in the lot next to the road and hike about 1½ miles down an easy trail to the mile-long strand that ends at a plunging waterfall at Taylor Point. The trail continues from Taylor Point to the mouth of the untamed Hoh River, a distance of about 20 miles over the rugged headlands; consult National Park headquarters (360)452-4501, before hiking this portion of the trail.

The mouth of the Hoh River is more easily reached by continuing on Highway 101 past Forks to the turnoff to Oil City, and then taking the 15-mile-long gravel road to the Hoh's north shore. We've seen cougar tracks on the trail and herds of elk swimming the river here, as well as hundreds of brown pelicans and arctic terns fishing at the river's mouth. The narrow trail winds along the riverbank and ends at an impressively deep, and wide, pile of driftwood. Across the Hoh River is a small band of Quileute families, living on a few acres of land reserved for them by presidential decree in 1893.

North of La Push is Rialto Beach, also part of Olympic National Park. You can see Rialto Beach across the Quileute River from La Push, but to get there you must backtrack toward Highway 101. Take the Mora/Rialto turnoff and continue past the Mora campground, in deep woods, to the large, paved parking lot, with information kiosk and restrooms. The hike on Rialto Beach is richly rewarding. The surf pounds the steep shore with a satisfying roar. Huge red cedar logs, remnants of the logging era when the big cedars were being cut upriver, are strewn across the rocky beach. Most visitors walk a few feet from their cars, find a spot to sit against the big logs, and watch the surf. You can hike north on Rialto Beach about 2 miles to Hole in the Wall, a natural arch in the rock and a great place to poke about in tide pools.

From Hole in the Wall, you can continue to hike the wilderness beach all the way north to Ozette Village (see the Ozette listing in the Makah section) and on to Neah Bay, a distance of about 45 miles, best traveled at low tide. Creeks along the way are tea-colored by natural tannin and unsafe to drink; water must be portaged. Information, Ozette Wilderness camping permits, and maps of Olympic National Park beach and mountain hiking trails are available from park headquarters in Port Angeles, (360)452-4501.

Why the Beach Rocks Are Flat

"When all the people in the world were spirits, Raven was invited to a feast. He intended to gamble while there, so he took his disks and invited the other guests to join him in a game. Raven whirled his disks. The others spun their disks. No one could beat Raven, however, because his disks were special spirit disks. As he whirled them, he called in his spirit power and sang his spirit song. 'The moon always shines at night!' he sang. And wily old Raven could not be beaten because his spirit power was stronger than anyone else's.

"When Raven won the game, his opponents could not pay. The game was being held on the beach, and Raven looked at the water and said, 'Make the water roll back and give me power over it and we will be even.' So Raven was given control of low tide. You can still see Raven's gambling disks covering the beaches at La Push and Rialto— they are the flat, round stones that spin in the undertow when the tide goes out." *(This Quileute story is one of many versions of why the rocks are flat along this section of the Olympic Peninsula.)*

Paddlers' Sun

Quileute elder Helen Harrison was a major force in organizing the Quileute's 1,200-mile, round-trip canoe journey from La Push to British Columbia, so it's natural she'd call her gift shop "Paddlers' Sun." In the shop, which was added on to a mobile home, you can purchase baskets made from cedar bark, bear grass, and raffia; wood carvings; and prints and silver jewelry; Most of the items were hand-crafted by students and elders of the tribe. Sales of black-and-white postcards of La Push, reproduced from the tribe's archives, help support the Quileute Tribal School's cultural enrichment program. Feel free to ask Mrs. Harrison questions about La Push: she's lived here all her life and is a fluent speaker of both English and Quileute.

Paddler's Sun, across from Ocean Park Resort and next to the grocery store in La Push. Summer hours, 10am–5 pm daily; winters, most days noon–5 pm. Best to call first: (360)374-9033 or (360)374-6942.

Taholah: *Quinault*

The Quinault Reservation is neighbor to Olympic National Park, Olympic National Forest, and the Olympic Coast National Marine Sanctuary. The villages are isolated from the rest of Washington's coastal resort towns. There are two scenic public roads on the reservation, U.S. 101 and State Route 109—which ends at the reservation's major village, Taholah, a long inhabited site at the mouth of the Quinault River. Where longhouses once faced the water, Taholah has been platted into a grid of streets serving single-family houses, with two sports fields and a seafood processing plant. The village is in the middle of 23 miles of unspoiled Pacific coastline.

The Quinault signed a treaty with the U.S. government in 1855, allowing them to remain in the heart of their ancestral land. Eventually, other tribes moved there as well. The Quinaults prefer to be addressed as the Quinault Indian Nation. The Nation consists of Quinault, Queets, Quileute, Hoh, Chehalis, Cowlitz, and Chinook descendants.

Many visitors come to Taholah to buy fresh and smoked seafood. Fewer know of the reservation's fabulous Quinault River birdwatching, fishing, kayaking, or dugout canoe tours. All tours include an escort by knowledgeable and courteous tribal members.

The largest reservation in western Washington, the Quinault Indian Nation is a huge triangle (208,150 acres) of mostly forested land at the southern edge of Olympic National Park. The swift, clear Quinault River runs through Lake Quinault (visible from Highway 101) on its way to the ocean.

The scenic coastal Hwy 101 wraps around the Quinault Reservation, touching its eastern boundary at pristine Lake Quinault. Just south of the lake you can take a shortcut to Taholah on the Moclips Hwy. Watch for signs. From the south, between the coastal towns of Aberdeen and Hoquiam, take Hwy 109 all the way to Taholah.

Forestry Tour

Most of the Quinault Nation's old-growth trees have been logged. The Bureau of Indian Affairs, which managed the land, gave out large, long-term contracts to a few logging companies. The companies, in turn, made enormous profits while their logging practices destroyed whole watersheds, filling salmon-spawning streams with wood debris. In 1971, the Quinault Tribe risked arrest in order to protest these practices by blocking roads into logging units. Their effort to bring the destruction to public attention worked; the tribe gained support locally and took over the management of their remaining forests.

To reverse more than 100 years of ecological damage, the Quinault plant more than a million trees a year, as well as rehabilitate streambeds. The young forests, planted with diverse species, are healthy, with ferns, mushrooms, blackberries, bear grass, and multitudes of shrubs and wildflowers. Tribal foresters offer guided tours of their new forests, which are a haven for herds of Roosevelt elk, black bear, blacktail deer, bald eagles, cougars, and many other animals.

Quinault Natural Resources Department, PO Box 189, Taholah, WA 98587; (360)276-8211.

Hiking, Fishing, and Bird-Watching

The western Olympic Peninsula has a wide variety of birds, from bald eagles and osprey to rufous-sided hummingbirds, cormorants, and little sandpipers. Brown pelicans are annual visitors to the Quinault River, sometimes traveling in flocks of up to 200. Lake Quinault boasts over 20 pairs of trumpeter swans, which nest along its shoreline. Teaming up with local Audubon chapters and WINGS, an international bird-watching organization, Quinault tribal member Mike Marchand offers several unusual bird-watching tours. Ride with Marchand in a traditional Quinault River cedar canoe, (outfitted with a small motor) from Lake Quinault downriver to Point Grenville, south of the river's mouth. Kayak groups may also contact him for a two-day tour that includes an overnight campout on the river's bank.

Winter or summer, Quinault guides can take you steelhead and trout fishing on the Quinault, Humptulips, Queets, and Salmon Rivers or on Lake Quinault. Guides must always accompany hikers on the reservation, or you can pick up a daily pass at the Administration Complex, 1214 Aalis, Tahola, to use the Quinault coastal beaches open to the public.

For a list of tribal tour guides, contact the Quinault Department of Community Development, PO Box 189, Taholah, WA 98587; (360)276-8211.

Quinault Pride Seafood

The Quinault Tribe established Quinault Pride Seafood, a seafood processing plant in Taholah, to market local fishermen's catches. During the peak season, more than 80 people are employed. Fishers deliver daily, and within hours the catch is cleaned and processed. Begun in a wooden shack in the 1950s, Quinault Pride is now in a spacious building overlooking the Quinault River, with state-of-the-art equipment to fast-freeze, can, and smoke seafood.

You can buy alderwood-smoked fish in handsome paper boxes or handcrafted wooden gift boxes with braided rope handles. Variety gift packs include smoked razor clams, sturgeon, albacore tuna, and three kinds of salmon, including rare Quinault blueback salmon. The small shop also sells cards, gift baskets, baseball caps, T-shirts, and fishing gear and will ship orders anywhere in the world. Free factory tours (no canned speeches).

Land of the Quinault, written and published by the Quinault Department of Natural Resources, describes the tribe's early history, culture, and struggle for self-governance. You can order the award-winning book from Quinault Indian Nation, PO Box 189, Taholah, WA 98587; (360)276-8211.

Quinault Pride Seafood, 100 Quinault St, Taholah, WA 98587; (800)821-8650 or (360)962-2180. Call for an order form and price list, or visit the packing plant. Open 8am–5pm weekdays; closed Sat–Sun.

Quinault National Fish Hatchery

In 1976, the Quinault Tribe opened their hatchery on Cook Creek, a small stream that flows under the Moclips Highway. Each year the hatchery produces over 8 million chinook, chum, and coho salmon, as well as steelhead. Visitors are welcome to tour the facility during working hours. The information center at the hatchery displays mounted specimens of adult fish and explains the fish life cycle.

Quinault National Fish Hatchery, PO Box 80, Neilton, WA 98566; (360)288-2508.

Quinault Indian Nation Dancers

Tribal historian and cultural expert Reggie Thunderbird Ward, Sr is the lead singer, drummer, and storyteller for the Quinault Indian Nation Dancers. The dancers combine song, dance, and drama to tell legends and share the Quinault culture. They have

Although Quinault seafarers hunted seals through the early 1900s using sail-powered canoes, the art of canoe building was suspended when the U.S. government declared a moratorium on seal hunting in the 1930s (it is still in effect today). Decades passed before tribal members once again carved a canoe. That canoe, launched April 10, 1994, bears the Quinault name Mayee (the Beginning). Two more have since been completed.

performed at major events throughout the region, for the Discovery Channel, and are available for performances.

Contact Reggie Ward, Sr, 3124 Pacific Ave, Hoquiam, WA 98550; (360)532-5503.

Seven Feathers Artist and Craftsperson Cooperative

Throughout Taholah you will find carvings and totems on schools and other community buildings. The Nation even has a sign ordinance that prescribes carved wooden signs for all public buildings. Art, clearly, has a place in the heart of the community. So much so that Quinault artists Randy Capoeman, Michael Cardwell-Snqhepi'wes, and Guy Capoeman (a renowned canoe carver) were among a group that co-founded the Seven Feathers cooperative in order to promote the seven bands that form the Quinault Indian Nation. Randy Capoeman makes prints, drums, cards, and T-shirts. Cardwell-Snqhepi'wes (a Salish word, meaning "spirit") is a member of the American Institute of Certified Planners who works with the tribal planning department. Guy Capoeman carved the Mayee canoe, performs with the Quinault Indian Nation Dancers, and exhibits his work in metropolitan galleries.

For more information about arts in Quinault, contact Michael Cardwell-Snqhepi'wes, Seven Feathers Artists and Craftspersons Cooperative, PO Box 40, Taholah, WA 98587; (360)276-4796.

Oakville: *Chehalis*

The Chehalis are known for their skill as fishermen and for their fine basketry. Located on the Chehalis River at Oakville, their reservation occupies the former site of one of their largest ancestral villages. They were called the *Chehalis,* which means "people of the sand," because all of their villages were situated on the sandy banks of the Chehalis River, including two very large villages near present-day Elma and Grand Mound. The Lower Chehalis and Upper Chehalis spoke different dialects of the same coast Salish language. During the 1850s, they banded together, refusing to move to the Quinault Reservation where they had been assigned. With the help of an Oakville teacher, adults over the age of 18 homesteaded the land that is today incorporated into the Chehalis Reservation. Today, about 575 people are enrolled as tribal members; around 250 live on the reservation at Oakville. At their tribal office, you can buy a copy of *The Last Canoe,* which documents the carving of the last Chehalis canoe; and *The Chehalis People,* which tells the tribe's history. Smoked salmon, caught from the Chehalis River, can also be ordered from the tribe.

Chehalis Tribal Center, 420 Howanut Rd, Oakville, WA 98568; (360)273-5911. From I-5, take the Oakville/Rochester exit. Travel 8 miles west on Hwy 12, turn left on Anderson Rd, and go to the top of the hill. At the stop sign, take a right, go past a church, and watch for signs. Open weekdays, 8am–4:30pm.

Hazel Pete Institute of Chehalis Basketry

Hazel Pete teaches Chehalis-style basketry year-round at her home, on a portion of the original 90-acre parcel that was homesteaded by her great-great-grandmother Jane Moxley (Guma). Hazel Pete learned basketry from her grandmothers, who shared the homestead, and then taught gathering and basketmaking to her own family. Today her nine children, who live throughout the United States, come home each year to participate in the family's Thanksgiving weekend basket sale. They gather materials such as cattail from the marshes and sweet grass from the mouth of the Chehalis River, and then weave baskets under their mother's direction. The great-grandchildren weave angels, cattail dolls, and bookmarks; the grandchildren and adult children weave the more complicated baskets. Collectors come from all over the world to buy Pete family baskets. Members of the extended family have put themselves through college by making baskets and telling stories. Hazel Pete herself returned to school in her 60s, and received her Bachelor of Science degree from Evergreen State College, and master's degree in Indian education from the University of Washington.

Hazel Pete's basketry can be seen at the American Indian Community House Museum in New York City, the Institute of American Indian Art in Santa Fe, at the University of Washington Burke Museum in Seattle, and the Washington State Capitol Museum in Olympia. She also teaches basketry spring and fall, to anyone interested, at her home in Oakville.

The Hazel Pete Institute of Chehalis Basketry, 137 Anderson Rd, Oakville, WA 98568; (360)273-7274 (after 4pm). From I-5, take the Oakville/Rochester exit and on Hwy 12, travel 8 miles west. Turn left on Anderson Rd, and travel one mile to the top of the hill. The house is on the left hand side of the road, past the stop sign.

WESTERN OREGON & NORTHERN CALIFORNIA

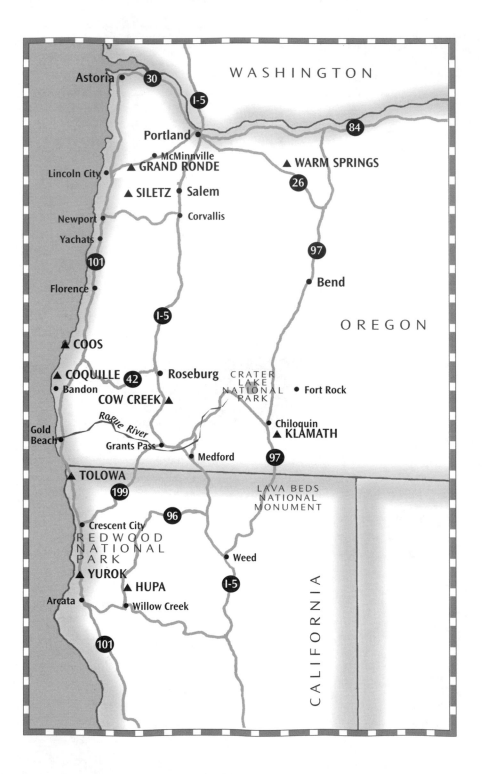

WESTERN OREGON & NORTHERN CALIFORNIA

Prior to European contact, numerous tribes lived on the coast, rivers, and forested mountain ranges that now constitute western Oregon and northern California. However, during the 1800s, epidemics decimated entire villages south of the lower Columbia River. A 100-mile-long Indian reservation was established along the coast, from the capes of Tillamook to the sand dunes south of Florence, to hold the remaining Indians of western Oregon.

Today two small tribes still live near the central Oregon coast: the Confederated Tribes of the Grand Ronde (just west of McMinneville's wine country) and the Confederated Tribes of Siletz Indians (about 25 miles inland of Lincoln City). About 100 miles south, in Coos Bay and Bandon, you can meet members of the Coos and Coquille tribes and learn about villages and landmarks along the coastal shoreline.

In Redwood National Park, on California's northern coast, three tribes still quietly practice their traditional religions and fish for salmon on the Smith and Klamath

Rivers. In Partridge Point State Park, Yurok houses, a dance house, and a sweat lodge have been re-created in an architectural style that once lined the rivers and bays.

Inland about 60 miles, the Hupa Tribe offers eco-tours, raft trips, and cultural tours of their valley along the crystal-clear Trinity River. Far inland, at the headwaters of the Klamath River, you can pick wocus (the edible fruit of a lily pad) with the Klamath Tribe, learn about the tribe's legends of the eruption that created Crater Lake, and visit the lava beds where Modoc leader Captain Jack held off the U.S. cavalry through the winter.

Portland Metropolitan Area

Portland, Oregon, is situated on land once inhabited by Native peoples, yet like other metropolitan cities in the Pacific Northwest, it focuses very little on those tribes. Both Multnomah County and the region's most spectacular waterfall, Multnomah Falls, are named after the Multnomah Band of Chinook Indians who lived on the shores of the Columbia and Willamette Rivers, where Portland is now located. Multnomah Channel, a narrow waterway 14 miles north of Portland that flows along the west bank of Sauvie Island, is also named after the band. Although five archaeological digs have been completed on Sauvie Island, few people know that Multnomah Chinooks once occupied the island. Stone figures carved of basalt, unearthed from the Sauvie Island sites, are part of the Oregon History Center's collection. The few Multnomahs who survived the epidemics that swept through the lower Columbia and all of Western Oregon in the 1830s intermarried or were moved to reservations in the 1850s—some of them to Grand Ronde near the central Oregon coast.

Like its sister cities of Vancouver, British Columbia, and Seattle, Washington, Portland offers a broad taste of Native American art, literature, and culture through its galleries, bookstores, and museums. The Bureau of Indian Affairs regional headquarters are located in Portland, as are the offices of the Affiliated Tribes of Northwest Indians (ATNI), which represents 54 tribes from six states. The Columbia River Inter-Tribal Fish Commission, a consortium of four tribes with fishing rights on the Columbia River, also has an office in Portland. More than 11,000 "urban Indians," who have moved to Oregon from all over the United States, live within the city limits and co-sponsor an annual powwow each summer at Portland's Delta Park, near the airport. (For more suggestions of Native sites near Portland, see the Columbia River Gorge & Basin chapter.)

Children's Museum

"Living Legends: American Indians Today," at Portland's Children's Museum, invites kids 5 to 10 years old to explore a community center, fish on the Columbia River, camp in a teepee, attend an intertribal powwow, and try out different rhythms in the dance arbor. The exhibit showcases Northwest Indian life as well as the contributions made to our society by Indian peoples, such as democracy, recycling, and respect for the environment.

Children's Museum, 3037 SW 2nd Ave, Portland, OR; (503)823-2227. Open daily 9am–5pm. Exhibit hours may differ. Call for hours. Admission $3.50.

Oregon History Center

Across from the Portland Art Museum, on a pleasant pedestrian avenue of trees and rose gardens called the Park Blocks, is the Oregon Historical Society's museum, library, and photograph collection.

Native American collections include basketry, beadwork, leatherwork and stonework representing many Northwest tribal groups, including Oregon's Paiute, Tillamook, and Wasco, and Idaho's Nez Perce. Artifacts from the collection are exhibited on a regular basis. Research using the Native American collections can be arranged by contacting the director of Museum Collections. Access to records is currently through a manual catalogue card system. Computerized access to the collections is being developed. Collections are shared with other museums, including all Native American museums in Oregon and southwest Washington.

Aross the Columbia River from Portland, you can see "living history" at Fort Vancouver, the original site of a Hudson's Bay Company trading post. The fully reconstructed fort includes an Indian trade store furnished with trade goods of the period. (See "Fort Vancouver" in the Columbia River Gorge & Basin chapter.)

The photograph collection, housed in the center's library, includes over 1,000 images relating to Northwest Indians. The earliest images are sketches, including one of a Native fisherman with a dip net at Willamette Falls, made during the 1840s. Photographs are arranged by subject, and detailed cross-references include tribal identity, when known.

The manuscripts collection, also housed in the center's library, covers the missionary/pioneer era through the reservation era, mostly through firsthand accounts. Most letters, drawings, interviews, and diaries are from missionaries, pioneers, military men, and Indian agents. A few manuscripts were penned by Indians.

The Oregon History Center is also home to the Oregon Folk Arts Program, which awards teaching fellowships to traditional artists. Their work is often on display in the museum.

The museum's gift shop has a large selection of Native-related books, maps, art prints, cards, and gifts, including a line of products, based on a Wasco basket elk design, that helps support the center, as well as Indian education programs.

Oregon Historical Society, 1200 SW Park Ave, Portland, OR 97205; (503)222-1741. In downtown Portland. Museum, library, and gift shop hours differ, call for hours. Admission $4.50.

Portland Art Museum

The Portland Art Museum was one of the first art museums in North America to recognize the "art" in Indian artifacts and to purchase a major collection. The Axel Rasmussen Collection, purchased in 1948, brought to Portland 500 objects collected in the 1920s and 1930s in Southeast Alaska and British Columbia. A school superintendent from the midwestern United States, Rasmussen was in British Columbia at the time that Native winter ceremonies and potlatches were outlawed. Tribal members were forced to give up ceremonial items to Indian agents in order to bail family members out of jail; these items are the source of many Northwest Coast collections of art and artifacts. Much of Rasmussen's collection came from Alert Bay (see Alert Bay and Quadra Island in the British Columbia chapter). It includes Chilkat blankets, an 8-foot-long ceremonial potlatch serving bowl, bentwood boxes, masks, frontlets, and household items.

The art museum's Elizabeth Cole Butler Collection of Native American Art contains traditional artwork such as basketry and Plains Indian beadwork. Butler, of Choctaw ancestry, began collecting in 1970, purchasing from dealers and at auctions.

The museum has also purchased contemporary artwork by Northwest Indian painters Jim Lavadour, Rick Bartow, and others.

Traveling exhibitions of Indian art, such as a collection of 1800s children's clothing and toys, as well as major shows of North American contemporary work, are periodically displayed. Traditional Indian artists also demonstrate their skills in (sometimes week-long) workshops through the Pacific Northwest College of Art, which adjoins the Portland Art Museum's building.

Portland Art Museum, 1219 SW Park Ave, Portland, OR 97205; (503)226-2811. In downtown Portland. Due to major shows that will interrupt normal daytime hours and exhibits, call the museum for current hours, exhibits, and admission charges.

Powell's City of Books

The largest bookstore in North America, with more than half a million titles, Powell's City of Books includes 5,000 new and used books both by and about Native Americans. Most are grouped in the Native American section, though some are interspersed in the rare book, literature, poetry, or language sections of the store. Northwest Native writers, such as Coeur d' Alene/Spokane writer Sherman Alexie, Spokane poet Gloria Bird, and Warm Springs poet Elizabeth Woody are well represented. Buyer Susan Wentland doesn't censor the old books, which she considers a rich source of bias that contributes to our understanding of past federal policies: among the titles you might find *Our Wild Indians,* written in 1885 by Colonel Richard Irving Dodge (aide-de-camp to "Indian fighter" General William Sherman). What you won't find in the Native American section, says Wentland, are "new age" authors, who she believes misrepresent Native spirituality.

Powell's City of Books, 1005 W Burnside, Portland, OR 97209; (800)878-7323 or (503)228-4651. At the corner of 10th and Burnside in downtown Portland. For a schedule of readings at Powell's, ask to be put on the mailing list. Open Mon–Sat, 9am–11pm; Sun, 9am–9pm.

Quintana's Galleries

The Quintana family owns two galleries of Native American art in Portland, both downtown. The largest of the two, Quintana's Gallery of Native American Art, is in Portland's charming Old Town, near the Willamette River, in the historic Merchant's Hotel building. High ceilings allow Quintana's to display massive Northwest Coast house posts carved by such Alaskan artists as Metlakatlan David Boxley, as well as large screens and triptychs, by Aleut carver John Hoover. All work sold in the Old Town store is by contemporary artists and includes many Northwest Coast–style dance masks, rattles, and potlatch bowls carved from cedar and alder. The gallery also displays work by Inuit and Eskimo stone and ivory carvers, and Southwest jewelry and paintings. Frequently, artists demonstrate their craft, such as Navajo rug weaving, in the gallery. New shows often open with Native drumming, singing, and dancing.

The Quintana family's second gallery, North American Indian, Inc., has an extensive collection of antiquities for sale, including baskets, beadwork, jewelry, and Navajo rugs, as well as original photographs, photogravure, and goldtones produced by Edward S. Curtis, who photographed Indians in traditional clothing from 1898 to 1928.

Quintana's Gallery of Native American Art, 139 NW 2nd, Portland, OR 97209; (503)223-1729. In Portland's Old Town. Open Tues–Sat, 10:30am–5:30pm. North American Indian, Inc, 816 SW 10th St, Portland, OR 97205; (503)223-4202. Across the street from the Multnomah County Library. Open Tues–Sat, 10:30am–5:30pm.

Visit ATNI Offices

Drop by the offices of the Affiliated Tribes of Northwest Indians (ATNI) and pick up a complimentary copy of the "Northwest Indian Travel Guide and Map" (while they last). This brochure features Native attractions, arts, cultural centers, tourist facilities, and businesses throughout the Northwest; the map identifies reservations and Native lands. The ATNI offices also have a small inventory of books and video tapes, as well as arts, gift boxes of Native foods, and other products made by member tribes. Signed copies of this book are also available.

ATNI was formed in 1953, when tribal leaders in the Northwest grew concerned about the federal policies (termination acts) that would abolish tribal governments. Following successful efforts to stop such policies, the tribal leaders maintained the coalition, believing it could help ensure a better life for their people today and for generations to come. Today, ATNI represents 54 Northwest tribal governments from Oregon, Idaho, Washington, Southeast Alaska, northern California, and western Montana.

ATNI, 222 NW Davis, Ste 403, Portland, OR 97209; (503)241-0070. Located in Old Town above Quintana's Gallery of Native American Art. Copies of the "Northwest Indian Travel Guide and Map" brochure are also available through the mail ($2; bulk quantities over 50, $0.25 each). Trip planning for groups available upon request.

Grand Ronde: *Grand Ronde*

Most tourists didn't give Grand Ronde, a little whistle-stop town on Highway 18 between Portland and the beaches of Lincoln City, a single thought—until the Spirit Mountain Casino complex was built right next to the road, announcing an Indian presence. Even fewer knew that Grand Ronde was the northern end of the Confederated Tribes' Trail of Tears, the 69,000-acre Coastal Reservation where almost all the Indians living in northwestern Oregon were forced to move. Among those who were marched to Grand Ronde through the inland valleys were the Chinooks, who lived along the lower Columbia River; Tillamooks, who came from the northern Oregon coast; the Santiam, Tualatin, and Yamhill; the Calapooia Indians, Luckiamute, Hanchuyuk, Chepanefo, Chelamela, Winnefilly, Mohawk, Tekopa, and southern Yoncalla people from the rivers in the mid–Willamette Valley; and Molalla bands who were driven from the western slopes of the Cascade Range. A few people also came from the Umpqua and Rogue River valley of southern Oregon. All of the tribes had been ravaged by smallpox, measles, and influenza epidemics and attacked by white vigilantes who called themselves "exterminators." As they moved onto the reservation, each group settled in its own area, each speaking its own language. Eventually all spoke Chinook jargon, the language used between fur trappers and Indian traders. Today, everyone on the Grand Ronde Reservation speaks English, and Chinook is the only Native language remaining.

Over time, the 69,000-acre reservation shrank to a mere fraction of its former size. As settlers took more of the land, boundaries established between the tribes also dissolved, and the Indian groups were united by a common reservation government, intermarriage, and participation in the Ghost Dance and Indian Shaker religion. They also worked together in the Willamette Valley's hop fields. By the late 1800s, most of the reservation's inhabitants had been converted to Catholicism, due to the efforts of Father Adrien Croquet. An unusually kind and well-loved missionary, Croquet came to Grand Ronde in 1860 and built a church and mission boarding school that was run by nuns for 35 years.

The Dawes Severalty Act reduced the tribes' land holdings drastically. After each head of household received 160 acres of land within the reservation, about 25,971 acres of "surplus" land was returned to the U.S. government. By the time the government terminated all its treaty agreements with the Grand Ronde tribes in the 1950s, only 597 acres were left in the reservation. The land was controlled by a trustee who was appointed by the government, and given the dictate to dispose of it. He sold it to private interests for $1.10 an acre. Each tribal member received $35.

Some of the tribes that had given up their land in the 1850s and moved to the Grand Ronde Reservation, such as the Tualatins, never received any compensation for their losses. When the federal government terminated its services to the reservation, there were few jobs. As a result many tribal members moved away. In 1970, tribally owned land and buildings consisted of 2.5 acres and a tool shed.

The Toolshed

If there were a shrine to perseverance, the toolshed on the Grand Ronde Reservation would be it. In 1974 the toolshed, sitting on 2½ acres, part of the cemetery grounds, became the headquarters from which an elected tribal council began to work for restoration of treaty rights. On November 22, 1983, one of the most important dates in Grand Ronde history, the federal Restoration Act gave the tribe recognition once again. Five years later the Grand Ronde Reservation Act gave the tribe 9,811 acres of public BLM-managed timberland in Yamhill County. Income from the timber was the seed money for the tribe. There was a price to pay, however. The tribes had to agree not to export timber or compete in the local timber market for 20 years, to set aside 30 percent of the money for economic development, and to give Yamhill and Tillamook Counties 20 years' worth of payments for tax and timber revenues lost from the land taken for the new reservation. Ironically, the land they received from Congress was some of the very land they had given up, without compensation, in the 1800s.

The tool shed is next to the tribal cemetery on Grand Ronde Road. New tribal headquarters are at 9615 Grand Ronde Rd, Grand Ronde, OR 97347; (503)879-5211.

Martha Jane Sands Bronze

As a child, Martha Jane Sands survived a massacre in the Rogue River valley by hiding in a beaver dam. She grew up on the Grand Ronde Reservation, married a white gold miner, raised a family, and carried on the tradition of the Rogue River basket weavers. She traded her handmade baskets throughout the Willamette Valley for food and clothing for her family. A revered elder, teacher, and guardian of tribal culture, she died in the early 1900s. Great-grandson Lon Mercier sketched Sands' picture from a photograph taken shortly before her death, and his portrait served as the basis for the bronze statue that now sits in the tribes' Spirit Mountain Casino foyer. True to Mercier's sketch, Martha Jane sits on the ground, barefoot, as she always liked to be. Her strong hands hold a nearly completed basket, made of hazelnut switches. Her granddaughter, Gertrude, sits at her feet, hazelnut switches clutched in her small hand, learning to weave. Hand-tinted prints of Mercier's rendering of Sands are available at Spirit Mountain Casino at Grand Ronde on Highway 18.

Shortly after the statue of Mary Jane Sands was installed in the casino foyer, people began to lay flowers at her feet and to tuck money around her skirts. The tribes decided to donate the money to local Head Start programs.

Spirit Mountain Casino, 27100 SW Salmon River Hwy (Hwy 18), Willamina, OR 97396; (503)879-2350. The casino is adjacent to Grand Ronde, between McMinneville and Lincoln City.

Nelson's Checkermallow

When Grand Ronde tribal members discovered that several specimens of a rare plant was growing on their building site, they transplanted them onto 2 acres of a tribally owned field and waited through the winter to make sure the plants would thrive. Nelson's Checkermallow (*Sidalcea Nelsoninia*) grows in the wet prairie in the Willamette Valley. The tall plant, with its small pink blossoms, lives 20 to 30 years and is a favorite of butterflies. The tribes hope to build a nature trail through the wet prairie ecosystem, near the South Fork of the Yamhill River. It would include plants the tribes used for medicine, basket making, and food, such as willow, hazelnut, and maidenhair fern.

Basket Weaving

Basketry and quilt making were primary industries for the Grand Ronde Tribe at the turn of the century. A few examples of baskets are behind glass cases at the Grand Ronde Tribal Center. Visitors can also see the trade beads Martha Jane Sands was wearing when she walked barefoot to the reservation in 1860, a mortar and pestle for grinding camas lily bulbs, and photographs of St. Michael's Church and its school.

Grand Ronde Tribal Center, 9615 Grand Ronde Road, Grand Ronde, OR 97347; (503)879-5211. Call first for permission to visit, and directions.

Spirit Mountain

Spirit Mountain Casino is the size of two city blocks, built in the round. The exterior brick is set in a basket-weave design similar to those woven at Grand Ronde a century ago. Proceeds from the casino will be used for education, housing, and medical services for tribal members. Spirit Mountain Casino gets its name from a hill, visible northeast of the intersection of Grand Ronde and Hebo Road. The hillside was used by tribal members for vision quests, which followed fasts and meditation. Spirit Mountain, owned by a timber company, is recognizable by the treeless area near the summit.

Siletz: *Siletz*

For many, the Oregon coast is a 350-mile-long public playground. Tillamook Bay, the sand dunes of Pacific City and Florence, the cliffs of Depoe Bay, and the big aquarium and bayfront of Newport are well known to most Oregonians. But for 10 years in the mid-1800s, the entire central Oregon coast was all Indian reservation—and as bleak a place as any internment camp.

The reservation's northern boundaries were at rugged Cape Lookout in present-day Tillamook County, its southern boundaries below present-day Florence—a stretch of more than 100 miles of scenic coastline. Beginning in 1856, Indians from all over western Oregon were marched at gunpoint to the Coast Reservation. The tribes' "Trail of Tears" is a tragic counterpoint to the famous emigrant Oregon Trail. Although it is rarely mentioned today, thousands of archived documents detail the removal of more than forty tribes from their homelands.

Few of the people arriving at the Coast Reservation spoke the same language. Many came from isolated river villages, where they had lived in small bands of 30 to 150 people. Those speaking the same language clustered together on the reservation and began the labor of trying to survive. Eventually they learned where to fish (the D River in Lincoln City was a favorite salmon-harvesting spot), where to gather shellfish, and where to find plants for food, medicines, and basket materials. They cleared land and built houses. In exchange for ceding their lands, the government provided tools and building materials as well as sugar, lard, coffee, and flour that arrived by ship in Yaquina Bay.

The tribes learned to speak to each other in sign language and Chinook jargon (the trader's language, composed of Northwest Indian languages, French, and English).

In 1865, the reservation was cut in half to make way for a railroad route to the coast. The middle of the Coast Reservation, which included 200,000 acres surrounding Yaquina Bay (present-day Newport), was opened to white settlement and speculation.

Ten years later all of the reservation was opened to white settlement, except for one 30-mile strip between Lincoln City and Newport, which came to be known as the Siletz Reservation. In the

In September 1995, 20 descendants of the Rogue River Tututni Tribes retraced the steps of their exiled great-grandparents. Carrying an eagle staff and stopping to pray at sites where relatives had died during the exodus, the 20 descendants ran more than 239 miles of coastal highway, from Siletz to their tribes' former homelands on the Rogue River.

1890s even this small part was "allotted." Each Indian family received a small plot of land. The rest was declared "surplus" and became public domain. In all, more than 1 million acres of premium land was taken from the reservation.

In the 1950s, the Confederated Tribes of Siletz Indians were struck another blow when they were officially terminated by the federal government. The Siletz tribal government was formally disbanded but continued to meet anyway, without federal recognition or support. Their remaining few acres were sold. The tide turned, finally, in 1977: after years of lobbying and legal battles, the U.S. Congress once again recognized the Siletz. In 1980, legislation was passed that returned some scattered parcels of land, about 3,600 acres. To get the reservation bill passed, the Siletz had to agree to give up hunting, fishing, and gathering rights guaranteed by their first treaty with the U.S. government.

The Siletz Reservation today consists of 3,900 acres of mountainous forestland, 230 acres surrounding the Rock Creek Fish Hatchery, and 36 acres in the town of Siletz. Siletz is between the coastal towns of Lincoln City and Newport, 24 miles up the Siletz River, on Highway 229. The area of town called Government Hill was the site of the original Indian agency, boarding school, and cannery. Depot Slough, where provisions were unloaded from the ships docking in Yaquina Bay, is near the town of Siletz.

In 1990 the Siletz Tribe's economic development group bought property at Lincoln City to build a convention center and a casino, to raise money for tribal housing, health programs, and environmental rehabilitation of the Siletz River and watershed. Ironically, the price they paid for just 10 acres of beachfront property was more than twice what they received for the loss of more than a million acres of the Coast Reservation.

Siletz Culture and History

It's difficult to interpret Native history from what you see in busy Lincoln County and along the Siletz River, but it's possible to cobble together some bits and pieces. Take Highway 101, 4 miles south of Lincoln City, to Highway 229 and drive the winding road along the Siletz River. Between clearcuts are long stretches of alder and maple, and turnouts overlooking the river.

At Siletz, visit the Siletz Tribal Cultural Center on Government Hill. Before shelter was built for the hundreds of Indians arriving at the Siletz Reservation, the military raised administration buildings, a school, and a blockhouse on Government Hill. Now a deeply shaded park with carefully tended lawns, the 36-acre site contains a cemetery and veterans' memorial, a handsome cultural and community center, and powwow grounds. In 1994 more than 30,000 people attended the annual Nesika Illahee Powwow, held every second weekend in August for three days.

Siletz Tribal Cultural Center; (800)922-1399 or (503)444-4294. From Siletz take Logsden Rd to the marked road and follow that to the top of Government Hill. Free.

Ceremonial Dance House

A cultural revival is under way for the Siletz, who are maintaining the language, dances, and ceremonial regalia of their ancestors. In honor of their past, the tribe has completed a traditional dance house in a grove of trees, the first structure of its kind on the Siletz Reservation since the 1870s. A pitched roof, supported by the round trunks of large fir and cedar trees, shelters the earthen dance floor and central fire pit.

The Ceremonial Dance House is open to the public only by prearranged tour. Contact Selene Rilatos at the Siletz Tribal Cultural Center, (800)922-1399 or (503)444-4294.

Eel Study

The population of lamprey eels, once thick in the Siletz River, has declined drastically in the last few years. An ongoing study was initiated, with funding from Oregon State University's Native Americans in Marine Science program, and continues under a grant from the U.S. Forest Service. The tribe has published an eel study handbook that documents the tribe's use of eel as a traditional food. The current study focuses on documenting the life cycle, ideal habitat, and decline of the eels. Fishermen and others using the river help by reporting sightings of lamprey eels to the tribe.

Anyone wanting to assist in the eel study is welcome. Contact the Siletz Tribe's Department of Natural Resources; (800)922-1399.

Kayaking the Siletz River

The Siletz Valley is almost completely surrounded by the river. Inner-tubers, kayakers, and canoers can put in at Hehe Illahee Park (it means "happy place" in Chinook jargon), and float the loop to the boat ramp at the old mill site. Boaters can pull out and walk only four or five blocks back to the parking lot at Hehe Illahee, but it's a daylong float on an inner tube, a bit faster with a paddle. (Be prepared for a fast ride in early spring or to portage over exposed riverbed during summer's low water.) Farther downriver, some of the best canoeing and non-whitewater kayaking on the coast is found between Morgan Park (milepost 18) and Strom Park (between mileposts 13 and 14) on Highway 229, between the mouth of the Siletz River and the town of Siletz.

If you need clearer directions for the Siletz River loop, contact the Siletz Tribe's Department of Natural Resources, in the tribal administration building behind Hehe Illahee Park: 201 SE Swan St, PO Box 549, Siletz, OR 97380; (800)922-1399. Hehe Illahee Park, Morgan, and Strom Parks, all on Hwy 229, have parking lots and paved boat ramps. Free.

Siletz Tribal Smokehouse

The land where the Siletz Tribal Smokehouse store sits, on the south side of the famous arched Depoe Bay bridge on Highway 101, was allotted to "Depot Charlie," a worker at the army depot at Yaquina Bay. His family eventually changed their last name to DePoe. Sunset Investment Company bought his land in 1927, platted a town site, and named it after Charles—Depoe Bay. The "t" was changed to an "e" by the U.S. Post Office.

The Smokehouse is both a gift shop and an outlet for the tribe's smoked salmon, albacore tuna, and sturgeon. First soaked in brine then alder-smoked, the fish has a firm texture and a rich smoky taste. Buy it fresh from the cold case (smoked oysters and fresh-cooked Dungeness crab on ice too, in season), along with cold-smoked lox and smoked beef jerky. The smokehouse will vacuum-pack and freeze selections on the premises and ship them to your home.

You can buy smoked salmon in attractive red boxes, as well as salmon pâté (made of smoked salmon, cream cheese, and herbs) in tins—neither require refrigeration until after they're opened. The smokehouse will also make up custom gift packages of Blue Earth gourmet jellies, cranberries, smoked Tillamook cheese, and their own smoked products in fragrant pine boxes and ship them for you. No preservatives or colorings are added.

Look here also for Native American gifts, Ken Hatch's Northwest Coast–style hand-carved seals and whales, T-shirts, and free tide tables.

Siletz Tribal Smokehouse, 272 SE Coast Hwy, PO Box 1004, Depoe Bay, OR 97341; (541)765-2286. Depoe Bay is between Lincoln City and Newport on Hwy 101. Open daily, year-round.

Depot Slough Historical Site

You can see the remains of Depot Slough at the junction of Highway 20 (from Corvallis to Newport) and Highway 229. Follow the marsh of cattails about a mile north along Highway 229 to the Lincoln County interpretive sign that marks the slough landing site. Provisions for the Coast Reservation were unloaded from ships at Yaquina Bay and portaged through Depot Slough, then taken by horse and wagon to the raft/ferry that crossed the Siletz River. Although most of the slough has been filled, Highway 229 generally follows the original supply route.

Log Cabin Museum

One room of Lincoln County's log cabin museum in Newport is dedicated to the Siletz Reservation, although the collection is small. Why so little art and regalia? There was a long period in federal Indian policy during which traditional ceremonial dances and religious practices were forcefully discouraged, except for approved "exhibitions." The collection includes prime examples of period exhibition dance regalia—made with turkey feathers and dime-store materials because of difficulty in obtaining traditional materials near the turn of the century. Look here for a few pictures of Fourth of July parades through Newport, as well as fascinating early pictures of the Siletz school and one of the area's first stores, built on Government Hill. The museum library, in the Victorian house next door, contains early photographs and newspaper clippings, and the gift shop sells a book by Leone Kasner that describes how basket weavers "carried the culture" from ancestral lands to Siletz during the relocation.

Log Cabin Museum, 579 SW 9th, Newport, OR 97365; (541)265-7509. Call for hours. Free.

Nesika Illahee Powwow

Be part of the "Circle of Friendship" at the Siletz's annual powwow, held the second weekend in August on Government Hill in Siletz. Activities include crowning royalty, competition dancing all three days, and a salmon feast on Sunday afternoon. Arts and crafts and food booths too.

Shuttle buses run to the Nesika Illahee Powwow from the bottom of Government Hill in Siletz every 15 minutes. For information, contact the Siletz Tribal Cultural Center, (800)922-1399. Free.

Coos Bay: *Coos, Lower Umpqua, & Siuslaw*

Coos Bay is home to the Coos Indians. Located on a broad shallow bay, estuary, and salt marsh, their land is carved by sloughs and is rich with clams, fish, and nutritious sea plants. Surrounded by rounded hills and dunes on its north shore, the bay is protected from open seas by rocky Cape Arago, the southern promontory at its mouth. Today, the whole cape is state parkland: Cape Arago, Shore Acres, and Sunset Bay State Parks form a network of trails along the dramatic southern shore of Coos Bay. The high forested cliffs, carved with small crescent beaches, offered the Coos Indians village sites safety from canoe raids. One of those sites, Baldya'ka, on the cliff above Sunset Bay, is the proposed location of an interpretive center for the Coos Indians.

The Coos Tribe consists of three groups who once lived on more than 100 miles of the central Oregon coast, between present-day Waldport and Coos Bay. The Siuslaw and Umpqua, who lived on three major rivers north of Coos Bay, about 25 miles apart, are part of the present-day Coos Tribe. Like other southern Oregon tribes, they had the misfortune of living in an area coveted by mining companies. In 1853 the Coos Bay Commercial Company, a joint stock company, was formed in the Rogue River valley expressly to explore, stake mining claims, and settle Coos Bay. In just two years, miners had extracted more than $1.9 million in coal and gold from the Coos Bay area.

Three years after the miners arrived, peaceful Coos Indians were forced from their villages at Coos Bay and from along the nearby Umpqua, Siuslaw, and Alsea Rivers. Under armed guard, nearly 700 people marched to Fort Umpqua, on the sand spit on the north side of the mouth of the Umpqua River. In November, as the weather turned from Indian summer to winter squalls, the new superintendent of Indian affairs cut off the refugees' food rations. He claimed no treaties had been signed, and if they had, he said, he didn't know about them.

In 1859, about 400 remaining Coos and Lower Umpqua Indians were moved from Fort Umpqua to Yachats Prairie on the north side of Cape Perpetua. Today the area is a popular coastal town with soaring property values, but in 1859 the Indian refugees subsisted there on shellfish torn from the rocks at low tide. Most of the land they were supposed to farm at Yachats was sand or timber-covered slopes. In their first five years at Yachats, more than half the Coos Indians died from exposure and starvation. Conditions were so terrible that Indians periodically fled to their old homes in Coos Bay, only to be rounded up by the U.S. Army and returned.

Over the next 16 years, the land at Yachats was laboriously cleared and fenced. Indians erected barns and homes. But in 1875, Congress closed the whole southern part of the reservation, including Yachats and Siuslaw (present-day Florence), and threw all the land open for settlement. Thus, the Coos Indians came home to Coos Bay. Many intermarried with whites. Some worked as wood choppers or domestic laborers for room and board; some found seasonal work during the cranberry harvest.

It wasn't until 1984 that the Confederated Tribes of Coos, Lower Umpqua, and Siuslaw Indians were finally recognized by the U.S. Congress. Their recognition was based on a treaty they had signed at Empire in 1855, which the government had first denied, then ignored. Today, the tribe owns less than 20 acres in the former city of Empire, a strip of marginal businesses between the town of Coos Bay and the cape.

The Coos tribal office is in downtown Coos Bay, the largest city on the southern Oregon coast. Feel welcome to stop at the tribal hall, built on the few acres owned by the Coos Tribe, and at the tribal office in Coos Bay, where you can buy a videotape about the tribe and purchase their Blue Earth gourmet foods.

Coos Tribal Hall

Although it was built in 1941, the little Coos Tribal Hall holds more history than many buildings three times its size. Not much larger than a cottage, it was built for the tribe by the Bureau of Indian Affairs on 6 acres of land donated to the Coos in 1940 by the Empire Development Company. The tribe has added a few acres of land to the property, recently restored the shingled, cottage-style building, and built another small structure next door to house health care services for tribal members. The tribal hall has a small exhibit of Coos history. You are welcome to visit, but call first.

Coos Tribal Hall, 338 Wallace, Coos Bay, OR 97420; (541)888-3536.

Blue Earth Gourmet Foods

The name Blue Earth comes from a lengthy Coos creation legend that begins when two young "traveling men" drop five blue disks in the water that covers the world, and create land. At the end of their creation of birds, animals, and humans, both men shoot arrows into the sky. The arrows interlock and the men climb them like a ladder to the skies, stop to admire the beautiful world they have created below, and then disappear. TgE'En, blue earth, can still be seen under the sea.

Two of the young men's creations—vine blackberries, which grow wild in the clearcuts of Coos Bay, and cranberries, which are farmed in the wet peat bogs inland—are the basis for the Coos Tribe's Blue Earth gourmet food products. The tribe teamed up with a licensed gourmet and developed a tangy blackberry chipotle chili-pepper sauce, sweet blackberry syrup, wild blackberry/honey spread, brandied cranberry sauce, dried cranberry and wild rice stuffing, blue cornmeal pancake and waffle mix, and Indian fry bread mix.

You can order the products separately or in attractive gift boxes. Order them by phone (pancake mix and blackberry syrup nestled in a handsome wooden crate are $11.95), or buy them at selected retail outlets in the Coos Bay area.

Two outlets that carry Blue Earth foods are Klahowya, a Native American gift shop on Highway 101 in North Bend; (541)756-5958; or the House of Myrtle-wood, at 1125 S 1st, Coos Bay; (541)267-7804.

Blue Earth Gourmet Foods, Confederated Tribes of Coos, Lower Umpqua and Siuslaw Indians, 455 S 4th, Coos Bay, OR 97420. For a retail order form, call (541)267-5454.

Shoot an Arrow into the Air

Recordings of songs, oral literature, and language and basketry, clothing, and hundreds of pages of manuscript notes collected by anthropologists and linguists are stashed in archives and museums thousands of miles away from Coos Bay. The "Captured Heritage" project, which seeks to find data and copy it onto microfilm and tape, has been ongoing since 1990. An excellent 28-minute video of the Coos, Lower Umpqua, and Siuslaw peoples' history, *Shoot an Arrow into the Air*, was produced in 1995 as a result of cultural resource coordinator Don Whereat's search for historical documents. His daughter, Patty, is working with her father to put the tribe's complex language on CD-ROM.

In the 1850s Oregon's coastal Indians had an estimated 10,000 tales— all committed to memory. Etiquette dictated that when a person spoke, the listener tried to repeat verbatim what was said. Working with their elders, children learned to repeat every tale they were told.

Order the videotape from the Coos Tribe, 455 S 4th, Coos Bay, OR 97420; (541)267-5454. $25, including handling and shipping.

Baldya'ka on Cape Arago

A U.S. Coast Guard station and lighthouse stand today on an old Coos village site, Baldya'ka (pronounced *bald-yakka*). The site, high on a bluff, overlooks the Sunset Beach State Park and the Pacific Ocean, west of the town of Coos Bay. Baldya'ka, like many Coos villages, was built high above the sea for fortification from canoe raids for slaves. The Baldya'ka site is not open to the public.

Below the village site is a cliff-sheltered crescent beach (present-day Sunset Beach State Park), which was probably used for fish dry-ing, food preparation, and as a put-in for canoes. Offshore is Chief's Island, where a lookout watched for raiders, and Squaw Island, with 40-foot-high sheer rock walls, where women and children fled dur-ing raids. Explorer Jedediah Smith reported seeing the village in his 1828 journals. Squaw Island, now with a steep trail to the top, is ac-cessible at low tide from Sunset Beach State Park.

Follow the signs to ocean beaches and Charleston from Hwy 101 to the three state parks on Cape Arago (campgrounds, hiking, beaches, overlooks). Sunset Beach State Park is the first park you'll come to. The tribe is trying to raise $15 million for an inter-pretive center and reconstructed village site at Baldya'ka, in cooperation with state agencies and the Coast Guard. Tax-deductible donations are gratefully accepted. Contact the tribe at 455 S 4th, Coos Bay, OR 97420; (541)267-5454.

South Slough National Estuarine Research Reserve

Once home to the Coos Indians, who lived along its shores, South Slough is one of the few estuaries in the Northwest still in its wild and natural state. Follow a 3-mile trail along Hidden Creek to the salt marsh and tide flats, take a short hike along Wasson Creek, or launch kayaks and canoes into the long fingers of Coos Bay. The reserve's interpretive center contains several exhibits about estuarine ecology and the flora and fauna of South Slough. Summer workshops include explorations on the mud flats, wild edibles, and bird-watching.

South Slough National Estuarine Research Reserve, PO Box 5417, Charleston, OR 97420; (541)888-5558. South Slough is located 4 miles south of Charleston (west of the town of Coos Bay) on Seven Devils Road. Open summers, daily; weekdays only, Sept–May. Free admission. Call for a summer schedule of classes.

Hunting Lodge, Florence

A *hitsi,* or hunting shelter, stands near its original site on Heceta Head, the Siuslaw Tribe's former hunting grounds. It was recon-structed a few years ago by Florence Boy Scout Troop 777 with the guidance of the Coos Tribe. Surrounded by a split-rail fence, the pit-style shelter, built into the side of a bank and barely large enough for two people, was one of many in the coast range providing shelter for hunters from high winds and rain.

The hunting lodge is 8 miles north of Florence on Hwy 101. To reach the trailhead, follow Herman Peak Road up the hill on the north side of C&M Stables. (About a mile from the south side of Heceta Head to the Coast Horse Trail.) Ride your horse or hike to the site, between miles 11 and 12 on the 18-mile trail along the ridge. There's a hitching post for horses at the site.

Historical Riverboat Rides, Florence

A bit of Siuslaw Indian history is narrated on board a sternwheeler that travels up the Siuslaw River from the "old town" dock at Florence, about 30 miles north of Coos Bay. The small Siuslaw Tribe was one of the few coastal tribes in Oregon allowed to remain on their original village sites along the Siuslaw River. Descendants are the source of some of the information shared with passengers during the 6-mile journey upstream. The boat, a 65-foot, double-deck replica of the sternwheelers plying the Columbia River at the turn of the century, goes through the estuary, past old homesteads, cannery sites, railroad bridges, and other points of interest, including an old Siuslaw fish weir on the North Fork.

Westward Ho! PO Box 3023, Florence, OR 97439; (541)997-9691. Located at Florence's "old town" dock. Historical tours (1½ hours) begin at 11am daily (except Tues and Sun), May–Oct. Off-season schedule is 1pm, Sat only.

Bandon: *Coquille*

The small town of Bandon, Oregon, boasts gigantic haystack rocks offshore, as well as a picturesque white lighthouse perched on the north jetty at the mouth of the Coquille River. No wonder it's a favorite destination for tourists, who also visit its cheese factory on the highway and the cranberry-candy factory in the old part of town near the river.

Few visitors, however, realize that Bandon and the shoreline on both sides of the lower river were once home to the (Gwuh-see-ya) bands of Miluk-speaking Indians, also known as the Lower Coquille Indians. Athabascan-speaking bands also occupied the Coquille River upstream, near what are now the towns of Coquille and Myrtle Point. More than 300 Native sites in the area have been documented—from rock shelters and petroglyphs to burial grounds and villages. On the south side of the Coquille River at Bandon, on the site of the present-day green-shuttered Coast Guard station, was the village called Na-Cu-Ce-Tun. About half a mile away, at the mouth of the river, stood a massive haystack rock the Na–Cu–Ce–Tun people called Grandmother.

In 1851, the Na–Cu–Ce–Tun village was shelled by the U.S. Army in retaliation for an attack on white surveyors. The villagers rebuilt their cedar plank houses and moved back in. But on the night of January 28, 1854, in an unprovoked attack, 40 gold miners surrounded the village, and began firing into the villagers' houses, gunning down those who resisted or tried to escape. Then they burned the village to the ground. (One of the leaders of the massacre was William Packwood, a great-grandsire of Oregon's former senator, Bob Packwood.)

The adjoining bands of Coquilles were eventually forced from their homes and removed to a temporary reservation at Port Orford, south of Bandon, along with Indians from the Rogue, Chetco, Pistol, and Sixes Rivers in southern Oregon. By this time, more than half of the Coquilles had been murdered or had died of disease. In 1856, the remaining Natives in the area were forced to abandon their villages and move to the Coast Reservation. In 1903, the Army Corps of Engineers dynamited the Grandmother Rock to build the two jetties that today enclose the river.

More than 140 years after the Coquilles moved to the Siletz Reservation, the U.S. government recognized them as a separate tribe. Soon afterward, in 1990, the Port of Bandon returned about 1¼ acres of the site where the Grandmother Rock used to guard the river. In 1993, the tribe built Heritage Place on the site. This three-story, assisted-living residential facility, with views of the ocean, the lighthouse, and the river, is open to grandparents of all races, and is home to several Coquille grandmothers and grandfathers. You are welcome to visit.

Heritage Place, 1000 6th Ave W, Bandon, OR 97411; (541)347-7502.

The Grandmother Rock

Many people have taken a seat on one of the big rocks on the Coquille River jetty to fish or just watch the ocean waves crash on the beach. But few know that the rock they sit on, colored an unusual serpentine green laced with white crystal, is fairly uncommon in the world. According to geologists studying the West Coast subduction zone, the Grandmother Rock was created by extremely high compression far under the earth's surface. The rock then rose and broke through the earth's crust before it could be transformed further by the heat. The Coquille River jetties, made of the fractured remains of the Grandmother Rock, are one of the largest collections of blue schist anywhere in the world. After the Grandmother was blasted apart by dynamite, according to one version of a local story, "an Indian man came down out of the forest and warned the mayor that Bandon would burn three times for what it had done." To date, the city has burned twice—once in 1916, and again in 1936, when more than 480 buildings went up in flames.

Coquille Economic Development

Coquille tribal member Bruce Anderson grew up in Coos Bay, Oregon, while his mother, a schoolteacher, struggled for years to restore government recognition of the Coquille Tribe. Anderson played football for Willamette University, then played NFL football for the Rams, Giants, and Redskins for six years. Later, he became a Wall Street stockbroker, and owned his own plastics company. When the tribe was restored, the Coquilles called Anderson out of retirement to return home and help lead them to prosperity. As president of the tribe's Economic Development Corporation, and with the assistance of financial partners with deep pockets, Anderson helped build the Mill Bay Casino on the North Bend waterfront, 100 units of new housing, and a 400-acre industrial park. He also dug the first 500 acres of a cranberry farm and is negotiating with the Bureau of Land Management to obtain 59,000 acres of forestland to provide timber for area mills, making the tribe self-sufficient and the second largest employer in Coos County.

Coquille Tribe, PO Box 1435, Coos Bay, OR 97420; (541)267-4587.

Canyonville: *Cow Creek*

The North and South Umpqua Rivers, which flow toward the ocean from the foothills of Mount Mazama, are two of the most beautiful rivers in Oregon. In the upper reaches they pool around big boulders and rush through narrow canyons. In the spring, the wildflowers in the meadows and along the banks of the Umpqua are so plentiful that nearby Glide, Oregon, has held a wildflower festival every April for the past 25 years to show off nature's bounty.

Five Indian groups made their homes along both the North and South Umpqua. One of those, the Cow Creek Band, has built new tribal facilities at Canyonville, which is located just off Interstate 5 south of Roseburg, where two creeks enter the South Umpqua River. In 1996 the Cow Creek Band plans to open a four-story hotel next to their casino in Canyonville.

The Past

The Cow Creeks once built permanent winter camps along rivers and creeks, to make use of the abundant resources. From along the Rogue River and Umpqua Divide, they would gather huckleberries; at South Umpqua Falls (where the tribe still holds its annual pow-wow), they fished for salmon and hunted in the surrounding forests. Trees in the Jackson Creek watershed were prized for their medicinal value. In the spring, when camas carpeted the fields with blue flowers, the people dug the bulbs from the ground, using a stick made of Indian arrowwood with a point as hard as steel. They also gathered tarweed seeds, hazelnuts, wild onions, acorns, mushrooms, and vitamin-rich lambs-quarters. Yerba buena leaves were used fresh or dried to make tea, which is still a favorite today. Fish weirs were made from hazelnut sticks, and one of the Natives' only musical instruments, a fife, was made from the dry stalks of wild parsnip.

During the early 19th century, the Cow Creek territory was an important rendezvous site for fur traders. Many of the French traders married into the tribe, and tribal names such as DuMont, LaChance, Rainville, Pariseau, Rondeau, and Thomason clearly stem from that time. In the 1840s, an influx of white settlers swept into southern Oregon via the Applegate Trail. Beginning near the Shoshone-Bannocks' land in eastern Idaho, the trail crossed the mountains between Crater Lake and Mount Shasta, turned north toward the Willamette Valley, and finally ended at Jason Lee's mission near present-day Salem, Oregon. Following Indian trails that parallel today's Interstate 5, the Applegate passed right through the heart of Cow Creek territory.

When gold was discovered on Jackson Creek in southern Oregon, hundreds of miners moved up from the goldfields of California and filed claims on streams and riverbanks. Hydraulic mining muddied the rivers with mining debris, destroying salmon runs. Farmers homesteaded camas meadows, blocking the Cow Creek from their most important source of food. Epidemics ravaged the tribe.

The treaty that the Cow Creeks eventually signed was a sad mockery. It was negotiated in one day with people who did not speak the English language and who did not understand the concept of land ownership. The Cow Creeks were reimbursed 2.3 cents an acre for their 800 square miles of land at a time when Donation Land Claim buyers were paying the government $1.25 an acre for the same land. Later, the Cow Creeks joined the Rogue River Indians in the Rogue River Indian Wars. When Indians were rounded up and marched to the Coast Reservation, many hid in the hills, only to be hunted down by contractors hired by the Bureau of Indian Affairs (a division of the

War Department). Present-day tribal members are descendants of those who successfully hid from the contractors.

The U.S. government ignored its treaty with the Cow Creek Tribe until 1956, at which point it officially terminated the tribe without the members' knowledge or consent. After successfully presenting its case to Congress in 1980, the tribe negotiated a settlement of $1.5 million for its remaining 700 enrolled members. The tribe invested the entire $1.5 millon in an endowment, from which they have drawn annually only the earned interest. They bought 50 acres at Canyonville, their only land holdings. All the tribe's earnings have been spent on economic development.

Pioneer-Indian Museum

In 1969, a group of Cow Creek tribal members joined pioneer descendants and founded the South Umpqua Historical Society to establish a pioneer-Indian museum in Canyonville. The little museum is on the original Applegate Trail. Cow Creek legends and recovered artifacts establish the tribal existence before the eruption of Mount Mazama, which formed Crater Lake.

Pioneer-Indian Museum, 421 W 5th St, Canyonville, OR 97417; (541)839-4845. Open Thurs–Sun afternoons, year-round. Free.

Tours

In conjunction with the South Umpqua Historical Society and the Tiller Ranger District, the Cow Creek Tribe has developed a tour brochure and map for the Canyonville area, one of the oldest settlements in Oregon. In the summer of 1996, for the celebration of the sesquicentennial of the Applegate Trail, a tour route will extend up the South Umpqua River to Crater Lake.

Tourist information and a walking tour map of Canyonville is at a kiosk at the foot of 5th St on the south end of Pioneer Park in Canyonville. For more information about tours, contact the Cow Creek Tribal Office, 2400 Stewart Pkwy, Roseburg, OR 97470; (541)672-9405.

Klamath: *Klamath*

From the broken rim of southern Oregon's Mount Mazama, 7,100 feet above sea level, there are two views. One is of ultramarine blue Crater Lake, 1,000 feet below the rim, created by a series of violent volcanic explosions. The other is of the valley floor, the Klamath basin, a lovely mosaic of soft greens, yellows, and blues. The basin, once part of a huge Pleistocene lake that covered most of southeastern Oregon, is now reduced to marshes and shallow lakes spreading across the arid land for nearly 100 miles.

Though it seems at first glance devoid of history, the basin holds many surprises for travelers: not only were 9,000-year-old sandals discovered at Fort Rock, and stories of the Modoc War well documented at Lava Beds National Monument but contemporary Klamaths can take you into the marsh and explain how their people lived so well for so long in the harsh climate of southeastern Oregon.

Highway 97 weaves through the ancient lava flows that cover most of central Oregon. In the north, the highway skims John Day Fossil Beds National Monument. In central Oregon it slices through a section of Newberry National Volcanic Monument, the major source of obsidian used for arrowheads and knife blades by Indians all over North America. In the south, in the shadow of Mount Mazama, it threads its way between extensive marshes and lakes, the ancestral home of the Klamath and Modoc Indians.

Just over the California border, Highway 97 enters Lava Beds National Monument, home of the Modoc and site of the Modoc War with the U.S. cavalry in 1870. Both the Modoc and Klamath were witnesses to Mount Mazama's explosive volcanic eruption 6,800 years ago. Both the explosion and the gradual renewal of the basin after the cataclysmic event are chronicled in their legends.

The Klamaths' aboriginal lands are the birthplace of three rivers—the Williamson, the Wood, and the Sprague—and an abundance of sweet, freshwater springs that feed the marshes. These were once the source of all food and shelter for the Klamaths on the north end, the Yahooskans in the east, and the Modocs in the south. Today the Klamaths, Modocs, and Yahooskins, who were moved together onto the huge Klamath Reservation near the northern marsh and Klamath Lake, are landless. Terminated by the federal government in the 1950s, many moved to the cities. A core of people remain on their aboriginal lands, with a tribal office just south of Chiloquin.

Chiloquin

The little town of Chiloquin, at the junction of the Sprague and Williamson Rivers, was until the 1850s, Mbusaksuwas (means "good flint-making place"), one of the largest permanent Klamath villages in the area. People lived here in round lodges with insulating woven tule-mat flooring. Few household items from that time remain in the area. The largest collection of Klamath utensils, baskets, fishhooks, weirs, nets, bows, arrows, and other necessities are held in the archives of Chicago's Field Museum. Even though Chiloquin was in the center of the Klamath Indian Reservation, during the reservation era about half the town was occupied by white settlers.

Both Natives and non-Natives live in Chiloquin today. Klamath guides can take you to sites along the river where their great-grandfathers fished, to natural stream crossings, to old trails, to other village sites along the Williamson and Sprague Rivers, and to Cave Mountain, the Klamaths' creation site.

Contact the Klamath Tribe, PO Box 436, Chiloquin, OR 97624; (541)783-2095, in advance of your visit to make arrangements.

Klamath Lands

Termination of the Klamath Tribe began during a 1945 Lake County Chamber of Commerce meeting with a motion made by Eugene Favell. But congressional legislation to liquidate the tribe's land holdings by condemning them was orchestrated by Secretary of the Interior Douglas McKay, a former car dealer and former governor of Oregon. He appointed three friends to oversee the legislation in 1955. Other "management specialists" appointed by McKay were Lake and Klamath County real estate developers. Lake County, one of the poorest counties in the state, was blocked in 1995 by federal court from acquiring former reservation lands now in Fremont National Forest.

Picking Wocus

Lynn J. Schonchin, great-grandson of Modoc leader Captain Jack, his graying hair tied back in a neat ponytail, jumps onto a solid spot on the marsh's edge, leans over the water, and plucks a green seed pod about the size of a large fig. It is the fruit of the lily pad the Klamaths call *wocus*. He slits open the fruit and squeezes out hundreds of plump seeds, the same color as the lily's butter-yellow bloom. When the seeds ripen to a soft gray, they are ready to harvest. Sun-dried, roasted, and ground like wheat, the seeds make a highly nutritional cereal that can be stored through several winters. Boiled, it's similar to bran; dried, it's crunchy like Grape Nuts cereal, delicious with dried or fresh wild plums.

The tribal archives include 225 legends recorded on computer disks, a plant gathering manual, and a Klamath and Yahooskin phrase book.

Heritage and Cultural Tours of the Klamath

Klamath guides can show you Crater Lake, Fort Rock, Klamath Marsh National Wildlife Refuge, and Cave Mountain at Chiloquin. You can also see the Victorian-style Indian agency buildings on the northern end of Klamath Lake (now privately owned), the Council Grove in the Wood River valley where the Klamaths' treaty with the U.S. government was signed in 1864, and Fort Klamath. Tours can also include the fishing, gathering, and village sites on the marsh and lake, and the Klamath's hatchery on the Sprague River. You can also ask for someone to accompany you to Modoc Captain Jack's lava fortress—a maze of caves, clefts, and gullies in a lava flow, and the site of the 1870 Modoc War.

To arrange a tour contact the Klamath Tribe, Hwy 97, south of Chiloquin, PO Box 436, Chiloquin OR 97624; (541)783-2095.

Klamath Lake and Marsh

The Klamath Basin, comprising a network of more than 100 miles of springs, rivers, lakes, marshes, and wetlands, covers land from southeastern Oregon into northern California, from the valley east of Crater Lake all the way to the lava beds northeast of California's Mount Shasta.

Little dolls woven of tule reeds, a species of bulrush, were not toys, but were given to each girl child by her grandmother. The child kept the doll, which carried the wisdom of the household, throughout her life until she herself was a grandmother and passed "Grandma's wisdom doll" down to her own granddaughter.

—Klamath Gordon Bettles, Cultural Heritage Specialist

Birders come from all over the world to see the spectacular waterfowl migrations in the spring and fall, when thousands of ducks and geese converge on the Tule Lake marsh, Klamath Lake, and Klamath Marsh. Twenty-four species of hawks, owls, and falcons live here year-round. The largest concentration of bald eagles in the Lower 48 also winters here.

Most of Tule Lake and Lower Klamath Lake, below the town of Klamath Falls, was drained in the early 1900s. Upper Klamath Lake, the big lake visible from Highway 97, which nearly fills the valley between the towns of Chiloquin and Klamath Falls, is only 4 to 12 feet deep.

North of Chiloquin, the Klamath Forest National Wildlife Refuge on the Klamath Marsh is bisected by a paved road. About half the marsh is diked for grazing land; the other half has been restored in the last four years. Listen for the throaty call of red- and yellow-winged blackbirds and look here for raptors (especially rough-legged hawks), great blue herons, and cinnamon teals. Great horned owls perch on road-side markers at night. On the east side of Klamath Marsh, in a stand of oak and ponderosa pines, is another of the Klamaths' old village sites. There's no sign of the village now, but you can walk along a forest service road that ends 5 miles south at Wocus Bay and imagine what it might have been like. The area is visited regularly by Native people whose families once lived here.

Hwy 97 follows the Klamath basin from one end to the other. To cross Klamath Marsh, take Silver Lake Road north of Chiloquin off Hwy 97 and head east. Three roads, including Hwy 97 and Hwy 140, loop around Klamath Lake. For detailed maps and an excellent guide to the basin's wildlife, look for A Birder's Guide to the Klamath Basin, published by the Klamath Basin Audubon Society, for sale in the tribe's Natural Resources Department, 116 E Chocktoot St, PO Box 436, Chiloquin, OR, 97624; (541)783-2095.

To catch ducks at night, fires were built in stone basins on the stern of the canoe. The birds, attracted by the light, fluttered into the air, flew toward the fire, and got tangled in up-raised nets made of nettle fibers.

Fort Rock

According to their legends, the Klamath people found refuge in the caves of Fort Rock when Mount Mazama exploded 6,800 years ago. It's possible that they were able to travel to the rock shelter by canoe, since the marsh system, the vestiges of what was once a huge Pleistocene lake, probably extended all the way from Klamath Lake to Fort Rock, about 45 miles north. Certainly the Klamaths used Fort Rock as shelter; woven sandals found in a Fort Rock cave were carbon-dated as being 9,000 years old. Archaeologists have been excavating the caves since 1938, when more than 40 sandals were discovered, and have recently excavated the old marsh bottom, finding even more evidence of occupation that dates back at least 13,000 years. The Klamaths' sacred mountain, 8,196-foot Yamsey, is between Mount Mazama and Fort Rock.

Fort Rock is a good spot for a picnic on the long drive south; a mom-and-pop grocery store is nearby, as is a small pioneer museum.

To reach Fort Rock, travel south on Hwy 97 from Bend, and then take Hwy 31 east at La Pine. On Hwy 97, from Klamath Marsh, take the Silver Lake Hwy east through the middle of Klamath Marsh, past Yamsey Mountain.

The Klamaths and Modocs designed a mud-shoe for walking in the soft marshes. It was made of willow and round like a snowshoe. Their canoe poles were split at the bottom, to hook plant stems and pull the boats canoes through shallow waters.

Traditional Bows and Arrows

Tribal member Ivan Jackson has researched Modoc culture for more than 14 years. Based on this knowledge, he uses juniper, yew, chokecherry, wild rose, and serviceberry woods collected near the marshes to make traditional Modoc arrows and bows. Such arrows are rated by collectors as some of the strongest and truest in the world. Arrow tips are made of carved mountain mahogany (also called ironwood), and both arrows and bows are painted with red ocher, yellow, and green pigments obtained from the lake bed.

For more information, contact Ivan Jackson at (541)356-2197.

Native Fish Hatchery

Since 1988, the Klamath Tribe has funded scientific research on two endangered species of mullet: the Lost River sucker and shortnose sucker. For the first two years, fisheries biologists learned how to raise the delicate fish in a hatchery environment; now the focus is on genetics, larvae predation, vegetation, chemistry, and water-level studies as a baseline for understanding the ecology of Klamath Lake. No fish are released from this hatchery. "There's no reason to," says one biologist, "until we find out what is killing them in the river and lake." The tribe has given staff biologists free rein to investigate the problem—all studies are subject to unbiased peer review by out-of-state scientists. The facility is near the old Braymill lumber mill in Chiloquin, near the tribe's ceremonial site on the Sprague River.

Signs that herald the fish coming upriver to spawn: (1) Falling snow changes from hard powder to large, fluffy "fish blanket" flakes. (2) The fish constellation ("Orion's belt") appears on the southwestern horizon.

To see the research station, a fascinating place filled with glass beakers and big fish tanks, contact the tribe's natural resources department, 116 E Chocktoot St, PO Box 436, Chiloquin, OR 97624; (541)783-2095.

Kintpuash (Captain Jack)

In 1870, disenchanted Modoc chief Kintpuash, known as "Captain Jack," led the Modoc Tribe back to their Tule Lake homelands across the California border and refused to return to the Klamath Reservation, where they had been forced to move. Pressured by the settlers, troops from Fort Klamath were dispatched to bring the Modocs back to the reservation by force. As the troops burned the Modocs' Tule Lake village, the tribe fled into the lava beds that came to be known as "Captain Jack's Stronghold." The incident was highly publicized on the East Coast, and sympathies were with the Indians until two negotiators were killed. Then the government increased its forces, bringing in more than 1,200 troops to fight 60 Indian men. The Indians held them off for nearly four months in the only major Indian war fought in California.

In 1873, Captain Jack, Boston Charley, Schonchin John, and Black Jim (all nicknames) as well as several other Natives were executed by hanging, in an aspen grove adjoining Fort Klamath at the upper end of Klamath Lake. The remaining members of the Modoc Tribe were exiled to the Quapaw Reservation in Oklahoma, where many of them died. The present-day Modoc Tribe of Oklahoma are descendants of only seven prisoners of war, many of them women and children. About 140 Modocs were exiled to the Klamath Reservation.

> *"The Modoc word for old Fort Klamath, where the Cavalry hung Captain Jack, means 'around the neck,' so that we'd never forget what happened there."*

The bodies of the men hung outside Fort Klamath were decapitated and their heads sent to the Army Medical Museum in Washington, D.C. There, a collection of at least 3,000 skulls of Indian men, women, and children was used in a "cranial study" to correlate intelligence with skull size. The project was abandoned when the skulls of some Native peoples proved to be larger than that of Daniel Webster, considered the standard of genius at the time. The Smithsonian Institution's department of anthropology inherited the collection.

Modoc Lynn Schonchin, whose great-grandfather was executed with Captain Jack, has researched the Modoc Wars and is an excellent source of information. An educator, he may be contacted for summer tours or lectures through the Klamath Tribe. The Fort Klamath site (a monument and small cabin) and the old grove of aspen where the execution took place (unmarked, south of the cemetery) are on Hwy 62, a few miles south of the town of Fort Klamath. Watch for Fort Klamath signs

Lava Beds National Monument

Captain Jack and 60 male Modocs were able to defend themselves against 1,200 troops of the U.S. cavalry for more than four months, in the dead of winter, by withdrawing to the tortuous landscape of the lava beds at the edge of 94,000-acre Tule Lake. The natural clefts and gullies, caves, overhanging ledges, and jagged boulders were formed about 30,000 years ago after the eruption of a nearby volcano. The lava beds continued to form until the last volcano erupted 1,000 years ago. Lava tubes and dozens of caves, some filled with ice year-round, were well known by the Modocs, who lived on the shores of the nearby marsh. The lava beds provided an almost impenetrable citadel that failed only when the army cut off the Modocs from their fresh water supply. Free interpretive handouts and maps are available at Lava Beds National Monument Visitor Center. Also look for a lengthy (but inexpensive) booklet that maps a self-guided walk through 23 sites, outposts, defense lines, firing positions, and fortifications with hand-built rock walls, including the cave where Captain Jack's family hid during the siege.

Lava Beds National Monument Visitor Center, PO Box 867, Tulelake, CA 96134; (916)667-2282. The visitors center is at the south end of the lava beds, off Hwy 139. (Take Hwy 39 south from Klamath Falls to the town of Tulelake and drive about 15 miles through the lava beds to the campground, picnic area, and visitor center at Indian Well. $4 per car. Best times to visit are May–Oct. Wear sunblock and good boots, and watch for rattlesnakes on the trails.

Northern California Coast:
Tolowa, Yurok, & Chilula

The California gold rush of 1849, which began with the discovery of gold in the mountains of northern California near San Francisco, determined Indian policy. Fearful that any large Indian reservation might place tribes on top of a potential gold strike, Indian land ownership was confined to "rancherias." Native peoples had to determine the area of most importance to them—for example, the clam beds in a bay or a fishing hole on a river—and then the entire tribe was confined to that one spot. Rancherias were often less than 100 acres for an entire tribe.

Rancherias are private, but you're welcome to stop by tribal offices. The Tolowa's Rancheria and tribal office is at the mouth of the Smith River on Hwy 101.

On the northern California coast, near the Oregon border, the first rancheria is Tolowa Rancheria, which today looks like a small subdivision, at the mouth of the Smith River. Another small rancheria is next to the Smith River, several miles to the east. Nearby, farmers grow fields of white Easter lilies on land that gently slopes to the beach.

The next 40 miles of coastline, from Crescent City to Eureka, is Redwood National Park. Highway 101, which winds through nearly 40 miles of the park, is one of the state's most scenic drives, with access to sandy beaches, rocky headlands, and shady groves of towering redwoods, many of them over 2,000 years old and 300 feet tall.

It may come as a surprise that the Redwoods National Park region is home to three Native tribes: the Tolowa, the Yurok, and the Chilula. Perhaps more surprising, these tribes continue to perform traditional sacred dances within the park boundaries—as they have on this coastline for centuries. You can learn about the tribes by visiting Redwood National Park headquarters in Crescent City or in Orick. Best of all, visitors can walk through a replica of a traditional Yurok village site in Patrick's Point State Park, near the town of Trinidad. Two museums in the area display extensive private collections of northern California basketry.

Visitors can also drive to the mouth of the Klamath River near Requa to watch Natives catching salmon, then drive up to the brow of the cliff, 600 feet above the river, to the Klamath Overlook and the trailhead of the 25-mile-long coastal trail along the cliffs. Summers, the park service at Orick offers morning kayaking near the river's mouth. The Avenue of the Giants, a 33-mile byway through the oldest redwood groves on the coast, will give you an idea of how the forest looked before white contact and logging.

Pick up free detailed maps showing the trails, campgrounds, and picnic areas of Redwood National and State Parks from park headquarters (1111 2nd St, Crescent City, CA 95531; (707)465-4113). An informative 16-page pamphlet, "Living in a Well-Ordered World: Indian People of Northwestern California," is also available.

An Inside Perspective

Thumbs up for *News from Native California: An Inside View of the California Indian World*. This quarterly magazine, available from Heyday Press, is devoted to California Indian history and culture, contemporary issues, and myth, with contributions from Native American scholars and others.

Heyday Press, PO Box 9145, Berkeley, CA 94709; (510)849-0177. Cost is $19 a year for four issues. Also available are Heyday's free catalogue of Native American titles and California Indian art notecards.

Tolowa Rancheria at Smith River

The Tolowa Tribe has two rancherias, one up the Smith River and one at its mouth, both about the size of a large cul-de-sac, where they have struggled to survive for over a century. Drive into the Smith River Rancheria, off Highway 101 on North Indian Road, and follow the road past the Indian Shaker church, built along the cliffside in 1928, and past the cemetery overlooking the Pacific Ocean, to a small park overlooking the mouth of the Smith River. The Talowa chose this former village site, which they call Nelechundun, because it gave them access to the river so they could continue to fish for salmon and dig clams on the beaches.

Smith River Rancheria Tribal Center, 501 N Indian Rd, PO Box 239, Smith River, CA 95567; (707)487-9255. Visitors are welcome to stop at the tribal center, but call first for an appointment and directions to the office.

Three Feathers Cafe at Crescent City

Doug (Miwok, from Fresno, California) and Donna (Paiute, from Escondido, California) Lindsay own a small roadside cafe in Crescent City. It sports pure Indian/frontier kitsch: arrows stick out of the walls among framed pictures of the Lone Ranger and Tonto, beaded moccasins, cradleboards, and coonskin caps. Portions are very generous (especially thick, juicy hamburgers on oversized buns, smoked beef ribs on sourdough bread, and Indian tacos), and all are under $5. All meats, including buffalo, are extra lean and ordered fresh daily. Doug's Indian Chef's Salad, topped with chicken, smoked sausage, ham, and cheese, takes up half the 1950s yellow-and-chrome diner counter, and easily feeds two. For dessert, try the extra-light fry bread topped with fresh fruit and real whipped cream.

Three Feathers Cafe is on Highway 101, in front of the Humboldt County fairgrounds. You can't miss it: the building is painted turquoise.

Three Feathers Cafe, 451 Hwy 101 N, Crescent City, CA 95531; (707)464-6003. In front of the Humboldt County fairgrounds. Open for lunch, dinner weekdays; breakfast, lunch, and dinner Sat and Sun; closed Mon.

"End of the Trail" Museum

A gigantic statue of Paul Bunyan still shoulders his ax outside the Trees of Mystery tourist attraction, as he has since the place was built in the 1940s. In a wing next to one of the biggest souvenir stores this side of San Francisco is the owner's private collection of Indian artifacts, including a large number of extraordinary woven hats made by local Yurok and Hupa women. Most were purchased by the owner, Marylee Thompson Smith, in the 1940s and 1950s; some were gifts. We hesitate to recommend this collection because it displays Indian burial items that may offend. We include it, however, because some Native people told us that they have a long, amicable history with the owner and are grateful that she allows them to borrow items, such as shell-adorned dresses, from the collection for ceremonial use.

"End of the Trail" Museum and Trees of Mystery, PO Box 96, 1550 Hwy 101 N, Klamath, CA 95548; (707)482-2251. Open daily, year-round. No charge for gift shop or museum.

Klamath Overlook

"In the beginning there were only spirits. One day the Creator called them together to ask what they wanted to be—trees, rocks, or animals. Oregos, the helpful one, chose to be the Guardian rock at the mouth of the Klamath River. She tells the salmon when the rains have swollen the rivers and it's time to come back." That's the terse message on the sign at the edge of the Klamath Overlook; no doubt the story is longer and better in a face-to-face telling.

Salmon used to run all the way through the coastal range of northern California to the marshes of Klamath Lake in eastern Oregon, and from there up the Sprague, Wood, and Williamson Rivers to spawn. Fishers at the mouth of the river knew which fish were theirs by the density of the eggs packed inside the females; those more densely packed were destined for spawning tributaries far upstream. Fish were caught in weirs, but enough salmon were always let through to feed the people upstream. Today fishers fish from boats at the river's mouth and can, freeze, wind-dry, and smoke their catch.

You can see the Guardian rock from the impressive Klamath Overlook, 600 feet above the river, by turning west on Requa Road from Hwy 101 and continuing up the hill to a clearly marked parking lot at the head of the 21½-mile coastal trail.

Redwood National Park Center, Orick

The park information center at Orick displays Yurok baskets and basket materials from Redwood National Park's collection, as well as photographs of Jim and Josie Marks's fish camp at the mouth of Redwood Creek. A rough-hulled, 18-foot redwood dugout canoe, shaped like an ocean-going cargo canoe, is also on display; a brochure explains the lumps of wood inside, which symbolize the boat's nose, heart, lungs, and kidneys and give the canoe life.

During summers, check the park schedule for cultural demonstrations by Yurok artists and lectures.

Redwood National Park Information Center, PO Box 7, Orick, CA 95555; (707)400-3461. On Hwy 101, 1 mile south of Orick, on the beach; open daily year-round.

Kayak at the mouth of the Klamath River with National Park Service interpretive guides who tell you a bit of the history of the river while you're on the water. Kayaks, paddles, and life jackets are provided. No kayaking experience necessary. Donation of $6–$10 per person. Contact Redwood National Park Information Center at Orick for times (summers only); (707)488-3461.

Sumeg Yurok Village at Patrick's Point

In a quiet, grassy field speckled with white daisies and purple lupine, tucked away from the campgrounds, playgrounds, beaches, and tide pools of Patrick's Point State Park, is a replica of a traditional Yurok village. Three family houses made of split redwood lashed together with hazelnut and spruce roots, look almost Japanese in design. Each house is surrounded by pavement made of smooth, flat stones. The doorways are small and perfectly round; to enter you must crawl in on your knees. You crawl onto a platform at ground level that was used to store items such as food, firewood, and cedar boxes that held ceremonial regalia. Living space was about 3 feet below ground, insulated by the earth and centered around a square fire pit. Pick up a self-guided village tour brochure at the park gate. Yurok docents conduct tours of the village by appointment.

Patrick's Point State Park, 4150 Patrick's Point Dr, Trinidad, CA 95570; (707)677-3570. Take Patrick's Point Drive off Hwy 101 between Big Lagoon and Trinidad. Open daily year-round; you can tour the site from 8am until dusk. Park entrance fee is $3 per car at the gate.

Clarke Memorial Museum, Eureka

Founded by Cecile Clarke in 1960, this is one of the most extensive collections of Yurok, Karuk, and Hupa baskets in the world. Clarke befriended many Indian families when she taught their children in school. Most of the baskets in this collection were purchased by her. Oral-history audio tapes of interviews with 17 northwestern California basket makers are available (by appointment), and photographs of the tribes are exhibited in the museum's hall. Contact the museum for information about basket-weaving classes with Yurok Vera Ryerson.

Clarke Memorial Museum, 3rd and E Sts, Eureka, CA 95501; (707)443-1947. Open Tues–Sat afternoons. Donations.

Hoopa Valley: *Hupa*

The emerald-green Trinity River, rushing through rocky canyons covered with oak, cinnamon-barked madrona, pine, and fir, slows as the gorge widens into the Hoopa Valley in northern California. The flat valley, 7 miles long and about a mile wide, is the ancestral home of the Hupa Tribe, which lives there still. The valley is on the drier east side of the giant redwood groves, 60 miles inland from the California coast.

Every two years, determined by a phase of the moon, the Hupa Tribe's traditional people shed their T-shirts and jeans, or suits and ties, and don ceremonial kilts, headgear resplendent with the feathers of red-headed woodpeckers, and deerhide dresses adorned with seashells. Thus garbed, they dedicate a week to a ritual "world renewal prayer." The White Deerskin Dance begins at one end of the valley, with dancers moving each day to the next prayer site. The dance continues aboard dugout canoes, becoming The Boat Dance, and crosses the Trinity River. Reaching the opposite shore, the dancers drag trunks packed with regalia and camp gear up a steep trail. They finish the dance near the summit of Bald Hill, overlooking the Hoopa Valley. Their prayer asks for abundance for everyone in the world. Some say that the reason the world is now so far out of balance is that the rest of us have forgotten how to dance.

In the Hoopa Valley, there is a reconstructed village site built of sacred Port Orford cedar on the stone foundations of the original houses. One of the foundations is known to have been that of a medicine person's house because it contains a smooth stone engraved with calendar marks and the phases of the moon.

Yet, in every other way, the Hoopa Valley seems to be a modern place. The shopping center and high school look like any other. The local cafe and service station do a booming business. Kids swim in the river and ride their bikes through town. No one lives in the reconstructed houses—modern houses are far more comfortable.

Forestry and logging are central to the valley's economy, but now that the Bureau of Indian Affairs no longer makes decisions for the tribe, these industries are conducted in a more thoughtful manner than elsewhere. With only 12 square miles of property, taking meticulous care of the land for future generations is the essential work of the tribal council and its nationally respected leadership.

> *"All history is seen from Hoopa Valley, the center of the Hupa world, the place where according to legend 'people came into being.' It is family history . . . the story of a culture still remembered, still cherished, and—one rejoices at the miracle—still very much alive."*
>
> **—Malcolm Margolin, reviewer for the California Historical Society Quarterly,** *in his review of tribal member Byron Nelson, Jr's book,* **Our Home Forever** *(available from the Hupa Tribal museum gift shop).*

Hupa Tribal Museum

Every other August, all of the Hupa Tribal Museum's ceremonial clothing, including deerskin dresses and aprons, disappear from their glass cases, checked out to dancers to wear during ceremonies. Missing, too, are a few of the women's bowl-shaped caps with stunning geometric designs woven of hazel sticks, willow roots, porcupine quills, bear grass, and the black stems of maidenhair fern. This museum is different from any other in the United States; it's a repository for individuals' private artifact and basket collections. Owners can remove items for their own use at any time.

That's not to say the museum is ever empty. Hundreds of baskets, including those that hold tobacco, an integral part of medicine ceremonies are exhibited, as well as headdresses made of the bright-red-feathered crowns of woodpeckers. Look here too for carved elkhorn purses, canoes, baby baskets and rattles, and dentalium-shell currency wrapped with the colorful skin of the "money snake" and strung on threads made from iris stems.

During an hour-long tour, you can visit a village site, learn about the ceremonial dances, and discover the meanings of basket designs and other items in the museum ($10 per person). Two-hour tours include a trip to the top of Bald Mountain for a scenic overview of the Hoopa Valley ($20 per person).

Fine artwork is for sale in the museum, including a few woven caps from private collections as well as Hupa artist George Blake's silverwork, elk antler purses, and gold jewelry. (His work is also displayed in both the Smithsonian Institution and Phoenix's Heard Museum.)

The hundreds of seashell beads, acorns, and dried juniper berries that adorn Hupa ceremonial dresses make a soft, tinkling sound when a dancer makes the slightest move. Each dress has its own sound. Imagine the world being so quiet that you could hear the difference.

Hupa Tribal Museum, PO Box 1348, Hoopa, CA 95546; (916)625-4110. On the left in the shopping center complex behind the Best Western Tsewenaldin Inn. Open daily, year-round, except weekends during the winter. Free admission. Discounted tour prices for groups.

Trinity River, Hupa Raft Trip

Aurora River Adventures offers day-long raft trips that begin in the town of Hoopa. There is a tour of the valley, museum, and an original village site, with its restored houses, sweat lodge, and ceremonial dance grounds. After lunch the group heads upriver for a 3-hour raft trip down the scenic and remote Tish Tang Gorge, a gentle ride through Class II rapids that the *San Francisco Chronicle* called "a plunge through both white-water rapids and the culture of the Hupa Indians." As the raft passes ancient village sites, Hupa guides regale rafters with stories about the history of the tribe, pointing out places of spiritual quests, medicine training, and food, medicinal, and gathering sites. There's a rest stop along the way at an abandoned village site, where you can enjoy a bite of traditional Hupa smoked salmon and a taste of acorn soup. Kids as young as 7 are allowed on the trip, which is an easy one for first-time rafters.

Aurora River Adventures is based at Camp Kimtu, a private 12-acre campground on the Trinity River near the town of Willow Creek; PO Box 938, Willow Creek, CA 95573; (800)562-8475 or (916)629-3843. Six people to a raft; wear swimsuits. Offered May–Oct (warmest times are June 15–Sept 15). Raft trips are endorsed by the Hupa Tribe. Adults $90, children under 11, $50.

Tsemeta Forest Nursery

The Hupa Tribe raises more than 700,000 trees annually in their silva-culture (tree-growing) greenhouses. Coastal redwood, giant sequoia, ponderosa pine, incense cedar, and other conifers are grown from seed. Foresters collect seed by climbing the tall trees and picking ripe pinecones. Seedlings are sold all over the world to large growers—from Christmas tree farmers to the U.S. Forest Service and timber companies. Native species, such as deerbrush, buckbrush, elderberry, and western redbud, are grown for erosion control. The tribe also maintains a tree seed bank in cold storage. Seedlings are sold in 6-inch and 10-inch containers for as little as 25 cents each.

Tsameta Forest Nursery, 123 Marshall Lane, PO Box 368, Hoopa, CA 95546; (916)625-4206. Off Hwy 96 in the valley's north end, past the shopping center. Call first.

Eco-tours

Hike with a Native guide through a rare Port Orford cedar grove and listen for an answering hoot when he calls endangered spotted owls; see where biologists are photographing the elusive fisher (an animal similar to a weasel) and identifying it by its footprints; and learn about the Hupa Tribe's innovative, award-winning forestry practices during this 2-hour eco-tour of the reservation. The hike ends with a refreshing swim in the Trinity River, weather permitting.

For custom tour information, contact Thomas Imfeld, (916)625-4275

Assist Tribal Biologists

Gain valuable insights and experience assisting tribal wildlife biologists and foresters as a research assistant on one of their many projects on the reservation—from clearing trails and replanting to helping record wildlife observations (a marbled murrelet count, for example). You bring your gear and camp in a reserved site on the Trinity River, are fed three square meals a day, and get treated to a raft trip downriver at the end of a challenging 10 days of work; cost $1,200.

For more information, contact Bill Wilkinson, (916)625-4206.

Best Western Tsewenaldin Inn

From the stucco motel's balcony you can see the morning sun sparkling on the Trinity River. The Best Western Tsewenaldin Inn and an adjoining shopping center are built on the site of an ancient

Hupa village, near a bend in the river. Except for the modern build-ings and parking lot off Highway 96, the area probably looks about the same as it always has. Pronounced "say-when-ALL-din," the motel's name means "the place of happy meetings." All 19 rooms and two suites of the two-story building, built in 1991, have views of the river, as does the small conference room. An enclosed, shaded patio surrounds a pool and spa. However, there is a trail from the motel to the river, where more hardy souls can wade into the cold stream or just sit on the riverbank, perhaps with the rolls, cold cereal, coffee, and juice that are complimentary each morning in the motel lobby. These are nice folks; if you want to fish, they'll hunt up a for-hire guide to go with you.

Best Western Tsewenaldin Inn, Hwy 96, Hoopa, CA 95546; (800)528-1234 for Best Western's central reservations, or (916)625-4294. Room rates are $65–$80. Open daily, year-round.

Humboldt County Library

In 1991 the tribe built their library based on the ancient Hupa house design. Hand-hewn cedar planks cover the exterior, and the moon-shaped doorway and sloped roof echo the lines of the Hupa's first, subterranean dwellings. From the street, its landscaping makes the building appear to be barely above ground. The design is particularly appropriate because the library is a memorial to Kim Yerton, a young Hupa woman who, in the 1970s, compiled archival documents and photographs of Hupa history, culture, and art from the Smithsonian Institution and Chicago's Newberry Library. Her work is now col-lected and preserved in the library's repository for others to use.

Humboldt County Library, (916)625-4447. Across from the high school. Call for hours.

COLUMBIA
RIVER GORGE
& BASIN

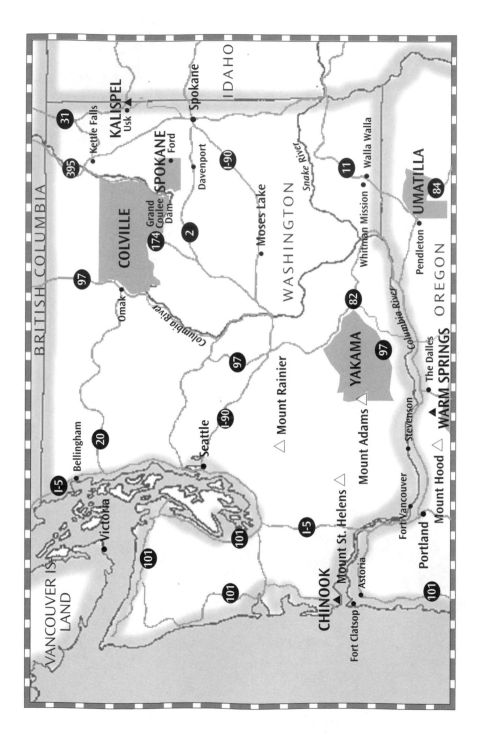

THE COLUMBIA RIVER GORGE & BASIN

The snub-nosed prow of an 800-year-old dugout canoe, unearthed from a Chinook village site on Washington's southern coast and donated to the Ilwaco Heritage Museum, is a treasure to today's Chinook tribal members. It's a reminder of the days when their ancestors controlled the Washington and Oregon coastlines north and south of the mouth of the Columbia River. The Columbia served as a superhighway for tribes living along it and along the extensive network of tributaries. Canoes could travel nearly 400 miles eastward from the Columbia's mouth, squeezing through a narrow gorge and portaging over a wall of water at Celilo Falls, before the river turned north for another 500 miles to present-day Canada. Along the way, tributaries such as the Deschutes, Umatilla, Walla Walla, Snake, Yakima, Okanogan, and Spokane Rivers greatly expanded the reach of the network, connecting the Columbia to the mountains and high plateaus of present-day eastern Oregon and Washington, Idaho and Montana, and farther. The Snake River, a major river system itself, extends as far east as Wyoming.

For centuries, hundreds of Indian villages, encampments, and fishing sites lined the riverbanks of the

Columbia Gorge and Basin. In their journals, American explorers Lewis and Clark reported that along the Columbia River they were rarely out of sight of an Indian village. More than 50 Chinook villages lined the lower Columbia, a stretch of about 150 miles.

By the early 1800s, however, epidemics had wiped out nearly 90 percent of the Native populations on the lower Columbia River. Today, none of the original villages remain, except in the hearts of tribal members who fight to protect ancient burial sites from development. Near the mouth of the Columbia, visitors can see Fort Clatsop, where Chinook chief Comcomly, who had exchanged gifts with ship captain Robert John Gray in 1792, greeted Lewis and Clark in 1805. The Chinooks' small tribal office is in the town of Chinook, on the river's north side. Across the Columbia River from the Portland International Airport is Fort Vancouver, a reconstructed Hudson's Bay trading post that was, in the 1830s, the center of the fur trade as well as the provisioner for immigrants arriving via the Oregon Trail.

East of Portland, among the dramatic cliffs and rock formations of the Columbia Gorge, visitors can see petroglyphs and pictographs left on the rocks by the river's earliest human inhabitants, or learn the story of the Bridge of the Gods from a Native guide. Indians still build scaffolding along the river, catching salmon in the traditional way with long-handled dip nets. Within a few hours of Portland are three Indian reservations that welcome visitors: Warm Springs and Umatilla in Oregon, and Yakama in Washington. Up north, the Columbia divides the Colville and Spokane Reservations in Washington. Our most northern point is the small reservation of the Kalispel Tribe, on the banks of the Pend Oreille, a Columbia River tributary.

THE LOWER COLUMBIA

Lower Columbia River: *Chinook*

The gatekeepers of the mouth of the Columbia River were the Chinook Indians. Their villages were the first point of contact for all of the canoe tribes entering the river from the Pacific Ocean. Later, the Chinooks were the first Natives the European traders and explorers encountered when they crossed over the bar and into the mouth of the Columbia. Chinook chiefs, in a manner similar to the kings of European countries, married their daughters to trading partners, including Europeans, successfully forming strong trade alliances.

The Chinooks are the only Pacific Northwest tribe whose story is told in the video series "Indians of North America," by Schlessinger Video. You can purchase the 30-minute tape at the Ilwaco Heritage Museum gift shop (115 SE Lake St, Ilwaco, WA 98624; (360)642-3446), or order it directly from the video company; (800)843-3620.

With the consent of the Clatsop Band of Chinooks, American John Jacob Astor, in 1811, built the first fur-trading fort in the region at present-day Astoria. The British fur traders followed a decade later, building their trading post upriver.

Trade with Europeans had its down side. Smallpox, measles, and malaria decimated the Chinooks and other tribes of western Oregon. A four-year round of "fever and ague," which broke out during the summer of 1830 at Fort Vancouver, emptied most of the villages along the Columbia River. In the 1850s Chinook survivors who hadn't married into settlers' families were moved to various reservations.

Today, people of Chinook ancestry live all over the Northwest. About 1,600 tribal members are actively seeking federal recognition. The Chinooks rent a 1920s schoolhouse for their tribal office in the town of Chinook, Washington, on the north side of the Columbia, across the river's mouth from Astoria, Oregon. Visitors are welcome.

Chinook Indian Tribe, PO Box 228, Chinook, WA 98614; (360)777-8303.

Ilwaco Heritage Museum

The prow of an 800-year-old dugout canoe is displayed, along with stone tools, baskets, cedar handwork, and turn-of-the-century photographs, in one room of this tiny museum in Ilwaco, a fishing town north of Chinook on the Washington coast. The canoe was unearthed in an archaeological dig and given to the museum. Everything else on display was donated by local people, many of Chinook ancestry.

Ilwaco Heritage Museum, 115 SE Lake St, Ilwaco, WA 98624; (360)642-3346. Admission $2. Open daily, most of the year. Call for hours.

Fort Clatsop National Memorial

Explorers Lewis and Clark spent three months in the winter rain with the Clatsop Band of Chinooks at Fort Clatsop. The Clatsops taught the men methods of tanning hides, hunting, and gathering food, and provided them with clothing and shelter. The Clatsops also contributed to the party's botanical research and shared their knowledge of local waterways. Lewis and Clark's journals documenting the Clatsop culture provide important historical records of the tribe. Near Astoria, Oregon, a memorial site commemorates this period of Northwest history. There is a reconstructed fort, a canoe landing, exhibits of Clatsop culture, and occasionally historic interpretations presented by costumed narrators.

Fort Clatsop National Memorial, Box 604-FC, Astoria, OR 97103; (503)861-2471. Near Warrenton, west of Astoria. From Hwy 101 or Hwys 26 and 30, follow well-marked signs to Fort Clatsop. Open daily in summer; call for calendar of events. Summer admission $2. In winter, grounds and the small center are open daily; free.

Chinook Jargon

The European traders and Native tribes developed a language called Chinook jargon to communicate with one another. Chinook is a combination of Pacific Northwest Indian languages, primarily Nooksack and Chinook, and English and French. Many place names in the

Northwest, such as Seattle's Alki Beach and the Washington coast village of La Push, as well as words such as *tyee* (chief) and *illahee* (the earth) stem from Chinook jargon. For very thorough information about this language, refer to *Chinook: A History and Dictionary of Chinook Jargon,* by Edward H. Thomas (Binford & Mort Publishing, 1970). It's available from Fort Clatsop National Memorial, Box 604-FC, Astoria, OR 97103; (503)861-2471.

Chief Comcomly Memorial

Chief Comcomly was a young man and hereditary chief of the Chinooks when Captain Robert Gray sailed into the mouth of the Columbia River in 1792. The chief welcomed Lewis and Clark at the end of their journey in 1805, and helped the Astor fur traders survive their first few winters near present-day Astoria. Comcomly died at the age of 66 of the fever that swept the lower Columbia River in 1830. He was buried in a raised war canoe near his village, Quats-A-Mts, on the north shore of the Columbia River, where the Astoria bridge touches the Washington shore.

To keep the grave from being robbed, his family moved Comcomly's body to a burial site in a nearby forest. A young Hudson's Bay Company naturalist and physician, Meredith Gairdner, secretly exhumed the body, decapitated it, and took Comcomly's head with him to Hawaii. He eventually sent the head, packed in a box, to his friend, a Dr. Richardson, in England. The skull lay in the Royal Naval Hospital Museum in Gosport, England, for 117 years before it was returned to the Astoria Historical Society in the early 1950s. In spite of the Chinooks' pleas for its return to them for burial, the skull was displayed as a curiosity in the society's Flavell House museum for more than 20 years. In 1961, the town of Astoria, Oregon, raised a memorial, a black burial canoe cast in concrete, to Chief Comcomly on its highest hill.

Comcomly's skull was finally returned to the Chinooks in 1972, but only after the tribe had threatened legal action, notified the press, and proved they had purchased a headstone and burial plot. Comcomly's remains were reinterred by his family in an Ilwaco graveyard north of his old village site.

To see Comcomly's memorial in Astoria, take 16th St to the top of the hill and follow signs to the Astoria Column. To read a copy of the letter Gairdner wrote and sent to his friend Dr. Richardson, contact the Chinook Indian Tribe, PO Box 228, Chinook, WA 98614; (360)777-8303.

Fort Vancouver

A stockade and five major buildings, including an Indian trade shop stocked with replicas of trade goods, have been reconstructed on their original footings at the old Hudson's Bay Company's Fort Vancouver. Fort Vancouver National Historical Site is in Vancouver, Washington, on the north bank of the Columbia River, 15 minutes from downtown Portland.

The 1820s British fashion that fueled the Hudson's Bay Company was a felted top hat made from sheared beaver pelts. But when the king of England appeared in public wearing a hat made of real silk, everyone had to have one. Trade shifted from the Pacific Northwest beaver to silkworm cocoons from China.

The original British fort was built between 1827 and 1829. Located near the center of a network of long-established Indian trade routes and annual trade fairs held in the Columbia Gorge, the fort was actually a warehouse that supplied 20 to 30 smaller trading posts throughout the Northwest.

Many of the items offered for trade with the Natives were novelties, such as mirrors, clay pipes, rum-soaked tobacco, bells, Jew's harps, and popular Venetian-cut glass beads. A shipment of windup toy dogs from China traded out immediately. More practical trade items included metal hatchet blades and knives, flint, square nails, windowpanes, metal pots, china, cloth, and blankets. Most in demand were the hanks of beautiful faceted glass beads, which Natives used to adorn garments and personal possessions. They were as coveted as cut diamonds are today, and easily transported for trade. The official currency at the trading posts (determined by the Hudson's Bay Company) was beaver pelts, which were plentiful and easily caught with the metal traps available at the company store.

Reconstructed on the fort grounds are the Indian trade shop; the chief factor's residence and kitchen, furnished with period antiques; a fully stocked blacksmith shop; a bakery; a shipping warehouse; and a period flower and vegetable garden. The stockade and bastion are also reconstructed; they were originally built to defend against American boundary threats, not against Indian attacks. When the fort was excavated in 1948, more than a million artifacts were uncovered, including thousands of trade beads that had fallen through the large cracks in the Indian trade shop floor. The beads are on display in a hallway adjoining the shipping warehouse.

Fort Vancouver National Historic Site, 1501 E Evergreen Blvd, Vancouver, WA 98661; (360)696-7655. Located within the city limits of Vancouver, across the Columbia River from Portland. From I-5, take the Mill Plain Blvd. exit and follow the signs. From I-205, take the Vancouver exit, go west on Hwy 14 for 5 miles, and then turn right on Grand Blvd. Open daily, 9am–5pm; tours hourly during the summer months; live demonstrations on weekends. Admission $2 per person; $4 per family.

Columbia River Gorge

Columbia Gorge Interpretive Center

Located in Stevenson, Washington, the Columbia Gorge Interpretive Center was built primarily to house eclectic collections donated to the Skamania County Historical Museum from former residents of the Columbia Gorge. There are donations from Baron Eugene Fersen, a Russian refugee who thought his 29-acre plot near Prindle, Washington, was a spiritual vortex; Donald Brown, who owned the largest collection of Catholic rosaries in the world; and amateur archaeologist Emory Strong, who spent 40 years recording petroglyphs, pictographs, and ancient village sites in the gorge (information the tribes generally did not share with non-Indians).

Unfortunately, Strong also "salvaged" artifacts, digging up hundreds of stone tools, trade beads, mortars, and pestles, and taking them for his private collection (a practice now against federal law). His family gave the entire collection and his library to the interpretive center, which houses both in a room intended to resemble Strong's den. A founder of the Oregon Archaeological Society and author of two books, *Stone Age on the Columbia* and *Stone Age in the Great Basin*, Strong may have encouraged thousands to appreciate the region's first inhabitants. However, his methods inspired a rash of digging and a plundering of sites that the Indians regard as sacred ground.

Also on display at the interpretive center are a life-size model of traditional Indian fishing scaffolding and a replica of the McCord Creek Fishwheel, a device used to scoop salmon out of the rivers for the canneries.

Columbia Gorge Interpretive Center, Hwy 14, Stevenson, WA 98648; (509)427-8211. From Oregon, cross the Bridge of the Gods at Cascade Locks and travel 1½ miles east toward Stevenson. Open daily, summer, 10am–7pm; winter, 10am–5pm. Admission $5.

Salmon, Scaffolding, and Dams

To catch the salmon migrating upstream to spawn, Natives once used such tools and devices as stone weights, seine nets, harpoons, leisters, willow and stone weirs, gill and set nets, dip nets, and baited bone chokers on hemp lines. Just 150 years ago, nets were still being made of silky Indian hemp, laboriously gathered, prepared, and twined by the women before it was woven into nets.

During the past 80 years, 81 dams have been built on the Columbia River and its tributaries. Thousands

Native fishing artifacts— including nets, weights, and evidence of weirs— have been found at sites near The Dalles, Oregon. Some of the artifacts have been dated to 9,000 years old.

of rapids, eddies, and falls have disappeared beneath slackwater pools. Villages, fishing camps, and trails along riverbanks, used by Indians for at least 10,000 years, are now underwater. Today, most Indians have turned to modern fishing methods and gear.

In the Columbia River Gorge, however, some Natives still employ traditional fishing methods. Standing on wooden scaffolding attached to the river's basalt outcroppings, they scoop salmon out of the water with long-handled dip nets. You can see Indians fishing from scaffolding at Cascade Locks Port Marina Park in Oregon, and at the mouth of the Klickitat River at Lyle, Washington. One of the most exciting places to watch fishermen work is at the falls at Sherar Bridge, on the Deschutes River, southeast of The Dalles.

A large ball of woven Indian hemp twine, about the size of a softball, was worth a horse in trade. The twine was strong enough to hold a 900-pound sturgeon.

A life-size model of traditional Indian fishing scaffolding is on display at the Columbia Gorge Interpretive Center in Stevenson, Washington. Also on display is a 40-foot replica of the McCord Creek Fishwheel. This non-Native invention scooped millions of ready-to-spawn salmon out of Northwest rivers to feed the canneries, a practice that dangerously depleted Columbia River salmon runs in the early 1900s.

Scaffolding is left up year-round. For more information on the salmon fishery, as well as several excellent videos explaining Indian positions on salmon issues, contact the Columbia River Inter-Tribal Fish Commission, 729 NE Oregon, Portland, OR 97232; (503)238-0667.

Native Tours of the Columbia River Gorge

Poet and professional storyteller Ed Edmo, of Shoshone and Yakama descent, offers tours of the Columbia River Gorge from a Native perspective. His tours begin at the Cascade Locks, where Edmo tells the Indian legend of the Bridge of the Gods. The tour then travels upriver to Celilo Falls and the Memaloose Island overlook, east of The Dalles. Edmo grew up in The Dalles during the 1950s; he remembers when Celilo Falls was submerged by The Dalles Dam.

When Edmo was young, only one local restaurant—Johnny's Cafe—served Indians. Now his tours usually include a stop at Johnny's, for coffee and a snack. The cafe was opened by Polish immigrant John Wantalak, who ran it with his wife, Nancy, for 24 years. Their daughter, Barb Tumilson, now owns it.

Arrange tours with Ed Edmo by reaching him in Portland; (503)256-2257. Johnny's Cafe is at 408 E 2nd, The Dalles, OR 97058; (541)296-4565.

James Selam and Nch'i-Wana

James Selam was born in 1919 at Rock Creek, Washington, and raised along the Columbia River between Celilo Falls and the John Day River. As a child he lived in a tule mat longhouse at Blalock, Oregon. He would travel with his parents to fish at Celilo Falls, and to pick berries and hunt at what is now called Indian Heaven Wilderness near Trout Lake, Washington. Selam is bilingual, a fluent speaker of both the Sahaptin language and English.

Tule is a bulrush that can grow up to 10 feet tall. Collected from marshes, dried stems can be woven into large mats. Tule mats, laid like shingles against a sturdy framework, are excellent insulators from the cold because their interior structure is similar to Styrofoam.

For 14 years, Selam and his family have shared their encyclopedic knowledge of their environment with University of Washington ethnobiologist Eugene S. Hunn. Hunn and Selam co-authored the book *Nch'i-Wana: The Big River* (University of Washington Press, 1990), which has overturned many misconceptions about Native Americans. In the book Selam and Hunn explain the term "hunting and gathering" as it applies to Columbia River tribes. Their "root gathering" was actually a carefully timed harvest of bulbs and tubers; one person would collect an average of 50 pounds a day. The Indians' taxonomy defines plant species to an even finer degree than does scientific Latin.

James Selam spends several weekends each summer at the Flying L Ranch in Glenwood, Washington. There he teaches seminars and leads workshop participants to his tribe's favorite camas meadows, huckleberry slopes, and fishing sites, many of which are still in use. In the evenings, Selam narrates a slide show and tells stories in the lodge's comfortable living room.

Sahaptin is a root language, like Latin or Chinese, with many dialects. A complex language that is difficult to learn, it was spoken by tribes in the mid-Columbia River region. A number of elders and traditional tribal members in the area still speak Sahaptin dialects.

To take James Selam's workshop, or receive a free catalog of classes, contact the North Cascades Institute, 2105 SR 20, Sedro Woolley, WA 90204, (360)856-5700.

Memaloose Island

Memaloose Island was the largest of the Indian funeral islands in the Columbia River Gorge, and one of the few islands not completely submerged by the dams. The deceased were taken to the island by canoe and interred in small wooden grave houses.

The Bonneville Dam, completed in 1937, submerged all but a small portion of the island's original 4 acres. Families removed the remains of the deceased to higher burial grounds before the dam was completed. Today, what is left of the island is visible from Interstate-84. The gravestone that can be seen from the riverbank is that of Victor Trevitt, a white man from The Dalles who, before his death in 1883, said he'd rather face eternity with the Indians than with the whites.

To view Memaloose Island, follow I-84 east of Hood River for 10 miles to a rest stop overlooking the river.

Maryhill Museum of Art's Basket Collection

The Maryhill Museum of Art is housed in a two-story mansion that stands completely alone, high on a grass-covered hill above the Columbia River Gorge. Early on, the building became a museum—housing the Queen of Romania's furniture and personal items, sculptures by Rodin, and a large collection of Indian baskets from the Columbia River Gorge.

The baskets were collected by Reverend W. C. Curtis, pastor of the First Congregational Church at The Dalles, and his son, Winterton. Responding to the rage for American Indian baskets, inspired by the Arts and Crafts Movement of the early 1900s, the two men bought dozens of Columbia River Gorge baskets directly from Klickitat and Wasco basket weavers. In the 1940s, Winterton Curtis donated the collection to Maryhill Museum.

To really appreciate the arduous labor of basket making, enroll in one of the museum workshops. Some of the best basket weavers in the world teach there, including Nettie Jackson, whose work has been chosen for the Smithsonian's collection.

At the museum's gift shop, look for curator Mary Dodds Schlick's *Columbia River Basketry: Gift of the Ancestors, Gift of the Earth* (University of Washington Press, 1994). The gift shop also sells a video on basket making featuring Northwest weavers, *Baskets of the Northwest People, Gifts from the Grandmothers.*

Maryhill Museum of Art, 35 Maryhill Museum Dr, Goldendale, WA 98620; (509)773-3733. Cross the Columbia River from Oregon at Biggs Junction on Hwy 97. Open 9am–5pm daily, Mar 15–Nov 15. Admission $5.

Petroglyphs at Horsethief Lake State Park

The most famous petroglyph in the Columbia Gorge is the large-eyed Tsagaglalal, "She Who Watches," chipped into stone high on a cliff overlooking an ancient village and trading site across the Columbia River from The Dalles, Oregon. You can see "She Who Watches" and other petroglyphs and pictographs today in Horsethief Lake State Park. (The area is protected and closed to the public except for tours led by park staff.)

Carbon-dated to a period of time between 1700 and 1840, "She Who Watches" is thought by some to represent a guardian spirit or be a warning sign to stay away from an area where many people sickened and died of smallpox and other epidemics. For centuries the area near the petroglyph was a major gathering spot for Indians from up and down the Columbia River, who converged there for trade fairs. During such gatherings, contagious diseases could have spread rapidly—which may have prompted the creation of "She Who Watches." There is additional evidence that this petroglyph may be associated with death and epidemics: in the area numerous traces of cremation burials (a rare practice in the Columbia Gorge region) have been found, as well as images—carved in bone, stone, and antler—associated with burial offerings. But such interpretations remain highly controversial.

Horsethief Lake State Park is on Hwy 14, east of Murdock, WA; (509)767-1159. From The Dalles, Oregon, cross the Hwy 97 bridge. To view the petroglyphs, you must arrange a narrated tour with a park ranger. (The park grounds are patrolled to protect the petroglyphs.) There is usually one tour a day, Apr–Oct, Fri–Sat, starting at 10am. Reservations a must; may be a small fee.

Lone Pine Tree Village

The lone pine tree is gone, and a few buildings do not a village make. But the humble, weather-burnished shacks create a startling contrast to the nearby spillways of Bonneville Dam. There is a little Indian Shaker church that was moved here from its original site on the highway but fits in well with the other unpainted buildings, which were constructed by settler Henry Gulick for his Indian wife, Harriet, around 1896. If you look carefully, you'll see fishing scaffolding hanging on the cliffside—signs of a traditional fishing site still in use.

Lone Pine Village is visible on the edge of the cliff behind the Shilo Inn, exit 87 off I-84 at The Dalles, Oregon. The village is accessible on foot through the breezeway from the inn's parking lot.

Celilo Falls

Dams provide cheap hydroelectric power, water for irrigating the rich plains east of the Cascades, and stairsteps of pools for barging wheat from the irrigated fields to the international port of Portland.

These were the reasons given for constructing The Dalles Dam and others like it along the Columbia River during the 1940s. Little heard in the rush to create these technological "miracles" were the voices of the Indian people the length of the Columbia, whose cultures were built around the annual migrations of plentiful salmon. Celilo Falls, in the lower Columbia, and Kettle Falls, in present-day eastern Washington, were two of the great Native fishing sites on the Columbia, where salmon were easily caught with nets as they fought their way over the falls. Before the dams were built, water cascaded over these basalt cliffs with a roar that could be heard for miles. But in the 1940s Celilo Falls was silenced by The Dalles Dam, and Kettle Falls was silenced by the Grand Coulee. Dam builders included fish passages at The Dalles, but Grand Coulee, with no fish passages, blocked salmon from the upper river with its wall of concrete. Today, with 81 dams on the main river and its tributaries, the Columbia is a series of large lakes, and the once-abundant native stocks of salmon are nearing extinction.

Celilo Park is just off Interstate 84, at the edge of Celilo Lake (the lake created by The Dalles Dam). The little park looks as if it is stepping right into the lake. If the dam were to break, Celilo Park would find itself perched on a rock shelf above the reborn roaring falls. Under the placid lake lie rock cliffs that drop more than 100 feet and extend all the way across the river. This is the site of the former Celilo Falls, which was one of the most important and famous Native fishing sites on the Columbia.

One of the most well-known photographs of the Columbia region is of Indian fishermen netting salmon at Celilo Falls. You can see it and other photographs, and hear the story of Celilo Falls, at both the Yakama Cultural Heritage Center in Washington and the Museum at Warm Springs in Oregon. Warm Springs tribal member and poet Elizabeth Woody writes of the silencing of the falls and its effect on the psyche of Indian people of the region. Her books are available from booksellers throughout the region.

Indian people of the Columbia River, many of them from the Yakama and Warm Springs Reservations, hold an annual First Salmon ceremony, welcoming the first spawning salmon each spring, in the longhouse at Celilo Village. Separated from the river by the freeway, Celilo Village consists of a few trailers and houses—all that remains of the original village.

Celilo Park (a highway rest stop with a boat ramp) is about 10 miles east of The Dalles, off I-84. The longhouse at Celilo Village is rarely open to guests, except during the annual First Salmon ceremony. The date is announced in local newspapers each spring.

Toppenish: *Yakama*

For more than a century the Yakima Valley, in south-central Washington, has been drawing down water from nearby rivers to irrigate its 350,000 acres of fruit orchards, hop farms, and wineries. Once dry grassland, the irrigated valley is today Washington State's breadbasket. Although the valley floor receives only 8 inches of rain a year, perfectly adapted native plants once grew here in abundance. These desert plants provided the bulk of the Native diet. Roots and berries were carefully harvested so they would reseed themselves and never had to be planted, cultivated, or watered. In this way Native peoples lived without dams or irrigation.

The 14 tribes and bands of the Yakama Indian Nation are the Palouse, Pisquouse, Yakama, Wenatchapam, Klinquit, Oche Chotes, Kow was say ee, Sk'in-pah, Kah-miltpah, Klickitat, Wish ham, See ap Cat, Li ay was, and Shyiks.

The word "Yakama" comes from their Salish-speaking neighbors. It means "a growing family" or "a tribal expansion." They spelled it "Yakima," like the nearby town of Yakima, until 1994, when the Confederated Tribes passed a resolution to revert to the original spelling of Yakama, as written in the Treaty of 1855.

The Yakama Nation's travel agency provides airline reservations with on-site ticketing, Amtrak and hotel reservations, and car rentals. Visitor information packets, including a calendar of events, can be obtained by writing to the Tourism Program, Yakama Nation, PO Box 151, Toppenish, WA 98948; (509)865-2030 or (509)865-5121. Offices are open Mon–Fri, 8am–5pm.

The Confederated Tribes and Bands of the Yakama Indian Nation live on 1.3 million acres of forest, range, and agricultural land. One of the largest reservations in the United States, the Yakama Reservation is one and a half times larger than the state of Rhode Island.

The predominant physical and spiritual landmark of the Yakama Indians' territory is the snowcapped peak of 12,276-foot Mount Adams, south of the Yakima Valley. The Yakama name for the mountain, Pahto, means "standing high," a name used for all of the volcanic peaks of the area—Mount Rainier, Mount St. Helens, and Mount Hood.

Today, the Yakama elders are revered as the historians and teachers of the Confederation's spiritual heritage and traditional culture. The word "respect" is not used lightly among the Yakamas. Most of the 8,560 tribal members own land near the towns of Toppenish, Wapato, White Swan, Brownstown, Harrah, and Union Gap. Visitors are welcome to stop by the tribal headquarters, which is in a large complex of buildings within the city limits of Toppenish. The one-stop complex also includes a restaurant, gift shop, theater, library, cultural heritage center, and RV park. Visitors can see historic Fort Simcoe on the reservation and view murals in the city of Toppenish depicting Native heritage. On the reservation, you can walk along trails in a protected wildlife refuge or drive over Satus Pass to the section of the spectacular Mount Adams Wilderness run by the tribe, for alpine camping and hiking.

Nipo Tach Num Strongheart was born on the Yakama Reservation in the town of White Swan, west of Toppenish. At age 11, he joined Buffalo Bill's Wild West Show. Later he was an actor in several Holly-wood films, and was a technical advisor on Indians for Hollywood film studios.

Yakama Nation Cultural Heritage Center

The Yakama Nation Cultural Heritage Center was designed by internationally known architect Pietro Belluchi and tribal consultants, based on the Yakamas' traditional tule mat–covered longhouse. It was built on ancestral lands of the Yakamas. Inside the large build-ing are a gift shop, library, theater, and the first trib-ally owned museum built in the Northwest.

It's best to tour the museum exhibits with a guide who can explain how objects on display were made. Permanent exhibits include an earthern lodge made of willow branches, reeds, grasses, and mud, of the kind that were used as permanent dwellings thousands of years ago in the valley and along the Columbia River. There is also a tepee made of tule mats as well as a re-creation of the fishing grounds at Celilo Falls, and fishing gear, tools, and baskets. Don't miss the "Indian Time Ball," a string diary made from hemp twine. Over the years, the string is knotted in a special way and rolled into a perfectly round ball to record the significant events in a woman's life. Six new exhibitions are mounted in the museum throughout the year.

Yakama culture is alive and well: many traditions are still practiced with reverence by some tribal members, who live by gathering food in the same way as their ances-tors did, practice their Native religion, and speak both English and their native Sahaptin.

In the same building housing the museum is a user-friendly one-room library with an emphasis on Native American culture. More than 12,000 volumes in the Native American section were donated by Nipo Strongheart, a Yakama descendant. Included in the collection are 30 books of legends written for chidren. Strongheart's books can be used only in the library.

First-run movies are shown at the center Thursday through Sunday for about half the price of other theaters. The 400-seat auditorium, with its stage light-ing, is also used for lectures, presentations, and other entertainment. A recent event was a fashion show of women's buckskin dresses, most made before the turn of the century, adorned with beadwork and porcupine-quill embroidery.

Yakama Nation Cultural Heritage Center Complex, 280 Buster Rd, PO Box 151, Toppenish, WA 98948; (509)865-2800. From Hwy 97, take the Buster Rd exit. The complex is next to the highway. The museum is open daily. Museum admission $4. The library is open Mon–Sat. The theater is open for both films and events. Call the number above for museum, library, and theater hours and special events.

Heritage Inn Restaurant

Luk-a-meen, a traditional Yakama Indian dish of button-sized dumplings with flakes of fresh or smoked salmon, served with Indian fry bread, is a common meal for Yakama families. Chef Britt Whipple of the Heritage Inn Restaurant, at the Yakama Nation Cultural Heritage Center, says the dumplings remind him of Hawaiian poi, but made with flour. In other regions of the west, luk-a-meen can be flavored with buffalo, venison, or elk, but Yakamas always use fresh salmon. Whipple has sparked the inn's menu with other items from Native American traditions, mostly from the Southwest (Papago cactus salad, corn salsa, buffalo stew, Pueblo barbecued pork). Most traditional Yakama foods, except for fresh salmon, are too labor-intensive to serve in a commercial restaurant. Don't leave without ordering a piece of pie made with tart huckleberries from the slopes of Mount Adams.

Unique heritage dinners are served to large groups booking the restaurant to experience Yakama tradition. The meal includes *sshaxu chuush* (saltwater clams), *waykaanish* (salmon) or *ayay* (trout) or *pay'umsh* (stuffed game hen), wild rice, *luk-a-meen* and fry bread, dessert, and coffee. The meal is enhanced by traditional dancing and storytelling. Guests leave with a small souvenir.

Heritage Inn Restaurant, 280 Buster Rd, PO Box 151, Toppenish, WA 98948; (509)865-2551 or (509)865-2800, ext 740. From Hwy 97, take the Buster Rd exit. The complex is next to the highway. Open daily for breakfast, lunch, and dinner. Espresso cart. Excellent Sunday brunch (with huckleberry crêpes). Reasonable prices. Reservations recommended.

Yakama Nation Resort RV Park

The Yakamas, recognizing that roaming RVers were in need of an encampment in the Yakima Valley, have installed a first-class (AAA-approved) RV park with 95 full hookup spaces (50 amps), tent camping area, swimming pool, showers, hot tub, laundry, basketball court, jogging track, and other amenities. The most popular lodgings are

14 colorfully decorated tepees, raised and ready for groups of up to 10 people per tepee, each with an outdoor fire pit.

Yakama Nation Resort RV Park, 280 Buster Rd, Toppenish, WA 98948; (800)874-3087 or (509)865-2000. Next to the Yakama Nation Cultural Heritage Center complex (see above), accessible by footbridge over the canal. Reasonable prices.

Yakama Art

"When you walk into our house it looks like the place exploded," says Norma Jack, who works at the Yakamas' summer camp in the mountains, teaching Native kids how to tan hides and how to make dance bustles, drums, cedar bark baskets, and featherwork for pow-wow fancy dancing regalia. "It's just one big workshop," says Jack. She suggests that learning how to make things is a form of watchfulness. "You learn from elders by watching and trying to imitate them, until you get it right." Numerous Indian artists raised by their grandparents remember playing with cast-off materials, such as small scraps of cattail and spruce root or beads, at the feet of a grandmother or grandfather, and then imitating until they became skilled themselves.

At the Real Yakama Fruit and Produce stand you can buy fresh apples, melons, apricots, and other seasonal fruit and vegetables grown by Yakama tribal members. Collectible Yakama Nation apple labels are for sale as well. The stand is 20 miles west of Toppenish, on the outskirts of Yakima, on Highway 97; (509)877-7256 or (509)865-5121. Open seasonally when crops are being harvested.

Arts and crafts created by Yakama tribal members are always sold during special events held on the reservation. Following are some of our recommendations.

The largest art event of the year is the Speelyi-mi Arts and Crafts Trade Fair, held annually in mid-March for more than 30 years. It usually takes place in the Yakama Nation Cultural Heritage Center's "winter-lodge" room, next to the museum; (509)865-2800. An admission fee is charged.

The Cultural Heritage Center's gift shop offers clothing, including traditional wing dresses and jingle dresses (dresses adorned with dozens of cone-shaped bells that jingle when the wearer dances), vests, skirts, and embroidered or printed jackets and caps from all over the Northwest. There's a large selection of jewelry on display in glass cases, much of it from the Southwest. You'll also find locally made beaded wallets, key chains, and other souvenirs. Ask clerks to point out gifts made by Yakama craftspeople.

You can buy art directly from the makers on tribal paydays in the main hallway of the Yakamas' administration offices. We've found some real gems here—a tiny handwoven basket hanging from a beaded necklace, for example. Beadwork, deerskin moccasins, and other crafts are for sale at lower prices than in stores; and artisans have time to chat about how they make their crafts. From Highway 97, at the Toppenish intersection, go west on Fort Road. The administration building is the first large building you see on your right (509)865-5121. It's okay to park in the lot out front and walk in.

In downtown Toppenish, Windflower 'Latit' Indian Trading Company (7A S Toppenish Ave, Toppenish; (509)865-1888) carries Yakama-made baskets, drums, and jewelry. At Inter Tribal Sales (2 Buena Way, Toppenish; (509)865-7775), Tom Estimo, Sr., designs handsome wool coats for men, women, and children using Indian-motif fabric milled in nearby Pendleton, Oregon. They're all hand-sewn at his store.

Delores George and her children often make the work sold in the Wapenish American Indian Trading Post (702 W 9th St, Wapato; (509)877-4554). She also sells Native American arts and crafts and beadworking supplies. Open daily, except Sunday. Wapato is between Toppenish and the town of Yakima, on Highway 97.

Tribally owned Mount Adams Furniture (180 E Jones Rd, Wapato; (800)821-9774 or (509)877-2191) produces chairs and ladder-back rockers, ottomans, and other contemporary furniture made of Columbia River alder wood and custom upholstered in Native American–design fabrics. The factory showroom is open to the public.

Internationally known silversmith Steve Gunnyon, of Yakama ancestry, opens his Wapato studio to visitors on request. Call for an appointment and directions; (509)877-4862.

Toppenish National Wildlife Refuge

A small portion of the Yakima Valley's natural ecosystem is preserved as Toppenish National Wildlife Refuge, in the heart of the Yakama Reservation. It is actually three refuges connected by a stream. Natural grasslands and nesting cover more than 1,000 acres, with another 580 acres flooded to create wetlands. Corn, barley, wheat, and alfalfa are sown to keep wintering birds from consuming nearby commercial crops. The refuge is a great place to bird-watch, except during hunting season, mid-October through mid-January. In the spring mallards, shovelers, and wood ducks trail ducklings; by summer's end, the shorebirds drop in during their southern migrations. Fall and wintering birds include pintails and Canada geese. You can see some of the birds from Highway 97, but it's best to take the less-traveled Old Goldendale Road to see eagles, hawks, herons, gulls, egrets, and terns. Thousands of songbirds also nest in brush along Toppenish Creek, which connects the three refuges. Expect to hear the hoots of great horned owls; watch for deer and muskrats (and signs of badgers' burrows). For hiking trails, take Highway 97 south from Toppenish to parking sites on Robbins Road and Pumphouse Road. No camping or overnight parking.

Write or call for maps from Toppenish National Wildlife Refuge, 21 Pumphouse Rd, US Hwy 97 S, Toppenish, WA 98948; (509)865-2405.

Hunting, Fishing, and Camping Permits

Canada geese, game birds, and rabbits can be hunted on the Yakama Reservation with a valid permit. You'll also need a current map of areas open to hunters. No big-game hunting, or hunting of any other animals, is allowed. Fishing is allowed in certain reservation streams, pursuant to tribal regulations. Permits and maps are available at sporting goods stores, motels, and other outlets in the towns of Toppenish and Yakima, but not directly from the tribe. Prices change seasonally. The tribe also has a fish pond where children under 12 can fish without a permit. Ask for the "Feel Free to Hunt Map" available from Toppenish National Wildlife Resource Management; (509)865-6262.

Camping at Mount Adams (Pahto)

In 1972, President Richard Nixon helped the Confederated Tribes and Bands of the Yakama Indian Nation regain their sacred mountain, Pahto, lost in treaty negotiations in 1855. Millions of acres of pristine wilderness are now managed by the Yakamas, with the 21,000 acres of the Mount Adams Wilderness open to the public from July 1 to September 30. The tribal area ("Tract D" of the wilderness area) almost entirely encompasses the mountain's broad east slope and includes four gorgeous campgrounds on three high mountain lakes (Bench, Mirror, and Bird). The lakes are stocked with foot-long cutthroat trout raised in Yakama hatcheries. At elevations above 4,700 feet, the lakes are accessible via primitive roads (a Honda Civic can make it; a loaded RV can't). Bird Creek Meadows, just below Mazama Glacier, where small streams trickle through fragile subalpine glades, is filled with thousands of wildflowers in the early summer. Hikers can take an easy 5-mile loop from Bird Lake Trail up to Bluff Lake's viewpoint, and then to the Trail of the Flowers (stay on trails through the meadows). Continue on to the Hellroaring Overlook, and then head back down via the Crooked Creek Falls Trail. Campsites are first come, first served; weekends are busiest. Bench Lake has 41 campsites; Bird Lake has 21; Mirror Lake, 6; and Sunrise Camp, 12. Drinking water and rest rooms are available at all except Sunrise Camp. Trailer hookups are not available.

The best way to reach Mount Adams Wilderness Area (Tract D) from the Yakama Reservation, about a 90-minute drive, is south on Hwy 97 over scenic Satus Pass to Goldendale, then west on 142 to the Glenwood cutoff. Continue to Trout Lake. The Mount Adams Ranger Station, in Trout Lake, has detailed maps of the area; 2455 Hwy 141, Trout Lake, WA 98650; (509)395-3400. Open daily, 8am–4:30pm. For information about hiking and camping in the tribe's section of the wilderness, contact the Forestry Development Program, Yakama Nation, PO Box 151, Toppenish, WA 98948; (509)865-5121, ext 657.

Pah Ty-Muu Thla-Ma Dance Company

More than 100 young people perform traditional music and dance in the Pah Ty-Muu Thla-Ma (Messengers of the Healing Generation) Dance Company under the direction of founder Sue Rigdon and cultural director Willie Selam, and with the guidance of tribal elders through the Wapato Indian Club. "The inexplicable truth of the performance is gathered from a spiritual pool that has been replenished over generations, back to the time of Creation," says Rigdon, who founded the program in the Wapato schools 23 years ago. "The mystical training from the elders of our people enables us to teach the children a way to draw from this pool of collective knowledge and energy."

Audiences are often deeply moved during the Pah Ty-Muu Thla-Ma's hour-long performances. This is work from the heart and takes years of preparation. Whole families are involved in handcrafting the traditional dance regalia—from beaded deerskin moccasins and clothing to feather bustles. "When the children dance for you, they are conveying a message of reverence toward the past, environmental care, brotherhood, and peace that transcends time and race," says Rigdon. The group includes non-Indian students as well. Dances and songs are drawn from Indian cultures all over North America, as well as those originating in the Columbia River basin. The group is accompanied by the Selam Family Drum, men trained in the centuries-old spiritual discipline of "Na-Ti-Tayt" singing.

Pah Ty-Muu Thla-Ma dances for state, national, and international multicultural conferences, and for special events, such as Treaty Days, held in June. Contact Sue Rigdon at Wapato Middle School; (509)877-2173.

Yakama Nation Review

The journalists' office in the little cinder-block building next to the tribal center on Fort Road look like any other small-town weekly newspaper office—stacks of paper burying the desks and bookcases spilling over onto the floor. The 12-page weekly paper, subsidized by the tribe, is packed with Yakama Indian news, intelligent editorials, impassioned letters to the editor, and a calendar of events, as well as Native American news from all over the country. It keeps the tribe informed and is an eye-opener for non-Indians.

Subscriptions are $26 a year from Yakama Nation Review, PO Box 310, Toppenish, WA 98948; (509)865-5121.

Toppenish Murals

A few years ago the Toppenish Mural Society started painting the town with historical murals. Now nearly 80,000 visitors a year come to gape at the town's past, illustrated on more than 40 buildings by muralists. Some depict local Indian history. Most portray the settlement and farming of the Yakima Valley in the years since 1830. Those illustrating Indian history include *The Indian Stick Game, Signing of the Treaty—1855, The Blanket Traders, Indians' Winter Encampment, Cow Camp,* and *Haller's Defeat. The Rhythms of Celilo,* which shows Indians fishing from scaffolding thrust over the Columbia River at Celilo Falls, is painted on Pacific Power and Light's building at the corner of Third and Elm.

Narrated, mule-drawn wagon tours of the murals are offered by two companies. Conestoga Tours, (509)865-2898, offers stagecoach, covered-wagon, and trolley tours, Apr–Nov. Mural Tours, (509)697-3385 or (509)865-4515, has tours on a horse-drawn trolley, a covered wagon, and a buggy. Neither are Native-owned, but sometimes tours leave from the Yakama Nation Cultural Heritage Center. Pamphlets with self-guided tours are available from the Toppenish Mural Society, 11A S Toppenish Ave, Toppenish, WA 98948; (509)865-6516.

The American Hop Museum

The Yakima Valley is one of the world's largest suppliers of hops, producing over 25 percent of the world's crop. Before modern machinery, Yakama tribal members played a vital part in the harvest. Many Yakama elders remember the tepee encampments to which they returned, with bruise-swollen hands, after picking hops all day under the scorching sun. At the end of the season, Native women gathered twine on which the hop vines had grown, to reuse in weaving projects. A mural and bronze statue of a Yakama woman with a basket of hops commemorate their hard work. Both are in the Old Timers Plaza in the center of town. The American Hop Museum, which houses hop memorabilia from all over the world, contains several photographs of Native laborers.

The American Hop Museum, B St (near E Toppenish Ave), Toppenish, WA 98948; (509)865-4677. Open 10am–3pm daily, May–Oct 31, weekends the rest of the year. Small admission fee.

Fort Simcoe State Park

Fort Simcoe State Park, about 30 miles west of Toppenish on Fort Road, is a beautiful grassy area at the foot of the Simcoe Mountains. Next to a bubbling creek and surrounded by a shady grove of oaks, the site was once a large encampment where a number of important trails converged. It was also the beginning of the trail from the Yakima Valley, through a gap in the mountains, to the Yakamas' fishing sites on the Columbia River. Known as Mool Mool ("Many Springs"), it was the home of Yakama leader Skloom, one of the signers of the Treaty of 1855; it was also used as a tepee encampment in the summer and early fall when food was gathered.

A bugle regiment from the U.S. Ninth Infantry Division was stationed at the site in 1856 under Robert Selden Garnett. The infantry was presumably there to keep the Indians safe from aggressive settlers. The real reason, however, was that Nisqually chief Leschi, from the Puget Sound area, had ridden over the Cascade Range to warn the inland tribes that the treaties offered by Territorial Governor Issac Stevens were not in their best interest (see the introduction to the Western Washington chapter).

The troops renamed Mool Mool Simcoe Valley after the Yakama phrase *sim quwe,* which means "a dip between two hills like a saddleback." It later was the site of both the headquarters for the Bureau of Indian Affairs' Yakama Agency and a boarding school for Indian children.

The area was named a historic site in 1956, but the sparkling white buildings and barracks there now are reconstructions. All four homes, including one representing the turn-of-the-century boarding school, are appointed with period furnishings. It's a beautiful place for a picnic on the lawn, but the history of Fort Simcoe is not so pleasant. After the "Indian Wars" of 1856, won by the U.S. cavalry, say our sources, soldiers randomly lynched young Indian men and left their bodies hanging in the trees all across the Yakima Valley to quell any further resistance.

Fort Simcoe State Park, 5150 Fort Simcoe Rd, White Swan, WA 98952; (509)874-2372. Thirty miles west of Toppenish; follow Fort Rd from Toppenish west to the end of the pavement. The park is open Apr–Oct from 6:30am to dusk. Buildings are open Wed–Sun, 9am–4pm; or by appointment. Free admission.

Indian Painted Rocks

On the outskirts of the town of Yakima near the Yakima Sportsmen State Park campground, pictographs are painted on a 70-foot-high cliff of columnar basalt.

The area was undeveloped when the cliffside was made part of the state park in the 1950s. Now megastores and houses surround it. Still, that doesn't diminish the awe people feel about the rock art, which extends across the basalt wall for about 400 feet. Anthropologists surmise that the Indians painted the cliffs from canoes at a time when the valley floor was submerged by a prehistoric lake. The area's cultural significance was recognized as early as 1924, when the Northern Pacific Railroad Company gave Yakima County the title to 17.6 acres around the cliffs to protect the pictographs. Nonetheless, the paintings have suffered plenty of abuse. Water leaking from a wooden irrigation flume kept them continously wet, and contruction blasts for a second flume buried some of them in talus. Early-day Yakima merchants even painted ads over the pictographs. Most of the ads have faded away by now, leaving the ancient paintings intact, a remarkable testament to the original paint formula of pure minerals mixed with fish oil and other organic substances.

Follow signs on Powerhouse Rd south of Hwy 12 between Gleed and Fruitvale (the old Chinook Hwy). Park your car on the shoulder of the road and follow the trail to the cliffside.

Local and regional news is published biweekly in Spilyay Tymoo (Coyote News) by the Confederated Tribes of Warm Springs. Its offices are in the basement of the historic girls' dorm of the tribal school at 1115 Wasco Street. For a subscription, write PO Box 870, Warm Springs, OR 97761; (541)553-1644. The cost is $9 a year, or $15 outside the United States.

Warm Springs:
Warm Springs

The Warm Springs Reservation begins on the southeastern flanks of Mount Hood, where tribal people still pick their year's supply of wild huckleberries, and descends through cinnamon-barked ponderosa pines to the sagebrush-covered high desert of central Oregon, where the sun shines almost year-round.

The 600,000-acre reservation, 1½ hours from Portland, is home to three tribes who arrived here after signing the Treaty of 1855. The first two tribes to arrive were from the Columbia River Gorge area, today about an hour's drive from the reservation. Like the Indians who lived at the mouth of the Columbia, one of these tribes spoke a dialect of Chinook. The other spoke Sahaptin. Both tribes traditionally used these lands to gather food. Included in the agreement they signed with the U.S. government was the right to fish, hunt, and gather food in usual and customary places, including the Columbia River and some of its tributaries. The Northern Paiutes, who arrived on the reservation 20 years later, were hunters from northern Nevada and southeastern Oregon; they spoke Shoshone. Today they are together called the Confederated Tribes of Warm Springs.

Each spring a traditional Root Feast ceremony is held in the tribal long-house. Elders select those who will dress in traditional clothing and basket hats and dig roots for the ceremony with original tools. During the day of the feast, there are worship dances, prayers, and blessings over fish, deer, pyaxi, lu'ks, xa'us, celery, mosses, and fruit For a thorough explanation of the Root Feast, see the exhibit at the Museum at Warm Springs.

The tribes' administration offices are housed in the town of Warm Springs, right off Highway 26, in a collection of historic and modern brick and wood-frame Indian agency buildings. Nearby is the splendid Museum at Warm Springs, with the largest tribally owned collection of artifacts in the United States. About 14 miles north of the museum is Kah-Nee-Ta Resort and Village. Just south of the reservation, the Deschutes, Crooked, and icy Metolius Rivers converge behind Round Butte Dam, creating Lake Billy Chinook, one of the largest recreational lakes in Oregon. In the spring the desert floor blooms with hot pink phlox, blue camas, and chartreuse wild buckwheat. Wild iris clings to the banks of the rivers, its bright yellow flags resplendent against the rimrock.

The Museum at Warm Springs

The Museum at Warm Springs is an inspired work of art. Even if the museum were empty, the building would be a monument to the land and the ancestors of the Warm Springs people. A creek flows around volcanic boulders at the entrance; thick fir columns support the ceiling. The rooflines echo the form of a tule mat dwelling, a plank house, and a travois; the exterior brick walls are set in a traditional basket-weave design.

When the museum was conceived in the 1960s, tribal leaders knew that their traditions were fading. Not only were the languages and old ways disappearing but speculators in Native American art were paying cash for family heirlooms. The heirlooms were then resold to private collectors and museums, disappearing from the reservation forever. Concerned that their children were losing their heritage to strangers, the tribes decided to establish their own museum. They allocated $50,000 a year to buy heirlooms for the museum, and spent more than $900,000 for artifacts and historical photographs. They appropriated another $2.5 million in 1988 to underwrite construction of the award-winning $7.5 million museum.

Artist Pat Courtney Gold drives all the way to Oregon's eastern border to gather the natural materials she uses in basket making: Indian hemp (which is spun into cordage), the red bark of Indian dogbane, tule reed, the entire leaf of cattails, sedges, and wild grasses. Pat is available to lecture on traditional and contemporary Columbia Basin art, basketry, and Wasco Indian culture; (541)553-3331.

The most stunning display in the self-guided museum tour is a replica of a wedding among the Wasco, one of the tribes in the Confederation. The gift-giving aspect of the ceremony is narrated as a spotlight shines on each member of the wedding party and the exquisitely beaded and woven gifts they are exchanging. One gift is a horse dressed in vivid beaded trappings. The faces were cast from those of Wasco tribal members living on the reservation today and seem very real.

There are also models of dwellings: a Paiute wickiup, a Warm Springs tepee, and a Wasco plank house. In an intimate circular room, you can sit and listen to "Songs of Our People," a 20-minute videotape of drumming and singing. The program includes a fragment of a ceremonial Washat and Feather religious song, a powwow round dance, energetic stick-game songs, and one song sung when gathering roots. In another alcove is a gallery of historical photographs showing the early days on the reservation, accompanied by recordings of elders discussing their childhoods.

None of the items in the museum's collection is anonymous, as is usually true of Native items in museum collections. Each of the 200 cornhusk bags made by master weavers, 150 Klickitat baskets, and rare Paiute willow baskets has a known history. Identifying some of the objects was a challenge to the tribe. A hollow piece of sheep's horn, carved and lidded, was a mystery until one elder remembered its purpose: women once kept sunburn salve in it, and used the salve when going into the desert hills to dig the year's supply of roots and bulbs.

Elders and artists give day-long "Living Tradition" presentations at the museum on weekends, from Memorial Day weekend through Labor Day. Lectures cover topics such as traditional knot tying, sally bags (a basket style unique to the Columbia River area), cedar-root basketry, Paiute artifacts, and tribal landmark history. The presentation might include powwow fancy dancing by the Spotted Eagle Dancers, performances by the Dry Creek singers and dancers, and poetry readings by author Elizabeth Woody.

The museum complex includes a gift shop (look for Lillian Pitt's raku ceramic masks and Pat Courtney Gold's baskets) and the Changing Exhibits Gallery, featuring Indian art.

The Museum at Warm Springs, PO Box C, Warm Springs, OR 97761; (541)553-3331. On Hwy 26 at the town of Warm Springs, 1½ hours from Portland. Open daily, 10am–5pm. Admission $6. Museum members receive a gift shop discount, unlimited admission, invitations to events, a subscription to the museum's quarterly newsletter, and other benefits.

Kah-Nee-Ta Resort and Village

Kah-Nee-Ta was the Indian name of the woman who once inhabited the canyon floor along the Warm Springs River. Her name means Root Digger, and it's safe to assume that it was a name given to her by tribal elders because she was an especially gifted food provider. The resort that bears her name was built in the early 1970s, in the Warm Springs River canyon.

The spring water bubbling from the ground near the Warm Springs River is *hot,* but it doesn't smell like sulfur—two big reasons for the resort's popularity. From the air, the 139-room lodge resembles an arrowhead with a handsome swimming pool in the center. The doors to the rooms are painted bright orange, which makes the lodge look dated. But lit up on a frosty winter night, the doors look like 139 campfires glowing around the steaming swimming pool. There is also a tepee encampment consisting of canvas tepees raised on real lodgepoles over concrete floors with wood-burning fires inside. It's kid heaven. The tepees are right next to the miniature golf course and an Olympic-size hot springs pool that features decks, diving boards, and fountains shaped like bears clutching salmon.

The resort complex also includes RV parking spaces, 25 fully furnished cottages, a gift shop, tennis courts, and an 18-hole golf course.

You can rent horses from Warm Springs chief Delvis Heath (a former rodeo competitor) for trail rides, or take an easy trip down the Warm Springs River in a kayak. A full-time recreation counselor is on hand at the swimming pool office.

Ask at the resort's main desk for "Gary the Gard'ner's" 25-cent maps of the resort grounds, which explain the geology and plants of the area. Hand-printed and reproduced on a copy machine, they look like pages torn out of his journal. "Well, I hope I haven't confused anyone beyond recovery," he scribbles in the middle of the page containing his geo-hike map. It's a good way to shift your kids' attention to the rocks and wildflowers of the canyon. Easy-to-read hiking and bike trail maps are free.

Fry bread and huckleberry preserves are served with dinners in the lodge's Juniper Room, overlooking the canyon. Lunch is served in the Pinto Grill. Salmon is a specialty here, as well as "Bird in Clay" (Cornish game hen stuffed with wild rice and baked and served in its own clay pot). Popular outdoor salmon bakes are featured Saturdays from Memorial Day weekend through Labor Day. Fillets are skewered on alder sticks, a traditional method, and baked around an alderwood fire. Gift shop on premises.

Kah-Nee-Ta Resort and Village, PO Box K, Warm Springs, OR 97761; (800)554-4786 and (541)553-1112. Follow the signs from the Simnasho exit on Hwy 26 or from the town of Warm Springs on Hwy 26. Charter airlines land at the Madras airport, 25 miles from the resort. Commercial airlines land at the Redmond airport, 52 miles from the resort. Resort room and suite rates are $100–$295, double or single occupancy; no tax. Open daily, year-round.

A poet and professor of creative writing at the Institute of American Indian Arts in Santa Fe, New Mexico, Elizabeth Woody has written three books of acclaimed poetry and prose. Luminaries of the Humble and Seven Hands, Seven Hearts were published in 1995. Her first, Hand into Stone, won a 1988 American Book Award. Her books are available from the Museum at Warm Springs gift shop and from booksellers throughout the Northwest.

Warm Springs Fish Hatchery

Spring Chinook salmon and steelhead come up the Warm Springs River from April through July—some of them wild stock that have been coming back to the river for thousands of generations. Sorted from hatchery fish at a small dam, the wild fish are allowed to continue their spawning migration upstream. The crystal-clear, narrow Warm Springs River runs through a mostly untouched canyon; the fish hatchery is one of the few places on reservation property open to visitors. During the winter, ponds are frozen over and snow covers the ground, but from April through September you can watch the huge salmon swimming in the tanks, as well as the young fish churning as they wait to be released.

Warm Springs Fish Hatchery, PO Box 790, Warm Springs, OR 97761; (541)553-1692. From Hwy 26, take the Simnasho exit to Junction 3, and follow the signs to Kah-Nee-Ta. Watch for fish hatchery signs on your right. Open daily 7:30am–4pm.

Pendleton: *Umatilla*

The sagebrush is a soft dusky green and shadows are lavender against the rolling fields of wheat along the Umatilla River canyon. In the distance are the Blue Mountains, a ribbon of hills stretching from north to south as far as the eye can see, like an indigo wave on the horizon.

The Umatilla Indian Reservation, about 4 hours east of Portland, adjoins the town of Pendleton at the foot of the Blue Mountains in northeastern Oregon. Descendants of the Umatilla, Walla Walla, and Cayuse Tribes share the small reservation. All three tribes were speakers of the Sahaptin language, and all three once shared the Columbia River basin at its eastern end, from the John Day River to the river's big bend near Walla Walla. The Cayuse also shared territory with the neighboring Nez Perce. Both the Cayuse and Nez Perce acquired horses in the early 1700s and became extraordinary horse breeders.

When white fur traders made their way into the area in the early 1800s, the dominant Cayuse seized the opportunity to increase trade, encouraging the establishment of a fur-trading fort at the confluence of the Columbia and Walla Walla Rivers. White accounts of the Cayuse describe them as reserved and imperial; their own language describes them as "the superior people." By the mid-1800s, the Cayuse's herds of horses numbered in the thousands, grazing bunch-grass growing in the meadows and valleys from the John Day River to the Wallowa Mountains.

At the time of white contact, the Cayuse, Umatilla, and Walla Walla Tribes lived in semipermanent, narrow, tule mat lodges, often 60 feet long. It was not uncommon to have 10 families living together within a lodge, each with its own family fire. Mud baths and sweat houses were close to home.

A virulent attack of measles hit the tribes after the last wagon train of the season pulled into Marcus Whitman's mission near Walla Walla, shortly after Whitman returned from the East Coast, where he had arranged to help more emigrants enter the area. On November 29, 1847, after burying their children who had died in the night, a group of enraged Cayuse men, suspicious of Whitman's true motives, killed the missionaries and took 50 people hostage. This incident came to be called the Whitman Massacre.

Consequently, the Umatilla, Cayuse, and Walla Walla Tribes were forced to sign a treaty with the U.S. government, ceding more than six million acres of land, leaving them with 245,699 acres.

Umatilla Reservation

The Slater Act of March 3, 1885, and the later Dawes Act divided the reservation up into parcels, assigned allotments to families, and gave the rest to white homesteaders, eroding the tribes' lands further. The land is still called the Umatilla Reservation, but its 120,000 acres is today a checkerboard of Indian and non-Indian ownership. The reservation adjoins Umatilla National Forest, forming a wildlife corridor with Ochoco, Wallowa-Whitman, and Malheur National Forests—the tribes' former territory, now all public land that dominates Oregon's northeast corner. Additional thousands of acres of public land adjoining the reservation are owned by the Bureau of Land Management and are leased to ranchers.

The Umatilla River flows through the reservation to the Columbia River from artesian springs. The word "Umatilla" means "water rippling over sand."

The reservation is bisected by Interstate 84. Five miles east of Pendleton on Interstate 84, take exit 216 and travel north ¼ mile to the tribe's information center in the Wildhorse Gaming Resort. A hotel, golf course, RV park, and the Tamustalik Cultural Institute are being built on this site.

Tamustalik Cultural Institute

Across the nearly 2,000-mile-long Oregon Trail flowed people, goods, and ideas. The opening of this route in the 1840s drew tens of thousands of settlers. Heralded as one of the greatest mass migrations in the annals of human history, the overland travel of the pioneers had an indelible impact on the Indians of the region. The 13-million-dollar Tamustalik (pronounced ta-MUST-ah-luck) Cultural Institute, being built on 640 acres behind the Wildhorse Gaming Resort, will tell the story of the Oregon Trail from the Indian point of view for the first time.

Groundbreaking for the institute began on the 140-year anniversary of the Treaty of 1855. The project, which includes a walk through history, a gallery devoted to the memory of the Cayuse horses, a huge art gallery, a gift shop, and outdoor encampments, is expected to be completed by the summer of 1997.

A donation entitles you to have your name, or the name of a loved one, permanently recognized on the center's "Noo nim lough te we" ("our friends") wall sculpture.

Funds may be sent to the Tamustalik Donations Fund, Umatilla Indian Reservation, PO Box 638, Pendleton, OR 97801.

St. Andrew's Mission

Cayuse chief Taawitoy asked missionaries visiting Fort Walla Walla in 1838 to baptize his infant child. Nine years later, the chief gave the

Catholics a log cabin on the banks of the Umatilla River for their first mission. The priests set up housekeeping just a few weeks before the Whitman Massacre; shortly after the massacre, their cabin was burned to the ground. The priests were given another cabin in 1864, and added a church and boarding school; Jesuits took charge in 1888.

The present-day mission, open to visitors, was built on higher ground in the 1930s, in California mission style, with stucco walls and red-tiled roof. The small church, still in use, contains hand-carved wooden statuary from Romania and is decorated with Native beadwork, altar cloths, and blankets. Wooden crosses on the oldest graves in the nearby cemetery were destroyed by wildfire in the 1950s, but many burial sites are marked with headstones.

St. Andrew's Mission. Take Hwy 30 east to St. Andrew's Rd. Call first for a tour of the mission; (541)276-6155.

Crow's Shadow Institute

Crow's Shadow Institute, a nonprofit arts facility, is in the old St. Andrew's Mission schoolhouse, which adjoins St. Andrew's church. It includes a printmaking workshop and room in which guest artists can teach. Nationally known artist James Lavadour, a tribal member and contemporary landscape painter who grew up on the Umatilla Reservation, co-founded the institute with his wife, JoAnn, also an artist. Their goal was to help the many other Indian artists living in rural eastern Washington and Oregon with their professional development.

James Lavadour's work is represented in Portland by the Elizabeth Leach Gallery, but he maintains a studio at Crow's Shadow. Two other artists from the Umatilla Reservation have national reputations as well: painter PY Minthorn studied at the Institute of American Indian Arts in Santa Fe and now lives in Washington, D.C. Beadworker Maynard White Owl Lavadour, whose work is in major museums and metropolitan galleries, lives on the Umatilla Reservation and works out of his home.

*Marilyn Whirlwind, the doctor's receptionist on CBS's Emmy Award-winning series **Northern Exposure**, was played by Elaine Miles, whose parents are Cayuse and Nez Perce. Elaine is skilled in traditional arts (she's beader Maynard Lavadour's cousin), and is also a prize-winning traditional dancer.*

Crow's Shadow Institute (in the schoolhouse adjoining St. Andrew's church), Rt 1, Box 517, Pendleton, OR 97801; (541)276-3954. Take Hwy 30 east to St. Andrew's Rd and watch for signs. Look here for postings of art events as well as tribal members' studio hours and phone numbers.

Doris Bounds Collection

Hermiston resident Doris Swayze Bounds collected deertail-adorned ceremonial dresses, beaded and cornhusk bags, cradleboards, and other items throughout her life, including a cornhusk diaper bag and the first moccasins given to her by her Nez Perce nanny. Bounds, a banker, was adopted in a formal ceremony by the Montana Blackfeet in 1965, and was a friend of the Umatilla. She accumulated more than 3,000 items over the years, many of them given to her for safekeeping. Her collection, one of the largest of its kind in the United States, will be housed in its own wing, in the Hall of Native Peoples, at the High Desert Museum, just south of Bend, Oregon, a drive of several hours from the Umatilla Reservation through John Day Fossil Beds National Monument.

High Desert Museum, 59800 S Hwy 97, Bend, OR 97702; (541)382-4754. You can get to the museum from the Umatilla Reservation by heading south on Hwy 395 to Hwy 7, then driving through John Day Fossil Beds National Monument (the original border of Cayuse territory) and Ochoco National Forest to Bend, about a 3-hour drive. After a stop at the museum, you can loop back to Portland north on Hwy 26 through the Warm Springs Reservation. The High Desert Museum is open 9am–5pm daily, year-round. Admission $6.25.

Cayuse Horses

The Cayuse horse was distinctive, with a large head, muscular little body, and long mane and tail—a descendant of the Spanish mustang brought to the New World by the conquistadors. Bred for their intelligence, toughness, and endurance, the horses were adorned in elaborately beaded masks, martingales (breastplates that drape over the chest), and ribbons and feathers. The breed virtually disappeared when the animals were killed by the U.S. cavalry in an effort to extinguish the Cayuse's will to fight. Nearly all of the remaining wild horses, considered a nuisance by ranchers, were rounded up in the 1950s, loaded into boxcars, and shipped to slaughter. The neighboring Nez Perce lost their horses much the same way.

Fortunately, in the 1920s, remnants from wild herds that had strayed into remote areas were gathered by a packer and mapmaker for the U.S. Geological Survey. He registered and bred the strays over the years to preserve the bloodlines. Antone Minthorn, chairman of the Umatilla Tribe's General Council, remembers Cayuse horses from his childhood and plans to bring them back to the reservation. When the Tamustalik Cultural Institute opens, an entire gallery will be devoted to honoring the Cayuse horses and annual roundups.

The Pendleton Round Up and Happy Canyon Pageant

The Pendleton Round Up, held every September on the rodeo grounds in downtown Pendleton, would be just another rodeo if it weren't for the Indians' 200-tepee encampment, top-name country-western performers, and the "Let 'er Buck Room" bar. However, the Round Up is just as well known for the Happy Canyon Pageant held nightly during the rodeo.

Today's Round Up has its roots in Native tradition: The tribes once raced their horses during their own roundup, held where the arena now sits. It was such a popular event that the tribes and the townspeople sat down together in 1909 to brainstorm a rodeo extravaganza. In addition to the Pendleton Round Up, they devised an energetic pageant about Pendleton's mixed heritage, the Happy Canyon Pageant. The first segment begins in an idyllic Indian world threatened by storm clouds and ends with the tribe sadly dismantling their tepees while someone sings the sentimental "Indian Love Song." The stage goes dark and then bursts to life with the raucous arrival of the settlers and a slapstick parody of frontier Pendleton.

Recently the pageant has generated some controversy. Defenders claim the pageant memorializes a way of life that ended abruptly. "You'd have to have a heart of steel not to feel sad about it," says one tribal member. Critics counter that Indians didn't disappear; they're still here, going to Pendleton schools and buying their groceries like everyone else, and argue that although stereotypes may make a play more entertaining, there's nothing funny about the pageant's portrayal of Pendleton's Chinese laborers in coolie hats.

Regardless of how the pageant may change, however, the Pendleton Round Up will continue to be a much anticipated event in the Indian community. The Indians hold private ceremonies on the reservation before entering the rodeo grounds. Then Indian families and friends set up their canvas tepees in the encampment that adjoins the rodeo grounds, and gather to enjoy dancing, drumming, and singing—a treasured family and community event.

Pendleton Round Up, PO Box 609, Pendleton, OR 97801; (800)457-6336. The rodeo grounds are at 1205 SW Court on the west side of downtown Pendleton. Pendleton adjoins the Umatilla Reservation. Visitors may walk through the Round Up's Indian encampment, where crafts, art, souvenirs, and fry bread and other treats are for sale. The Pendleton Round Up is held over a 4-day period each September. The Happy Canyon Pageant takes place Thurs–Sat evenings during the Round Up. Round Up tickets range from $7 to $17.50; pageant tickets are $7–$12.

Jackson Sundown

A member of the Chief Joseph band of Nez Perce who survived the Nez Perce War as a young boy, Jackson Sundown became one of the best bronc riders in the country.

In Pendleton, he was a Round Up crowd favorite, earning his way to the bronc-riding semifinals four years in a row and winning third place in 1915. When he was named Outstanding Rodeo Performer of the Year, the Round Up awarded him a golden belt buckle. That same year, at the age of 50, Sundown won the world champion bronc-riding title.

A 1916 photograph of Jackson Sundown, taken when he was named Outstanding Rodeo Performer of the Year, is part of a series of sepia-tinted note cards, posters, and silk-screened T-shirts available at the Wildhorse Gaming Resort's gift shop.

In 1972, Sundown was posthumously inducted into the Round Up Hall of Fame, for his outstanding performance as a rodeo cowboy. When he wasn't on the rodeo circuit, Jackson Sundown lived on the Flathead Reservation in northwestern Montana.

Located on the Pendleton rodeo grounds, the Round Up Hall of Fame is an absorbing collection of memorabilia, including photographs of all the Happy Canyon Pageant court and some of their regalia. The photographs of Sundown show the intricate floral beadwork on his gauntlets, indicative of the quality of beadwork being done at the turn of the century. The Round Up Hall of Fame is located under the south grandstand on the rodeo grounds.

Round Up Hall of Fame, PO Box 609, Pendleton, OR 97801; (541)276-2553. Open year-round. Free admission. Call for hours.

National Forests and Wilderness Areas

The 1½-million-acre Umatilla National Forest was once Cayuse and Umatilla territory filled with grazing horses. Threaded with un-improved trails, the mostly pine forest includes heavily timbered slopes, grassland ridges and benches, and bold granite outcroppings. Elevations range from 1,900 to 7,000 feet. Summers are warm and dry, with cool evenings. Expect snow in the winter. The primitive trails often cross small clear creeks without bridges. The forest supports over 200 species of birds, including several kinds of woodpeckers. In April, watch for wild turkeys. Hummingbirds pass through or return to nest in April and May. Bighorn lambs are born in late May. Elk calves and fawns are dropped in June and July.

You can also follow Highway 395 south of Pendleton for 8 miles to McKay Creek National Wildlife Refuge to see gulls, sandpipers, killdeer, pheasants, partridges, and golden and bald eagles during summer months. In winter waterfowl, mostly Canada geese and ducks, live on the refuge.

Another pretty spot is North Fork Umatilla Wilderness. On the Umatilla Reservation, follow the Umatilla River Road (all roads on the reservation are open to the public unless posted) to Gibbon and continue along the river on Forest Road 32 to North Fork Umatilla Wilderness. Take time to look closely at the cliffs on the way, which are covered with wildflowers and fluorescent green moss in the spring. Bring binoculars to look for waterfowl, wild turkeys, chukars, and woodpeckers in the ponderosa pine groves along the river, as well as nesting birds in the willows. On either side of the Umatilla River are steep, wooded cliffs that rise to plateaus covered with native bunchgrass. The wilderness area offers 27 miles of trail, with climbs of 2,000 to 5,400 feet. Horses are allowed; motorized and mechanized vehicles, including mountain bikes, are not. Anglers may fish for wild native trout and steelhead with a state permit, available in local sporting goods stores. Watch for elk and deer, as well as blue and ruffed grouse. Several trailheads begin near Umatilla Forks. A favorite short hike is the Beaver Marsh trail used by schools in outdoor education classes. Beavers have flooded the last section of the trail; if you tread quietly, you may see them at work.

For free road maps call the Oregon Department of Tourism; (800)547-7842. For free maps and brochures about national forests in the area, stop at Umatilla National Forest headquarters, 2517 SW Hailey, Pendleton, OR 97801; (541)278-3716.

Indian Lake Campground

Indian Lake Recreation Area has a tribally owned campground open to the public next to a pristine 80-acre artificial lake in the Blue Mountains. A full-time attendant is on duty during summer months to monitor the 42-site campground. Amenities include running water, cooking grills, fire pits, picnic tables, and rest rooms. The lake is stocked annually with trout. Only nonmechanized boats and boats with electric outboards are allowed. The annual fish derby is held on Father's Day, with cash prizes.

For Indian Lake Recreation Area campground reservations, call (541)443-3338 or (541)276-3873. The campground is 18 miles southeast of Pilot Rock, Oregon (on Hwy 395), at an elevation of 4,200 feet. Watch for signs.

Pendleton Woolen Mills

The histories of the Pendleton Woolen Mills and the area's Indians are intertwined. The tribes of the plateau (eastern Oregon,

Washington, Idaho, and Montana) traditionally wove heavy blankets from mountain goat hair, with a warp of vegetable fibers. The mill, built on the Umatilla River in 1896 near the western border of the Umatilla Reservation, began mechanically weaving wool blankets but modified the complex Indian designs over the years, until they became the more simple patterns of the present day. The mill is operated by the non–Native Bishop family, descendants of the original owners.

Pendleton blankets are today a favorite gift among Indian people. The blankets are exceptionally well loomed, and the company incorporates into their blanket patterns both Native-style designs and Native ideals, with their Legendary Blanket series. The first Chief Eagle Robe was dedicated to Chief Seelatsee of the Yakama Tribe, and in 1985 the company honored Chief Clarence Burke of the Umatilla Tribe. The company has also recently issued the Hope Series, a limited edition of blankets designed by Indian artists; sales benefit the American Indian College Fund.

Pendleton Woolen Mills, 1307 SE Court Pl, Pendleton, OR 97801; (541)276-6911. The mill sells clothing, handbags, yardage, and blankets as well as seconds, 8am–5pm daily. There are four free guided tours daily, Mon–Fri. For a free catalogue of the Hope Series blankets, contact the American Indian College Fund, PO Box 367, Camden, NC 27921; (800)987-3863.

Whitman Mission National Historic Site

This historic site near Walla Walla, 40 miles north of Pendleton, for years told only one side of the conflict between the Cayuse and the missionaries. Now, however, it attempts to incorporate the Cayuse point of view in its interpretation of the Whitman Massacre. Marcus and Narcissa Whitman and most of their family were murdered on this site by a handful of Cayuse men who had watched half of their tribe die from smallpox and measles after the missionaries' arrival. The Catholic-hating newspapers of the day blamed the Jesuits, who had arrived only four days before the massacre, for inciting the Indians. However, the men who killed the Whitmans believed that the missionary was deliberately killing the tribe's children while his own lived, as well as encouraging a flood of pioneers to invade and ruin Indian lands. After the massacre, several Cayuse men were rounded up at random, tried in a kangaroo court, and hanged in Oregon City (the end of the Oregon Trail), a part of the story most accounts leave out.

Whitman Mission National Historic Site, Rt 2, Box 247, Walla Walla, WA 99362; (509)529-2761. Seven miles west of Walla Walla on Hwy 12. The interpretive center *is open 8am–4:30pm daily. Park grounds are open dawn to dusk. Admission $2; children under 17 free. A 10-minute orientation slide show is shown every half hour. Trails to the mission, graves, and monument are self-guided.*

Raphael's Restaurant and Catering

Raphael Hoffman is a member of the Nez Perce tribe, and her namesake restaurant, located in Pendleton, offers one of the best dining experiences in the region. Located in the historic Roy Raley House, the restaurant contains three intimate dining rooms decorated with Indian art, and a small bar (try the wild huckleberry daiquiri). The food shows a distinctive Native American touch: wild greens in the dinner salads, huge portions of hickory-smoked prime rib, succulent salmon wrapped in spinach and smothered with wild huckleberries, and marinated quail finished with a sauce seasoned with juniper berries. Wild game such as rattlesnake and elk are featured during fall hunting season. Wines include a good selection of moderately priced Northwest vintages.

Raphael's Restaurant and Catering, 233 SE 4th St, Pendleton, OR 97801; (541)276-8500. On the corner between Court and Dorion in downtown Pendleton. Full bar. Moderate prices; credit cards and checks accepted. Call for dinner hours.

THE UPPER COLUMBIA

Nespelem: *Colville*

The Columbia River runs north to south through the middle of eastern Washington, a vast, mostly undeveloped area that ranges from wheat fields to pine forest and desert. The Colville Reservation, near the U.S.–Canada border, occupies a spectacular landscape that resembles the setting of a Western movie—rimrock canyons, boulder-strewn sagebrush prairies, clear mountain streams, azure lakes in bowls of solid granite, and forested mountains. The Columbia River wraps the reservation's southern and eastern borders, and the rushing Okanogan River defines its western edge. Among the better-known attractions and events here are Grand Coulee Dam and the Omak Stampede. Among the lesser-known are the Colville Confederated Tribes museum, historic Catholic mission, and annual powwow. The reservation is surrounded on three sides by national forest lands, including the Pasayten, Glacier Peak, and Lake Chelan-Sawtooth Wilderness, which together make up the largest roadless area in the four Northwest states.

Both the Colville Reservation and Fort Colvile were named after Andrew Colvile, British director of the Hudson's Bay Company. Government Indian agents often chose English or American names for reservations because they had difficulty both pronouncing and spelling Indian place names. Tribal members prefer the spelling "Colville" to "Colvile."

Before European settlement, Indians lived along the upper Columbia River and its tributaries, both in permanent villages and in fish camps, as they followed the migration of salmon. The premier fishing grounds on the Columbia was at Kettle Falls, near the present-day Canadian border, a cataract so large that its roar could be heard for miles. Numerous tribes converged at the falls annually to catch their year's supply of salmon. In 1826, the Hudson's Bay Company built a trading post near Kettle Falls, exchanging furs for wool blankets, beads, and ironware. From 1826 to 1871, Indians coming to the falls brought beaver, buffalo, deer, and other hides—as many as 20,000 pelts a year.

Kettle Falls, as well as the site of the old trading post and what later would become the American Fort Colvile, is now submerged under Lake Roosevelt, created by Grand Coulee Dam. The trading post and fort are memorialized by a small stone monument in a stand of thick pines; a one-room cabin nearby is a replica of the first mission, St. Paul's. The site is an important one in Northwest history; summer fishing camps in the area date to A.D. 600.

The original reservation, so large it covered a third of the state of Washington, was established by treaty in 1855; by 1872, the reservation had been reduced to about 5 million acres. Three months later settlers again forced the government to rewrite the treaty and push 12 tribes from eastern Washington to an area between the Okanogan River and the Columbia River—creating today's Colville Reservation.

Of the 12 tribes who moved to the Colville Reservation, the Lake and Okanogan Tribes (who occupied the lands the whole length of the Okanogan River valley to its source in Canada) were the largest. They were joined by the Entiat/Chelan, Methow, Moses Columbia, Nespelem, Palouse, Sanpoil, Senijextee, Skitswish, and Wenatchis people—nearly all of the tribes of eastern Washington. All spoke dialects of the Salish language except for one band of Nez Perce, who spoke Sahaptin. This group, Chief Joseph's surviving band, was moved to the reservation when they returned from their exile in Oklahoma (see the Nez Perce section in the Idaho and Western Montana chapter). Chief Joseph, who died in 1904 while sitting outside his tepee on the Colville Reservation, is buried near the tribal headquarters at the town of Nespelem.

When the Lakes and other tribes signed the 1855 treaty that created the reservation lands, they retained their traditional fishing rights. During the annual salmon migrations, the tribes continued to meet and fish at Kettle Falls. Then, in 1941, Grand Coulee Dam was completed. This massive hydroelectric project drew an impenetrable concrete curtain across the Columbia River—creating 150-mile-long Lake Roosevelt, silencing Kettle Falls under 90 feet of water, and blocking salmon migration to the upper Columbia.

In 1906, "surplus" reservation land was put up for homesteading after 80 acres were allotted to each tribal member by the U.S. government. In 1916, the act that gave away the Indians' land was amended to reserve land for schools, mills, cemeteries, and missions. The rest of the unclaimed land was offered by the U.S. government for settlement: in a one-day land rush nearly the entire southwest side of the Colville Reservation was claimed by non Indians for homesteading. In 1956, ownership of still-undisposed land was returned to the Confederated Tribes of the Colville Reservation. Today about half of the 8,231 enrolled tribal members live on the reservation.

One of the most spectacular lake views in the Pacific Northwest is from graveled Omak Lake Road; which overlooks the deep (300- to 400-foot), blue-green Omak Lake In a granite basin. What you see here, except for a few small towns and roads, is almost exactly how this country looked when families lived along the banks of the Columbia River In pit houses 12,000 to 18,000 years ago.

Don't mistake, as many do, the town of Colville for the Colville Reservation. The reservation is about the size of Massachusetts and Rhode Island combined. One end of the Grand Coulee Dam project, which is visited by more than a million people a year, adjoins the Colville Reservation. Roads feed into the reservation from all directions. Except where posted, paved roads on the reservation are open to the public. The best towns for tourist services are Omak and the town of Coulee Dam.

A great way to see the reservation is to take a driving tour. The trip from Inchelium to Nespelem (in Salish, "the place of the beautiful valley") takes about an hour, across a forested mountain pass. When we reached the Nespelem Valley, the sun was obscured by sheets of rain that drew a gray curtain across the light like the color of the sky during a solar eclipse. Trees bowed in the wind. Thunderbolts struck around us in all directions. The rain hit with the force of a firehose, and continued until we drove across some imaginary line into the desert, where it abruptly stopped. Dry pavement. Blue sky. We liked the effect so much that we pulled off the road, turned around, and drove in and out of the curtain of rain again.

The most direct route to the Colville Reservation is to cross the Columbia River on Hwy 155 on the steel-girder bridge in front of Grand Coulee Dam, to the small town of Coulee Dam. Two free ferries cross the Columbia River to the reservation as well. On the southern border, a ferry leaves the town of Wilbur and docks at Keller, on the reservation. On the east side of the reservation, a ferry runs between Gifford, on Hwy 25, and Inchelium. Ferries leave Wilbur and Gifford daily, every half hour, 6:30am–10:30pm.

Luxury Houseboats on the Columbia River

The Confederated Tribes of the Colville Reservation maintain a fleet of 40 houseboats at two marinas on the shores of Lake Roosevelt. The fully furnished boats are 46 to 52 feet long, sleep 10 to 13 people, and are equipped with front and rear decks, full galleys, hot water, bathrooms with showers and tubs, and extras such as water slides and barbecue grills. You can also rent skiffs, runabouts, jetboats, or patio boats for waterskiing and exploring the nooks and crannies of the lake. In addition, the National Park Service and the Confederated Tribes operate more than 32 campgrounds in the area. Summer temperatures in the canyons range between 75 and 100 degrees Fahrenheit; water temperatures reach the 70s in August.

Recreational maps of the entire Lake Roosevelt area are available from National Park Service Headquarters, 1008 Crest Dr, Coulee Dam, WA 99116; (509)633-9441.

Houseboats can be rented from Keller Ferry Marina or from Seven Bays Marina, both on the Washington side of Lake Roosevelt. To reach Keller Ferry Marina, take US Route 2 to Wilbur, then travel north on Highway 21 for 14 miles. Kerry Ferry has a store; nearby are lakeside RV and tent campgrounds managed by the National Park Service.

Seven Bays Marina is 25 miles north of Davenport. It offers RV campers full hookups with lake views, marina store, laundry facilities, showers, waste disposal, and fresh water. To reach Seven Bays, take Highway 2 to the Highway 25 exit, then turn left on the Miles/Creston Road.

Roosevelt Recreational Enterprises Reservations Office, PO Box 5, Coulee Dam, WA 99116; (800)648-5253 or (509)633-0136. Lake Roosevelt is about 260 miles from Seattle and 70 miles from Spokane. Phone for a "Boating Adventures" brochure; "Lake Roosevelt Vacations," a brochure that explains houseboat rental in great detail; or reservations, rates, and campground maps. Houseboats are available Mar–Nov; reserve boats at least a year in advance for July and August. Cost is $1,045–$2,010 per week

*plus $300 deposit, sales tax, optional insurance, and gas and oil. Campground maps
are provided free with houseboat rentals.*

Lakefront Log Cabins

West of Inchelium, at Rainbow Beach Resort, you can rent a quaint
log cabin with a comfortable sitting porch overlooking North Twin
Lake. Cabin rentals include a small fishing boat equipped with an outboard motor. Some cabins have a wood range or fireplace. The mostly
undeveloped Twin Lakes, covering 1,500 acres and surrounded by
pine forest, are stocked with trout and bass. Tent and RV camping
areas are also available. The resort has a small grocery store, laundry,
gas and oil, and VCR rental; it also sells fishing tackle and licenses.

*Rainbow Beach Resort, PO Box 146, Inchelium, WA 99138; (509)722-5901.
Reservations essential.*

Wildlife

Elevations in the Colville Reservation range from 800 feet to over
7,000 feet. The reservation's forests, and shrub and grassland steppes,
provide ecological niches for more than 300 species of fish and
wildlife—from black bears to pond turtles. Three of Washington
State's rare loon-nesting grounds are here. We suggest you drive
slowly, or kayak or canoe, to see wildlife. A copy of tribal regulations
comes with reservation fishing and hunting permits. The permits
are sold at most convenience stores and marinas on the reservation,
as well as at nearby stores off the reservation. Note: Campgrounds
and public beaches are sometimes closed to nontribal members on
short notice.

*Before you leave home, direct all questions about camping, swimming, and fishing to the
Confederated Tribes of the Colville Reservation, Parks and Recreation Department, PO
Box 150, Nespelem, WA 99155; (509)634-8867.*

Colville Confederated Tribes Museum and Gift Shop

This small museum is rich in cedar baskets, fishing gear, and archival
photographs. Among the hundreds of photographs is one of Chief
Moses, of the Moses Columbia Tribe, who lived from 1829 to 1899,
hunted buffalo on the Great Plains as a young boy, and rode into
battles against the Blackfeet with Salish allies. Many members of his
family and tribe died in battles with the U.S. cavalry. Chief Moses
narrowly escaped being hung at Hangman Valley with other leaders
during the Indian Wars, and later, after negotiations with the U.S.

government, reluctantly moved to the Colville Reservation. Moses then provided refuge for many of the war chiefs in the region, including Nez Perce chief Joseph and Yakama chief Kamiakin. Their pictures are in the museum as well. (As this book went to press, the museum was moving to larger quarters in the former St. Benedict's Catholic Church.)

Colville Confederated Tribes Museum and Gift Shop, 502 6th St, Box 233, Coulee Dam, WA 99116; (509)633-0751. The town of Coulee Dam is on Hwy 155; the museum is in the former St. Benedict's Catholic Church. A sign on a white tepee, on the lawn in front of Grand Coulee Dam, points the way. Open Mon–Sat, 10am–6 pm. Admission by donation.

Mourning Dove

She had little formal education and labored during the day in the orchards and fields. But Christine Quintasket managed to write at night in a tent or cabin and by her life's end had published a novel, one of the first by a Native American woman, as well as a volume of short stories. The original draft of the remarkable *Mourning Dove: A Salishan Autobiography* was published in 1990, more than 50 years after her death. Scholar Jay Miller's preface discusses obstacles facing both the tribes of the Colville Reservation and individuals caught in the cross-cultural conflict well into this century. A good read. Available from the Colville Confederated Tribes Museum Gift Shop, 502 6th St, Coulee Dam, WA 99116; (509)633-0751.

Skolaskin Church

The humble wooden church on Highway 55, next to tribal head-quarters near Nespelem, is named after Chief Skolaskin (1839-1922), a respected prophet and medicine man who predicted the 1872 earthquake that shook the area. The Skolaskin Church, built in 1874, was moved from a village called Whitestone before the dam flooded the valley.

Outside the church is a weathered tree trunk. Look closely to see a human figure cut into the tree, distorted by 200 years of growth. Our guide suggested that some of the figures and symbols blazed in many other trees in the Okanogan Valley may have served both spiritual and directional purposes.

The Skolaskin Church is on Hwy 155, on a shaded lawn south of Nespelem at the tribal center. The church is closed, but it's a great spot for a photograph. Behind the church is a monument to the tribe's veterans.

St. Mary's Mission

The handsome St. Mary's Catholic Church, built in 1886 and restored 100 years later, is the centerpiece of St. Mary's Mission, today the Pascal Sherman Indian School. The mission is in a spectacular granite canyon, near the town of Omak, about 50 miles north of Grand Coulee Dam.

Indians wanted nothing to do with Jesuit father Etienne de Rouge until he saved a child from drowning in rain-swollen Omak Creek in 1886. That year Chief Smitkin gave de Rouge land to build the mission on a knoll above the creek. The historic mission is still used as a boarding school. Other buildings include those built in the 1920s, with wide covered porches reminiscent of Santa Fe's early architecture.

Priests used a cave behind the school for private meditation and prayer. Find the school's bus garage and ask anyone there to point the way to the cave. Near the cave is a pleasant waterfall over an irrigation dam; rocks there are carved with petroglyphs. Watch for rattlesnakes.

Pascal Sherman Indian School, Omak Lake Rd, Hwy 155, Omak, WA 90041, (509)826-2097. Watch for signs on Hwy 155, east of Omak. Register at the school's administration office first. A student or staff member may be available to show you around. Donations appreciated.

Chief Joseph's Monument

Probably one of the most epic stories in Western history is that of Chief Joseph's band of Nez Perce, who held off the U.S. cavalry during their 1,500-mile journey to Canada. After they surrendered near the Canadian border, the band was exiled to Oklahoma (see Nez Perce section in the Idaho and Western Montana chapter) Some of the band, including Chief Joseph (Heimont Toolyalaket), eventually returned and found a permanent home on the Colville Reservation.

Chief Joseph died on the Colville Reservation in 1904. A handsome monument to him, carved in white marble, stands in the Nez Perce cemetery at Nespelem. About a block away is another commemorative marker to Joseph, in a turnout on Highway 155. (The second marker, built and maintained by the Washington State Highway Department, is less than you'd expect for a man of Chief Joseph's stature, however.) To see the white marble monument, the Nez Perce request that you park next to the highway monument and walk to the cemetery, rather than kicking up dust or parking on the road that runs through a residential area. Please respect the Nez Perce people and do not enter the cemetery.

Look for the turnout on Hwy 155, south of Nespelem. The Nez Perce monument to Chief Joseph is clearly visible from the cemetery gate, under a lone tree.

Omak Stampede and Suicide Run

Horses prance and riders tense in anticipation as they wait for the signal to gallop over the brink and charge down the steep sandy hillside, swim the Okanogan River, and thunder to the finish line during the annual Suicide Run, the highlight of the four-day Omak Stampede. Held the second weekend in August, the Suicide Run harks back to tribal gatherings and overland races, in which horses zigzagged through trees, struggled up rocky hillsides, and plunged into rivers or lakes at the bottoms of steep sandy hills. The Suicide Run, the last leg of the traditional race, was added to the rodeo 60 years ago. Today the races are the Omak Stampede's main event, with two runs during the day and two after dark, lighted with flares.

Over 100 tepees fill the encampment near the rodeo grounds. Traditional fancy dancing, drumming and singing contests, and stick games go on during the four-day event. Booths featuring food and local and area Indian arts and crafts are open to the public.

For Omak Stampede and Suicide Run tickets and information, contact the Omak Chamber of Commerce and Visitor Information Center, 401 Omak Ave, Rt 2, Box 5200, Omak, WA 98841; (800)225-6625 or (509)826-1880. Held the second weekend in August. Also for purchase at the visitors center are videotapes of historic Suicide Runs and interviews with Indian participants.

Where's the Art?

More than 120 craftsmen and artists are on the Colville Reservation's artists registry, 39 of them graduates of the Institute of American Indian Arts in Santa Fe. However, it's difficult to find their work on or near the reservation. Some of the best artists sell their work at local church bazaars and other fund-raisers. Look for art at the Fourth of July Celebration Powwow grounds across from the tribal center in Nespelem; at the Omak Stampede and Suicide Run encampment the second weekend in August; or at the annual fall show of Colville art at the Confluence Gallery in Twisp, in the Methow Valley on Highway 20 (call for dates; (509)997-2787).

If you've never seen the raw materials used for beading, stop at the Bear's Den (Milepost 47, Hwy 155, Nespelem, WA 99155; (509)634-4922), a private home with hanks of tiny cut-glass beads hanging on the living room wall as well as baseball caps, shirts, and jackets with Native American emblems embroidered on them.

Storyteller Ken Edwards

Professional storyteller and oral historian Ken Edwards (Rainbow Cougar) has a repertoire of more than 1,000 Native American stories—from animal-people stories (such as Raven and Coyote) to more-recent true-life tales from Indian reservations across North America. He regales listeners at schools and colleges, as well as at Indian markets, fairs, powwows, museums, libraries, and bookstores. A versatile performer, Edwards can tell up to three or four hours of stories on any subject, including love stories on Valentine's Day and scary Native American stories on Halloween. He also has a fine arts degree from the Institute of American Indian Arts, Santa Fe, and his work illustrates numerous calendars, cards, and books sold nationally.

Ken Edwards, Rt 2, Box 72-S, Omak, WA 98841; (509)826-4744. An hour-long story-telling videotape is available from Edwards for $28, including postage and handling.

Traditional Dollmaker

Colville tribal member and cultural anthropologist Meg Orr has spent a lifetime collecting Native American dolls. Her mentor was Clara Moore, a Colville elder, who taught her at the age of 7 to carve dolls from soap, cover them with buckskin, and make wigs of horsehair. Orr is currently writing a book on Native American dolls and makes dolls for sale. She uses many different kinds of materials; most popular are cloth-bodied dolls dressed in vibrantly colored, 19th-century–style beaded buckskin dresses and shawls.

Meg Orr Dolls, PO Box 4188, Omak, WA 98841; (509)826-0904. Prices range from $20 to $350. By appointment or mail order only.

Kettle Falls Historic Sites

The falls, once one of the most important fisheries on the Columbia River, are now submerged under 90 feet of water; the rock islands that channeled the river to the falls are visible only on the rare occasions when the water behind Grand Coulee Dam is drawn down. A bridge on Highway 20 crosses the Columbia where the falls once roared.

The Kettle Falls Historical Center's "People of the Falls" exhibit, located in a warehouse-style building near the river, is an attempt to explain the importance of the falls using dioramas and limited artifacts. The exhibit falls short and is confusing—Southwest Indian art is on display, and the miniature "sweat lodge," made of green cedar boughs, is about as visually effective as displaying an unplugged jukebox to explain swing dancing. Still, it's worth a stop, if only for the newspaper clippings that have been enlarged and hung on the walls.

About a quarter of a mile from the center, in a pine grove, is a 1939 reconstruction of St. Paul's Mission church. There is also a monument to the area's first trading post. The single-room, cabinlike church was built in 1840 of hand-hewn pine by Father Anthony Ravalli. It is very different in style from the Cataldo Mission church, which Ravalli built with the Coeur d'Alene Indians in Idaho.

The Kettle Falls Historical Center and St. Paul's Mission are located off Hwy 395, on the east side of the Kettle Falls bridge; watch for a red-roofed building in the trees; (509)738-6964. National Park Service brochures explaining the area's history are free. The center is open May–Sept, Wed–Sun 11am–5pm (although the center sometimes closes early). Free admission; donations welcome.

Grand Coulee Dam

The dams were built on the Columbia River to make it easier to pump water out of the canyon to irrigate the desert; to produce the hydroelectric power needed to cheaply manufacture aluminum, build airplanes, and win World War II; to create inland shipping routes; and to create acres of lakes.

This upbeat message is delivered via loudspeakers and a laser light show projected on Grand Coulee Dam's blank concrete face every summer night after sundown, with a male narrator playing the part of the powerful but domesticated river. The Department of the Interior wrote the script for the laser light show. It does not disclose in depth how Indians feel about losing their ancestral villages and sacred sites along the river's submerged banks, or the cultural effect of losing the salmon. More than 1,000 linear miles of wild salmon spawning habitat were blocked when the dam was erected and no fish ladders were installed.

Grand Coulee Dam Visitor Arrival Center, Hwy 155, PO Box 620, Grand Coulee, WA 99133; (509)633-9265. Open daily; summer, open 9am until past dusk (until 11pm in June and July); winter, 9am–5pm. The laser light show, viewed from a small amphitheater facing the dam, is shown nightly after the sun goes down, May 30–Sept 30. In winter the center is open 9am–5pm.

Wellpinit: *Spokane*

According to Spokane oral historians, much of present-day northeastern Washington was once a huge lake that took several days to cross. Salish villages were all around the lakeshore and perched on various islands. Early one morning, a cataclysmic event overturned boats and created tidal waves that engulfed the villages. Some people fled to Mount Spokane as the entire lake was sucked out of the valley. The earth reeked of dead fish and game. The few people who survived eked out a meager existence until spring. When the snow melted, a roaring river cut its way over the rocks, bringing new life to the country. A waterfall roared to life, and its spray held a rainbow. This is the place the people decided to call home. The legend chronicles geologic fact—the dramatic Columbia River basin was shaped by a cataclysmic breaking of a natural dam that backed up a huge lake over the entire northeast corner of Washington State and the Idaho panhandle about 10,000 years ago.

The Spokane ("children of the sun") shared both their territory around the lake and the Salish language with the tribes that today make up the Kalispel, Coeur d'Alene, Colville, and Flathead Tribes. The Spokane consisted of three bands who lived along the Spokane River, a short tributary of the Columbia River with headwaters in Coeur d'Alene Lake. Spokane Falls, today the highlight of the city of Spokane, Washington, was the tribe's center of trade and fishing.

In 1808, the Hudson's Bay Trading Company built "Spokane House" next to the river, a large trading post that included a ballroom and horse track. It closed in 1825. By 1887, settlers had taken most of the rich agricultural land around Spokane Falls. Fearful that they would lose all their land, the three Spokane bands entered an agreement with the U.S. government to cede title and move to other reservations. Many moved to the Coeur d'Alene Reservation in Idaho and the Flathead Reservation in Montana before another agreement was reached to create the Spokane Reservation on the lower reaches of the Spokane River.

The Spokane Reservation encompasses a stunning landscape of conifer-covered slopes, basalt cliffs, and wheat and hay fields—most of which is undeveloped. It's bounded by the Spokane River on the southern border, and the Columbia River (Lake Roosevelt) on the west. The most scenic route to the reservation is from the city of Spokane on Highway 291, which follows the Spokane River to the reservation, then turns about a mile inland. A historic Catholic church is just off the road to Spokane tribal headquarters at Wellpinit, followed by the tribe's hatchery. Open to the public on the reservation's west side is Two Rivers, a recreation development at the conjunction of the Spokane River and Lake Roosevelt, as well as 32 small parks.

Two Rivers Resort

At the entrance to the Two Rivers Resort, on the reservation's west side, is a large sculpture cast by Spokane tribal member George Hill, depicting an Indian fisherman holding a spear and a salmon. Several horse sculptures cast in iron by another Spokane tribal member, George Flett, are perched on the slope above Two Rivers, memorializing the Spokane's herds of horses that were killed by the U.S. cavalry in the mid-1800s.

Two Rivers offers a large marina, an RV park, and a campground at the junction of the Spokane and Columbia Rivers (Lake Roosevelt). With the only floating store on Lake Roosevelt, the full-service marina also has 160 boat slips (many of which are covered) in a sheltered spot on the mouth of the Spokane River. Overnight moorage is available. The gas dock, with gas card service, is open 24 hours a day, as are rest room facilities with showers. Permits are available for fishing.

The adjoining RV park has hookups for 90, with water, power, and pumpout stations. The tent campground is on a promontory that juts into the confluence of the two rivers. Once a hay field, the campground is perfectly flat and newly landscaped with young pines. With 100 sites, it's a perfect place for group campouts.

Two Rivers Marina, 6828 C, Hwy 25 S, Davenport, WA 99122; (509)722-5500. For RV or campground reservations, call the on-site Spokane Tribal Parks Department; (509)722-4029. From the town of Davenport, south of the reservation on Hwy 2, take Hwy 25 and travel north for 25 miles until you cross the Spokane River. Marina, RV park, and campground are open year-round.

Public Campgrounds

Thirty-two gorgeous small parks are tucked into the trees along the Spokane River and on the shores of Lake Roosevelt; 16 are open to the public for camping and picnicking. All are marked with signs naming the parks (even No-Name Park) and are cared for by rangers from the Spokane Tribal Parks Department, who issue permits for camping and fishing. Campgrounds range in size from one to seven sites. All have shelters and fire pits or barbecues; most do not have potable water. Fresh water can be obtained at Two Rivers Resort.

Spokane Tribal Parks Department, 6828 B, Hwy 25 S, Davenport, WA 99122; (509)722-5500. The parks department at Two Rivers Resort is well marked. Stop there for maps of campgrounds, permits, and directions from the helpful staff. Overnight tent camping is $10; RV parking is $16. Some of the parks are closed periodically.

Alex Sherwood Memorial Tribal Center Museum

The small collection in this temporary one-room museum (the Spokane are planning a new cultural learning center and museum) reflects both traditional and contemporary life on the Spokane Reservation. Displays include arrowheads, ceremonial items made of beadwork, buckskin, and other natural materials. For sale at the museum is *Children of the Sun,* a booklet of history, culture, language, stories, and contemporary issues of the Spokane Tribe, written by tribal member David C. Wynecoop.

Alex Sherwood Memorial Tribal Center Museum in the Spokane Tribal Center, PO Box 100, Wellpinit, WA 99040; (509)258-4581. At Ford, cross the bridge onto Wellpinit Rd. and travel for 12 miles. The tribal center is in a stone building just past the four-way stop in Wellpinit. Open Mon–Fri, 7:30am–4pm. Free.

Spokane tribal member Gloria Bird's first collection of poetry, Full Moon on the Reservation (Greenfield Review, 1993), has received accolades. She teaches Native American literature and writing courses at the Institute of American Indian Arts in Santa Fe, New Mexico. Her book is available at the museum.

St. Joseph's Catholic Church

Around the time that St. Joseph's Catholic Church was built in 1912, tribal members from all over the region brought tepees and wagons to camp on the site. Spokane tribal members still make a pilgrimage to St. Joseph's each Easter. The church is a classic, with a bell tower and stained glass windows.

St. Joseph's Catholic Church At Ford, take the Wellpinit Rd and continue to the second road to the right (unnamed). The church is about ½ mile down that road, and is marked as a historic site by the Spokane Tribe. Usually open during daylight hours.

Spokane Tribal Fish Hatchery

The Spokane Tribal Hatchery is at Metamootels ("upwelling springs" in Salish), ice-cold springs that flow into Chamokane Creek, the Spokane River, and eventually the Columbia River. Here the Spokane Tribe annually raises 1.4 million kokanee salmon (a landlocked sockeye salmon that grows to about 3 pounds) and 530,000 rainbow trout, from both wild and hatchery stock.

The hatchery is a fascinating place to visit not only because of the pretty setting but also because of its displays, which include stone pestles and projectile points found on the site as well as artists' renditions of pit house dwellings and camas ovens (subterranean ovens used for roasting camas bulbs). Ask manager Tim Peone, who was raised on the reservation, about building camas ovens and eating the roasted lily bulbs when he was a child, and about annual root-digging ceremonies on the reservation.

Spokane Tribal Fish Hatchery, PO Box 100, Wellpinit, WA 99040; (509)258-7297. At the Ford/Wellpinit junction, go west toward Wellpinit for 2½ miles to Martha Boardman Rd., and watch for signs. Open daily; summer, 8am–4:30pm; winter, 9am–3:30pm. Call first for tours.

Cheney Cowles Museum

Located in the city of Spokane's historic Browne's Addition neighborhood, the Cheney Cowles Museum is the caretaker of one of the most significant American Indian collections in the United States. The museum's holdings include more than 35,000 items, mostly from the Plateau region of the Pacific Northwest, which encompasses the Spokane, Coeur d'Alene, Kalispel, Colville, Nez Perce, Kootenai, Flathead, Yakama, Umatilla, and Warm Springs Reservations. Because of size limitations, only about 150 items are exhibited at any one time. However, special American Indian exhibits are presented often.

Historic photographs are available for purchase from the museum's research library and archives, which also house manuscripts, maps, oral history tapes, and ephemera (researchers must make an appointment). Special events include art shows and lectures by members of the Colville, Spokane, Coeur d'Alene, and Kalispel Tribes. The Carriage House gift shop features a small selection of Native American art.

The museum sponsors an annual Friendship Dance the first Saturday in January that honors the traditions of the Plateau tribes (those of eastern Washington, Oregon, and Idaho), as well as a 10-day introductory course on Salish culture and language taught by a Spokane tribal member.

Clothing designer Betty David (2504 Castillo, #4, Santa Barbara, CA 93105; (805)682-5175), an enrolled member of the Spokane Tribe, makes unusually handsome shearling jackets decorated with Native American images, including horses, handprints, and adaptations of Northwest Coast clan designs. Jackets are custom made, in both adult and child sizes.

Cheney Cowles Museum, 2316 W 1st Ave, Spokane, WA 99204; (509)456-3931. Located in the Browne's Addition National Historic District, 5 minutes west of downtown. From I-90, take exit 280A; turn north on Walnut, then west on 2nd Ave. Follow signs. Open Tues–Sat, 10am–5pm; Sun, 1pm–5pm; Wed, until 9 pm. Admission $3.

Usk: *Kalispel*

In the late 1700s, 1,500 Kalispel Indians lived on the banks of the Pend Oreille River, a lovely, meandering stream that flows out of Lake Pend Oreille in present-day Idaho and runs north to Canada. The river flows north through a narrow valley in Washington State's Selkirk Mountains to Canada. The Kalispels lived in villages all along the valley, fishing for salmon on the river and killing deer for venison by driving herds into deep snow. By 1911 the tribe was down to only 100 members. They had lost most of their land to settlers, who claimed it as if it were unoccupied. Today the tribe owns just 10 miles along the Pend Oreille River, but a stunning 10 miles they are. In the spring, fragrant mock-orange blossoms along the roadside, and yellow lilies cover the forest floor. Hundreds of birds, including osprey, nest in the trees along the river or in the tall grasses along the riverbank. On the hillside is a path through the underbrush to a large cave, the New Manresa Grotto, where in 1844, missionary Pierre-John De Smet celebrated Christmas Mass with the Kalispels.

In a grassy meadow next to the river is the site of the Kalispels' largest village, photographed by Edward Curtis in 1910. There the tribe has built a ceremonial park. The buildings, which include a powwow dance arbor, are circular, designed of poles and cedar in the style of the original lodges and longhouses. In the spring, before the Salish Fair, Powwow, and Rodeo, the only sound in the park is the chattering of hundreds of swallows that swoop in and out of their mud nests under the roof of the open-air dance arena.

Enclosed by a sturdy fence in a lush pasture is the Kalispel Tribe's buffalo herd, which has grown to nearly 100 since 1978, when the tribe received 12 buffalo from the U.S. Fish and Wildlife Service. The tribe is now able to provide free meat to their elders. Heads and hides are also sold. And when the powwow comes around every year, guests are treated to a buffalo barbecue (see the appendix for dates and times of the Salish Fair).

Kalispel Reservation Tours

There's always someone who can show you around the little reservation; point out the many nests along the river, the buffalo, and the ceremonial park grounds; and take you up to the New Manresa Grotto (a short walk, but up a rocky hill, so wear sturdy shoes). Church services are still held each fall in the grotto, which has a gorgeous view of the river from both of its entrances. Ask for the tribe's free 37-page book, *The Kalispels: People of the Pend Oreille,* explaining their fascinating history. If you'd like a tour, please call in advance.

Kalispel Tribe, PO Box 39, Usk, WA 99187; (509)445-1147. Usk is located on Hwy 20, between the Canadian border and Spokane. Take the bridge across the Pend Oreille River at Usk. Just after crossing the bridge, turn left down a narrow road to the Kalispel Reservation. Tribal headquarters are well marked.

IDAHO
& WESTERN
MONTANA

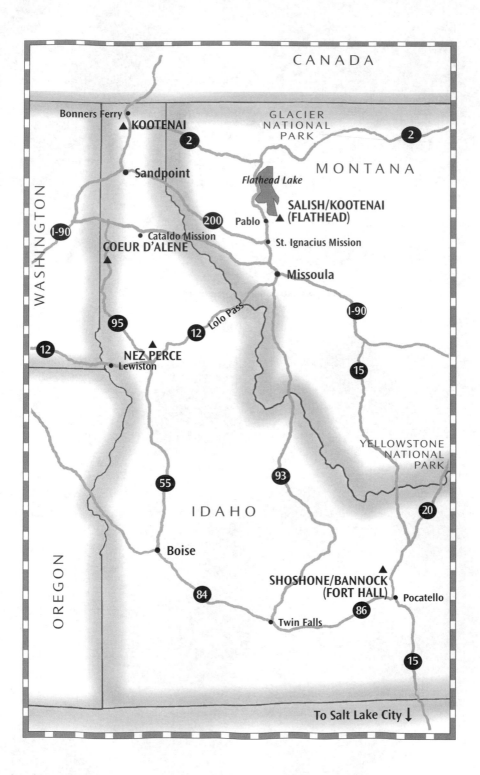

IDAHO & WESTERN MONTANA

The five tribes of Idaho and western Montana described in this chapter live in some of the most beautiful stretches of scenic wonderland in the West.

In Idaho, the Nez Perce Reservation adjoins the spectacular Hells Canyon, the deepest canyon in North America. In the heart of Idaho's Palouse country, the Coeur d'Alene Reservation encompasses rolling wheat fields, deep pine forests, and nearly half of Lake Coeur d'Alene. The Kootenai Tribe, who have no reservation, live in the town of Bonners Ferry on the Kootenai River in the northern Idaho panhandle, minutes away from world-class downhill skiing and some of the best fishing in the West. In the southeastern corner of Idaho is the Shoshone-Bannock's Fort Hall Reservation, at the edge of American Falls Reservoir near the Snake River, just south of the Sawtooth Mountain Range and Craters of the Moon National Monument. In Montana, just south of Glacier National Park, the Flathead Reservation encompasses lovely Mission Valley and half of the 28-mile-long Flathead Lake.

Not only is the scenery of this region spectacular but each tribe offers the traveler a unique cultural experience.

These tribes, whose territorial lands bordered those of the Plains Indians, all participated in buffalo and salmon harvests. Yet each has a fascinating history all its own. The Coeur d'Alene along with the interior Salish, for example, were among the first western tribes to invite Catholic missionaries into their territories. Nez Perce National Historical Park includes portions of the original 1,500-mile route of Chief Joseph's band of Nez Perce, who traveled by horseback and foot as they fled from the U.S. cavalry. The Shoshone-Bannock's land was a pioneer hub—nine emigrant trails, including the Oregon Trail, converged on their wintering grounds at Fort Hall, and they can show you the wagon ruts still visible there.

This is also the region to buy intricate beadwork, tepees, buckskin clothing, or a chandelier made from elk and deer antlers. The art created by tribes of this region more closely resembles Plains Indians' art, and is quite different from the art typical of British Columbia and Southeast Alaska Natives.

To visit all of the tribes and regions described in this chapter, you would need several weeks, especially if you wanted to include stops at Yellowstone National Park, Glacier National Park, and Hells Canyon. To save time, you can fly to towns adjoining reservations and then rent a car. You can fly from Portland and Seattle to Spokane, Washington (near the Coeur d'Alene); Lewiston (near the Nez Perce) and Pocatello (near the Fort Hall Reservation), Idaho; and to Kalispel and Missoula, Montana (at either end of the Flathead Reservation).

Before you begin your Idaho and western Montana adventure, write for free packets of information, which include good state maps and accommodations lists, from the Idaho Travel Council, PO Box 83720, Boise, ID 83720; (800)635-7820, and from Travel Montana, 800 Conley Lake Rd, Deer Lodge, MT 59722; (800)847-4868.

Lapwai: *Nez Perce*

The Nez Perce are famous for two tales of almost mythical dimension in the American imagination: that of Chief Joseph's cross-country flight from the U.S. cavalry, and that of their Appaloosa war horses. "Nez Perce" is what French fur traders named them; they refer to themselves as the "Nimiipu." They originally lived in three of the most rugged river canyons in the Northwest—the canyons of Idaho's Clearwater, Salmon, and Snake Rivers. The Snake's famous Hells Canyon, with its staircase rapids rushing through a chasm deeper than that of the Grand Canyon, contains more than 112 pictographs left by the Nimiipu's ancestors, in addition to well-worn trails down the canyon's steep walls. Hells Canyon today is the dividing line between the states of Idaho and Oregon. The Nimiipu also lived on the Oregon side of the canyon, in a verdant alpine valley in the shadow of the Wallowa Mountains. More than 75 Nimiipu village sites have been identified along the Snake and its tributaries. Some have been carbon-dated to 11,000 years, or about 500 generations; there are also indications of far older settlements.

The Treaty of 1855 ordered the Nez Perce to relinquish their ancestral territory and move to Oregon's Umatilla Reservation with the Walla Walla, Cayuse, and Umatilla Tribes. However, all the tribes so opposed this plan that Territorial Governor Isaac Stevens granted the Nez Perce the right to remain in their own territory, on the condition that they relinquish nearly 13 million acres to the U.S. government.

Today, the Nez Perce Reservation is much like an island surrounded by rivers. Nearly 90 percent of it is owned by non-Indians, and most of the plateau that once sprouted blue-flowering camas and other native plants is now planted with wheat and other grain crops. Tribal enrollment is approximately 3,300. About half live on the reservation, in small towns or on horse and wheat ranches. The tribe coordinates fish and wildlife management with sustained-yield forestry on about 47,640 acres, most of it off the reservation. Many places in Nez Perce

In 1806, a band of Nimiipu received explorers Lewis and Clark into their camp on the Clearwater River. Upon the request of Lewis and Clark's young Shoshone guide, Sacajawea, the Nimiipu graciously allowed the travelers to stay with them during the winter—probably saving their lives.

territory, such as the towns of Kamiah and Lapwai, still carry Nez Perce names.

Every year, thousands of visitors sign the register at Nez Perce National Historical Park, located on a wide, grassy clearing above the Clearwater River. The park includes a museum showing Nimiipu culture, several restored mission buildings, and a 100-mile-long, self-guided interpretive route that encircles the reservation. On this route, signs point out the creation site of the Nimiipu, the White Bird Battlefield, and a spot where explorers Meriwether Lewis and William Clark camped on the Clearwater River on their way to the Pacific Ocean.

The tribal center of government is a few miles down Highway 95 from Nez Perce National Historical Park, on Main Street in Lapwai. (Lapwai is a Nimiipu word meaning "place of the butterflies.") A few of the old Indian agency buildings remain at Lapwai, but mostly you'll see new housing, a modern school, the tribal office complex, Pi-Nee-Waus Community Center, and pastures filled with grazing Appaloosa horses.

Nez Perce Tribe, Pi-Nee-Waus Community Center, PO Box 305, Lapwai, ID 83540; (208)843-2253.

Nez Perce National Historical Park

Nez Perce National Historical Park is located on the site of the old Spalding (also called Lapwai) Mission, about 11 miles east of Lewiston, Idaho, on Highway 95. The mission was founded in 1836 by Presbyterian Henry Harmon Spalding and his wife, Eliza, who traveled west with Marcus and Narcissa Whitman in 1836. Both parties were sponsored by the Presbyterian American Board of Foreign Missions. The Whitmans went on to Walla Walla, Washington.

The park offers programs about Nez Perce culture, including a tour through the museum's artifacts collection, presented by park rangers three times a day during the summer and by request during the winter. The tour includes a gallery housing stunning horse regalia, distinctive cornhusk bags, and beadwork, most of it on loan from other museums. Watch the half-hour film, produced by Phil Lucas in his early career as a documentary filmmaker. The park also offers a scenic, self-guided, 100-mile-long tour route that encircles the reservation, with stops at historic landmarks such as the White Bird Battlefield, where the first battle between Chief Joseph's band and the U.S. cavalry occurred.

The park grounds are spacious. Spalding's original Presbyterian church, next to a creek, was built on the original Lapwai Indian village site, which had been occupied for thousands of years. The site today includes stones from the chimney of the Spalding Mission, and interpretive signs point out the locations of the former gristmill and sawmill. Watson's store still stands, and you can walk past the mission cemetery where the Spaldings and Nez Perce tribal members are buried. (Please keep in mind that the Nez Perce regard the old cemetery as a sacred burial ground. Even though it is surrounded by mowed lawns, to use it for picnics, Frisbee games, or any other recreational purpose would be disrespectful.) In 1971 the Nez Perce Tribe commissioned famed Nez Perce stone sculptor Doug Hyde to create a memorial tombstone for Josiah Redwolf, the last surviving veteran of the 1877 flight to Canada with Chief Joseph's band. The railroad tracks paralleling the river have a history as well—Chief Joseph rode a train along these tracks back to Lapwai when he returned to the West after his exile in Oklahoma.

The park's visitors center has a small gift shop stocked with books about the Nez Perce. Kevin Peters, a Nez Perce painter and sculptor who works as a park ranger, illustrated the cover of *Sapatqayn: Twentieth Century Nez Perce Artists,* a full-color catalog presenting 20 contemporary Nez Perce artists. The catalog is available for $12.95 at the historical park. Posters of the book's cover may also be available.

Nez Perce National Historical Park, National Park Service, PO Box 93, Spalding, ID 83551; (208)843-2261. About 11 miles east of Lewiston, Idaho. Take Hwy 12 east from Lewiston; at the bridge take the Hwy 95 south exit. Open daily. Admission free. Park rangers' programs are presented at 10am, 2pm, and 4pm throughout the summer and on request during the winter. June through Labor Day, Nez Perce artists demonstrate traditional and contemporary arts at the visitors center. Ask for free handouts on everything from edible plants to beadwork. Also ask for the free loop tour map, as well as a four-state map of 38 national park sites connected with the Chief Joseph story and Nez Perce culture.

Nee-Me-Poo National Historical Trail

After gold and other metals were discovered in Nez Perce country, the U.S. government negotiated a new treaty with the tribe, in the 1870s. Often called the "steal treaty," it stripped the Nez Perce of the Wallowa and Imnaha Valleys and the land at the confluence of the Snake and Clearwater Rivers—the site of the present-day towns of Lewiston and Clarkston.

Chiefs Joseph, White Bird, Looking Glass, Hushis-Kuate, Hahtelekin, and others refused to sign—and refused to move. The U.S. military assembled to force them to leave. Settlers, assured of their position, fenced the springs and ran cattle over fields of camas bulbs that had been carefully tended and harvested by the Nez Perce for hundreds of years. Just a few days before being moved to the new reservation, the bands assembled one more time. Emotions ran high. Some young men, furious over the earlier murder of family members by whites, left the camp and killed several settlers, setting off the Nez Perce War.

Carla HighEagle and JoAnn Kauffman sometimes offer week-long horseback tours over 100 miles of the Nez Perce Historical Trail. Each night concludes with a tepee and tent encampment in a high meadow, with Coyote stories told around the campfire. To see if tours are available, contact Heart of the Monster Tours, Kauffman and Associates, PO Box 1401, Kamiah, ID 83586; (208)935-0665.

One band of Nez Perce, pursued by the U.S. military, fled approximately 1,500 miles toward Canada before they surrendered in the Bear's Paw Mountains in northern Montana. The majority of the people fleeing were women, children, elderly, or sick. With their leaders (Chief Joseph among them), warriors, and 2,000 horses, the band fought for their lives in more than 20 battles along the trail. Upon surrender, the band was promised safe return to the Nez Perce Reservation. Instead, the survivors were shipped by train to a reservation in Oklahoma, where many more died. Eventually, some returned to the Nez Perce Reservation. Others stayed in Oklahoma. And others, like Chief Joseph, forbidden to return to Nez Perce lands, lived out their lives in exile on the Colville Reservation in northern Washington State.

Today the route followed by this band of Nez Perce is memorialized as the Nee-Mee-Poo National Historical Trail. History buffs can follow it, tracing the Nez Perce's escape route as it climbs over Lolo Pass, wheels south into present-day Yellowstone National Park, and then swerves north to Bear's Paw Battleground in eastern Montana, where Chief Joseph surrendered.

Follow the Nez Perce Trail, by Cheryl Wilfong (Oregon State University Press, 1990), provides a detailed three-in-one guide for the "mainstream, adventurous, or intrepid" traveler, and is packed with historical anecdotes and asides. You can order the book from the Northwest Interpretive Association, Nez Perce National Historical Park, PO Box 93, Spalding, ID 83551; (208)843-2261.

The Historic Loop Road

Part of Nez Perce National Historical Park is a 100-mile drive that encircles the Nez Perce Reservation. The drive includes 24 historic sites, among them the creation site of the Nez Perce. The loop stretches across a sun-drenched plateau, through wheat fields and pine forests, then drops into deep canyons. In early spring, when the wildflowers are blooming among the tall green grass, this is an especially pretty drive.

One site on the route is the White Bird Battlefield interpretive center, which commemorates the opening battle of the Nez Perce War of 1877. At this site, 70 Nez Perce warriors faced more than 100 United States soldiers and volunteers. Led by experienced fighters, the Nez Perce, with their well-trained horses, soundly defeated the larger and better-armed force. Knowing that more forces would be mounted against them, the Nez Perce moved on to the south fork of the Clearwater and began their long and bitter journey toward Canada. Today roads encircle the battlefield, allowing visitors to view the grassy ridges and knolls. A 16-mile-long loop tour around the battlefield begins at milepost 230 on Highway 95, almost 10 miles southwest of Grangeville.

From Highway 94 south of the national historical park, Route 64 is a short-cut from the west side of the reservation to the eastside town of Kamiah. The road is paved through the wheat fields, then turns to gravel as it descends into the Clearwater canyon with hairpin turns, drop-offs, and no guardrails—but stunning views (past your white knuckles gripping the steering wheel).

Another important site on the 100-mile loop tour is Heart of the Monster, the creation site of the Nimiipu. A mound of stone next to the Clearwater River (near the town of Kamiah), the site includes a shelter with a recording by Nez Perce elder Angus Wilson. In his Native language, Wilson narrates one of the many versions of the tribe's creation story.

According to one version of the creation story, Coyote was the creator of the world's animals. A huge monster that lived in the Kamiah area ate all of Coyote's creations for miles around. This angered Coyote, who decided to kill the monster. He allowed himself to be inhaled by the monster, and once inside, cut up its body into small pieces. When the monster's heart was hanging by a thread of tissue, Coyote warned all the little animals to run out the monster's orifices with its last breath. When Coyote cut the last thread, all the animals did escape, though some of them, such as the rattlesnake, were disfigured by their quick exit from the monster's body. When Coyote emerged he squeezed the heart, and the drops of blood that fell to the ground became the Nimiipu. The monster's heart and liver were left at the spot where he was killed, and were turned to stone to let everyone know that this is the place where the Nimiipu were created. At the interpretive site, a trail leads from the parking lot to the fenced Heart of the Monster, with picnic tables under the trees near the Clearwater River.

The Heart of the Monster shelter is open daily from sunrise to sunset, 2 miles south of Kamiah on Hwy 12. Cultural demonstrations take place at the site June–Aug. For more information, contact Nez Perce National Historical Park, PO Box 93, Spalding, ID 83551; (208)843-2261.

Mammoth Excavation

On the Clearwater River, just downstream from Heart of the Monster, archaeologists recently unearthed the bones of a mammoth. The creatures roamed North America for nearly 2 million years before they became extinct about 11,000 years ago. Archaeological evidence, including bones and spear points uncovered in the dig, indicates ancestors of the Nimiipu hunted mammoths with Clovis-style spear points chipped from stone. Mammoth, water buffalo, and other prehistoric mammal remains were also unearthed during a restoration project in 1994 at nearby Tolo Lake. The artesian lake and wet clay preserved fossil remains that may be one of the most significant finds in the West. As this book went to press, the mammoth's fossilized skeleton had been moved to the Chamber of Commerce office in Kamiah, but it may subsequently move to a local museum.

Kamiah Chamber of Commerce, 701 5th St, PO Box 189, Kamiah, ID 83543; (208)935-2290.

St. Joseph's Mission

In 1831, two Nez Perce and two Salish men traveled to St. Louis to inquire about the "white man's book of heaven," which they had learned of from French fur traders. In Salish culture, gaining spirituality meant having more ability to help others, and thereby more status. In seeking the newcomers' religion, they hoped to add to their spiritual wealth, not replace it. The Catholics answered the call of the Coeur d'Alene and the Salish; responding to the Nez Perce was the Reverend Henry Spalding, a Presbyterian missionary, who established a mission in 1836 at Lapwai. The Catholic "black robes" were latecomers, arriving in 1872 with Father Joseph Cataldo at the helm. The conflicts between the Presbyterians and the Catholics that had been going on for centuries in Europe continued in the western United States missions. The Protestants blamed the Catholics for supporting Indian resistance to white settlement. Spalding and others for a time also successfully fought Cataldo's desire to build mission boarding schools for the Indians, including the Nez Perce, that would prepare Indian students for higher education at the university he eventually built in Spokane, the present-day Gonzaga University. While Cataldo was well regarded, the Reverend Spalding's reputation was that of an extremely cruel and demanding man, intolerant of the Nimiipu's religion. Nez Perce Historical Park is built on Spalding's mission site.

Cataldo's original church, St. Joseph's Mission, is in a grove of trees in a pretty little valley near the town of Lapwai. It's a nice bicycle ride from the Nez Perce National Historical Park at Spalding, and a shaded spot to rest on a hot day.

St. Joseph's Mission. Follow Hwy 95 past Lapwai to the Mission Creek Rd turnoff. The single-room white church is in a grove of trees about 4 miles down the road. The church is open Thurs–Mon, Memorial Day through Labor Day. Guided tours are free. An annual mass, open to the public, is held in the church on the first Sunday of June.

Appaloosa Horses

One of the great thrills of visiting Nez Perce Reservation is seeing the Appaloosa horses, with their dappled backs and striped hooves, grazing in a pasture. Imagine these freckled beauties adorned with tinkling bells, brightly colored beadwork, and fringed leather threaded with glass beads. The Nez Perce were known for their skill in breeding strong horses, but were best known for the Appaloosa horse, which they called *mommon*. Named Appaloosa in the 1930s after the Palouse River, the horses were registered as a breed by non-Indian ranchers.

"We bred horses that would be sturdy, sure-footed, good-looking, with strong endurance for racing, that would survive winter — and some happened to have spots," says Allen V. Pinkham, Sr., founder of the Chief Joseph Horse Foundation. The nonprofit foundation was created with 14 head of Appaloosa horses donated by a New Mexico horse rancher and a $15,000 gift from actor Richard Gere; it seeks to reacquaint Nez Perce children with horsemanship. The Nez Perce Tribe lost more than 3,000 horses after the Nez Perce War of 1877, in which soldiers shot the tribe's horses. Today, the foundation's breeding program is adding the heart-strength of Turkmenistan Akhalteke war-horses to Appaloosa stock. Mares dropped their first foals in the spring of 1995. You can see the Appaloosas decked out in buckskin and bright beadwork at a number of Nez Perce events and parades throughout the year.

Several tribal members breed and sell Appaloosas, among them Rudy and Shirley Shebala, (208)926-0858; Bill and Bonnie Ewing, (208)843-7175; Bryce Corlin, (208)843-2134; Carla and Gordy HighEagle, (208)843-2907; Russ Spencer, (208)843-7167; Mario and Claudine Rabago, (208)843-2057; Nancy Wahobin, (208)935-0384; and Jon and Rosa Yearout, (208)843-2452. Best horse souvenir: a $10 black-and-white poster, a reproduction of an old photograph of a horse in beadwork tack and its rider, available from the Young Horseman Program, PO Box 305, Lapwai, ID 83540; (208)843-7333. Proceeds go to the Chief Joseph Horse Foundation.

Nez Perce Art

White Eagle Trading Post in Orfino sells only authentic beadwork, leatherwork, featherwork, and Native crafts; many of its items are made by owners and tribal members Larry and Pam WhiteEagle. Don't be put off by the treeless grounds around the shop. It's on the cleared site of the tribe's old lumber mill (on the banks of the Clearwater River, on Highway 1, east of Orfino; (208)476-7753).

From Highway 95, at Lapwai, you might be able to spot one of Connie Evans's Appaloosa-spotted canvas tepees set up in her backyard. Her custom-made tepees are weatherproofed, and some are painted. Make an appointment to look at or custom-order a tepee from Connie at Old West Enterprises; (208)843-5008.

Arthur Taylor weaves traditional flat cornhusk bags, a skill he learned as a child from Rose Frank, one of the Nez Perce's most respected weavers. Taylor works in the Nez Perce Cultural Resources Department in Lapwai. His work to help preserve Nez Perce culture and protect the pictographs in Hells Canyon leaves him little time for his art. As a result, his weavings are in high demand and are done mostly on commission. Taylor can be reached at (208)843-2967.

Brochures with photos of the artists and their works, including painters Nakia Williamson and John Wasson, stone sculptor A. K. Scott, and beadworker Allen V. Pinkham, Jr., are available from the Pi-Nee-Waus Community Center (on the corner of Main Street and Beaver Grade, PO Box 305, Lapwai, ID 83540; (208)843-2253). The center is off Highway 95, at Lapwai.

Understanding Nimiipu Territory

To fully appreciate the land that shaped the Nimiipu, you could begin your visit near the site where Chief Joseph's band had their summer camp, on the shores of Wallowa Lake in northeastern Oregon. This teardrop of clear water cupped in the eye of the Wallowa Mountains, near the town of Joseph, was shaped by a glacier and became the final resting place of Tuekakas (Old Chief Joseph), father of Chief Joseph.

Drive farther east, to the town of Imnaha, and follow the Imnaha River road south to Hat Point Overlook in Wallowa-Whitman National Forest. From the overlook you can see across the 7,900-foot chasm of Hells Canyon, although this isn't its deepest point. Retrace your route back to the town of Enterprise and travel over the hair-raising Rattlesnake Ridge (paved Highway 3) out of the Wallowa Valley and into the Snake River Canyon (caution: drop-offs and few guardrails). When you arrive at the deep-water ports of Lewiston and Clarkston, named after the explorers Lewis and Clark, think about how many times the Nimiipu traveled this same route and what they called this place—Tsemiiniicum ("place where two waters meet"). It was home to Nez Perce Chiefs Weeptes Sumpq'in, Looking Glass, and Timothy before the treaties were signed in the 1800s.

Hells Canyon

The Hells Canyon National Recreation Area covers 650,000 acres and has as its centerpiece the deepest river canyon in North America. More than 1,000 miles of trails, some of them in use for centuries, traverse this spectacular region. Although Hells Canyon, the aboriginal territory of the Nimiipu, is a protected river, access into the canyon by jet-boat is common, and jet-boat operators point out trails and several of 112 pictograph sites on their trips upriver.

Although the Nimiipu traveled throughout the canyon, hiking can be daunting: there are drop-off cliffs with steep, sliding rocky sections, poison ivy, ticks, rattlesnakes, and weather that ranges from 112-degree days in the summer to snowdrifts in the winter. But the payoff makes it worthwhile—views of bighorn sheep, elk, coyotes, river otters, eagles, and hawks in one of the most beautiful stretches of water in the world. You don't have to hike it to see the canyon. You can float the river with outfitters or jet-boat for more than 100 miles upstream from the towns of Lewiston and Clarkston at the confluence of the Snake and Clearwater Rivers.

For the Nez Perce Tribe's recommendations for river outfitters, call the tribal office; (208)843-2253. (Any outfitter using a Nez Perce guide gets our vote.) For additional information on recreation in the canyon and adjoining Eagle Cap Wilderness, call Wallowa-Whitman National Forest, Baker, Oregon, (503)523-6391; Hells Canyon National Recreation Area in Lewiston, Idaho, (208)743-3648; in Riggins, Idaho, (208)628-3916; and in Enterprise, Oregon, (503)426-3151. For information on environmental issues in the canyon, contact Hells Canyon Preservation Council, PO Box 908, Joseph, OR 97846.

Lolo Trail

The Nimiipu traveled the Q'ueseyn'ueskit (a Nez Perce word meaning "trail to buffalo country") over the mountains to hunt buffalo with the Crow Indians. Now called the Lolo Trail, the deeply embedded route was the main corridor to the Plains; it began in Nez Perce territory, followed the Clearwater River, and passed through Salish territory in Montana's Bitterroot Valley, south of Missoula. Some of the elders from various tribes have good stories to tell about the trail, which was still in use when they were young.

Today you can travel 100 miles along the high divide of the original trail (Forest Service Road 500), which was widened into a narrow, single-lane dirt road in the 1930s. It's treacherous, full of potholes, and clear of snow only from mid-July until late fall. At the highest point in the trail (7,033 feet), you will find one of the many rock mounds where Indians once left symbolic messages, in the form of feathers, beads, and other objects, for others using the trail.

Highway 12 and Lolo Pass, the main road from Lewiston, Idaho, over the mountains to Missoula, Montana, parallels the Lolo Trail. It follows the Lochsa River and the Middle Fork of the Clearwater, both protected under the Wild and Scenic River system. It's a paved highway with many pullouts for watching deer, elk, and moose. A surprising number of pedestrian bridges cross the rivers to trailheads.

There are 1,500 miles of hiking trails along Lolo Pass into Clearwater National Forest's 1.8 million acres, although not all of them are maintained. Elevation is from 1,600 to 7,000 feet, nights are always cool, and the area is covered with snow December through May.

Pick up maps and camping information at Clearwater National Forest headquarters, 12730 Hwy 12, Orofino, ID 83544; (208)476-4541.

Plummer: *Coeur d'Alene*

The Coeur d'Alene Indian Reservation, located south of the resort town of Coeur d'Alene in Idaho's panhandle, occupies a fraction of the tribe's original territories. An arrowhead-shaped piece of land, the reservation includes the edge of the western Rockies, half of Lake Coeur d'Alene, and portions of the fertile Palouse country. French fur traders named the tribe *Coeur d'Alene*—"heart of an awl"—saying they were the finest traders in the world. The tribe's trade involved year-long trips to the Pacific coast as well as to the Great Plains to exchange goods. They called themselves *Schee chu'umsch,* which, in their native Salish language, means "those who are found here."

The Coeur d'Alene Indians lived in large permanent villages along the Spokane and St. Joe Rivers, near Lake Coeur d'Alene and Hayden Lake and on parts of the large prairie known today as the Palouse country, an area of about 5 million acres. They enjoyed a close relationship with the inland tribes of Canada and the Northwest, sharing a common language and fishing grounds, intermarrying, and attending big trade gatherings and celebrations.

One of the first Catholic missions in the West, the Cataldo Mission was established on the St. Joe River in the early 1840s.

Because of flooding, it was moved to a bluff overlooking the Coeur d'Alene River in 1848. A new church and parish house were erected there and still stand today, both part of Old Mission State Park.

Silver was discovered in the Idaho panhandle in the 1870s, setting off a frenzy of mining activity. The Coeur d'Alene Indian Reservation, established in 1873, originally included all of Lake Coeur d'Alene. By a series of treaty agreements, the reservation was reduced to its present size. The tribe is currently working to reacquire what they have lost, buying back land that is often in high demand. The tribe is also in court, battling a railroad, seven mining companies, and the state of Idaho, trying to reacquire Lake Coeur d'Alene and seeking aid in cleaning up lead, zinc, and cadmium contamination in local lakes and rivers.

At least 72 million tons of mine tailings were discharged into the Coeur d'Alene River and flushed into Lake Coeur d'Alene in less than a century of mining. Even though most of the heavy metals have sunk to the bottom, and even though Lake Coeur d'Alene may look perfectly clear and lovely, anyone exploring creek beds near the old Kellogg mines east of Coeur d'Alene can readily see the impact of mining.

In addition to the old Cataldo Mission east of Coeur d'Alene, historic buildings still stand on the reservation, including the old Indian agency and the girls' living quarters and classrooms at the De Smet Mission. In nearby Rosalia, a battle monument marks the spot where Lt. Colonel Edward Steptoe and 150 U.S. cavalry soldiers were defeated by local tribes in 1858. Adjacent to the reservation is Steptoe Butte, the highest point in the Palouse and one of the most important sacred sites of the Coeur d'Alene. Now a state park with a road to the top, it offers visitors a breathtaking 360-degree vista from the summit.

The Cataldo Mission at Old Mission State Park

The restored Cataldo Mission Church is one of the oldest standing churches in the West and the oldest building in Idaho. Its unique construction alone—thick walls made of woven sticks and grass and plastered with clay mud—sets it apart from other old buildings in the region.

The church and parish house sit on a hill on the old mission grounds, today a state park, above the Coeur d'Alene River. Interstate 90, which cuts through northern Washington, Idaho, and Montana, roars past the still-pastoral setting of the mission. Nonetheless, it's easy to imagine the days when the Cataldo Mission was created from what was once wilderness.

The stately Greek-revival church was designed by Father Anthony Ravalli, a member of Father Pierre-John De Smet's Sacred Heart group of missionaries. Ravalli had studied art and architecture in Italy, in addition to theology, philosophy, mathematics, and medicine. Under Ravalli's direction, tribal members quarried stones in the mountains and cut trees with an adze, dragging both to the site on carts. A pair of handprints is still visible on an interior wall in a small room behind the altar. The church's high ceiling is stained blue with juice pressed from huckleberries.

Below the church and parish house, a modern interpretive center has been built into the hillside. An excellent narrated slide show tells about the history of the mission, the construction of a military highway closeby, and the 1917 flooding of the mission farmland with contaminated waters from the mines. The interpretive center includes a small but exquisite collection of beadwork from the early 1900s, as well as recent Native artwork. You can also pick up a brochure for a self-guided tour of the mission grounds.

Standing inside the spacious church, park rangers, sometimes robed in cassocks, talk about the mission from the viewpoint of an 1840s mission priest. They also discuss church furnishings, paintings, and statuary, pointing out details such as the crack in the statue of Mary, which begins at the corner of her eye and, like the trail of a salty teardrop, runs down the front of her robe.

For an evocative account of inland Salish tribes (including the Coeur d'Alene) and early Catholic missionaries, read Sacred Encounters: Father De Smet and the Indians of the Rocky Mountain West *(University of Oklahoma Press, 1993). Written by Jacqueline Peterson, with the help of tribal elders, it's filled with archival and contemporary photographs. Available at Old Mission State Park and from most Northwest booksellers.*

Every August 15, the Coeur d'Alene Tribe sets up tepees on the mission grounds to celebrate the annual Feast of the Assumption, with a pilgrimage from the mission cemetery to the church for Mass. Some of the procession songs have their roots in pre-Christian traditions, as does some of the ceremony that follows. Afterward there is a traditional Indian dinner, served picnic-style, and drumming, singing, and dancing. The public is invited to attend.

Old Mission State Park, PO Box 30, Cataldo, ID 83810; (208)682-3814. The park is 24 miles east of Coeur d'Alene on I-90. Admission $2 per vehicle; open daily, year-round.

The Old Indian Agency

Turn-of-the-century Indian agency buildings are in a cluster on a hill near the tribe's newer administration headquarters. The buildings overlook the prairie, with Steptoe Butte in the distance. Woods surround the agency center, and the entire area within a 5-mile radius is a wildlife refuge. In the Joseph Garry Building, you can purchase books about tribal history and pick up a list of Indian-owned businesses, which include grocery stores, a trading post, restaurants, motels, and gift shops.

Coeur d'Alene Tribe Administration, Rt 1, Box 11 FA, Plummer, ID 83851; (208)686-1800. Open 7:30am–4pm weekdays. Just south of Plummer, on Hwy 95, take Rt 11 west (it's marked by a sign with an arrowhead on it). Follow Rt 11 up the hill several miles, through small farms and woodlands. You'll think you're on the wrong road, since it seems such an unlikely spot for the agency to be built, but in the old days the area was accessible via a railroad that stopped on the south side of the hill.

Mary Immaculate Girls' Boarding School

The three-story brick dormitory, one of the few buildings left standing on the historic De Smet Mission grounds, is visible from Highway 95 at De Smet, on the south end of the reservation. Built in 1919, after two previous structures had burned to the ground, the dormitory is typical of early 1900s Indian boarding school dorms. The first floor is all parlors and offices; the second floor contains spacious classrooms and a chapel with the original stations of the cross still on the walls. Under the sloped eaves of the attic are wide-open dormitories where Indian children as young as 3 years old slept in rows of beds. Used as a day school until 1972, the building's classrooms are now home to a sewing training center, Lewis & Clark College's extension campus, and the tribe's Department of Education. The building, which is on the National Register of Historic Places, is open to the public for tours.

Coeur d'Alene tribal members make and sell tepees in traditional Plains or Coeur d'Alene style. Made of heavy canvas with rope reinforcements, tepees are 12 to 20 feet in diameter and cost $250–$450 (not including poles). From the tribe's Cut-and-Sew workshop, Mary Immaculate Girls' Boarding School; (208)274-2403, ext 2492.

Mary Immaculate Girls' Boarding School. At De Smet, on Hwy 95, take De Smet Rd, and turn onto Moctelme (the state's highway department spells it "Moctelme") Rd. Call in advance to arrange a tour of the building; (208)274-2403, ext 2492.

Stick Game Tournaments

Around 30 teams gather each year outside the Coeur d'Alene casino, on Highway 95 north of Worley, to play "stick game." The sound of singing fills the air as teams sit on the ground, facing each other, under a striped circus tent strung with electric lights.

Each team begins with five counting sticks and a pair of finger-length game pieces made of bone—one marked with colored stripes, the other plain. A team member hides the bones from the opposing team in his or her hands, challenging the other team to guess which hand holds the marked bone. Guess right and you get a counting stick on your side; guess wrong and you lose a stick. The team that acquires all the sticks wins. In the old days, blankets, saddles, baskets, guns, and even horses were used as collateral for bets instead of currency.

The crux of the game is the skill of distraction. As the bones are passed from hand to hand under a scarf, other team members hammer on drums or on the pole lying in front of them, shake rattles and noise-makers, and sing loudly. Particularly effective songs are handed down through families, and players sing their most distracting songs when the game becomes close. When the game is played at night, by firelight, as it was in the old days, it is even more challenging and memorable.

Annual stick game tournaments are held in August at the Coeur d'Alene casino. Teams begin playoff competition on Friday night, continue on Saturday, and play all night through Sunday afternoon. The casino crew serves plenty of coffee. Bystanders can bet on the game. The winning team takes home at least a $10,000 purse. Expect crowds.

The Red Bird Memorial Horse Races are tribal member Cliff Sijohn's memorial to his grand-father, Red Bird. Red Bird used to take a string of 25 to 30 horses to Canada each year and race them all summer. The 1-day event, held in his honor, takes place each fall and features traditional Indian horse races. Between events, there are stick-horse races for all ages. Call Cliff Sijohn for details at (208)686-7402.

The Coeur d'Alene casino is located on I-95, 30 miles south of Coeur d'Alene near Worley; (800)523-2464. The stick game tournament is held each August; call for dates.

Battle of Tohotonimme

"Remember the Battle," reads the sign at the entrance to Rosalia, Washington, a small town about 17 miles west of the Coeur d'Alene Reservation. Rosalia lies in the shallow, 6-mile-long valley along Pine Creek, next to the hillside. There, in 1858, Lieutenant Colonel Edward J. Steptoe lost a battle against 600 to 1,200 Indians from all over the region, led by the Coeur d'Alene. History books say that Steptoe and his men, surrounded by Indians, made a clever escape over the hillside in the middle of the night. Coeur d'Alene tribal members whose ancestors fought there say that the peace was nego-tiated with the help of Catholic priests, and that Steptoe and his men were then allowed to leave.

There are also different versions of why the skirmish began. Steptoe and his men entered Palouse and Coeur d'Alene territory fully armed, with two howitzers. They were questioned by the Coeur d'Alene about their intent. The battle began after gunshots were fired.

After their surrender, Steptoe and his men returned to Fort Walla Walla on the Columbia River. News of their loss prompted the U.S. Army to send in General George Wright, along with armed troops and wagonloads of ammunition, to move the Indians permanently to reservations. Wright's tactics for breaking Indian resistance were horrific. He called meetings with important chiefs to discuss peace, but when the chiefs arrived, dressed in ceremonial regalia befitting the occasion, Wright had them hanged. He was also responsible for the destruction of thousands of horses that belonged to the tribes—a loss that effectively crushed the tribes' economy. For extra effect, Wright and his men bludgeoned and shot foals in front of their Indian owners. (The slaughter of 800 captured ponies along the Spokane River occurred at milepost 292, on Interstate 90.)

In his popular novel **Reservation Blues** *(Atlantic Monthly Press, 1995), Coeur d'Alene-Spokane tribal member, author, and poet Sherman Alexie places General George Wright in a contemporary setting, as an employee of Cavalry Records, and uses "screaming horse" imagery throughout the book. Alexie referred to Carl P. Schlicke's* George Wright: Guardian of the Pacific Coast *and Benjamin Manning's* Conquest of the Coeur d'Alenes, Spokanes, & Palouses *for historical background.*

Steptoe Butte State Park

Adjoining the Coeur d'Alene Reservation are the rolling hills of the Palouse, some of the most fertile farmland in the world. (The French word *Palouse* means "grass blowing in the wind.") Created during ice-age windstorms, the topsoil here is 32 feet deep. In the heart of the Palouse is solitary Steptoe Butte, the Coeur d'Alene's sacred mountain, towering more than 1,000 feet above the valley floor. Its peak was a site of meditation, prayer, and ceremony for centuries. The butte, covered with downy grass, is solid rock, 500 million years old. The narrow, paved road to the butte follows tidy wheat fields edged with colorful wildflowers. From the picnic tables sheltered by stubby pines at the foot of the butte, the road spirals to the top, which has been scraped flat and paved for a parking lot. In summer, a steady warm wind carries the sweet scent of wild roses, wheat, and dry grass. As the sky darkens, the glow of the city of Spokane lights the sky to the northwest. It is still possible to be alone, with views in all directions, on top of this solitary summit.

The gated road to Steptoe Butte State Park, (509)549-3551, is open from dawn until dusk (or until the gatekeeper shows up to close it). Take Hwy 195 to the town of Steptoe. At Steptoe, turn east on the county road. Drive for 5–7 miles until you see Steptoe Butte Rd. Eight picnic sites. Free.

Chatq'ele Interpretive Center

In 1908, the U.S. Congress carved out 5,505 acres of land and 2,333 acres of lakebed from the Coeur d'Alene Indian Reservation's marsh, woodlands, and open meadows to create Heyburn State Park.

The park includes what is actually four small lakes that pooled together with Lake Coeur d'Alene after a dam was built on the Spokane River. The navigable St. Joe River feeds Lake Coeur d'Alene near Heyburn State Park; the river's swift current and original riverbed is still marked by a line of partly submerged cottonwood trees. You can get a good look at it by hiking the 3-mile Indian Cliff Trail in the park. Stop at the Chatq'ele Interpretive Center at Rocky Point, east of Plummer, for trail maps of Heyburn State Park. The interpretive center is located in an old lakefront log lodge, built in 1934 by the Civilian Conservation Corps. A small but lovely display includes unusual Coeur d'Alene buckskin jackets and leggings trimmed with white ermine skins, and beadwork created with both European glass beads and older bone beads. There's a "Discovery Corner" for kids. A member of the tribe is on hand to explain Coeur d'Alene traditional culture. Be sure to ask to view an award-winning video about the tribe's effort to clean up Lake Coeur d'Alene, *Paradise in Peril,* as well as tapes of storytelling by tribal elders.

Chatq'ele Interpretive Center, Rt 1, Box 139, Plummer, ID 83851; (208)686-1308. From Hwy 95 at Plummer, go east on Hwy 5 for 5 miles to Rocky Point. Watch for signs. The park offers boat launch facilities, beaches, picnic areas, and overnight camping. The park and interpretive center are open summers only. Call to check on fees and dates the park is open.

Bonners Ferry: *Kootenai*

The Kootenai people are geographically split: part of the tribe lives in Montana (see Flathead Reservation section in this chapter). Another group lives in Canada and a third group lives in Idaho. The tribe was separated when Britain and the United States drew the boundary between Canada and the United States right through the middle of Kootenai ancestral lands, which stretched from Yellowwood Falls in mid-British Columbia all the way to Great Falls in Montana and south to the border of Yellowstone National Park. Today, just a few hundred Kootenai people live on their original ground in Bonners Ferry, Idaho, a little farming valley in the state's northern panhandle that is surrounded by snowcapped mountains. Just 31 miles from Schweitzer's world-class downhill skiing, Bonners Ferry also adjoins the Snow Creek Recreation Area in the Selkirk Mountains, which offers cross-country skiing and snowmobile trails that are maintained throughout the winter.

Surrounded by national forest, the Kootenai people living in Bonners Ferry do not have a reservation, but they do own a first-rate hotel on the banks of the Kootenai River, one of Idaho's premier fishing streams. They also raise nearly 20,000 white sturgeon every year in one of the most unusual fish hatcheries in the Northwest.

Kootenai River Inn

The 48-room Best Western Kootenai River Inn is built on the banks of the Kootenai River. The area is gorgeous year-round but is especially so in the fall, when the quaking aspens turn bright yellow against the fresh green of the pines. About 30 miles north of Sandpoint, Idaho, the hotel is the jump-off spot for four seasons of away-from-the-crowds recreation: golf, hiking, whitewater rafting, hunting, fishing, skiing, and snowmobiling—all of which can be arranged through the hotel. The Springs Restaurant and Lounge overlooks the river and is open for breakfast, lunch, and dinner. Use of the indoor pool, sauna, Jacuzzi, steam room, and fitness area is free with your room.

Kootenai River Plaza, Bonners Ferry, ID 83805; (800)346-5668 or (208)267-8511. Room rates are $80–$225. Open year-round.

> **A Century of Survival,** *dedicated to "our stubborn, strong-willed, long-suffering ancestors," is a short, lively, easy-to-read, Kafkaesque account of Kootenai history, written and published by the tribe in 1990. Available for $8.95 (includes postage and handling) from the Kootenai Tribe, PO Box 1269, Bonners Ferry, ID 83805; (208)267-3519.*

Kootenai Tribe Fish Hatchery

Visit the Kootenai Tribe Fish Hatchery and you will see one of most unusual fish nursery operations in the Pacific Northwest. The hatchery raises white sturgeon: big, prehistoric-looking fish that have been landlocked in fresh water since the end of the last ice age, about 10,000 years ago. The female fish first spawn at the age of 24 and weigh more than 100 pounds, then spawn again every 4 to 6 years.

When brood stock began to dwindle, fishery biologists performed Caesarians on the mother fish to remove their eggs. Today, egg production is controlled with hormone injections. About 20,000 baby sturgeon are confined and fed in tanks until they're 2 years old and about 16 inches long, at which time they're released into the Kootenai River. The fish are a sight to behold. Visitors are welcome at the hatchery during business hours (fish biologists know where all the river's good fishing holes are, too—for cutthroat trout, kokanee, Dolly Varden trout, and landlocked lingcod).

Kootenai Tribe Fish Hatchery, PO Box 1269, Bonners Ferry, ID 83805; (208)267-3519. Call for directions and best times to visit.

Pablo: *Flathead*

There are several stories about how the Flathead Indian Reservation, in western Montana, got its name. One is that fur traders mistakenly thought the inland Salish people had the same head-shaping custom as the coastal Salish, who shaped their infants' heads with gentle pressure in the cradleboard, "flattening" their foreheads. Perhaps Salish-speaking relatives from the coast were visiting at the time the fur traders showed up in Montana. Another story is that the sign-language motion identifying the Salish was pressing both sides of the head with the hands.

Whatever the reason, "Flathead" doesn't accurately describe the handsome Salish or the Kootenai people, who share the Flathead Reservation in western Montana. Nor does it remotely begin to describe the beauty of the Mission Valley, south of Glacier National Park, which nestles against the impenetrable spine of the Mission Range. The Salish called these mountains the "backbone of the world." The ax-blade peaks of the towering, dark-blue Mission Range define the whole east side of the reservation, which comprises more than 1.3 million acres. The glacier-carved valley begins in the south with the hilly grasslands of the National Bison Range, home to hundreds of buffalo, antelope, and elk, flattens into rangeland, and ends in the north at the 28-mile-long Flathead Lake.

Highway 93, a two-lane highway, cuts through the middle of the reservation's Mission Valley, past big-sky cattle ranches, the pow-wow grounds at Arlee, the historic St. Ignatius Mission, Ninepipe National Wildlife Refuge, the People's Center at Pablo, and the tribally owned first-class resort hotel, KwaTaqNuk, on the south shore of Flathead Lake.

The Salish and Kootenai Tribes originally shared a huge area that stretched from southern British Columbia, northern Idaho, and northern Washington to western Montana. The 1855 Treaty of Hell's Gate took away most of their land, exchanging millions of acres for promises never kept. The tribes ended up with more than 1.3 million acres, including the forested slopes of the Mission Range and the southern half of Flathead Lake (a line was mapped right through the middle of the lake). Some Kootenai people were already living on the western shore of Flathead Lake on Dayton Creek, and they entered into the treaty agreement in 1855 to keep their land. Their descendants live there to this day.

The reservation was divided into allotments by a government act in 1904, 20 years before Native Americans were allowed to vote. Each of the 2,378 tribal members was allowed 80 acres of agricultural land or 160 acres of grazing lands. Unclaimed lands were opened for homesteading and sale. Tribal members who refused to claim their allotments, as a way of saying no to the scheme, were "assigned" land, some of it literally bare rock under a thin layer of soil and grass. Since 1940, the Salish and Kootenai Tribes have been buying back land within the reservation that was lost to homesteaders.

One group of Salish Indians refused to move. Chief Charlo held out against settlers in the beautiful Bitterroot Valley, south of Missoula, for 20 years until forced to move to the Flathead Reservation. Not one to hang his head, Chief Charlo led his people into the Flathead Reservation settlement of Arlee on horseback, proudly dressed in their finest regalia. But his family says that he was never the same again, embittered by broken promises and the loss of the Bitterroot Valley.

Today about 100 tribal members farm or ranch. Estimated tribal enrollment is about 6,700. The tribe has built an alternative high school and the Salish Kootenai College, oversees five timber operations, and has control of the valley's electric service. They have also written one of the most stringent water quality and shoreline protection acts in the state of Montana, if not the United States, to protect Flathead Lake from the impact of unregulated construction. Determined to protect the reservation, the tribe also requested a pristine-air designation from the Environmental Protection Agency in 1979; designated the reservation a nuclear-free zone in 1984; and, in 1982, created one of the first tribal wilderness areas in the country as part of its commitment to saving habitat.

Confederated Salish and Kootenai Tribes, PO Box 278, Pablo, MT 59855; (406)675-2700. Write for their free brochure and map listing 39 sites to visit on the reservation. Free Montana road maps are available from Travel Montana; (800)847-4868 or (406)444-2654.

KwaTaqNuk Resort at Flathead Bay

KwaTaqNuk (pronounced "qua-TUCK-nuck") is Kootenai for "where the water leaves the lake." The KwaTaqNuk resort hotel is perched on the western shore of Flathead Lake, near the headwaters of the Flathead River. The resort has all the amenities: two swimming pools, spa, espresso cart, and 112 spacious guest rooms with balconies offering an astounding view: the ice-capped Glacier Mountains to the north and the Mission Range across the broad windswept, blue-green lake. The small town of Polson, mostly non-Indian owned, is right behind the hotel. Bears occasionally lumber along the waterfront, and a family of mink sometimes slinks into view. Seagulls mingle with bald eagles and osprey over the lake, and migrating tundra swans have been seen in flocks of 800 or more along the shore.

In the summer, there may be a tepee on KwaTaqNuk's lawn—referred to with a grin as the "traditional suite" by hotel staff. You can't sleep in the tepee, although blankets and pillows have been found in it on occasion.

Few would guess that this Best Western hotel is tribally owned—except that the captions under the 45 historic photographs decorating the lobby and public halls actually name the Indians in the pictures, and document when and where the photographs were taken. These pictures of the tribal chiefs and leaders were gathered from various museum collections, and all those pictured were identified by descendants living on the reservation. The hotel's meeting rooms are named after these famous chiefs. Another tip-off about Native ownership: Indian fry bread is served with meals in the hotel's dining room. And the bright red flag of the Flathead Nation whips in the wind on the flagpole on the hotel lawn.

Guest rooms are large, with roomy tiled baths, classic wicker chairs, and comfortable beds. All public rooms, including a sun-splashed lounge, dining room, and even the swimming pools, have the same stunning views and decks. The hotel has two gift shops (carrying mostly Western art), a boardwalk along the lake, a full-service marina, excursion and twilight cruises on the tribe's sightseeing boat, and nearby golf and whitewater rafting. Reserve in advance for paddleboats, canoes, ski boats, fishing boats, and wind-surfing equipment from Flathead Surf-n-Ski at the hotel's marina.

Best Western KwaTaqNuk Resort at Flathead Bay, 303 US Hwy 93 E, Polson, MT 59860; (800)528-1234 or (406)883-3636. Open year-round. Rates $49–$128. Peak season is July–Aug. Spring and fall travelers are virtually guaranteed rooms with a view (but bring a warm coat; it can snow here in May). Nonsmoking and wheelchair-accessible rooms available, also a conference center and banquet rooms. No charge for kids 16 and under in the same room. Water-sports rentals: Flathead Surf-n-Ski, KwaTaqNuk Resort, PO Box 1161, Polson, MT 59860; (800)358-8046 or (406)883-3900.

Flathead Lake and River Cruises

Flathead Lake water levels are lowered in the winter to ready the lake basin for glacial runoff in the spring. By mid-June water levels are normal, the lake is clear, and the little (50-passenger) cruise boat, the KwaTaqNuk *Princess,* makes three rounds of the lake a day, through September 30. Cruises are narrated by the captain or a tribal member. The 1½-hour Bay Cruise takes you up through "the narrows," a chain of forested, stepping-stone islands in the glacier-carved lake basin. For a few dollars more, take the 3-hour cruise up to Wildhorse Island, east of the Kootenai town of Elmo. Accessible only by boat, Wildhorse Island State Park is home to wild horses, bighorn sheep, and deer. Twilight cruises leave the dock at 7:30pm daily.

Arrange cruises on the KwaTaqNuk Princess *through KwaTaqNuk Resort, 303 Hwy 93 E, Polson, MT 59860; (406)883-2448. Rates are affordable, and discounts are available for families, seniors, and groups. The boat is also available for private charters.*

The People's Center

The stone building is built close to the ground, with a copper door that glows in the morning sun and a white-pine arbor encircling the lawn. From the sky, the grounds and building resemble an eagle. The People's Center was created by volunteers, who painted the walls, put together the exhibits, and donated family heirlooms. The story of the Salish-Kootenai is told by the people themselves, instead of being interpreted by outsiders. Think of it as the heart of the reservation, thrown open to the public.

At the entrance are four floor-to-ceiling cedar poles on which realistic carvings depict animal and bird tracks and plant and water life. The People's Center includes an interpretive center, gift shop, and a large room for events, cultural classes, and demonstrations. Although the exhibits are labeled, it's best to ask at the desk for a guide, who can point out such things as how dried buffalo bladders were worn much like a modern-day fanny pack. Audio tours are provided in the Salish and Kootenai languages with English translations. The gift shop sells only Native art, with a special emphasis on tribal members' art and work from other Northwest tribes. In addition to fine beadwork, silver jewelry, and antler lamps and chandeliers, the shop also sells locally made T-shirts, books, and audio- and videotapes. The video *We Live in a Circle,* produced by the Salish Kootenai College Media Center, is available for $10; it presents the history of the center and describes the rich culture of the Salish and Kootenai peoples.

The People's Center, Hwy 93 W, PO Box 278, Pablo, MT 59855; (406)675-0160. The town of Pablo is about 10 miles south of Flathead Lake, on Hwy 93. The People's Center is raising funds for collections acquisition and exhibit development; membership ranges from $10 for students to $100 for patrons. Admission $2. Open daily, Apr–Sept, 9am–9pm. Open Mon–Fri, Oct–Mar, 9 am–5pm.

Native Ed-Venture Tours

Hire a Native guide for the day. The People's Center offers five tours through Ed-Venture Tours, all of them under $45 per person and some lasting as long as a day. The half-day "Heritage and History—Focus on the Arts" tour includes the center, historic St. Ignatius Mission, local galleries, and artists' homes. "Bears, Bison, and Birds" takes a look at the National Bison Range, the Mission Range, and tribal wilderness areas, with an in-depth explanation of the tribe's efforts to manage its diverse ecosystems. The "Powwow Tour" includes attendance at one of the tribe's special celebrations with a Native guide to explain the songs, dances, and ceremonies and to introduce visitors to dancers and artists. In addition to a number of community events, the tribe hosts two major powwows, the Arlee Fourth of July Celebration and the Standing Arrow Powwow, held the third weekend in July. Be prepared to stay late, since most powwows continue until at least midnight. The center also arranges custom tours, including hikes, river floats, and overnight stays with Native families. Visitors can learn firsthand about reservation life from those who live it daily. We loved our tour. Don't forget to tip your guides; they really earn the money.

Native Ed-Ventures, The People's Center, Hwy 93 W, PO Box 278, Pablo, MT 59855; (800)883-5344 or (406)883-5344.

Kerr Dam Vista Point

Where Kerr Dam now stands was once a spectacular waterfall, considered by the Kootenai Indians as the center of their spiritual world. From the unpaved parking lot, it's some 320 wooden stair steps down to the end of a narrow granite ledge (with a covered shelter perched on the end) overlooking the dam and the dramatic Flathead River Gorge. Built in the 1930s with Indian labor, the dam seems to have grown into the sheer rock walls of the gorge. In spite of the concrete and the spillways, this is a breathtaking vista. We spent an hour with our guides here, admiring the view. Montana Power leases the dam from the Flathead Tribe, sharing hydroelectricity profits with the tribe to the tune of about $12 million a year, and will continue to do so until the lease expires in 2015.

The *Place of the Falling Waters* documents the building of Kerr Dam and how it forever altered the spectacular falls. The documentary series includes interviews with tribal elders, newsreel footage, rare photographs, and aerial footage of the reservation. Produced in 1991 by Salish Kootenai College and Native Voices Public Television

Workshop at Montana State University, this set of three ½-hour programs, now on video, won the Silver Apple Award at the National Educational Film and Video Festival.

Roads to Kerr Dam are unmarked and hard to find. Ask for directions from the People's Center or at the KwaTaqNuk Resort's reception desk. The Place of the Falling Waters video series, which includes all three programs, is available from Salish Kootenai College, Hwy 93 W, PO Box 117, Pablo, MT 59855; (406)675-4800.

National Bison Range

At one time, 30 to 70 million buffalo roamed the Plains, before they were deliberately destroyed by European settlers in an effort to tame the West for farming and cattle ranching. By 1873, only 100 buffalo remained in the wild. That year, Walking Coyote, a Kootenai tribal member, returned to the Flathead Reservation from Musselshell River country with five orphaned calves and began to rebuild the herd. Two white ranchers bought descendants of Walking Coyote's breeding stock, and between 1907 and 1909, three reserves were carved out of Flathead Reservation land by President Theodore Roosevelt and Congress to save the animals from extinction. Today 350 to 500 bison roam 18,500 fenced acres of the National Bison Range, mostly hilly, dry grasslands on the reservation's south end.

The buffalo and the wild grasses that grow on the rocky, arid land are perfectly suited to each other. The native grasses are dryland-adapted: while most plants grow from their tips, these grasses grow in clumps from the base of their stems and continue to grow after their tops are grazed off. But of course, on the National Bison Range it's the shaggy beasts that get all the raves, not the slender grass. You may also spot antelope, white-tailed deer, elk, mule deer, bighorn sheep, mountain goats, bears, and coyotes.

Begin at the National Bison Range visitors center (well marked, off Highway 212), and pick up a map with excellent explanations of how this ecosystem works. Although the area next to Mission Creek on the northern part of the range looks perfect for a picnic, stay in your car and slowly drive the dirt roads; don't walk. Bison can outrun a horse and will charge and gore with their pointed horns. They're especially nasty during the breeding season, from mid-July to August. This is one of the reasons the tribes preferred to run them over cliffs to break their necks when slaughtering them for food and hides, instead of facing them head on.

National Bison Range, 132 Bison Range Rd, Molese, MT 59824; (406)644-2211. The visitors center is off Hwy 212 and is well marked.

Ninepipe and Pablo Wildlife Refuges

The Ninepipe and the Pablo National Wildlife Refuges cover about 4,500 acres of water, marsh, and upland grasses, harboring about 190 species of birds. On the migratory flyway, the refuges are home to 80,000 Canada geese, blue herons, cormorants, redheads, pintails, snow geese, coots, and other waterfowl. Ninepipe refuge is 5 miles south of the town of Ronan. The Pablo refuge is north of the Ninepipe refuge, 3 miles northwest of the town of Pablo. Also see birds at the Nature Conservancy's Safe Harbor Marsh, north of the town of Polson and west of the "narrows" on the west shore of Flathead Lake, visible in the distance from KwaTaqNuk Resort.

The Confederated Salish and Kootenai Tribes provide a free map of the Flathead Reservation's recreation and conservation areas. For more information contact the Tribal Fish and Game Office, PO Box 278, Pablo, MT 59855; (406)675-2700.

Trading Posts

There are four colorful "trading posts" on the Flathead Reservation, all of them on Highway 93. The term comes from the fur-trading posts built all over the Northwest in the last century, when beaver pelts were in high demand.

Modern-day trading posts sell Indian antiquities, new Pendleton blankets and vests, arts and crafts (such as new beadwork), contemporary Indian art, and supplies. Some offer tidbits of local history as well. Doug Allard's Flathead Indian Museum & Trading Post (Hwy 93, PO Box 460, St. Ignatius; (406)745-2951) displays beautiful old beadwork, as well as portraits of Indian leaders, in a large room adjoining his two-story store.

Preston Miller has moved some of the oldest hand-hewn log buildings on the Flathead Reservation to his trading post, including the 1862 Indian agency building from the town of Jocko and the 1885 Ravalli railroad depot. The historic buildings make his Four Winds Trading Post (Hwy 93, PO Box 580, St. Ignatius; (406)745-4336) worth a stop, especially with a guide from the People's Center, who can give you the Indian perspective on the old buildings.

Other trading posts include the Jocko River Trading Post (Hwy 93 N, PO Box 630221, Ravalli; (406)745-3055) and the Polson Bay

Trading Company (320 Main St, Polson; (406)883-3742). For tips on how to buy Indian art, look in the appendix of this book.

St. Ignatius Mission National Historic Site

The narrative posted at St. Ignatius Mission National Historic Site describes several delegations sent by the tribes to bring back the "black robes." Fur traders had brought with them Iroquois trappers who had told of Catholic rituals and beliefs that seemed very similar to Salish and Kootenai spirituality. Narratives say there were "language difficulties," so it is hard to know what exactly the delegations were seeking. Some say it was the power and the "medicine" of the "black robes" that the tribes wanted, and some say that the Jesuits fitted the prophecy of Shining Shirt, a prophet who had seen a vision of men wearing long black dresses and signs of the cross.

There's a great deal of personal satisfaction (and large tax benefits) to be had in returning stone tools, baskets, beadwork, masks, and other items to the tribes and their museums, who can't afford to buy them. If you have an item you'd like to return, but don't know who made it, contact the Affiliated Tribes of Northwest Indians at 222 NW Davis, Suite 403, Portland, OR 97209; (503)241-0070.

The first mission was built in Salish territory by Father Pierre-John De Smet on the Bitterroot River, south of Missoula, Montana. In 1854, Jesuit missionaries built a second mission, on a site the Salish called *snieleman,* a word that meant "the surrounded" (because the mission was surrounded by mountains). Their log cabin, sawmill, flour mill, printing press, carpentry shop, and blacksmith's shop were the first in the Mission Valley. The town where the mission was built was named after the church, St. Ignatius. By 1899, with the help of tribes now confined to the Flathead Reservation, the missionaries built a massive brick church with 58 murals painted on the interior walls. The church still stands, as do several of the small log cabins that were moved next to it (look inside for photographs of the boarding school and gardens). The three-story dormitories of the boarding school, run by the Ursuline Sisters, are gone, however.

To reach St. Ignatius Mission National Historic Site, look for signs on Hwy 93 at the town of St. Ignatius. Don't worry, you'll find it; the church is the biggest building around. The church and adjoining log cabins are open daily.

Recreation Areas and Campgrounds

Nine trailheads enter a 93,000-acre tribal wilderness area, on the west side of the Mission Range, then proceed to more than 100 high-country lakes and ponds, including "kettle lakes," big potholes left by retreating glaciers. Wilderness–area campgrounds, maintained by the tribe, are undeveloped. You must pack in fresh water and pack out garbage. In mid-July, 10,000 acres are closed when the grizzly bears show up to feed on ladybugs and army cutworm moths above McDonald Lake. Take precautions when camping here at any time of the year.

Whitewater stretches of the Flathead River for rafting and river kayaking are accessible from boat ramps below Kerr Dam. Boats with motors (15 horsepower maximum) are allowed on most reservation lakes and the river. All boats must be pulled from Flathead Lake when not in use to protect the water from gas and oil seepage.

Tribal Fish and Game Office, PO Box 278, Pablo, MT 59855; (406)675-2700, ext 595. The tribe's brochure and map, available at the People's Center (see "The People's Center" in this section), lists 23 state and tribal parks for tent and trailer camping, picnicking, fishing, and wildlife viewing on the reservation's high mountain lakes, wetlands, and streams. All are first come, first served. Peak season is Jul–Aug. Campers, fishers, and hunters need to obtain inexpensive use-permits, available at the People's Center, posted gas stations, and sporting goods stores.

Char-Koosta News

Founded in 1957 by tribal leader Walter McDonald, the tribal newspaper *Char-Koosta News* was established to inform the Salish and Kootenai about the consequences of "termination," a Congressional plan to destroy Indian tribes' self-determination and sovereignty. The *Char-Koosta News* is still published weekly by the Confederated Tribes in Pablo and is on newsstands each Friday. The paper's title combines the names of the last two traditional chiefs—Charlo of the Salish Tribe and Koostahtah of the Kootenai Tribe.

Char-Koosta News, PO Box 278, Pablo, MT 59855; (406)675-3000. Subscription $25 a year, out of state; $45 a year, foreign. Call for a complimentary issue and subscription form.

Pocatello: *Shoshone-Bannock*

The geography of the Shoshone–Bannock ancestral lands alone is impressive. It includes parts of Montana, Idaho, Yellowstone National Park, and northern Utah, Nevada, and California. Today, the Shoshone and Bannock Tribes' Fort Hall Reservation is on potato-growing land on the upper reaches of the Snake River in southeastern Idaho, halfway between Yellowstone National Park and Salt Lake City. The reservation's name, Fort Hall, comes from a trading post that was built on the tribe's wintering grounds near the Snake in the early 1800s. Nine emigrant trails, including the Oregon Trail, passed through Fort Hall. If you look closely, you can still see ruts from the wagons in the tall grass.

The Shoshone and Bannock Tribes were hunters who followed big-game migrations and fished for salmon. When horses were introduced in the early 1700s, the tribes began to travel great distances, pursuing buffalo across the Plains and into New Mexico and Texas. Guns, ammunition, and horses soon gave their armed Blackfoot and Sioux enemies the upper hand, pushing the Shoshone and Bannock back into the Rocky Mountains by the beginning of the 19th century.

The Shoshones had long formed alliances with the Cayuse in eastern Oregon. When the European fur trappers arrived, the Shoshones did the same thing with the trappers, trading horses for guns to arm themselves against Athabascan and Sioux Indians driven westward from the Plains by settlers.

Sacagawea is probably the best-known Shoshone, a member of the Lemhi band. She was kidnapped as a child and was sold or traded to the fur trapper Charbonneau when she was a teenager. Accompanied by Toby, a Shoshone guide, and his four sons, she began her mission to lead explorers Lewis and Clark across the Rocky Mountains to the Pacific Ocean shortly before the birth of her son.

The Lewis and Clark expedition was followed by fur traders and then by massive emigration through Shoshone lands by pioneers, with disastrous consequences for the fragile desert ecology. Livestock uprooted camas beds; game was hunted almost to extinction; and when settlers put down their roots, land was fenced and entry denied to the Native peoples, who depended on seasonal hunting and fishing for their food. Tension mounted with each new encroachment. The removal of Shoshone Indians from areas of land desired by non-Indians resulted in the massacre of more than 250 Shoshones in southeastern Idaho in January 1863. An 1867 presidential executive order established the 1.8-million-acre Fort Hall Indian Reservation, to which the Boise Shoshone were relocated from their western territory. The Fort Bridger Treaty of 1868 confirmed the arrangement, but a survey error reduced the reservation to 1.2 million acres in 1872. The Bannock Wars of 1878 were a final attempt by independent Native hunters to fight for their traditional existence.

From 1885 to 1914, the reservation was cut into allotments of 160 acres to each adult and 80 acres to each child. The tribes lost half of their reservation, including Lava Hot Springs and what is now the city of Pocatello, through a series of agreements between the tribe and the federal government.

The Bottoms

The old maps call the Bottoms, a rich river delta in the heart of the reservation, "Indian Wastelands." But the Bottoms is anything but a wasteland. Fed by artesian springs and the Blackfoot, Portneuf, and Snake Rivers, the Bottoms is a cool oasis in a desert landscape—huge meadows of waist-high grass, nodding sunflowers, tangles of willows and cottonwoods, and clear, cold streams swimming with trout. Slightly lower in elevation than the surrounding benches, the area was a perfect winter camp, where Indians pitched wickiups covered with elk hides for shelter. The wind and snow blew straight across the surrounding benches but drifted only lightly into the Bottoms. The bubbling springs that lace the meadows kept the ground soft while the desert above froze solid. Except for Lava Hot Springs, 40 miles away, the Bottoms land was the warmest wintering place in the region. The warmth also meant an abundant supply of fish and game—rabbits, antelope, deer, and bison—all through the winter. Because of frozen ground elsewhere, Indians for years buried their dead in the quicksand of the Bottoms; Chief Pocatello (for whom the nearby town of Pocatello is named) was buried here in the late 1800s; weights were attached to his body, and he was lowered into the quicksand.

Chief Pocatello saw his father hanged by white settlers between the upraised and braced yokes of three wagons, fostering his hatred of immigrants. Pocatello's band of 450 Northwestern Shoshones was almost totally wiped out at Bear River on January 29, 1863, by a Colonel Conner and his "California volunteers." It was the largest military massacre of Indians in the history of the United States, even larger than the one at Wounded Knee. Only seven members of the band survived.

The Bottoms is loaded with history. Archaeological evidence supports Shoshone claims that the Bottoms has been a winter camp and gathering place for at least 15,000 years. In the last 200 years, emigrant, freight, and stage roads passed through the Bottoms on the old Indian trails; it was a resting spot on the route of at least nine major emigrant trails from the Midwest.

Fur traders in search of beaver pelts began trapping here in 1810. The first fur-trading post, Fort Hall, was built in the Bottoms in 1834 by Nathaniel Wyeth, and was later an important supply and rest stop for settlers on their way west. Between 1842 and 1852 nearly 200,000 settlers passed through Fort Hall, sometimes 5,000 at a time. Members of the 1843 Great Emigration led by Marcus Whitman passed through here, as did more than 3,000 Mormons on their way to settle what is now Salt Lake City, Utah.

The spot where the trails safely crossed the Snake River is now underwater, flooded with backwater from a dam built at American Falls in 1925. The reservoir, rising higher each year, now threatens to flood the Bottoms and the pile of rocks marking the site of the original Fort Hall trading post.

A portion of the Bottoms was purchased by the Bureau of Reclamation in 1924 for 15 cents an acre. Today, the Bottoms is fenced grazing land for the tribe's 400 head of buffalo. It is a haven for wintering birds, and a habitat for bald eagles in cottonwood snags above the Snake River.

Mosquitoes are fierce here in the summer. "No one could ever figure out why the white men erected a year-round, permanent fort there," says Robert "Red" Perry, Sr., who was born to a Bannock/Sioux mother on the reservation. Even Marcus Whitman, in his journals, complained about the ferocity of the mosquitoes in the Bottoms. Wear long-sleeved shirts, jeans, socks with shoes, and plenty of bug repellent when you visit—or try crushing willow branches with a stone and rubbing the juice on exposed skin.

Access to the Bottoms is restricted. The only way you can enter the area is if you are accompanied by a tribally endorsed tour guide (see "Reservation Tours" later in this section) or purchase a $30-a-day seasonal fishing permit. All others must get permission from the tribal business council. Inquire at the Tribal Fish and Game Department for fishing permits, (208)238-3743, or at the Fort Hall Administrative Office, (208)238-3700.

Old Fort Hall

A number of fur-trading companies, attracted by the large colonies of beavers living in the marshland, trapped in the Bottoms before Nathaniel Wyeth built his trading post there in 1834. Wyeth, a New England businessman, arrived in the Bottoms in July 1834 with $3,000 worth of trade goods after his deal to supply the Rocky Mountain Fur Company had fallen through. Stuck with the trade goods, he erected the Fort Hall Trading Post near the Snake River, a few buildings made of hand hewn cottonwood, thus challenging the powerful Hudson's Bay Company. Wyeth built a tailor shop to make cotton and wool shirts for the Indians—and employed Indians there to make moccasins and tanned buckskins for the trappers. However, Hudson's Bay quickly put him out of business, and in 1837 Wyeth sold Fort Hall to Hudson's Bay. By 1847, at the peak of emigration, Fort Hall included a two-story store, mill, lumber room, blacksmith, storehouse, dining hall, and two-story house. But by then most of the game, beavers, and buffalo were gone; the fragile ecology of the Bottoms had been nearly destroyed by too much hunting and too many people. The Shoshones, who had lived well on seasonal game before the trappers came, were reduced to eating roots. Hudson's Bay Company had abandoned Fort Hall by the 1850s. By 1864, most of Fort Hall had been torn down and the logs used to build a stagecoach station.

A replica of the old trading post was established by the Bannock Historical Society, at Ross Park, in nearby Pocatello.

To visit the Fort Hall Replica, take exit 67 off I-15 to S 5th Ave and the top of Lava Cliffs. In summer the park is open daily 9am–7pm. Small admission fee. For more information, call the Fort Hall Replica, (208)234-7091, or the Bannock County Historical Society, (208)232-7051. The Rotary Rose Garden Visitor Center is at the base of the replica and can provide other local information and maps, 2605 S 5th Ave, Pocatello, ID 83204; (208)234-7091.

Shoshone-Bannock Tribal Museum

People seem to linger a long time in this small museum near the interstate, perhaps because it has such a personal feel to it. Museum staff, tribal members themselves, seeded the museum's collection with their own family treasures. Here you might meet the granddaughter of the woman you see posed in an 1885 photograph wearing a dress adorned with polished elk teeth. And you'll see the dress itself hanging nearby.

The museum's wonderful collection of photographs arose from a call to the Shoshone-Bannock community to comb through their attics for historic pictures. A few are formal portraits taken by Benedicte Wrensted, who photographed more than 300 Fort Hall individuals in her Pocatello studio in the late 1800s. The community's photos were copied by the museum, some of them from glass negatives, and hung on the wall. Over the last several years, most of the people in the photographs have been identified by relatives and friends who have wandered into the museum.

Unusual items, such as eagle-bone whistles from past Sun Dances, a willow-frame cradleboard and water jug, and a buffalo-bone paint set, are on display. Kids go nuts over the stuffed buffalo in the center of the room. A gift shop offers books, beaded items, and other things made on the reservation. A calendar of historic photographs from the Fort Hall Reservation and several posters are on sale.

Shoshone-Bannock Tribal Museum, PO Box 793, Fort Hall, ID 83203; (208)237-9791. The museum is on Simplot Rd., just off I-15, exit 80. Open Apr–Oct, Mon–Sat, 10am–6pm. Winters by appointment only. Admission $1; 12 and under, free.

Good Shepherd Mission

The little red Episcopal church behind the cemetery on Mission Road was built in 1904 and is on the National Register of Historic Places. The original church bell, mounted on a small tower outside the church, is rung with a bell cord for Sunday morning services conducted by Vicar Joan Laliberte. Inside the church, the sun shines through original stained glass windows; eagle-feather staffs are mounted over the altar. The old mission schoolhouse next door, in its original condition except for vinyl-covered floors and a modern kitchen, is available for Episcopal retreats.

Good Shepherd Mission, PO Box 608, Fort Hall, ID 83203; (208)237-9479. It's on Mission Rd; you can't miss it.

Fort Hall Boarding School

Except for the laundry building and weathered dairy barn, the old government-run Fort Hall boarding school has been torn down. It's no surprise, said our guide. Children used to chew the bulbs of white death camas to make themselves sick enough to get out of school. His mother, who attended school there as a child, remembered the $1 reward for truants who were brought back with a rope around their necks. The school closed in the mid-1930s. German prisoners of war were housed in the old school buildings during World War II. The unmarked graves of German prisoners of war may be found south of the school site.

A colonnade of old cottonwoods leads to the school site, under the old water tower. A photograph of the school is in the Shoshone-Bannock Tribal Museum. Other historic buildings, all built by the Fort Hall Indian agency, some of them prior to the turn of the century, are in a four-square-block area and are still used by the tribe. The old commissary and physician's quarters, sandstone courthouse, and superintendent's quarters still stand, as does the old Oregon Shortline railroad depot, moved from its original site. For a tour of the old buildings on the Fort Hall Reservation, call the Shoshone-Bannock Tribal Museum; (208)237-9791.

Reservation Tours

Rusty Houtz, a bronze sculptor, former professional rodeo cowboy, and movie extra (he appeared in the 1950s' *The Tall Man* and numerous episodes of *Bonanza*), gives tours of the reservation when he's not behind the counter of the Shoshone-Bannock Tribal Museum. Houtz's grandfather was Shoshone, his grandmother Bannock. Short tours include the Bottoms, the springs, historic buildings, viewpoints, the ruts of the Oregon Trail, and a stop at the tribal museum; longer tours may include a loop drive to Lava Hot Springs and the Bear River massacre site. Arrange tours through the Shoshone-Bannock

Tribal Museum; (208)237-9791.

Robert "Red" Perry, Sr., was born on the reservation to a Bannock-Sioux mother and Irish trapper father. He offers tours of the Bottoms or a drive around the reservation and peppers his tour with personal anecdotes, opinions, and stories. Tours are 2 to 2½ hours long. A second, 4½-hour tour originates at Fort Hall, continues to the old military fort at Lincoln Creek, explores portions of the emigrant trails, including the Oregon Trail, and then circles back to the reservation. Contact Robert Perry, Sr., at (208)238-0097 or (208)241-0557.

Clothes Horse Trading Post

The baby holds her legs in the air, as all infants do—gazing in wonder at the miracle of her own feet enveloped in buckskin moccasins as soft as velvet, the top hand-stitched with tiny glass beads in a pattern of bright blue flowers. Made of "Indian-tanned" leather that has been lightly smoked, the moccasins will hold their sweet campfire smell and vibrant design long after the baby has grown, and even after the moccasins have been framed and hung on the wall as a piece of art.

More than 300 Shoshone-Bannock men and women produce hand-stitched beadwork in their homes, providing the local tribal store with, literally, a wall full of dazzling moccasins for sale. There's no other trading post like this in the Pacific Northwest. Many of the moccasins are fully beaded across the top of the foot to the toe with florals and geometrics. High-tops, ankle, and slipper styles are made in sizes that range from infant to adult 16, and widths from narrow to wide. Prices range from $25 to $200 a pair, depending on quality of hide and difficulty of beaded design.

Fully beaded checkbook covers, coin purses, belt buckles, earrings, and headbands are also for sale. The most prized work is the hard-to-find porcupine quillwork, a technique that predates European cut-glass beads. Look also for Edgar Jackson's collectible beadwork, notable for both its intricate design and its tiny beads. Whimsical buckskin dolls, many of them dressed in beaded regalia and on horseback, are made by the Ottogary family. The store also carries a full line of Western wear, boots, and Western art.

Because of the sharp quills that protect them from most predators, porcupines move slowly when approached, curling up to protect their soft underbellies. Quills are gathered by throwing a blanket over the porcupine. A porcupine doesn't throw its quills. Instead, sharp barbs on the quills hook into the blanket, like cactus spines, and pull away from the animal when the blanket is removed. Hollow quills can be dyed; they are then twisted and flattened as they are sewn into intricate patterns that give a garment a textured, luminous look.

Clothes Horse Trading Post, PO Box 848, Fort Hall, ID 83203; (208)237-8433; in the trading post complex off I-15, exit 80. Open Mon–Sat, 8am–8pm; Sun, 10 am–6pm.

Call for a color catalog of beadwork ($2); custom orders for beadwork are taken as well.

Annual Shoshone-Bannock Indian Festival

The full moon rises behind the dry hills, crickets are chirping, and in the distance is heard the drumbeat calling hundreds of dancers into the outdoor arena. They are gathered between cars and tepees, tents and campers, putting on the last touches of feathered and elaborately beaded regalia; the youngest, 3 and 4 years old, spontaneously dance in place while they wait to join the dancers already in the circle. There are speeches and prayers, a grand entry that may take up to 2 hours, then dance contests that last until 2 or 3am.

You can buy a buffalo T-bone steak, burgers, buffalo stew and fry bread, buffalo sausage and eggs, and Indian tacos made with buffalo meat at the Oregon Trail Restaurant, a tribally owned cafe; just off Interstate 15, exit 80. Open daily 6am–midnight. Accommodations are in nearby Pocatello, on Interstate 15. For help with accommodations, contact the Pocatello Chamber of Commerce, 343 W Center St, Pocatello, ID 83204; (208)233-1525.

Not everyone watches the dancing—in a nearby building, stick game tournaments are going on, with teams lined up in lawn chairs facing each other, shaking rattles, pounding drums, and singing to distract their opponents as the game's bones change hands. In the dark, children run in all directions, darting between the craft and food booths, laughing, throwing water balloons at each other; the baseball diamond becomes a nighttime playground. A mother unloads a crate of canned pop from the back of her van; her young daughter loads it into two barrels of ice and joyously counts the $58 in the till. Earlier in the day, the grandstand was nearly full for the wild and woolly All-Indian Rodeo and Indian Pony Relay Races, while 300 pounds of buffalo meat roasted over coals in a pit—a traditional giveaway dinner that includes baked potatoes, chili, and watermelon.

The Annual Shoshone-Bannock Indian Festival is one of the largest Indian gatherings in the West, with some 600 of the best dancers in North America competing for nearly $40,000 in prize money. As if this weren't enough, the All-Indian Men's and Women's Sanctioned Softball Tournament goes on at the same time—with teams competing from all over the country. More than 50 arts and crafts booths and food concessions circle the grounds.

The Annual Shoshone-Bannock Indian Festival, (208)238-3700, is held Thur–Sun, the second weekend of August, every year at the Festival and Rodeo Grounds in Fort Hall. The grounds are off I-15, exit 80, approximately 1 mile west on Simplot Rd. A small admission fee is charged at the gate, good for all events. Non-Indians are welcome.

APPENDIXES

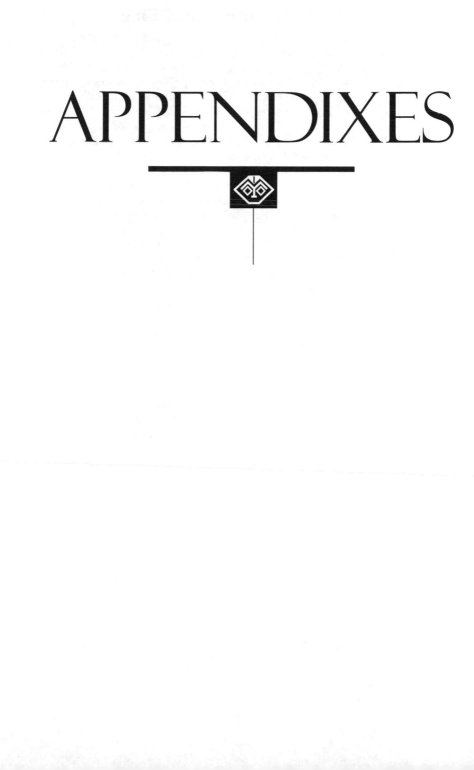

Sacred Ceremonies and Sites

Because Native peoples welcome visitors so warmly, sharing their traditional stories, songs, dances, and foods, visitors are sometimes surprised to learn that certain lands or religious ceremonies are closed to them. But as in any religion, Native ceremonies, symbols, and places are sacred, and are not to be shared with strangers in a casual way. Nor is sharing intended to deepen the pockets of outsiders, who pretend to sell Native spirituality to the general public. Spiritual teaching is not for sale; when the time is right, it is given without charge. Your respect and consideration regarding this are deeply appreciated.

There is another reason that tribes are cautious with their spiritual teachings. During the late 1800s and early 1900s, the federal government vigorously suppressed Native religions and ceremonies. Regulations were passed that banned all practices, including dancing, singing, burial customs, sharing wealth with family and tribal members, and holding gatherings off the reservation. During this time, religious practices had to be conducted in secret. The fear still exists that those days may return.

In addition to protecting the sacredness of their religious ceremonies, Native peoples have tried—often in vain—to protect sacred grounds. However, during the past century, countless sacred sites— honored by more than 500 generations of tribal peoples—have been desecrated by everything from strip mining to building construction. Some sites are unknowingly desecrated by hikers or campers who stumble onto a site and want to take home a souvenir. However, those "souvenirs" are usually important religious items meant to remain at a specific place, or are funerary items meant to stay with the deceased. Archaeologists, driven to learn what they could about Native peoples, have for years failed to consult with the tribes or with family members before removing items that had been deliberately placed. Perhaps the most painful desecration of all has been the casual removal of the dead from family graves.

If you should ever find remains, petroglyphs, or other items, take note of where you found them—but do not remove them. Alert the nearest tribe and the state historic preservation office. Looting on federal or tribal lands is a crime. When a tribe is willing to share historic sites and cultural areas, we have included them in this book. You can also contact each tribe's cultural committee, which considers requests for information (see the list of tribal offices in this appendix).

For more information about historic sites, battlefields, and monuments, we recommend George Cantor's *North American Indian Landmarks: A Traveler's Guide* (Gale Research, 1993), or David Hurst Thomas's *Exploring Ancient Native America: An Archaeological Guide* (Macmillan, 1994). Both books include contributions by Cheyenne writer/poet Suzan Shown Harjo, who heads The Morning Star Institute, a cultural and arts advocacy organization in Washington, D.C. Harjo's well-known poem *Sacred Ground* follows; Harjo rewrote it especially for this book, creating new verses about Northwest sacred sites.

Sacred Ground

eagles disappear into the sun
       surrounded by light from the face of Creation
       then scream their way home
              with burning messages of mystery and power
some are given to snake doctors and ants and turtles and salmon
       to heal the world
              with order and patience

some are given to cardinals and butterflies and yellow medicine flowers
       to heal the world
              with joy, with joy

some are given to bears and buffalos and human peoples
       to heal the world
              with courage and prayer

messages for holy places
       in the heart of Mother Earth
       deep inside the Old Stone Woman
              whose wrinkles are canyons
       in the roaring waters and clear blue streams
       and bottomless lakes
              who take what they need
       in the forests of grandfather cedars
       and mountains of grandmother sentinel rocks
              who counsel 'til dawn

messages for holy places
       where snow thunder warns
       and summer winds whisper
              this is Sacred Ground

Sacred Ground at Spirit Falls
       where small round stones have secrets
              that clear-cutters can never discover

Sacred Ground at Steptoe Butte
       where wild roses in grasslands dull the roar of microwaves
              and screams of Tohotonimme ponies in the night

Sacred Ground at Mount Graham
       where Apaches pray for a peaceful world
              invisible through the vatican telescopes

Sacred Ground at Bear Butte
       where Cheyennes and Lakotas hide from tourists
       to dress the trees in ermine tails and red-tail hawk feathers
              and ribbons of prayers to the life-givers

Sacred Ground at the San Francisco Peaks
      where Navajos and Hopis dodge ski-bums and bottles
      to settle the spirits
            where they walk

Sacred Ground at Snoqualmie Falls
      where condo-dwellers and hydro-sellers
      cannot harness power
            at the center of Creation

Sacred Ground at Chota
      where even Tellico's dam engineers
      hear Tsalagee voices
            through the burial waters

Sacred Ground at Thunder Mountain and Mount Adams
      Kootenai Falls and the Jemez Mountains
      where vision-questers seek gifts of the Spirit
            and fire clouds and walking waters stand guard
Sacred Ground at Badger Two Medicine and Crazy Mountain and the
Black Hills
      Red Butte and Chief Mountain and the Sweetgrass Hills
      where miners have drills for arms
            and gold in their eyes
Sacred Ground at the Medicine Wheel
      and all the doors to the passages of time
      to Sacred Ground of other worlds
            where suns light the way
            for eagles to carry messages
            for fires on
                      Sacred Ground

                            —*suzan shown harjo*

Powwows

The word *powwow* comes from the Native peoples of the Northern Woodlands. Named after their spiritual gatherings of medicine people, powwows were a time for healing and prayer. In later years, Europeans witnessing powwows wrongly concluded that the gatherings were merely social events. Peoples of the Northwest held similar gatherings for spiritual, social, and economic reasons. Through large gatherings, individuals sought marriage partners from other tribes, and trade was conducted up and down the coast and across the continent.

Contemporary powwows

Powwows and celebrations are still held today throughout the Northwest. They present a wonderful opportunity for cultural exchange. Most powwows are open to the public. Some are huge events. A recent powwow in Vancouver, B.C., for example, drew several drum groups, more than 600 dancers, and over 20,000 spectators. A powwow can last for a few hours, all night, or for as long as two weeks. Powwows are alcohol- and drug-free.

Powwows are usually held in outdoor powwow arbors; sometimes they take place in gymnasiums or ballrooms. Today's powwows still mirror the past and include a feast provided by the hosts for the honored guests. At the Shoshone-Bannock Festival in Idaho, or the Arlee Powwow in Montana, the community will most often host a buffalo feast; at the Treaty Day Celebrations along the Columbia River or a powwow in the Puget Sound area, you'll be offered a salmon dinner.

Today, powwows are still spiritual events. Special prayers are made to the creator, with thanks for all that's been given. The people ask for blessings for the powwow grounds and dancers. Special ceremonies are conducted for those dancers returning after a prolonged absence due to a death in the family. There are honoring songs and special dances offered for veterans, and memorials for loved ones, name-givings, giveaways, or whenever an eagle feather drops in the arena.

During these ceremonies, be respectful of the silence and stand when others do. For example, everyone stands during the "Grand Entry" and "Honor Dances," to pay respect to the flags and the dancers. If you have questions, wait until after the ceremony to ask them. There is usually an information booth or stand where powwow committee members are available to answer your questions and provide directions.

Traditional games, sometimes called hand game, stick game, or bone game, are played at all hours in arbors, tents, or other covered buildings. Canoe races, rodeos, horse races, and baseball tournaments often accompany the dances. Vendors selling traditional and contemporary arts and crafts, shawls, blankets, music tapes, and food are reminiscent of the trade that was prevalent in historic gatherings.

Most powwows are inter-tribal, with dancers and drum groups from throughout the United States and Canada. In recent years, the larger powwows have offered thousands of dollars in prize money to the dancers and drum groups.

The Dancers

The drum is the center of the powwow, the heartbeat of the nations, drawing the people together. Dancers fill the arena during the inter-tribal dances, from the smallest child able to bounce to the rhythm, to the grandmothers and aunties dressed in intricately beaded buckskin dresses with fringe that gracefully sways to each drum beat.

Each tribe has its own traditional dances and songs. These dances are rarely performed during contemporary powwows; they are held for special ceremonies and celebrations. The dances you'll see at a contemporary powwow are adapted from the Plains Indians and shared by tribes throughout the United States.

A favorite of the audience, because of their fast steps and swift turns are the fancy dancers, whose colorful outfits may be elaborately beaded and adorned with feather bustles. Traditional dancers, the proud bearers of culture, wear prized heirlooms, such as eagle feathers, that may have been passed down for generations. Their outfits are a strong contrast to contemporary fancy dancers, who lean toward bright neon colors, the better to catch the eye of the judges. The grass dancers' outfits, fringed with yarn and ribbons, resemble the graceful swaying motion of the prairie grass.

Shawl dancers wear a long-fringed shawls over beaded or ribbon dresses; their dances are said to be inspired by the butterfly, moth, hummingbird, and other small birds. Jingle dresses are adorned with hundreds of cone-shaped bells made from tobacco can lids; each bell is said to represent a prayer to the creator.

The dance area must be respected. Do not enter it unless the master of ceremonies invites you with a call for an "inter-tribal" or "round dance." The round dance, sometimes called a "friendship dance," is performed by facing the center of the arena in a large circle. Follow the dancer beside you.

Powwow Etiquette

At the Peoples' Center in Pablo, Montana, guides are available to help explain how the powwow works. They introduce the visitors to dancers and artists. Many other tribes are following suit. If guides aren't available, you need to know that there are a number of customs and ceremonies that may occur.

- Powwows are like large extended family gatherings. Friends and families make plans each year to meet at different gatherings; many have attended the same gatherings for generations. Families may bring their tepees, with the local hosts providing the tepee poles. Never enter a tepee without an invitation; these are private homes during the powwow.

- Chairs surrounding the ring and the front seats of grandstands are reserved for elders and families of the dancers. Out of respect for the elders and dancers, do not stand in front of them, or sit in their chairs.

- Many powwows do not have seating. Bring along a lawn chair or blanket, but do not put them in front of the elders' seats.

- Casual street clothes are appropriate attire for spectators (jeans and T-shirts are okay, suggestive clothing is considered disrespectful). Women entering the dance ring should wear a shawl around their shoulders.

- It's generally acceptable to take photographs or videos of dancers inside the dance area for your personal use, but you should ask permission from the master of ceremonies or staff beforehand. Always ask permission before taking any individual's photograph outside the dance circle. Never publish a photo without permission of the dancer.

- Don't be offended or upset if someone does not respond to you. If you ask a question about something that a vendor or a dancer doesn't feel you need to know, they may just ignore the question. Silence is often considered more polite than a negative response or a refusal of a request.

Calendar of Events

The following is a list of some of the larger gatherings held in the Northwest. Some are called "powwows," some are called "celebrations." No matter what they are called, the public is welcome to attend. Call ahead for the exact dates and times, which often vary from year to year. Don't hesitate to ask questions if you're not sure what to wear, how to act, what to bring, or whether cash donations are needed.

Each tribe holds other community events as well. If you are planning to be on or near a reservation, call the tribe and ask whether any events are scheduled that are open to the public. Colleges and universities in major Northwest cities often have urban Indian organizations that sponsor powwows and events as well.

Alaska (Southeast)

June (in even years: 1996, 1998, 2000, and so on)

Gathering of Tlingit, Haida, and Tsimshian dancers and drummers, Juneau, AK; (800)344-1432. Arts and crafts.

Idaho and Montana

January–March

Annual Native American Art Association Show, Great Falls, MT; (406)791-2212. Powwow and parade.

Idaho and Montana *(continued)*

April–June

Annual Shoshone-Bannock Hand/Stick Games Tourney, Fort Hall Reservation, Fort Hall, ID; (208)238-8821.

Chief Joseph & Warriors Memorial Pow Wow, Nez Perce Reservation, Lapwai, ID; (208)843-2253.

Annual Arlee 4th of July Celebration, Flathead Reservation, Arlee, MT; (406)675-0160, (406)676-5280, or (406)675- 2700.

July–September

Shoshone-Bannock Indian Festival, Fort Hall Reservation, Fort Hall, ID; (800)497-4231 or (208)237-8774. Four-day festival with parade, powwow, rodeo, art exhibition, buffalo feast, arts and crafts.

Nee-Mee-Poo Sapatqayn and Cultural Days, Nez Perce Reservation, Spalding, ID; (208)843-2261. Horse parade, cultural demonstrations, speakers, drumming and dancing, arts and crafts.

Standing Arrow Pow Wow, Flathead Reservation, Elmo, MT; (406)675-0160.

Chief Looking Glass Pow Wow, Nez Perce Reservation, Kamiah, ID; (208)935-0716.

October–December

Reservation-wide Championship Wardancing, Flathead Reservation, St. Ignatius, MT; (406)675-0160.

Thanksgiving Day Pow Wow, Salish and Kootenai Nations, Flathead Reservation, St. Ignatius, MT; (406)675-2700.

Four Nations Pow Wow, Nez Perce County Fair Grounds, Lewiston, ID; (208)843-2253.

Oregon and Washington (Eastern): Columbia River Basin

January–March

Lincoln's Day Pow Wow, Warm Springs Reservation, Simnasho Longhouse, Simnasho, OR; (541)553-1161.

Speelyi Mi Arts & Crafts Fair, Yakama Reservation, Yakima, WA; (509)865-5121. Traditional exhibits, art show, daily entertainment.

Annual Father's Day Fishing Derby at Indian Lake, Umatilla Reservation, Pilot Rock, OR; (503)276-3873.

Washington's Birthday Pow Wow, Yakama Reservation, Toppenish, WA; (509)865-5121.

April–June

Pi-Ume-Sha Treaty Days Powwow, Warm Springs Reservation, Warm Springs, OR; (541)553-1161. All-Indian rodeo, endurance horse race, softball tourney, fun run, golf tourney.

Root Feast & Rodeo, Warm Springs Reservation, Warm Springs and Simnasho, OR; (541)553-1161. Traditional foods and ceremonies.

Annual Memorial Day Weekend "Open Jackpot Rodeo," Yakama Reservation, White Swan, WA; (509)848-3329.

Treaty Days Tinowit International Pow Wow and White Swan Annual All-Indian Rodeo, Yakima and White Swan, WA; (509)865-5121.

All-Indian Rodeo, Tygh Valley, OR; (541)483-2238. Western States Indian Rodeo Association–sanctioned rodeo, parade, helicopter rides, pony rides, western dances, fun run, arts and crafts, baseball tourney, Buckaroo Breakfast.

Eagle Spirit Father's Day Celebration, Yakama Indian Nation, White Swan, WA; (509)877-6754 or (509)848-3415. Camping, concessions, arts and crafts vendors, powwow, traditional gaming.

Annual 10-Day Encampment, Yakama Indian Nation, White Swan, WA; (509)865-5121.

Celico Wy-Am Salmon Feast, Celilo Village, OR; (509)848-3461.

Root Feast Celebration, Umatilla Reservation, Mission, OR; (541)276-3165.

July–September

Omak Stampede and Suicide Race, Colville Reservation, Omak, WA; (800)933-6625. Second weekend in August. PRCA–sanctioned rodeo with top stars, Native American encampment, world-famous race.

Spokane Falls Northwest Indian Encampment & Pow Wow, Riverfront Park, Spokane, WA; (509)535-0866. Every August. Dancing contest, Indian art auction, arts and crafts vendors, exhibits, modern dances, arcade.

Salish Fair and Buffalo Barbecue, Kalispel Tribe, Usk, WA; (509)445-1178. Dance competition, Native foods, arts and crafts.

Pendleton Round Up and Rodeo, Pendleton, OR; (800)524-2984. Happy Canyon Pageant, Native American encampment, Indian art auction, arts and crafts vendors, parade, rodeo.

Annual Golden Eagle Pow Wow, Yakama Indian Nation, Toppenish, WA; (509)865- 5121 (ask for AAOA).

Eagle Spirit Celebration, Yakama Reservation, White Swan, WA; (509)865-5121.

Spokane Indian Days, Tribal Fairgrounds, Wellpinit, WA; (509)258-4060.

October–December

Mid-Columbia River Pow Wow, Celilo Village, OR; (509)848-3461.

Restoration Celebration and Powwow, Siletz Reservation, OR; (541)444-2532.

Oregon (Western) and Northern California

April–June

Memorial Day Rodeo & Powwow, Klamath Tribe, Klamath Falls, OR; (800)524-9787.

July–September

Hoopa All-Indian Rodeo, Rodeo Grounds, Hoopa, CA; (916)625-4227. Western States Indian Rodeo Association–sanctioned rodeo, arts and crafts, dances.

Nesika Illahee Pow Wow, Confederated Tribes of the Siletz, Government Hill, OR; (800)922-1399 or (503)444-2532. Second week in August.

Hupa Tribe's Annual Sovereign Day Celebration, Hoopa, CA; (916)625-4211.

Grand Ronde Pow Wow, Pow Wow Grounds, Grand Ronde, OR; (800)422-0232.

All-Indian Rodeo and Barbecue, Klamath Tribe, Chiloquin, OR; (800)524-9787.

Klamath Treaty Days Celebration, Chiloquin, OR; (503)783-2005.

Washington (Western): Olympic Peninsula/Puget Sound

April–June

Chief Tahola Days, Quinault Indian Nation, Tahola, WA; (360)276-8211. Canoe races, baseball tourney, arts and crafts, food.

Annual Stommish Water Festival, Lummi Reservation, Bellingham, WA; (360)384-1489. War canoe races, footraces, tugs-of-war, traditional dancing, salmon barbecue, traditional bone game tournament, arts and crafts.

Sa'Heh'Wa'Mish Powwow and Art Fair, Squaxin Island Tribe, Mason County Fairgrounds, Shelton, WA; (206)426-9781. Traditional salmon bake, arts and crafts, entertainment.

Annual Native American Art Fair, Suquamish Tribal Center, Suquamish, WA; (360)598- 3311. Artists' displays and sales, Native foods.

Drummers Jam, Suquamish Tribe, Indianola, WA; (360)598-3311. Powwow drummers and dancers, arts and crafts; camping available.

Sharing of the Culture Annual Art Sale, Lummi Nation and Allied Arts of Whatcom County, Bellingham, WA; (360)384-2338.

July–September

Chief Seattle Days, Suquamish Tribe, Suquamish, WA; (206)598-3311. Annual celebration in honor of Chief Seattle, held annually since 1911. Memorial service, powwow, war canoe races, salmon bake, arts and crafts, dances, and entertainment.

Makah Days Celebration, Makah Reservation, Neah Bay, WA; (360)645-2201. Canoe races, parade, salmon bake, arts and crafts fair, dances, fireworks, traditional bone game tourney.

Annual Seafair Indian Days, Daybreak Star Indian Cultural Center, Discovery Park, Seattle, WA; (206)285-4425. Powwow, arts and crafts, salmon bake; camping available.

Annual Salmon Homecoming Celebration, Seattle, WA; (206)386-4320. Sponsored by Northwest tribes, Northwest Indian Fisheries, and City of Seattle. Four days of ceremonies, storytelling, forums, a powwow, and music to honor the salmon.

Muckleshoot Annual Pow Wow, Auburn, WA; (206)939-3311.

Puyallup Tribe Annual Pow Wow and Salmon Bake, Tacoma, WA; (206)597-6200.

October–December

Washington Indian Nations Art Celebration, Bellevue, WA; (206)665-1925.

Buying Native Art

Native art reflects each tribe's unique artistic heritage—whether it's the soft Wasco sally bags woven of wild grasses; the Tlingit, Haida, and Tsimshian totem poles carved from towering cedar trees; or the intricate glass beadwork of the Shoshone, adapted from the decoration of ceremonial regalia with dyed porcupine quills, elk teeth, and beads made of bone. Native artists draw inspiration from a continuity of culture. Even the most modern Native art is often guided by custom and culture. An Eagle Clan Tlingit artist would not carve the story of the Raven Clan without special permission. A basketmaker would not weave another family's designs without their approval.

The most important guideline to follow in purchasing Native art— especially for those who want something more than a simple souvenir— is to ensure the item's authenticity. When buying art from a gallery or a vendor, ask who made the item and what the artist's tribal affiliation is. A good gallery knows its artists or can get information about them; the best galleries mark each piece with the name of the artist and the tribal affiliation. If the sellers don't know who made the piece, there's a chance it is not Indian-made. Ask for information in writing. Many shops provide certificates of authenticity—even for the smallest items. If you're still not sure, call the tribe and ask. Every tribe has an enrollment office that keeps track of each of its members.

Don't be fooled by works marked "Indian-style," or "in the tradition of," or labels that describe the artist as having "Indian heritage." These descriptions are often used to get around federal and tribal laws. (The Indian Arts and Crafts Act protects buyers from imitations. The law provides stiff fines for those caught selling or promoting products as Indian-made if they are not.) No one can blame non-Native artists who are drawn to Native images and art—the bold forms and intricate design would capture any artist's imagination. In fact, some non-Natives have taught Natives traditional skills. However, these works, no matter how good, are only replicas of the real thing. Non-Indian artists with integrity do not claim that their work is authentic.

Some other guidelines for buying Native art:

* Remember that the ability to determine quality comes with time and observation. The more examples you see, the more you will appreciate the distinctions. At first, all totems and masks may look the same. After a while you can tell the differences in style and artist's work. Some galleries provide free printed materials that explain the art forms, or have reprints of articles about artists and motifs. Or ask the gallery to recommend a book on the topic.

* If you are going to invest in a major piece of art, buy a few books or magazines to learn what to look for. *Native Peoples, Indian Artist,* and *American Indian Art* magazines have articles on Native arts and cultures.

* Instead of relying on galleries, buy Native art from the artists themselves—at powwows, art markets, or special events. Don't be surprised if the artist is reserved. Artists are not always used to selling their work, and feel more comfortable discussing how a piece is made or how they learned their craft than trying to sell it.

* Don't be surprised by innovation and contemporary styles. Remember that culture is a living thing. Some of the jewelers and painters in the Northwest attended the Institute of American Indian Art in Santa Fe and have been influenced by the styles of the Southwest. Keep in mind that there's no such thing as "Indian art"—only art in whatever traditional or contemporary form that is produced by an American Indian, First Nations, or Alaska Native artist.

Traditional Gaming and Casinos

From modest bingo halls to lavish Las Vegas-style casinos, Indian tribes offer a full range of attractions for those who wish to court Lady Luck Indian style. Whether or not you are a gambler, you'll take a certain risk walking through these doors—you may have to challenge your attitudes and preconceptions of modern Indian people.

Visit, for example, the Wild Horse Gaming Center in Umatilla, Oregon. Created by Disneyland stagehands, its whimsical Western setting is clearly a place to drop your attitudes, along with your wallet, and have some fun. The Jamestown S'Klallam's Seven Cedars Casino in Washington, with its totems, grand longhouse-style entry, and immense cedar beams, opens into a first-class gallery featuring some of the finest artists from the Northwest. The Indian Head Gaming Center at Warm Springs, Oregon, has made major purchases of oil paintings and masks from Northwest Indian artists, and had the tribe's clothing factory design and produce the uniforms for their personnel. The Indian casinos will go out of their way to make you feel welcome—they provide classes for new players, handouts explaining the activities, and friendly employees to show you how to play even the most complicated games.

Participating in games of chance and skill is nothing new for Native tribes. For centuries, such competitions have been a serious sport for them, and the pot was worth much more than mere money. The Iroquois played lacrosse to settle land disputes with other tribes (much more civilized than war). Horse races were held throughout the Northwest, helping redistribute wealth as well as settle disputes. When Lewis and Clark came to the Northwest, they were dismayed by the amount of time Native peoples spent on social and recreational activities, ceremonies, dances, and gaming. Today, however, economists consider the amount of time spent on family and recreation a sign of an advanced civilization. Indeed, our ideas of play have come a long way.

In a strange twist of fate, the treaties that removed Indians from their traditional lands also protected their rights on the reservation to which they were assigned. Those treaties have given the tribes a competitive advantage in the business of gaming. In the 1980s, when the Cabazon Tribe in California decided to allow gambling on their reservation, nearby casinos were up in arms. The state of California took the tribe to court. The case went all the way to the U.S. Supreme Court, which declared that tribes were sovereign and had the same rights as any other government (or state) to allow gaming. Congress, in its response to the outcry, passed additional legislation that allows states a process with which to negotiate with tribes about instituting gambling.

Using games of chance as an economic option is not unique to the tribes. States such as Nevada and New Jersey have done the same; many churches raise funds from casino nights and bingo halls. And just as the states and churches use the money for the benefit of their constituents, the tribes use the money raised through the casinos to address the problems of poverty and unemployment on their reservations. For example, the Tulalip Tribe in Washington, which opened gaming operations in 1991, has seen unemployment on its reservation drop from 65 to 10 percent. They have also used proceeds to establish an elder-care facility.

So, when you visit an Indian gaming center, you're doing far more than courting Lady Luck. As one casino player said, "This is my way of donating money to the Indians, and having some fun while doing it." At many centers, you can buy Native art, learn a little about the tribe's culture, and enjoy a good meal—as well as have some fun. Some casinos (such as the one at Coeur d'Alene, Idaho) even host traditional Native games, such as hand-game tournaments, so you can see how it was all done in the past.

Casinos

Alaska

TLINGIT & HAIDA CENTRAL COUNCIL, 320 W Willoughby Ave, #300, Juneau, AK 99801; (907)586-1432. The council can provide you with a list of bingo halls and a schedule of games in Southeast Alaska.

Idaho

COEUR D'ALENE TRIBAL BINGO/CASINO, Coeur d'Alene Tribe, Junction of Hwy 58 and US 95, Worley, ID 83876; (800)523-2464. About 30 minutes south of the resort town of Coeur d'Alene. Video slots, pull-tabs; bingo Fri.–Sun. Gift shop; stick game tournaments in summer. Open daily, 24 hours a day.

FORT HALL BINGO AND CASINO, Shoshone-Bannock Tribe, I-5, Exit 80, Fort Hall, ID 83203; (800)497-4231. A few miles north of Pocatello, halfway between Salt Lake City, Utah, and Yellowstone National Park, on the Fort Hall Shoshone-Bannock Reservation. Pull-tabs; bingo Tues and Fri.–Sun. Concession stand, nearby restaurant and trading post with Native beadwork for sale. Open 10am–10pm daily.

KOOTENAI TRIBAL CASINOS. Kootenai River Inn, Hwy 95, Bonners Ferry, ID 83805; (800)346-5668 or (208)267-8511. Video slots; bingo Wed, Fri, Sun. Restaurant, forty-eight-room resort hotel overlooking the Kootenai River, pool, spa. Open daily, 24 hours a day.

Oregon

CHINOOK WINDS GAMING AND CONVENTION CENTER, Confederated Tribes of Siletz Indians, 1500 NW 40th, Lincoln City, OR 97367; (800)863-3314. Temporary facility until nearby casino and convention center overlooking Pacific Ocean opens. Video slots, card tables (blackjack, poker). Concession stand; accommodations nearby. Open daily, 24 hours a day.

COW CREEK INDIAN GAMING CENTER, Cow Creek Band of Umpqua, 146 Chief Miwaleta Lane, Canyonville, OR 97417; (800)548-8461. Off I-5, exit 99. Video slots, bingo, keno and card tables (blackjack, poker). Cafe, gift shop, motel. Open daily, 24 hours a day.

INDIANHEAD GAMING CENTER, Confederated Tribes of the Warm Springs Reservation, 1000 Main St, Warm Springs, OR 97761; (541)553-6123. At KahNeeTa Resort. Video slots, card tables (blackjack, poker). Delicatessen on site; children's arcade with latest video games; full-service resort with restaurants, accommodations, swimming, horse-back riding, golf course. Open 9am–pm daily.

THE MILL CASINO, Coquille Tribe, 3201 Tremont, North Bend, OR 97459; (800)953-4800 or (541)756-8800. A $10 million remodel of an old mill building on the Coos Bay waterfront. Video slots, card tables (blackjack, keno), bingo, pari-mutuel betting. Sports bar, arcade, family fun center, bayfront dining and retail shops. Free shuttle from your hotel. Open daily, 24 hours a day.

SPIRIT MOUNTAIN CASINO, Confederated Tribes of Grand Ronde, 28840 Salmon River Hwy (Hwy 18), PO Box 39, Grand Ronde, OR 97347; (800)760-7977 or (503)879-2350. Thirty minutes from Salem, McMinnville, and Lincoln City. Video slot machines, card tables (blackjack, poker), off-track betting, keno, pull-tabs, bingo, separate poker road, separate high-stakes room. Nonsmoking section. Family-style buffet dining room, full-service restaurant overlooking the Grand Ronde valley (accessible for families with children without going through the casino), deli, snack bar. Open daily, 24 hours a day.

WILDHORSE GAMING RESORT, Confederated Tribes of Umatilla Indians, 72777 Hwy 331, Pendleton, OR 97801; (800)654-WILD. A few miles east of Pendleton, off I-84. Video slots, off-track betting, live keno, bingo, sports events via satellite, card tables (blackjack, poker). Snack bar, restaurant, gift shop featuring Native art. Open daily, 24 hours a day.

Washington: Eastern

COULEE DAM CASINO, Confederated Tribes of the Colville Reservation, 515 Birch St, Coulee Dam, WA 99116; (800)556-7492 or (509)633-0974. Pull-tabs, slots, live keno. Delicatessen, espresso, gift shop with Native art and souvenirs. Open Wed-Sun, 10am-2am.

MILL BAY CASINO, Confederated Tribes of the Colville Reservation, 455 E Wapato Lake Rd, Mansen, WA 98831; (800)648-2946. Overlooking Lake Chelan. Slots, pull-tabs, card tables (blackjack, craps, roulette, red dog, mini-baccarat. Cafe, gift shop. Open daily, 24 hours a day.

OKANAGAN BINGO-CASINO, Confederated Tribes of the Colville Reservation, 41 Appleway Rd, Okanagan, WA 98840; (800)559-4643 or (509)422-3907. Off Hwy 997, just south of Omak, overlooking the Okanagan River. Video slots, bingo, pull-tabs. Concession stand, gift shop. Open weekdays 10am-2pm except in winter, when hours are shorter; call for information.

SPOKANE INDIAN BINGO AND CASINO, Spokane Tribe, Hwy 395, Smith Rd, Chewelah, WA 99109; (509)935-6167. Video slots, blackjack, pull-tabs. Bingo Mon, Wed, Sat, Sun. Deli, gift shop. Open 9am-midnight daily.

TWO RIVERS CASINO AND MARINA, Spokane Tribe, 6828-B Hwy 25 S, Davenport, WA 99122; (509)722-4000. Overlooks Lake Roosevelt (the Columbia River). Blackjack, craps, roulette, video slots. Snack bar; adjoining RV park, marina, and tent campground. Open daily.

Washington:Olympic Peninsula

CHINOOK INDIAN BINGO, Chinook Tribe, 10th and North Pacific, Long Beach, WA 98584; (360)642-4650. On the Long Beach Peninsula, off Hwy. 103, on the southern Washington coast. Nonsmoking area, restaurant. Open Sat–Mon, 10am–11pm. Games start at noon and 6pm.

LUCKY EAGLE CASINO, Chehalis Tribe, 11288 188th St SW, Rochester, WA 98579; (360)273-2000. Watch for exit signs on I-5, between Centralia and Olympia, to the Chehalis Reservation; the reservation is off Hwy. 12, a few miles past the town of Rochester. Craps, mini-baccarat, big 6, blackjack, Pai Gow, poker. Restaurant, sports bar, deli. Open 11am–4am daily.

SEVEN CEDARS CASINO, Jamestown S'Klallam Tribe, 270756 Hwy 101, Sequim, WA 98382; (360)683-7777. Near Sequim Bay on the Strait of Juan de Fuca; casino is built in the style of a longhouse, with seven hand-carved totem poles outside. Craps, roulette, big 6, red dog, multi-action blackjack, poker, bingo. Native fine-art gallery, souvenir shop, buffet-style dining.

Washington: Puget Sound Area

HARRAH'S SKAGIT VALLEY CASINO, Upper Skagit Tribe, 697 Darrk Lane, Bow, WA 98232; (800)427-7247 or (360)724-7777. From I-5, take the Bow Hill exit. Its tower and lights make the casino visible from the exit. Owned by the tribe; managed by Harrah's. Blackjack, roulette, craps, baccarat, keno, poker, bingo, craps, pull-tabs, game arcade. Gold card services, restaurant, nightly entertainment in the lounge, buffet, deli, gift shop with Native art and souvenirs. Open daily 11am–3am.

LITTLE CREEK CASINO, Squaxin Island Tribe, West 91, Hwy 108, Shelton, WA 98584; (800)667-7711 or (360)427-7706. Opposite the entrance to the Squaxin Island Reservation, south of Shelton, off Hwy. 101. Roulette, craps, mini-baccarat, money wheel, pull-tabs, poker, blackjack; bingo Sat.–Wed. Live entertainment Thurs–Fri. Restaurant, cafe, gift shop featuring tribal-logo clothing. Open daily noon–4am.

LUMMI CASINO, Lummi Indian Nation, 2559 Lummi View Dr, Bellingham, WA 98226; (360)758-7559. About 10 miles west of Bellingham, next to the landing for the ferry to Lummi Island. Craps, roulette, mini-baccarat, big six, red dog, pull-tabs, off-track betting, blackjack, Pai Gow, sic bow, poker, bingo. Cafe, gift shop. Open daily, 24 hours a day.

MUCKLESHOOT CASINO AND BINGO, Muckleshoot Tribe, 2402 Auburn Wy S, Auburn, WA 98002; (206)804-4444. Craps, roulette, Pai Gow, mini-baccarat, blackjack, poker, live keno, pull-tabs, off-track betting; afternoon, evening, and twilight bingo session daily, (206)735-2404. Fine restaurant, casual cafe, gift shop featuring local artists. Open 10am–6am daily.

NISQUALLY INDIAN BINGO, Nisqually Tribe, 12819 Yelm Hwy SE, Olympia, WA 98513; (360)459-8011. Gift shop. Open Wed.–Sun, 11am–1 am.

NOOKSACK RIVER CASINO, Nooksack Tribe, 5048 Mount Baker Hwy, Deming, WA 98244; (360)592-5472. Craps, roulette, red dog, blackjack, poker, Pai Gow. Buffet with Asian dishes, lounge with live entertainment on weekends, champagne brunch Sun, gift shop. Open 10am–6am daily.

PUYALLUP BINGO, Puyallup Tribe, 2002 E 28th, Tacoma, WA 98513; (206)383-1572. Three bingo sessions daily. Concession stand with breakfast and lunch items, food court, gift shop. Call for hours.

SUQUAMISH BINGO, Suquamish Tribe, 15347 Suquamish Wy, Suquamish, WA 98392; (360)598-3399. Off Hwy. 305, on the north side of the Agate Pass bridge. Facility is decorated with Northwest Coast art. Bingo, video bingo, pull-tab island with eighteen types of play. Snack bar, gift shop. Open 10am–10pm daily.

SWINOMISH CASINO AND BINGO, Swinomish Tribe, 837 Casino Dr, Anacortes, WA 98221; (800)877-PLAY. Just off Hwy. 20, north of the bridge over the Swinomish Channel, east of Anacortes. Blackjack, poker, craps, mini-baccarat, Pai Gow, sic bow, red dog, roulette. Bingo doors open at 5pm daily, matinees Fri–Mon; enclosed smoking room. Deli, gift shop, pull-tab bar, cafe between bingo hall and casino offering family dining. Open 10am–5pm daily.

TULALIP BINGO AND CASINO, Tulalip Tribe, 6410 33rd Ave NE, Marysville, WA 98271; (360)651-1111. Just off I-5 at Marysville, north of Everett. Blackjack, roulette, craps, poker, keno, pull-tabs; bingo daily. Restaurant, deli, gift shop. Open 10am–6am daily.

Tribal Administrative Offices

An Indian government may be referred to as a band, a tribe, or a confederation. The smallest unit, a band, usually refers to a family unit or a small group of people who lived together on their original lands. A tribe may include several bands of people who have the same language and culture. A confederation is made up of several tribes and bands who were moved to a reservation that is not in their original territory. An example of a confederation is the Yakama Nation, which is made up of 14 tribes and bands. Sometimes this nomenclature gets confusing, as when the Confederated Tribes of the Yakama Nation are simply referred to as the Yakama Tribe. The important thing to remember is that bands, tribes, and confederations have a special relationship with the U.S. government. They are nations within a nation, and have signed treaty agreements with the United States that are legal and binding. The following is a list of tribal offices in the Northwest (except for those in British Columbia).

All tribes have a governing body, which might include hereditary chiefs or elected officials or a combination of both. Tribes also have an administrative body that makes government, economic, and resource decisions for their people.

Alaska

Ketchikan Native Corporation
PO Box 7576
Ketchikan, AK 99901
(907)225-5158

Metlakatla Indian Community
PO Box 8
Metlakatla, AK 99926
(907)886-4441

Tlingit & Haida Central Council
320 W Willoughby Ave, #300
Juneau, AK 99801
(907)586-1432

California

Hupa Tribe
PO Box 1348
Hoopa, CA 95546
(916)625-4211

Idaho

Coeur d'Alene Tribe
Tribal Headquarters
Rt 1 Box FA
Plummer, ID 83851
(208)686-1800

Kootenai Tribe of Idaho
PO Box 1269
Bonners Ferry, ID 83805
(208)267-3519

Nez Perce Tribe
PO Box 305
Lapwai, ID 83540
(208)843-2253

Northwestern Band of Shoshoni
PO Box 637
Blackfoot, ID 83221
(208)785-7401

Shoshone-Bannock Tribes of the
Fort Hall Reservation
PO Box 306
Fort Hall, ID 83203
(208)238-3700

Montana

Chippewa Cree Tribe of the
Rocky Boy's Reservation
Rocky Boy Route, Box 544
Box Elder, MT 59521
(406)395-4282

Confederated Salish & Kootenai
Tribes
PO Box 278
Pablo, MT 59855
(406)675-2700

Oregon

Burns-Paiute Tribe
HC 71 100 Pa Si Go St
Burns, OR 97720
(541)573-2088

Confederated Tribes of Coos,
Lower Umpqua & Siuslaw
455 S 4th St
Coos Bay, OR 97420
(503)267-5454

Confederated Tribes of Grand
Ronde
9615 Grand Ronde Rd
Grand Ronde, OR 97347
(541)879-5211

Confederated Tribes of Siletz
PO Box 549
Siletz, OR 97380
(541)444-2532

Confederated Tribes of the
Umatilla Indian Reservation
PO Box 638
Pendleton, OR 97801
(541)276-3165

Confederated Tribes of the Warm
Springs Indian Reservation
PO Box 1299
Warm Springs, OR 97761
(541)553-3257

Coquille Indian Tribe
295 S 10th
PO Box 1435
Coos Bay, OR 97420
(800)622-5869 or (541)267-4587

Cow Creek Band of Umpqua
2400 Stewart Pkwy, #300
Roseburg, OR 97470
(541)672-9405

Klamath Tribes
PO Box 436
Chiloquin, OR 97624
(800)524-9787 or (503)783-2218

Washington

Chehalis Tribe
PO Box 536
Oakville, WA 98568
(360)273-5911

Chinook Tribe
PO Box 228
Chinook, WA 98614
(360)777-8303

Confederated Colville Tribes
PO Box 150
Nespelem, WA 99155
(509)634-4711

Confederated Tribes and Bands of
the Yakama Indian Nation
PO Box 151
Toppenish, WA 98948
(509)865-5121

Cowlitz Tribe
PO Box 2547
Longview, WA 98632
(360)577-8140

Duwamish Tribe
140 Rainier Ave S, #7
Renton, WA 98055
(206)226-5185

Hoh Tribe
HC 80, Box 917
Forks, WA 98331
(360)374-6582

Jamestown S'Klallam Tribe
1033 Old Blyn Hwy
Sequim, WA 98382
(360)681-4621

Kalispel Tribe
PO Box 39
Usk, WA 99180
(509)445-1147

Lower Elwha S'Klallam Tribe
2851 Lower Elwha Rd
Port Angeles, WA 98362
(360)452-8471

Lummi Indian Nation
2616 Kwina Rd
Bellingham, WA 98226
(360)734-8180

Makah Tribe
PO Box 115
Neah Bay, WA 98357
(360)645-2201

Muckleshoot Tribe
39015 172nd Ave SE
Auburn, WA 98002
(206)939-3311

Nisqually Tribe
4820 She-Nah-Num Dr SE
Olympia, WA 98503
(206)456-5221

Nooksack Tribe
PO Box 157
Deming, WA 98244
(360)592-5176

Port Gamble S'Klallam Tribe
31912 Little Boston Rd NE
Kingston, WA 98246
(360)297-2646

Puyallup Tribe
2002 E 28th St
Tacoma, WA 98404
(206)597-6200

Quileute Tribe
PO Box 279
La Push, WA 98350
(360)374-6163

Quinault Indian Nation
PO Box 189
Taholah, WA 98587
(360)276-8211

Samish Tribe
PO Box 217
Anacortes, WA 98221
(360)293-6404

Washington *(continued)*

Sauk-Suiatte Tribe
5318 Chief Brown Lane
Darrington, WA 98241
(360)436-0131

Shoalwater Bay Tribe
PO Box 130
Tokeland, WA 98590
(206)267-6766

Skokomish Tribe
N 80 Tribal Center Rd
Shelton, WA 98584
(360)426-4232

Snohomish Tribe
18933 59th Ave NE, #115
Arlington, WA 98223
(360)435-7900

Snoqualmie Tribe
18933 59th Ave NE, #114
Arlington, WA 98223
(360)435-1741

Snoqualmie Tribe
3946 Tolt Ave
PO Box 280
Carnation, WA 98014
(206)333-6551

Spokane Tribe
PO Box 100
Wellpinit, WA 99040
(509)258-4581

Squaxin Island Tribe
SE 70 Squaxin Lane
Shelton, WA 98584
(206)426-9781

Steilacoom Tribe
PO Box 88419
Steilacoom, WA 98388
(206)584-6308

Stillaquamish Tribe
PO Box 277
Arlington, WA 98223
(360)652-7362

Suquamish Tribe
PO Box 498
Suquamish, WA 98392
(360)598-3311

Swinomish Tribe
PO Box 817

La Conner, WA 98257
(360)466-3163

Tulalip Tribes
6700 Totem Beach Rd
Marysville, WA 98270
(360)651-4000

Upper Skagit Tribe
2284 Community Plaza
Sedro Woolley, WA 98284
(360)856-5501

INDEX